MARIOS KOUTSIAS

Consumer Protection and Global Trade in the Digital Environment

The Case of Data Protection

VDM Verlag Dr. Müller

Impressum/Imprint (nur für Deutschland/ only for Germany)

Bibliografische Information der Deutschen Nationalbibliothek: Die Deutsche Nationalbibliothek verzeichnet diese Publikation in der Deutschen Nationalbibliografie; detaillierte bibliografische Daten sind im Internet über http://dnb.d-nb.de abrufbar.

Alle in diesem Buch genannten Marken und Produktnamen unterliegen warenzeichen-, marken- oder patentrechtlichem Schutz bzw. sind Warenzeichen oder eingetragene Warenzeichen der jeweiligen Inhaber. Die Wiedergabe von Marken, Produktnamen, Gebrauchsnamen, Handelsnamen, Warenbezeichnungen u.s.w. in diesem Werk berechtigt auch ohne besondere Kennzeichnung nicht zu der Annahme, dass solche Namen im Sinne der Warenzeichen- und Markenschutzgesetzgebung als frei zu betrachten wären und daher von jedermann benutzt werden dürften.

Coverbild: www.purestockx.com

Verlag: VDM Verlag Dr. Müller Aktiengesellschaft & Co. KG
Dudweiler Landstr. 125 a, 66123 Saarbrücken, Deutschland
Telefon +49 681 9100-698, Telefax +49 681 9100-988, Email: info@vdm-verlag.de
Zugl.: PhD Thesis, University of Essex, 2007

Herstellung in Deutschland:
Schaltungsdienst Lange o.H.G., Zehrensdorfer Str. 11, D-12277 Berlin
Books on Demand GmbH, Gutenbergring 53, D-22848 Norderstedt
Reha GmbH, Dudweiler Landstr. 99, D- 66123 Saarbrücken
ISBN: 978-3-639-09060-4

Imprint (only for USA, GB)

Bibliographic information published by the Deutsche Nationalbibliothek: The Deutsche Nationalbibliothek lists this publication in the Deutsche Nationalbibliografie; detailed bibliographic data are available in the Internet at http://dnb.d-nb.de.

Any brand names and product names mentioned in this book are subject to trademark, brand or patent protection and are trademarks or registered trademarks of their respective holders. The use of brand names, product names, common names, trade names, product descriptions etc. even without
a particular marking in this works is in no way to be construed to mean that such names may be regarded as unrestricted in respect of trademark and brand protection legislation and could thus be used by anyone.

Cover image: www.purestockx.com

Publisher:
VDM Verlag Dr. Müller Aktiengesellschaft & Co. KG
Dudweiler Landstr. 125 a, 66123 Saarbrücken, Germany
Phone +49 681 9100-698, Fax +49 681 9100-988, Email: info@vdm-verlag.de

Copyright © 2008 VDM Verlag Dr. Müller Aktiengesellschaft & Co. KG and licensors
All rights reserved. Saarbrücken 2008

Produced in USA and UK by:
Lightning Source Inc., 1246 Heil Quaker Blvd., La Vergne, TN 37086, USA
Lightning Source UK Ltd., Chapter House, Pitfield, Kiln Farm, Milton Keynes, MK11 3LW, GB
BookSurge, 7290 B. Investment Drive, North Charleston, SC 29418, USA
ISBN: 978-3-639-09060-4

MARIOS KOUTSIAS

Consumer Protection and Global Trade in the Digital Environment

Acknowledgements

I would like to thank my family for its continuous help and support. I would like to thank my Professor Janet Dine for her precious guidance and advice. They made all this possible.

Contents

2

4

1. Introduction

In the last decade the world has experienced a radical shift in the traditional ways of conducting business. The emergence of technology as a factor of vital importance in the world economic framework gave rise to new business opportunities paving the way for the advent of the so called "new economy". The new economy encompasses all the economic activities performed in a digital environment. As a concept it includes the financial and commercial activities that can take place in the context recently shaped by new technologies. The advent of electronic commerce and the tide of changes it brought to traditional ways of engaging in commercial transactions along with the obvious advantages it brought to consumers and businesses –that are to be analysed later- led to the appearance of new challenges to legislators. The new challenges are closely related to the radical changes introduced by the Internet in the international economy. As the novel means of conducting business left its initial stage of development and entered an era evolving into an ambit of commercial transactions of international reach and importance, the first major problems and issues to be tackled appeared. The central matter of massive significance for the further development of e-commerce was immediately linked to the issue of "consumer protection". In other words all the factors involved in e-commerce such as the industry, national governments, supranational organisations and legislators realised at an early stage that the success of the digitally conducted commerce depends almost exclusively on the demonstration of trust on behalf of the consumers in the new type of commerce. Thus, the notion of "consumer confidence" evolved into a concept of primary importance for both consumers and industry. It also evolved into an issue that provided the basis for a new round of debate between different parts within a society such as consumer organisations and industry representatives and international factors with divergent legal, culture and economic views such as the European Union (EU) and the United States of America (USA). The differences in their approaches, which will be analysed further later, led to various discussions on the issue in question that underlined the importance of shaping an efficient commonly accepted policy. Although, the arguments expressed were based on sometimes widely different views all sides agreed upon the central issue of adopting measures to foster consumer confidence. The latter is universally accepted as a prerequisite for the development of e-commerce. In this framework the issue of data protection more specifically assumed a special role as it is more directly linked to the very subject matter of the new economy itself: personal information and its provision, dissemination and use. It is also directly linked to the most obvious challenges to the existing legal framework, protecting human rights and it is related to concepts as fundamental as dignity and personal freedom. Furthermore, it is one of the main parameters which fuel the lack of consumer confidence in electronically conducted transactions. Therefore, it is only natural that data protection stands at the core of the analysis of this book which seeks to detect the reasons of technical, cultural and historical nature behind the difficulties to agree on a common solution for tackling the problem and attempts to make certain proposals aiming at contributing to the ongoing discussions of dealing with this issue.

The main question emerging is "how traditional legal rules on consumer protection work in the information society?"[1]. The new landscape in world economy was deemed to bring a fundamental change to traditional legal principles and has already fuelled dramatic changes in particular areas of concern for legislators especially at the European level. It is the central thesis of this book that internet cannot flourish by showing disregard to Europe's rich humanistic traditions and legal culture. The book is going to analyse the legislative initiatives assumed in the EU in order to deal with the subject of protecting the consumers in respect to their privacy while conducting transactions in the digital environment. It is going to consider the regulations, directives and other pieces of European Law that regulate consumer relations in both traditional and electronic commerce. Analysis of the relevant directives will be provided along with a comparison of the approach adopted in the EU with that promoted in the other major player of international trade the USA. The integration of the European Union countries into a vast commonly regulated market had far reaching repercussions on world trade that led other countries to move towards the direction initiated by the EU. It will focus on the issue of data protection as the latter is shaped after the recent developments in the field of electronic commerce. The protection of personal data, as one of the most important aspects of consumer protection, has a far reaching effect on the market in question, especially after the passing of the Directive 95/46 on the protection of personal data, as is going to be demonstrated later and is closely related to

---

[1] Reich Norbert, Consumer Law and E-Commerce- Initiatives and Problems in Recent EU and German Legislation, ERA- Forum- 2-2001, p41.

2

prevailing cultural, philosophical, legal and societal values. In this book the historical developments that led to the particular legislative initiatives along with the sufficiency of the latter are going to be examined. There will also be an effort to initiate proposals for future reform or further adjustment of the current regime, so as to adapt in a more effective manner at the new challenges imposed by technological developments on the current state of law.

As Internet evolved into a market of global character with a massive impact on economy, trade flows and consumers the EU assumed several legal initiatives with an impact that extends much further from its already enlarged borders. As indicated above, the book is focused on the analysis of the "data protection" problem that seems to enjoy a strong link with the limited confidence that consumers have in the new means of commerce. It has emerged into an issue that touches upon both types of performing transactions and has assumed a central position in the arguments expressed by literature. The landmark EU Directive on "the protection of individuals with regard to the processing of personal data"[2] will be fully analysed, while necessary references will be made to the recent one on "electronic privacy"[3]. The EU emerged as a central figure in the forefront of the international trade players to inaugurate new initiatives at legislative level "due fundamentally to the way in which Internet applications are continuing to present new structures and revenue opportunities"[4] along with its constitutionally expressed objective to "harmonise the laws that could affect cross-border trade between member states when it is considered that there are fundamental differences between them"[5]. In this rapidly changing landscape the "European legislator wanted to guarantee judicial security and the confidence of the consumers"[6].

---

[2] Directive 95/46 of the European Parliament and of the Council of 24 October 1995 on the protection of individuals with regard to the processing of personal data and on the free movement of such data, Official journal L 281, 23/11/1995, p31-50.
[3] Directive 2002/58 of the European Parliament and of the Council of 12 July 2002 concerning the processing of personal data and the protection of privacy in the electronic communications sector, Official Journal L201, 31/7/2002, p37-47.
[4] Kariyawasam Rohan, Internet Interconnection: Where are we going?, Computer and Telecommunications Law Review, 2000, Sweet & Maxwell limited and Contributors, p187.
[5] Pearson E. Hilary, E-Commerce Legislation: Recent European Community Developments, Journal of Internet Law, accessed on 5/2/2002 on www.gcwf.com/articles/journal/jil_aug00_1.html .
[6] The original text reads: "el legislador comunitario desea garantizar la seguridad juridical y la confianza de los consumidores", Marta Pardo Leal, La directiva 2000/31 CE sobre el comercio electronico: su aplicacion en el ambito del Mercado Interior, Gaceta Juridica de la Union Europea y de la Competencia, 2000, n210, p38.

1.1 Outline of the Central Thesis of the Book

Privacy and more specifically data protection is an issue with deep roots in legal history and individual national cultures. Especially today it has an additional value and is of particular interest because it is a fundamental right whose essence and nature are in a phase of major transition seriously affected by significant changes occurred in the technological field. Privacy involves areas of law as diverse as human rights law, international trade law, single market regulations in the EU law context and telecommunications and internet legislation. It reflects and expresses a delicate societal balance between the need to further promote technological advances while maintaining the human rights guarantees established in the non digital era. Therefore, it possesses a twofold dimension which highlights its central status in the legal world while underlining the potential challenges in fully analysing its exact scope and application. It possesses a highly symbolic position in the European legal order and is a central characteristic of a legislative framework designed to effectively protect the European citizens. Simultaneously, in the new digital era it can be viewed as an anachronistic obstacle to further technological development, a right of the old regime unworthy of further protection in an era where transparency will substitute privacy as the principal feature of societal behaviour at least in the West. Privacy is currently even more significant than some years ago because after the emergence of the internet as a significant economic field, the right in question is deeply attached to the lifeblood of the new economy; information itself and of course its protection and use. It is *the* right directly linked with the very subject of the new electronic trade. Therefore, it is fundamental both for the protection of human rights *and* for the regulation of trade as well. Thus, privacy and data protection are rights falling within multiple and sometimes contrasting in terms of aims fields such as trade or internet law and human rights law. Therefore, the speciality of the issue in question lies in the necessity to thoroughly present and analyse both aspects of the privacy right as an integral part of human rights' protection and at the same time an element of single market or telecommunications legislation. The book is structured in such a manner so as to clearly reflect this dual nature of the privacy right. It attempts to highlight and focus on the multiple aspects of privacy so as to further illuminate the importance of the relevant right. In Chapters 2 and 3 privacy and data protection are presented from a commercial angle since the

4

relevant rights albeit recognised in many national legal orders, found their way to common regulation at EU level through legislative initiatives assumed in the framework of the single market. Data protection was a part of the relevant consumer protection legislation passed for the smooth function of the single market. The EU made the conscious choice to promote the regulation of common data protection principles and standards through its single market policy which anyway constitutes the cornerstone of the EU activities and achievements during the last half of the century. Chapters 2 and 3 provide a thorough analysis of the development of data protection legislation. It presents how the relevant rights gradually found their place in common EU wide legislation. It is necessary to fully understand the initial rise of privacy to prominence at the EU jurisdictional level before moving to present the current landscape and the future proposals.

In Chapter 4 an extensive analysis of the conceptual framework of the book is provided. This chapter focuses on the threats and challenges to privacy emerging from the new era which has internet as the main means of communication, commercial transaction and business tool at its centre. It is explained that the threats to privacy are inherent in the technologies of internet with the use of cookies and the exchange of data between the user's computer and the relevant commercial websites. Within this framework additional challenges to privacy are created by industries emerging from the commercial use of internet such as the direct marketing and profile advertising industries. It is explained that the radical shift in the way marketing campaigns are to be ran in the future presents novel challenges for privacy. Along with the human rights challenges, the chapters' analysis also point at the direction of consumer confidence as the main battle to be won on the front of convincing consumers to engage in on line activities and take advantage of the full capacities of the net. Therefore, the commercial aspect of privacy and data protection is present throughout the book in conjunction with the human rights aspects, because the nature of the rights in question renders this approach necessary. Protecting on line privacy is both an issue of human rights' protection and a necessary precondition for the commercial development of internet as consumer confidence stands at the core of the strategy for the commercial use of the net. This chapter also places a focus on the analysis of the delicate distinction between privacy and data protection, which has proved a difficult issue for academics worldwide and concludes with the issue of data retention with the analysis of the latest EU directive on the field. The latter is imperative as especially after 9/11 apart from the aforementioned fields of human rights and trade a third important dimension was added to the privacy equation; security. It is explained that depending on the actual national implementation of the directive in question, this piece of legislation can signal a major departure of the Union from its previous position on the issue seriously tipping the balance from human rights albeit in compromise with the current commercial reality to security. This chapter includes the analysis of the fundamental dimensions of the data protection and privacy problem now. With human rights, on line trade and security as the three basic dimensions, solutions have to be compatible with all aspects of the issue in question if they are to be implemented.

Chapter 5 adds to the analysis so far by presenting the evolution of privacy in international organisations and fora with an emphasis on the European experience. Naturally, Chapter 6 includes an extensive analysis of the Directive 95/46 on the protection of personal data in the framework of the single market. The rationale behind the thorough analysis of the directive is the fact it was the first EU wide legislative tool on the issue passed in the Single Market framework attempting to compromise the fundamental human right of privacy, as the EU explicitly now admitted privacy to be, with the function of the single market. The Directive set specific data protection principles for on line trade which are now common throughout the EU. It managed to influence major legal orders around the globe through article 25 on the transfer of data to third countries which led a wide range of jurisdictions to adopt the legislative patterns of the EU on the issue in question. The main problem remains the divergence between the two most important trade actors at international level; the EU and the USA.

The book will then embark on thoroughly explaining the rationale behind the divergence of approach on the two sides of the Atlantic which inhibits a common response to privacy risks at international level. It finds that the reason behind the divergence is of historical and cultural nature. Different historical developments have created a different set of principles and priorities which rendered a common approach challenging to achieve. Chapter 7 analyses the principal European legal orders in relation to privacy in the 20th century so as to find the historical, cultural and societal realities behind the European attitude towards privacy which led to the current legislative framework. Apart from the legal developments in mainly France and Germany, the choice was made to also present the relevant case law of the two main pillars of the European legal order; the ECJ and the ECHR. The rulings of the two top European Courts are used so as to shed further light in the way privacy and data protection and their exact scope, content and limitations are perceived at European level in interpretation of European legislation and conventions.

Chapter 8 complements Chapter 7 as it includes the respective analysis of the historical, cultural, societal and therefore legislative developments in the USA which led to the current more reserved attitude of the US legislature towards the protection of privacy. The respective developments are compared and contrasted so as to reach a conclusion on *why* the EU and the US have evolved in adopting divergent positions in relation to privacy. The US case law is analysed with the aim of providing a clear picture of the magnitude of divergence with the respective decisions of the ECJ or the ECHR.

Chapter 9 attempts to specifically lay out a range of concrete proposals for the future of data protection. It is the central thesis of this book that the European approach to privacy in the most appropriate as it is founded on the principle of fully respecting human rights while making the necessary realistic compromises which will enable the further development of internet as a commercial tool. The book includes specific proposals in this exact direction.

1.2 Brief history of Internet

"In 1876 Alexander Graham Bell was awarded a patent for the telephone. Its impact has been massive but 74 years were to elapse before 50 million subscribers were connected. Radio took 38 years to reach the same figure. With the PC only16 years elapsed. From its inception in 1993, the World Wide Web required only 4 years to acquire 50 million users"[7].

Although the majority of the people believe that Internet is a phenomenon that appeared only in the last decade the origins of it go back to the Cold War period when the U.S. government wanted to create a system that would "minimise the destruction caused by a nuclear attack"[8]. As a result of these efforts the U.S. military established the American Defence Department Network in 1969. The goal of limiting the effects of a nuclear attack at the computer system would be served by "decentralising control in a highly original way"[9]. The several individual computers of the system were allocated in

---

[7] Lloyd J. Ian, Electronic Commerce and the Law, Hume Papers on Public Policy: Volume 7, No.4, Edinburgh University Press, 2000, p1.
[8] Ruttley Philip, E.C. Competition Law in Cyberspace: An Overview of Recent Developments, [1998] ECLR 4, Sweet &Maxwell, 1998, p187.
[9] The same.

various places in USA, thus the destruction of the network could only be achieved if all command centres were destroyed. The computer network system developed by the US military department was named APRANET and by 1972 consisted of 37 individual computers. Furthermore, APRANET provided its users with the ability of communication through electronic mails. As the number of personal messages increased, the issue of security emerged as one of vital importance for the military authorities. Although, the latter created their own network under the name MILNET, the unprecedented structure and abilities of APRANET attracted the interest of various organisations such as universities and research institutions. By 1985 the capacities of the network were being used by a steadily increasing number of private and state bodies. It was at that period that the term "Internet" started to be used. The opportunities that had already emerged from the new way of communication became evident to a lot of parties, mainly in the US, which started to take into account the commercial dimension of the net. "The Internet from its US military origins has expended to span the whole globe"[10], thus the first area of economic life that flourished in such framework was the R&D sector, mainly because of the plethora of universities and research organisations that participated in the network. Now, it is considered as the "fastest growing free trade zone"[11] which emphasises the importance of regulating the main parameters of its commercial functions.

1.3 Definition of E-Commerce

According to the OECD:

"Electronic Commerce refers generally to all forms of commercial transactions involving both organisations and individuals, that are based upon the electronic processing and transmission of data, including text, sound and visual images. It also refers to the effects that the electronic exchange of commercial information may have on the institutions and processes that support and govern commercial activities"[12].

The development and further penetration of e-commerce has been impressive. The USA now have 215 million people on line, a figure which corresponds with 71% of its total population.[13] Recent reports demonstrated that "54% of the EU's population

---

[10] Evans D. Mark, Protection of Data on the Internet, Intellectual Property Quarterly, 2002, p53.
[11] Michael L. Rustad & Thomas H. Koenig, Harmonising Cybertort Law for Europe and America, 5 Journal of High Technology Law, 2005, page 13.
[12] OECD, Electronic Commerce: Opportunities and Challenges for Government, Paris, 1997, at page 11.
[13] See http://www.etcnewmedia.com/review/default.asp?SectionID=11&CountryID=93 for 2007 figures.

is now actively connected to Internet"[14]. Moreover, "the number of Europeans using broadband internet services grew from 30% to 42% only in a year between 2006 and 2007"[15]. Nowadays, an increasing array of commercial activities is taking place on Internet including advertising, on-line auctions, banking services, software promotion and exchange of a wide range of consumer goods and services. Its global infrastructure of telecommunication technologies and its open networks created the potential of a rapid growth rate in electronic transactions and paved the way for a new trend in global commerce[16].

---

[14] Eurostat Report: Internet access and e-skills in the EU27 in 2007, December 2007.
[15] The same.
[16] The dilemma "E-business or out of business" seemed to embody the basic concept on which the manager philosophy of various companies in Europe and US is based. See "The Economist", June 30th-July 6th 2001, at page 12.

2. Consumer Protection

Consumer policy constitutes one issue of growing importance for the EU. Recently it tends to occupy one of the places of primary importance in the priority list of the EU. As expressed by the European Commission nowadays "consumer policy involves: integrating consumer concerns in all EU policies"[17]. Thus, the importance afforded by the EU to the new dimension of consumer protection policies is evident and openly demonstrated. As the EU grows larger issues concerning citizens especially in their capacity as consumers assumes a place at the core of the Commission's concerns as a part of its highly publicised effort to achieve a greater degree of transparency in its functions and to bring the Union closer to its citizens. In this context, the Commission and the EU institutions in general needed to demonstrate their ability to tackle and resolve issues not only of "high policy" such as the constitutional reform or justice and home affairs issues but also matters more directly related to the everyday life of the European citizens especially when they act with their capacity as consumers in an integrated internal market.

Recent developments at both political and economic levels have fuelled the estimations that the EU is moving towards the aforementioned direction. As explained before the shift of the EU focus to more transparent everyday life linked policies will be integrated in the Union's strategy as a part of its effort to shape a stronger bond with the general public. Furthermore, from an economic point of view the globalisation of the world markets did offer a wider range of product variety to the consumers but it also gave rise to problems related to the lack of specific regulation of particular areas of consumer concern. Data protection has been ranked as one of the most important issues that impede the further development of transborder transactions[18]. Moreover, the further integration of the internal market, a goal constitutionally expressed as one of the most fundamental projects of the EU since the era of EEC, renders the need to facilitate the efforts of consumers to engage in transborder transaction via traditional or electronic trade imperatives. The EU has moved towards the achievement of this goal

---

[17] See http://www.europa.eu.int/comm/consumers/overview/index_en.htm , Overview of Consumer Policy as expressed by the relevant DG Consumer Protection. It constitutes the official position adopted by the Commission.
[18] See Press Release IP/03/81 of the Commission of the March 11th 2002. Accessed on July 23rd 2003 at http://www.europa.eu.int/rapid/start/cgi/guesten.ksh?p_action.gettxt=gt&doc=IP/02/381|0|RAPID&lg=EN&display= on "Most consumers not yet confident enough to shop cross border".

10

with the adoption of directives that are explicitly aimed at both protecting the rights of consumers and facilitating the functions of the internal market[19]. Thus, the proposed consumer strategy "is said to involve the establishment of open and competitive markets and the provision of good information, modern targeted consumer laws".[20] Finally, the dissemination and wide use of the new information technology facilities have introduced radical new methods of interaction between the markets and the consumers. By transforming the established relationship between the two aforementioned factors, the forming of a new framework within which consumers can effectively apply the rights they traditionally enjoyed emerged as an objective of central importance for the Commission. The latest technological developments have provided the necessary incentive for the Commission to reform its current state of legal tools and initiate a new round of legislation on consumer issues that can be equipped to face the challenges of the new era for both industry and the consumers. As it is stated by the Commission reports "consumers will have a profound role in unfolding the Information Society, being one of the driving and catalysing elements therein. Simultaneously, however, enhanced possibilities to do business give rise to legitimate concerns as regards consumer protection in the areas of privacy and marketing"[21]. Especially, in the area of data protection the changes brought by technology are enormous. Respectively, the need for reshaping the existing framework on consumer policies is compelling. As an indication of the changes already initiated, the very nature of some industries has been profoundly altered. The marketing industry for instance will need to resort less to huge advertising campaigns that entail huge expenses and try to appeal to all categories of consumers and more to marketing and advertising on an individual basis; marketing tailored according to the personal needs and preferences of individual consumers, an ability enabled by current technologic methods that can provide companies with such information. This of course leads to fears of privacy and personal data invasion matters that will be thoroughly addressed later. Thus, it is evident that all matters concerning the relevant industries and the consumers are closely inter linked and need common

---

[19] See Directive 95/46 on the Protection of Personal Data supra note 2. In its article 1 it states as its dual objectives the unimpeded flow of information aimed at facilitating the internal market **and** the protection of the European citizens' right of privacy.
[20] Howells Geraint, United Kingdom's Consumer Policy White Paper- A step in the right direction? , Consumer Law Journal, Volume 8, Number 2, Andover, Sweet & Maxwell, at p182.
[21] See the study produced by PriceWaterhouseCoopers for Health & consumer Protection DG. A summary can be accessed at
http://europa.eu.int/comm/dgs/health_consumer/library/surveys/sur20_en.html .

11

policy at European level. "By establishing an appropriate regulatory framework, consumer policy can foster the consumer confidence necessary for them to make purchases electronically. This confidence is a precondition if the market for e-commerce is to have a chance of fulfilling the more ambitious projections for its growth"[22].

The book is focused on what amounts to the greatest challenge to both consumer confidence and our legal culture as well: the threats that internet poses to our privacy. Privacy and more specifically data protection will stand at the core of the relevant analysis. The *basic thesis* of this book as mentioned above is that internet cannot flourish by showing disregard to Europe's humanistic traditions. It argues that Europe can achieve the development of on line commerce in line with the basic recognised rights and principles of its rich legal culture. Europe has founded its impressive development throughout the previous century on exactly this principle. Economic development took place in compliance with basic rights which in the European legal world were considered as "fundamental". Europe experienced its unprecedented growth in the aftermath of the Second World War in full compliance with the reinforcing of individual human rights in its domestic context; the creation of the EU right after the War based on the respect of those rights while having economic development as its basic aim stands as a vivid proof of Europe's achievements and clear political choices. There is no rationale behind any initiative which would undermine Europe's legal traditions and would associate internet's growth with a lack of respect to basic human rights such as the one to privacy. This would constitute a retreat from Europe's basic traditions on the one hand and would undermine the confidence of the consumers in the new medium on the other. The book therefore argues that respect of Europe's basic rights and traditions is compatible with the aim of efficiency which the new medium aims at achieving. If there is no respect of human rights on internet, then there will be no will to conduct on line transactions which would therefore limit the ability to develop e-commerce to its full capacity. Up to now Europe has proved that economic growth and development can indeed go hand in hand with the respect of human rights and its humanistic legal traditions; and it is argued that the same principle should stand

---

[22] The writer is not mentioned in the article. However, the article can be found in Consumer Law Journal, Consumer Policy Action Plan 1999-2001, Volume 7, Number 1, Andover, Sweet & Maxwell, 2000, at p62.

at the core of Europe's plans to develop on line trade as well. The book will cover the developments in the relevant field up to 2007.

2.1 The concept of Consumer Protection

Several parties both from industry and the legal world have tried to provide a common definition of the notion of consumer protection. Although, divergent opinions have been expressed it has been an object of wide agreement that "consumer protection programmes in any country encompass an extensive array of laws, regulations and practices that protect consumers against fraud, help ensure the respect of their economic interests and educate them about their rights, risks and responsibilities when they engage in a variety of transactions"[23]. At an early stage consumer protection law had been viewed as a part of law closely connected with environmental law. Later, it was perceived as an integrated aspect of the internal market process with no independent status of its own. Actually, the question of whether consumer law constitutes a distinctive part of law or not has been turned into the object of major debate both at literature and at political level. Laws protecting the public in its wider sense against the notion of fraud in the framework of product exchange date back to the beginning of the century and stem from the French legal tradition[24]. However, consumer protection as a developed field of legal instruments that covers a wide range of economic activities started to evolve in Western Europe much later. The first initiatives in the relevant field were launched in the UK motivated by the "Molony Report[25]" and in the USA after the President Kennedy's "special message to the Congress on protecting the consumer interest"[26]. President Kennedy described consumers as "the largest economic group in the economy" with "views that are often not heard". It was interesting that he made a direct link between consumer policy and quality of life stretching the importance of the sharp increase in US citizens' income during the respective period. It is also interesting

---

[23] FTAA Joint Government- Private Sector Committee of Experts on Electronic Commerce, Issue Briefing Notice by the Chair, Consumer Protection Issues in Electronic Commerce, accessed on 22/3/2002 at www.ftaa-alca.org/SPCOMM/derdoc/eci27e.doc .
[24] Loi du premier Aout 1905 sur la repression des fraudes.
[25] Committee of consumer protection final report, Board of Trade, Committee of Consumer Protection, Sessional Papers, 1961-62, Cmnd 1781, accessed on 22/6/2003 at http://www.bopcris.ac.uk/bop1955/ref477.html .
[26] Special message to the Congress on protecting the consumer interest, March 15 1962, President Kennedy, accessed on 25/6/2003 at http://www.presidency.ucsb.edu/site/docs/pppus.php?admin=035&year=1962&id=93 .

that he emphasised the importance of the advent of new technologies –of that chronological period- "that has outmoded many of the old laws and regulations and have made new legislation necessary". The speech is important for the subject because it provided for four fundamental consumer rights that were to influence consumer law worldwide. The right "to safety", the right to "be informed", the right "to choose" and the right "to be heard" have been promoted as the basis for an effective consumer protection since 1962.

In Europe the nature, scope and content of consumer law evolved into the subject of an open debate between parties with an obvious influence from the French legal tradition that views consumer policy matters in conjunction with the traditionally protective role of the state and the German stance that considered consumer law as a part of the civil law of the country. The parties within the EU that argue for the role of the state in assuring the protection of the consumers as the weakest link in the relationship involving commercial enterprises and individual consumers insist that "one can hardly speak about a genuine consumer policy at Community level[27]" before the entrance into force of the Maastricht Treaty that as will be analysed later provided for the first time for a constitutional basis of consumer protection law within the EU.

Thus, it is argued that before constitutional status was afforded to consumer protection, the precise definition of consumer has proved to be an equally controversial issue. The reason behind the controversy is weather the term "consumer" encompasses or not the notion of small enterprises or only the concept of a natural person. The central features of the debate is the relationship between a commercial business and a private individual from which it is deemed that most problematic issues in terms of consumer protection arise. This is the most fundamental legal relationship in consumer law as it forms the core of its regulatory purposes. The consumer is viewed as the part of the relationship that constitutes the weakest element that has to enjoy a legal safety net. However, in addition to that, "the role in which a person acts in the market has become relevant in legal policy"[28]. It has been recognised that "a consumer buyer might require additional forms of protection to those offered to a commercial buyer"[29]. At European level the concept "consumer" has been defined as "a person concluding a

---

[27] Bourgoignie Thierry, European Community consumer law and policy: from Rome to Amsterdam, Consumer Law Journal, Andover, Sweet & Maxwell, 1998, p443.
[28] Howells Geraint, Wilhelmsson Thomas, EC Consumer Law, Ashgate, Dartmouth, Sydney, Singapore, 1997, p1.
[29] The same.

contract for a purpose regarded as being outside his trade or profession"[30]. The particular definition is adopted by the text of the Lugano Convention on Jurisdiction in 1988 but was initially explicitly stated by the Brussels Convention on Jurisdiction and Enforcement of Judgments in 1968[31]. Furthermore, it was also included in Article 5 of the Rome Convention on the law applicable to contractual obligations[32]. The EU confirmed its definition in the recently adopted Council Regulation on jurisdiction matters[33] that reforms the regime established by the two aforementioned conventions. In Article 15 of the regulation the exact definition is incorporated as a part of the modern EU law. However, the definition has provided the grounds for a new round of dispute mainly between academics that was finally resolved by the European Court of Justice. Geraint Howells believes that the definition is stated in a clear manner leaving out of its scope "businesses and professional activities"[34]. Thus, only private individuals or natural persons acting for purposes outside their trade or profession fall into the definition of "consumer" and consequently can benefit from the protection afforded by the corresponding part of EU law. On the contrary, Stuyck argued that the following directives "limited the notion of consumer to natural persons while the consumer in the conventions can also be a legal person"[35]. However, the same wording has been subsequently introduced in several legislative initiatives such as the directive regulating certain aspects of the sale of consumer goods[36] in article 1 (2) (a) and in the directive on unfair terms in consumer contracts in article 2 (b)[37].

---

[30] See Article 13 of 88/592 EEC, Convention on Jurisdiction and the enforcement of judgments in civil and commercial matters, Lugano September 16th 1988, Official Journal L319, 25/11/1988, p 9-33. It can also be accessed at
http://europa.eu.int/smartapi/cgi/sga_doc?smartapi!celexapi!prod!CELEXnumdoc&lg=EN&numdoc=41988A0592&model=guichett .
[31] 1968 Brussels Convention on jurisdiction and the enforcement of judgments in civil and commercial matters, Official Journal C027, 26/01/98, p1-27. Article 13. Also available at
http://europa.eu.int/smartapi/cgi/sga_doc?smartapi!celexapi!prod!CELEXnumdoc&lg=EN&numdoc=41998A0126&model=guichett .
[32] EC Convention on the Law applicable to contractual obligations, Rome 1980, available at
http://www.jus.uio.no/lm/ec.applicable.law.contracts.1980/doc.html#1 .
[33] Council Regulation (EC) No 44/2001 of 22 December 2000 on jurisdiction and the recognition and enforcement of judgments in civil and commercial matters, Official Journal L 012, 16/01/2001 P. 0001 – 0023. Article 15. Available also at
http://europa.eu.int/smartapi/cgi/sga_doc?smartapi!celexapi!prod!CELEXnumdoc&lg=EN&numdoc=32001R0044&model=guichett .
[34] Howells Geraint, Wilhelmsson Thomas, EC Consumer Law, supra note 28 at p 3.
[35] Stuyck Jules, European Consumer Law after the Treaty of Amsterdam: Consumer policy in or beyond the internal market? ,at page 376.
[36] Article 1 (2) (a) reads: consumer: shall mean any natural person who, in the contracts covered by this Directive, is acting for purposes which are not related to his trade, business or profession.
Directive 1999/44/EC of the European Parliament and of the Council of 25 May 1999 on certain aspects of the sale of consumer goods and associated guarantees. Official Journal L 171, 07/07/1999 P. 0012 –

The role of the European Court of Justice in the interpretation of EU law has guaranteed its status as the institution of principal importance for European lawyers and member state judges. In its *Pinto*[38] judgment the Court preferred a narrow reading of the directive in question (the doorstep selling directive[39]) and assessed that only private individuals are to be afforded the protection assigned to "consumers". The Advocate General had proposed a more flexible and wide interpretation of the word "consumer" but the Court was not willing to adopt his position. More specifically the Advocate General argued that the status of the person in question could have been equal to that of a consumer since he engaged in a transaction outside the scope of his business activities and thus he was acting outside his "trade or profession". The Court as mentioned earlier was unwilling to extend the scope of the directive and the notion of consumer to that extent.

However, there was an ambiguity over the particular issue that was further underlined by the lack of coherence easily discernable in EU law when referring to the issue of defining the exact nature of consumer. Subsequent legislative initiatives on behalf of the Commission have extended the ambit of the term to cover "the person who takes or agrees to take the package or any person on whose behalf the principal contractor agrees to purchase the package or any person to whom the principal contractor or any of the other beneficiaries transfers the package"[40]. Therefore, it also covers for example "a businessman buying a business trip"[41]. The same line is followed by the Misleading Advertising Directive, which extends its protection to "persons

---

0016. Available also at
http://europa.eu.int/smartapi/cgi/sga_doc?smartapi!celexapi!prod!CELEXnumdoc&lg=EN&numdoc=31999L0044&model=guichett .

[37] Council Directive 93/13/EEC of 5 April 1993 on unfair terms in consumer contracts, Official Journal L 095 , 21/04/1993 P. 0029 – 0034, available also at
http://europa.eu.int/smartapi/cgi/sga_doc?smartapi!celexapi!prod!CELEXnumdoc&lg=EN&numdoc=31993L0013&model=guichett .

[38] *Criminal Proceedings against Patrice Di Pinto*, Reference for a preliminary ruling from the Cour d'Appel de Paris, Case C-361/89, [1991] ECR I-1189.

[39] Council Directive 85/577/EEC of 20 December 1985 to protect the consumer in respect of contracts negotiated away from business premises, Official Journal L 372, 31/12/1985 P. 0031 – 0033, also available at
http://europa.eu.int/smartapi/cgi/sga_doc?smartapi!celexapi!prod!CELEXnumdoc&lg=EN&numdoc=31985L0577&model=guichett .

[40] Article 2 (4) of the Package Travel Directive, Council Directive 90/314/EEC of 13 June 1990 on package travel, package holidays and package tours, Official Journal L 158, 23/06/1990 P. 0059 – 0064, also available at
http://europa.eu.int/smartapi/cgi/sga_doc?smartapi!celexapi!prod!CELEXnumdoc&lg=EN&numdoc=31990L0314&model=guichett .

[41] Howells Geraint, Wilhelmsson Thomas, EC Consumer Law, supra note 28 at page 4.

carrying on a trade or business or practising a craft or profession and the interests of the public in general"[42]. Thus, the directive adopts a broader definition of "consumer" wider than that of the Court in *Pinto*. In a subsequent case the Court has once again confirmed only the fact that "the term consumer refers solely to natural persons"[43] and not to an undertaking "even if it concludes a standard contract to acquire services solely for the benefit of its employees"[44].

It is quite interesting that the EU definition for the term "consumer" has influenced other strong players of world trade such as Canada. In the Principles of Consumer Protection for Electronic Commerce issued by the Canadian industry consumers are defined as "individuals who engage in electronic commerce for personal, family or household purposes"[45].

---

[42] Article 1 (2) of the Misleading Advertising Directive, Directive 97/55/EC of European Parliament and of the Council of 6 October 1997 amending Directive 84/450/EEC concerning misleading advertising so as to include comparative advertising, Official Journal L 290 , 23/10/1997 P. 0018 – 0023, available also at
http://europa.eu.int/smartapi/cgi/sga_doc?smartapi!celexapi!prod!CELEXnumdoc&lg=EN&numdoc=31
997L0055&model=guichett .
[43] Joined Cases C-541/99 and C-542/99 on Article 2(b) of directive 93/13/EEC on the meaning of consumer. Reference to the Court by the Giudice di pace di Viadana, accessible at
www.fs.dk/uk/acts/eu/d_fb1uk.htm .
[44] The same.
[45] Principles of Consumer Protection for electronic commerce, A Canadian Framework, Working Group on electronic Commerce and Consumers, Industry Canada, accessed on 22/2/2002, at
http://strategis.ic.gc.ca/SSG/ca01185e.html

3. The legal basis for Consumer Protection in the European Union

3.1 From the Treaty of Rome to the Treaty of Amsterdam

3.1.1 The Treaty of Rome

The Treaty of Rome, the founding Treaty of the then EEC, did not include any explicit reference to consumer protection not only as an independent policy branch of the EEC but also as an element of other aspects of European concern. There was just "an implicit reference to achieve this goal in Article 2 EEC, which provides that the Community shall have as its task to adopt measures to raise the standard of living"[46]. The only element signalling to the existence of a consumer protection element in the general policies of the EEC were some references in the body of the Treaty to the "peoples" of Europe and their interests. More concretely the preamble of the Treaty of Rome states that the six initial signatories are:

"Affirming as the essential objective of their efforts the constant improvements of the living and working conditions of their peoples"[47].

Article 2 of the Treaty included the increase of the standard of "quality of life" as one of the Community's basic objectives. This is usually viewed as an indirect reference to the body of consumers whose rights were dealt as a part of the Community's effort to raise the standard of living for its citizens. Of course by no means did a consumer policy emerge as an objective, not to mention a constitutionally protected one, but it was vaguely considered an aspect of the Community's manoeuvring to achieve an integrated internal market. Only in this framework could the protection of consumers find sufficient access to the highly focused on internal market Community agenda.

In Title II of the Treaty dedicated to agriculture in article 39 (1) (e) we can read that:

"The objectives of the common agricultural policy shall be to ensure that supplies reach consumers at reasonable prices"[48].

The Community was laying the foundations for one of its corner stone common policies, the Common Agriculture Policy, and provided for reasonably priced agriculture products. The consumers would reap the benefits of European integration mainly as the subjects of the internal market.

---

[46] Sideek Mohamed, Consumer Protection in the EC Financial Market, Consumer Law Journal, Volume 8, Number 3-4, Andover, Sweet & Maxwell, 2000, p383.
[47] Preamble of the founding Treaty of Rome, 1957, accessed at: http://europa.eu.int/abc/obj/treaties/en/entr6a.htm#11
[48] See: http://europa.eu.int/abc/obj/treaties/en/entr6d02.htm#Article_39

Furthermore, the European citizens (under this capacity were the consumers afforded protection under the Treaty of Rome) became the recipients of the advantages stemming from the inauguration of the Community Competition policy that since 1957 constitutes one of the most important pieces of EU legislation. Article 85 (3) declared agreements that otherwise would be prohibited under EC law as provisions compatible with the common market values if " they contribute to improving the production or distribution of goods or to promoting technical or economic progress, while allowing consumers a fair share of the resulting benefit"[49]. The underlining principle of the Treaty that placed consumers as the recipients of the positive effects of several sectors of EC policies was confirmed. The signatory parties shaped a range of policies aimed at enhancing the quality of services and products offered at EC level with obvious impact on consumer protection but they were not willing to add a consumer policy dimension to their initial plans because that would lead to the placement of impediments in the way of implementing an integrated internal market. The latter continued up to the mid nineties when it was to a very high level achieved the ultimate goal of the European Union.

The final reference to the consumers in the founding Treaty is detected again in the competition policy provisions in Article 86 (b). There it was stated that an abuse of dominant position must be deemed incompatible with the common market since it limits development "to the prejudice of consumers"[50].

However, it was viewed that with the provisions on the Free Movement of Persons, Services and Capital[51] along with the regulation of an effective competition law policy (mainly articles 85 and 86 stated before) the Treaty "proceeded on the basis that the consumer is the ultimate beneficiary of its economic objectives[52]". Thus, the "intensification of competition should serve the consumer by increasing the available choice of goods and services[53]" which would upgrade in a radical manner the quality of life of European citizens. Therefore, all the relative Treaty provisions "are indirectly part of EC consumer law and policy"[54].

---

[49] See: http://europa.eu.int/abc/obj/treaties/en/entr6d05.htm#Article_85
[50] See http://europa.eu.int/abc/obj/treaties/en/entr6d05.htm#Article_86
[51] See Title III of the Treaty. At http://europa.eu.int/abc/obj/treaties/en/entr6d03.htm#112
[52] Micklitz W. Hans, Weatherill Stephen, Consumer Policy in the European Community: Before and After Maastricht, Journal of Consumer Policy 16, Kluwer Academic Publishers, 1993 at page 285.
[53] The same.
[54] Ibid at page 286.

The inclusion of consumer policy in Community's interests as an aspect inherent in the common market may have deprived consumer protection of an independent status within the community agenda but it also had positive effects. The principal one was that it was seen as an aspect of the most prestigious goal of the recently founded Community. Therefore, although the community legislators had to deal with an issue lacking a clear constitutional basis, they managed to pass and implement a great number of directives concerning consumer protection based on article 100 of the Treaty. The relevant article allowed the Council to "issue directives for the approximation of laws...with a direct effect on the establishment and functioning of the common market"[55]. There was a burden imposed by the unanimity requirement introduced by the article but that was removed by the Single European Act, which will be examined afterwards, and in any case it didn't prevent the Community from adopting "approximately two hundred and fifty directives, aimed at harmonising the laws and regulations of member states[56]" in consumer related issues especially when the impetus was linked to the removal of "obstacles to the free movement of goods within the territory of the EEC[57]".

3.1.2 *The Single European Act*

The Single European Act (SEA) came into force on July 1st 1987. Its main aim was to institutionalise all the expansions of the competence of the EEC that had already taken place in the period after the ratification of the Treaty of Rome mainly at the level of the internal market policy. The latter as mentioned before still in the framework of the EEC constituted the most essential and of high profile objective of the Community policies. Therefore, in a step that now is judged as of vital importance for the elevation of the EEC to the EU level, which in simple words signals the passage of the European Community from a stage of pure financial goals to a stage where integration at political level is pursued, a new article was added. Article 100a is particularly significant as it constitutes a turning point in the way towards European integration. It is the article that came into force after years of discussions in the EC framework and paved the way for

---

[55] See Article 100 at http://europa.eu.int/abc/obj/treaties/en/entr6d05.htm#Article_100
[56] Bourgoignie Thierry, European Community consumer law and policy: from Rome to Amsterdam, supra note 27, p 443.
[57] The same.

the adoption of a more flexible and at the very end integrationalist approach on behalf of the Community.

"The Council shall acting by a qualified majority on a proposal by the Commission and after cooperation with the European Parliament and consulting the Economic and Social Committee adopt the measures....which have as their objective the establishment and functioning of the internal market"[58]. Thus, most of the barriers in reaching a commonly accepted decision concerning the internal market were effectively removed. Unanimity ceased to constitute a prerequisite for the achievement of a common position and the legislative process was significantly accelerated. The impact on consumer protection was immense since as explained before consumer protection was viewed as a by-product inherent in the internal market.

Article 100a (3) also supplemented by the SEA was also essential for our subject as it was the first time that "consumer protection" was mentioned in a text of constitutional dimension for the Community. The Commission in its proposals for the internal market will "take as a base a high level of consumer protection?"[59]. This article became the starting point for the elevation of consumer policy from the status of an aspect of internal market into a policy, which started to assume a more independent role and position in the Community agenda of priorities. It constituted the beginning of a new era for the shaping of consumer policy or even an independent consumer law within the context of the EC. However, it also provided the grounds for a new round of debate in literature as it led to the expression of widely conflicting opinions over whether the adopted provisions constituted a sufficient legal basis for the forming of an effective consumer policy or they were just an encouraging starting point for further development. Stuyck supported the view that "the SEA did not provide for a specific legal basis for consumer legislation"[60]. This opinion was also expressed by Micklitz and Weatherill who argued that "the SEA did not introduce a separate consumer policy title, therefore consumer policy remained an element in other policies"[61]. However, Nevenko in his article expressed the view that "a specific legal basis for consumer policy only appeared in 1987 with the adoption of the SEA which in the new 100a

---

[58] See article 18 of the Single European Act that supplements article 100a to the EEC Treaty. Available in pdf form at: http://www.eurotreaties.com/singleuropeanact.pdf
[59] See article 100a (3) as added in the EEC by article 18 of the Single European Act.
[60] Stuyck Jules, European Consumer Law after the Treaty of Amsterdam: Consumer policy in or beyond the internal market?, supra note 35 at page 378.
[61] Micklitz W. Hans, Weatherill Stephen, Consumer Policy in the European Community: Before and After Maastricht, supra note 52 at page 295.

required the Commission to take a high level of protection in the field of consumer protection"[62]. It appears more convincing that consumer policy was only beginning to assume a more prominent status in both political and legislative agendas of the community but still as a policy it lacked a concrete legal basis on which the commission could found a separate body of law and initiatives. Nevertheless, it must be noted that the SEA marked a turning point in conferring to consumer policy a more official status. But still there were many steps that had to be taken.

3.1.3 The Treaty of Maastricht

The Treaty of Maastricht or Treaty of the European Union (TEU) as it signalled the transformation of the up to that point EEC into the European Union is deemed to be the most significant constitutional text on the issue examined. The rationale behind this statement is the introduction – for the first time – of a new title devoted exclusively to consumer protection. Firstly, at article 3 (s) of the TEU it is explicitly provided that the various measures that the Community seeks to adopt in order to achieve its goals must include "a contribution to the strengthening of consumer protection"[63]. In addition to that the most important provision in the new Treaty regarding our issue was definitely 129a. This provision reads:

TITLE XI

Consumer protection

ARTICLE 129a

1. The Community shall contribute to the attainment of a high level of consumer protection through:

(a) measures adopted pursuant to Article 100a in the context of the completion of the internal market;

(b) specific action which supports and supplements the policy pursued by the Member States to protect the health, safety and economic interests of consumers and to provide adequate information to consumers.

---

[62] Nevenko Misita, Reconstructing the Consumer Committee: glossae marginalis, Consumer Law Journal, Volume 8, Number 1, Andover, Sweet & Maxwell, 2000, at pages 25 and 26.
[63] See article 3 (s) of the TEU at http://europa.eu.int/en/record/mt/title2.html

2. The Council, acting in accordance with the procedure referred to in Article 189b and after consulting the Economic and Social Committee, shall adopt the specific action referred to in paragraph 1(b).

3. Action adopted pursuant to paragraph 2 shall not prevent any Member State from maintaining or introducing more stringent protective measures. Such measures must be compatible with this Treaty. The Commission shall be notified of them.

It is very important to notice that it is the first time that a separate title is devoted to consumer protection that now was upgraded to one of the Union's policy goals with an explicit legal base in the Treaty itself. Therefore, consumer protection comes out of the shadow of the internal market and is effectively deprived of its character as a side area of it. The Commission after the ratification of the TEU had the necessary competence to propose legislation on consumer issues that were by no means related to the internal market.

Furthermore, article 129a (2) makes a direct reference to the procedure envisaged in 189b that has institutionalised the role of the European Parliament in the decision making process and approved qualified majority as a system of voting in the Council. This provision had further positive repercussions as it led to the upgrading of the role of the Parliament, which is the institution of the EU that stands closer to the European citizens and consumers. It is more keen to adopt positions that are beneficial to consumers. Moreover, the confirmation of the qualified voting that is now permanently established as the preferred pattern of voting had a major impact on the issue since it enabled initiatives that may have been hampered if unanimity was required.

There was, however, a limit on the ability of the Union to regulate in the sphere of the consumer protection, which was introduced by article 3b of the Treaty. The particular provision inserted the principle of subsidiarity in the list of the Community vocabulary as a principle of guiding nature for the planning of the Union's activities. According to the wording of the particular article: "The Community shall take action, in accordance with the principle of subsidiarity, only if and in so far as the objectives of the proposed action cannot be sufficiently achieved by the Member States and can therefore, by reason of the scale or effects of the proposed action, be better achieved by the Community"[64]. The Community was now called to act in cases where member states do not have the ability to achieve the desirable objective individually. Article 3s that required a "contribution to the strengthening of consumer protection" was perceived as a safeguard against the potential threat of putting another limit to the Community's ability to act. The European Parliament under its new reinforced status with its resolution of February 15th 1993[65] emphasised the necessity of preventing the principle of proportionality downgrading the level of consumer protection afforded by the EU. The Parliament supported the view that a wide decentralisation of consumer protection standards and a potential lack of harmonised policies on behalf of the EU will ultimately lead to the undermining of the offered protection in all member states. The latter will have a considerable impact on the common market, which is based on harmonised standards of function that are in force in all member states. It demonstrated the importance of consumer protection in all areas of community actions and concluded in supporting European level decision making. The repercussions of the more significant role afforded to the Parliament in the framework of the co-decision process implemented by article 189b of the TEU was already becoming obvious both in Brussels and in the European capitals.

The European Court of Justice on the other hand confirmed that article 129a has added another objective in the list of the Union but also stated that no horizontal direct effect can be assigned to the directives. As the Advocate General stated in *El Corte Ingles* "Article 129a of the EC Treaty does set the Community's clear aims, but, in view of its nature as a competence-conferring provision, it leaves relatively large margins of discretion as regards its implementation. Consequently, it lacks the very requirement that the provision in question should be sufficiently precise and unconditional"[66]. Finally, he concluded by emphasising that "if it were to be held that directives have direct effect in view of Article 129a, this would entail consumer

---

[64] Article 3b of the TEU. See http://europa.eu.int/en/record/mt/title2.html
[65] Resolution of the European Parliament on the application of the principle of subsidiarity to environment and consumer protection policy, Official Journal C 042, 15/02/1993 p. 0040, Available also at
http://europa.eu.int/servlet/portail/RenderServlet?search=RefPub&lg=en&nb_docs=25&domain=&in_fo
rce=NO&year=1993&month=&day=&coll=JO&nu_jo=42&page=40
[66] See paragraph 34 of the Opinion of Mr Advocate General Lenz delivered on 7 December 1995. Case El Corte Ingles SA v Cristina Blazquez Rivero. Case C-192/94, [1996] ECR I-1281, also accessible at http://europa.eu.int/smartapi/cgi/sga_doc?smartapi!celexapi!prod!CELEXnumdoc&lg=EN&numdoc=61
994C0192&model=guichett

protection directives being treated differently than other directives"[67]. Although, from a legal point of view this was a reasonable position it had led to discussions on whether regulations would constitute a more preferable tool to initiate consumer legislation.

The introduction of 129a (3) is also deemed as a further safeguard to consumer protection as it enables member states to adopt even stricter measures if they consider them necessary. Thus, the Union is setting a set of rules that is perceived as laying a minimum level of protection. The member states can build on these standards by introducing additional requirements. The harmonisation at minimum level and the scope of competence to extend the protection individually to the other aspects of activities is considered not only for consumer law but also for other areas such as environmental law a method of protection of an effective nature.

Despite the shortcomings detected in the TEU provisions it is important to notice that the Treaty introduced a legal basis for consumer legislation and an increased level of independence or maybe better autonomy of consumer policy within the framework of the EU agenda. The latter is highly significant since it provided the grounds for a row of directives that were issued concerning all levels of consumer related matters. Product safety[68], unfair contract terms[69], distance contracts[70], comparative and misleading advertising[71], price indication[72], alternative dispute

---

[67] See paragraph 35 of the relative opinion.
[68] Council Directive 92/59/EEC of 29 June 1992 on general product safety
Official Journal L 228, 11/08/1992 P. 0024 – 0032, available at
http://europa.eu.int/smartapi/cgi/sga_doc?smartapi!celexapi!prod!CELEXnumdoc&lg=EN&numdoc=31992L0059&model=guichett
[69] Council Directive 93/13/EEC of 5 April 1993 on unfair terms in consumer contracts
Official Journal L 095, 21/04/1993 P. 0029 – 0034, available at
http://europa.eu.int/smartapi/cgi/sga_doc?smartapi!celexapi!prod!CELEXnumdoc&lg=EN&numdoc=31993L0013&model=guichett
[70] Directive 97/7/EC of the European Parliament and of the Council of 20 May 1997 on the protection of consumers in respect of distance contracts, Official Journal L 144, 04/06/1997 P. 0019 – 0027, available at
http://europa.eu.int/smartapi/cgi/sga_doc?smartapi!celexapi!prod!CELEXnumdoc&lg=EN&numdoc=31997L0007&model=guichett
[71] Directive 97/55/EC of European Parliament and of the Council of 6 October 1997 amending Directive 84/450/EEC concerning misleading advertising so as to include comparative advertising
Official Journal L 290, 23/10/1997 P. 0018 – 0023, available at
http://europa.eu.int/smartapi/cgi/sga_doc?smartapi!celexapi!prod!CELEXnumdoc&lg=EN&numdoc=31997L0055&model=guichett
[72] Directive 98/6/EC of the European Parliament and of the Council of 16 February 1998 on consumer protection in the indication of the prices of products offered to consumers
Official Journal L 080, 18/03/1998 P. 0027 – 0031, available at
http://europa.eu.int/smartapi/cgi/sga_doc?smartapi!celexapi!prod!CELEXnumdoc&lg=EN&numdoc=31998L0006&model=guichett

resolution plans[73], injunction abilities[74], tobacco[75], consumer guarantees[76] were only some of the areas regulated on the basis provided by the TEU and later of course by the Treaty of Amsterdam to be analysed later.

3.1.4 The Amsterdam Treaty

The Treaty of Amsterdam agreed in 1997 introduced reforms in several sectors of EU activities. The most important of those concerned immigration and asylum issues where the reform was of massive scope. Nonetheless, the Treaty brought major changes also in the issue of consumer protection as it moved towards the direction of enriching the existing relevant provision of the Maastricht Treaty with new elements that contributed effectively to the elevation of consumer law and policies up to the level of an independent aspect of Community agenda. The Treaty added a new article in its body, article 153, which substituted article 129a inserted by the TEU. The new article reads[77]:

Title XIV

Article 153 (previously 129a)

1. In order to promote the interests of consumers and to ensure a high level of consumer protection, the Community shall contribute to protecting the health, safety and economic interests of consumers, as well as to promoting their right to information, education and to organise themselves in order to safeguard their interests.

2. Consumer protection requirements shall be taken into account in defining and implementing other Community policies and activities.

---

[73]98/257/EC: Commission Recommendation of 30 March 1998 on the principles applicable to the bodies responsible for out-of-court settlement of consumer disputes (Text with EEA relevance)
Official Journal L 115, 17/04/1998 P. 0031 – 0034, available at
http://europa.eu.int/smartapi/cgi/sga_doc?smartapi!celexapi!prod!CELEXnumdoc&lg=EN&numdoc=31 998H0257&model=guichett
[74] Directive 98/27/EC of the European Parliament and of the Council of 19 May 1998 on injunctions for the protection of consumers' interests
Official Journal L 166, 11/06/1998 P. 0051 – 0055, available at
http://europa.eu.int/smartapi/cgi/sga_doc?smartapi!celexapi!prod!CELEXnumdoc&lg=EN&numdoc=31 998L0027&model=guichett
[75] Directive 98/43/EC of the European Parliament and of the Council of 6 July 1998 on the approximation of the laws, regulations and administrative provisions of the Member States relating to the advertising and sponsorship of tobacco products
Official Journal L 213, 30/07/1998 P. 0009 – 0012, available at
http://europa.eu.int/smartapi/cgi/sga_doc?smartapi!celexapi!prod!CELEXnumdoc&lg=EN&numdoc=31 998L0043&model=guichett
[76] Directive 1999/44/EC of the European Parliament and of the Council of 25 May 1999 on certain aspects of the sale of consumer goods and associated guarantees. http://eur-lex.europa.eu/LexUriServ/LexUriServ.do?uri=CELEX:31999L0044:EN:HTML
[77] See the relevant article at: http://europa.eu.int/eur-lex/en/treaties/dat/amsterdam.html. Also available at Official Journal C 340 of 10 November 1997.

3. The Community shall contribute to the attainment of the objectives referred to in paragraph 1 through:

(a) measures adopted pursuant to Article 95 in the context of the completion of the internal market;

(b) measures which support, supplement and monitor the policy pursued by the Member States.

4. The Council, acting in accordance with the procedure referred to in Article 251 and after consulting the Economic and Social Committee, shall adopt the measures referred to in paragraph 3(b).

5. Measures adopted pursuant to paragraph 4 shall not prevent any Member State from maintaining or introducing more stringent protective measures. Such measures must be compatible with this Treaty. The Commission shall be notified of them.

There are certain differences with the respective text adopted in the Treaty of Maastricht, which as will be explained have as an obvious consequence a radical shift in the way the Union evaluates consumer policy. The most important new element is the formal recognition, at constitutional level now, of the fundamental rights of the consumers. Their rights to education, information and association[78] are afforded an official status. They become an integral part of community policy and a subject of protection and regulation on behalf of the European legislator. Moreover, it is now explicitly mentioned that the interests of consumers concerning the relative wide areas of health, safety and economy shall be promoted. Thus, consumer interests are now an element inherent in the planning of several policies at the EU level. Especially, the right to information included in the relevant provision was also recognised by the ECJ as an essential right of the consumers that can also place limits upon the ability of the member states to pass legislation "which denies the consumer access to certain kinds of information"[79]. This cannot even "be justified by mandatory requirements concerning consumer protection"[80].

---

[78] Freedom of association constitutes a fundamental right explicitly recognized by the Community. However, it was the first time that it was officially recognized as a consumer right.

[79] See Case GB Inno BM v Confederation du commerce luxembourgeois., Reference for a preliminary ruling: Cour de cassation - Grand-Duchy de Luxembourg. Case C-362/88. European Court reports 1990 Page I-00667. See Grounds of the judgment number 18. Also available at http://europa.eu.int/smartapi/cgi/sga_doc?smartapi!celexapi!prod!CELEXnumdoc&lg=EN&numdoc=61988J0362&model=guichett#MO

[80] The same.

27

Moreover, since the text of the Treaty afforded a constitutional status to the consumer's freedom of association, legislation was passed[81] in order to enable "qualified entities[82]" which refers to consumer bodies or organisations to bring a "cross border injunction[83]" on behalf of the "collective interests of the consumers[84]".

Paragraph two of the new article signalled a departure from the previous principle that defined consumer protection only in close relation to the internal market policies. Now according to the new wording consumer protection forms a requirement "that shall be taken into account in defining and implementing other community policies and activities[85]". The particular provision is extremely important as it deprives consumer protection of its nature as an element of the internal market and it elevates it up to the level of an objective or at least a parameter that must be taken into account in all community policies. Therefore, it effectively extended its ambit of application in increasingly important European policies such as environmental policies, the Common Agriculture Policy and of course Competition policy. Particularly, the CAP absorbs a great part of the capital provided by the community budget, thus the extension and the linking of consumer protection to parts of the Union's policy that occupy the top positions in its priorities list afford a new essence in it.

Furthermore, in paragraph three of the relevant provision a shift in the wording is easily detectable. The term "specific actions" which are planned to support member state policies enshrined in article 129 (1) (b) of the TEU is now reformed into the stronger term "measures" that are to be adopted pursuant to 95 for the completion of the internal market[86]. Measures as a term include legislative initiatives thus a step forward is decisively taken in this issue. Moreover, in the following provision[87] we read about "measures" that support, supplement and monitor the policy of a distinctive nature from the internal market pursued by the member states. The interpretation of the particular provision entails the confirmation of the previously analysed statement that consumer policy is now an integral part of other areas of law and community activities and can

---

[81] Directive 98/27/EC of the European Parliament and of the Council of 19 May 1998 on injunctions for the protection of consumers' interests. Supra note 76.
[82] Article 3 of the Directive.
[83] Article 2 of the Directive.
[84] Article 1 of the Directive.
[85] Article 153 (2) of the Treaty.
[86] Article 153 (3) (a) of the Treaty of Amsterdam.
[87] Article 153 (3) (b) of the Treaty of Amsterdam.

furthermore supplement by specific measures of legislative nature even initiatives assumed exclusively at a member state level.

3.1.4.1 The view of the European Commission on the Treaty of Amsterdam consumer provisions

The European Commission has issued a comprehensive guide[88] on the Treaty of Amsterdam, in which it provides an analysis of the basic elements of the constitutional text and its views and comments on the issues involved. The Commission regards the developments in the area of consumer protection as one of the "accomplishments"[89] of the Treaty in the area regulating the sphere of relations between the Union and the citizen. It concludes by underlining that "the new article 153 (ex article 129a) of the EC Treaty has the objective of ensuring a high level of consumer protection rather than simply contributing to such protection. Moreover, it emphasises promoting the consumers' right to information and education and their right to organise themselves in order to safeguard their interests"[90]. It also adds that "the Amsterdam Treaty markedly strengthens these policies at both Community and national level"[91]. It does not omit to focus on the importance of the new consumer protection provisions included in the Treaty that stems from the fact that "it binds all political players[92]" on the European stage.

3.1.5 The Treaty of Nice

The Treaty of Nice was negotiated under intense pressure from the imminent enlargement to Eastern Europe. It was primarily focused on the reallocation of the seats in the Parliament and the reforming and adjustment of the voting system in the framework of the other community institutions. Its primary goal was to prepare the grounds for the advent of ten new countries in the Union and to introduce changes in the function of Community institutions in order to enable their operation in a new

---

[88] The European Commission, The Amsterdam Treaty, A comprehensive Guide, Luxembourg, Office for Official Publications of the European Communities, 1999.
[89] See page 7.
[90] Ibid at page 48.
[91] See Amsterdam: Questions and answers. Available at: http://europa.eu.int/abc/obj/amst/en/qa.htm#7

enlarged Union with 25 members. Thus, the main concerns of the European leaders were not related to consumer protection at all but mainly to institutional matters. The landscape in consumer protection remained without any particular alteration.

3.1.6   *The proposed Constitution Treaty*

The Treaty of Nice was criticised for parts of its content especially related to institutional arrangements which were a result of negotiations and compromise between the member states. It was mostly related to the need to prepare the European institutions to the imminent big bang enlargement to the East and was rejected in the first referendum in Ireland. The will to renegotiate its content emerged only after some months following its ratification. Thus, after the Convention for the future of the European Union was convened, the way was paved for the introduction of a new Constitution of the European Union. The final text of the Constitution was presented by the President of the Convention in the European Summit in Thessaloniki on June 21st, 2003[93]. The final version of the Constitution had been shaped to a great extent during the Intergovernmental Conference of 2004, when, however, an agreement was not reached, because of the disapproval on behalf of Spain and Poland of the new voting rights in the Council. The Treaty was agreed in June 2004 at the end of the Irish presidency, and was signed in Rome on October 29th 2004. The new Constitution would have replaced the existing treaties if it had not been spectacularly rejected by French and Dutch voters in the respective referenda in May and June 2005. Since then, the EU is experiencing a constitutional limbo in the framework of which it agreed to afford itself years of "reflection" so as to contemplate its future destination, purpose and shape. Up to the time this book is written the European leaders had only agreed that they are not aware at least at this moment of how to deal with the hot potato of the rejection of the ambitious project by two of the core founding member states. President Sarkozy of France had proposed the adoption of a "Reform Treaty" which would keep the essence of the Constitutional Treaty while getting rid of the "federal" elements such as the establishment of a common anthem for the EU. In any case it is most likely that the Charter of Fundamental Rights where privacy related provisions are will find its

---

[92] The same.
[93] See the text at: http://www.europa.eu.int/eur-lex/en/archive/2003/c_16920030718en.html accessed on August 12th 2004.

place in the new Treaty too leaving therefore the landscape in relation to privacy intact. The provisions related to our subject are therefore presented as an indication of the importance of the issues in question for the European legal order as they found their way into important and highly symbolic parts of a text and a Treaty that was meant to be the "Constitutional Treaty" of Europe had the European voters refrained from expressing their loud disapproval over that and several other issues related to the project.

The relevant provisions in the draft Constitution are found in Part II of the Treaty, which incorporated the *Charter of Fundamental Rights* in an attempt to "contribute to a more positive human rights policy at the EU level"[94]. In Title IV under the title "solidarity" there is a new article that reads:

TITLE IV: SOLIDARITY

Article II-38: Consumer protection

Union policies shall ensure a high level of consumer protection

The interesting issue here is the fact that consumer protection is included in the Charter of Fundamental Rights section of the Treaty. This is of high symbolic importance as the protection of consumers now finds its place among the most basic of rights of the European citizens. Apart from the purely symbolic character of such an inclusion, it is doubtful, whether this clause will signal any significant difference in the actual status of consumer protection in the Union. Article 153 on Consumer Protection of the Treaty of Amsterdam included a provision in its paragraph two, where it rendered the consideration of consumer protection objectives in the designing of other community policies necessary. Such an explicit provision is now removed from the body of the relevant articles of the Constitutional Treaty. Thus, article II-38 will actually fill in the gap and play the role previously performed by article 159 (2) of the Treaty of Amsterdam. This remark can lead to the conclusion that apart from the "symbolic promotion" of consumer protection at the level of an aim of equal status with the rights included in the Charter, practically the landscape in consumer protection remains

---

[94] Gráinne de Búrca and Jo Aschenbrenner, in Steve Peers, Angela Ward, The European Union Charter of Fundamental Rights, Hart Publishing, Oxford and Portland Oregon, 2004, page 22.

absolutely the same[95]. This is because this provision "only declares ideals and principles without conferring any right or freedom at all…and…"this is aspirational, setting out programmatic objectives rather than judicially enforceable rights"[96].

The most extensive provision on Consumer Protection can be found in Part III of the Constitutional Treaty on the "Policies and the Functioning of the Union". More specifically, in Chapter III under the title "Policies in Other Specific Areas", in Section 6, the article III-132 on Consumer Protection reads:

SECTION 6

CONSUMER PROTECTION

Article III-132

1.   In order to promote the interests of consumers and to ensure a high level of consumer protection, the Union shall contribute to protecting the health, safety and economic interests of consumers, as well as to promoting their right to information, education and to organise themselves in order to safeguard their interests.

2.   The Union shall contribute to the attainment of the objectives referred to in paragraph 1 through:

(a)   measures adopted pursuant to Article III-65 in the context of the completion of the internal market;

(b)   measures which support, supplement and monitor the policy pursued by the Member States.

---

[95] As Aileen McColgan notes "Some of the provisions…are drafted so as to be incapable of meaningful enforcement…examples of these include Article 38". And taking into account article 51 (2), "It is difficult to imagine…that Art.38 will have a profound effect", see The EU Charter of Fundamental Rights, European Human Rights Law Review, 1, 2-5, 2004.
[96] Douglas Scott Sionaidh, The Charter of Fundamental rights as a Constitutional Document, European Human Rights Law Review, 2004, 1, 37-50.

3.   The measures referred to in paragraph 2(b) shall be enacted by European laws
or framework laws. Such laws shall be adopted after consultation of the Economic and
Social Committee.

4.   Acts adopted pursuant to paragraph 3 shall not prevent any Member State from
maintaining or introducing more stringent protective provisions. Such provisions must
be compatible with the Constitution. They shall be notified to the Commission.

This provision is almost identical with the respective one of article 153 of the
Treaty of Amsterdam. Consumer policy remains a field integral in the planning of the
internal market and the relevant goals will continue to be achieved in the framework of
the Union's internal market initiatives. Although, in the Treaty of Amsterdam context,
it was argued that consumer law achieved its independence as a separate field of law
with its own parameters and distinctive objectives, the new wording of III-132 leaves
no doubt over the incorporation of consumer policies in the internal market field.
Moreover, paragraph 2 is removed, but replaced by the new II-38 analysed above.
Paragraph 4, on the co-decision procedure with the European Parliament is also
removed, but this is because of the general institutional restructure and reform of the
Union that led to the reinforcing of the role of the Parliament in the legislative process.
According to article 19, "the EP shall jointly with the Council of Ministers enact
legislation", while article 33 states that "European laws and framework laws shall be
adopted jointly by the EP". Thus, the role of the Parliament has been upgraded to the
level of co-decision in the framework of legislative initiatives and therefore, paragraph
4 was immediately rendered unnecessary. Thus, the removal of both paragraphs does
not bring any new development in the field. Finally, both the principle of subsidiarity
(III-132 (2)(b)) and the central choice of promoting measures of minimum
harmonisation[97] (III-132(4)), analysed above, which were stated from the era of the
Maastricht Treaty, retain their position in the new text[98]. Thus, from the analysis of the
articles, it can be deduced that no significant change has been introduced to the
consumer protection regulatory regime at least at the level of a constitutional document.

---

[97] See Kenny Mel, stating that "minimum harmonisation asserts the validity of overarching public
interest objectives and allows member states to exceed standards laid down in the relevant directive", in
Globalisation, Interlegality and Europeanised Contract Law, 21 Penn State International Law Review,
2003, 569.

The area of consumer protection has of course evolved from the era of "the flanking policies of the early EEC years"[99] to a field important enough to be included in the Constitutional Treaty, but is still viewed as field integral in the Internal Market. This has assured the increased attention of legislators, who have passed a variety of directives in that context but, it has deprived the field of the ability to evolve on its own basis.

At this point and as we will start focusing specifically on data protection the analysis of the relevant constitutional provisions appears necessary. The constitutional codification of data protection is more impressive. The relevant right is included in Part I of the Treaty under the title "the democratic life of the Union" which basically includes the principles which stand at the very foundations of the EU as a union of democratic nations. It is ranked among principles such as the principle of democratic equality, representative democracy, and participatory democracy, Transparency of the proceedings of Union institutions, bodies, offices and agencies (articles I-45 to I-51). This is very important as texts of constitutional nature are "eminently dependant upon the historical, political etc context in the states they are supposed to govern"[100]. Thus, the inclusion of data protection on the very same part with the principles which have basically shaped the contemporary European constitutional and democratic culture reveals its significance especially in the light of the new technological developments in the European legal order and its newly established status as one of the most important civil rights for European citizens.

Part I of the Constitutional Treaty:

TITLE VI - THE DEMOCRATIC LIFE OF THE UNION

Article I-51 Protection of personal data

1. Everyone has the right to the protection of personal data concerning him or her.

2. European laws or framework laws shall lay down the rules relating to the protection of

---

[98] See also the arguments in Howells Geraint, Wilhelmsson Thomas, EC Consumer Law: Has it come of Age?, 28 European Law Review, 2003, 370.
[99] De Burca Grainne, The Constitutional Challenge of New Governance in the European Union, European Law Review, 2003, 28 (6), 814.
[100] Eivind Smith in Jack Beatson and Takis Tridimas, New Directions in European Public Law, Hart Publishing, Oxford, 1998, page 101.

individuals with regard to the processing of personal data by Union institutions, bodies, offices and agencies, and by the Member States when carrying out activities which fall within the scope of Union law, and the rules relating to the free movement of such data. Compliance with these rules shall be subject to the control of independent authorities.

It should also be noted that data protection will also find its place in Part II and more specifically in the Charter of Fundamental Rights which serves as a codification of Europe's fundamental rights which after their incorporation in the Treaty were obviously intended to assume constitutional recognition. Data protection will be a part of a catalogue which includes among others article II-61 Human dignity, article II-62 Right to life, Right to the integrity of the person, article II-64 Prohibition of torture and inhuman or degrading treatment or punishment, article II-65 Prohibition of slavery and forced labour, article II-66 Right to liberty and security, article II-67 Respect for private and family life, article II-69 Right to marry and right to found a family, article II-70 Freedom of thought, conscience and religion, article II-71 Freedom of expression and information, article II-72 Freedom of assembly and of association, article II-73 Freedom of the arts and sciences and article II-74 Right to education. Its inclusion with the most essential human rights and freedoms reveals the position reserved for it in the European legal order. In addition to that article II-68 extended the protection afforded by I-51 to all natural persons against the processing of personal data on behalf of the Union institutions to everyone against any processing of personal data to take place in contrast to the existing data protection legislation.

Part II of the Constitutional Treaty:
The Charter of fundamental Rights:
PREAMBLE:

"Conscious of its spiritual and moral heritage, the Union is founded on the indivisible, universal values of human dignity, freedom, equality and solidarity... To this end, it is necessary to strengthen the protection of fundamental rights in the light of changes in society, social progress and scientific and technological developments by making those rights more visible in a Charter... This Charter reaffirms, with due regard for the powers and tasks of the Union and the principle of subsidiarity, the rights as they result, in particular, from the constitutional traditions and international obligations common to the Member States, the European Convention for the Protection of Human Rights and Fundamental Freedoms, the Social

Charters adopted by the Union and by the Council of Europe and the case-law of the Court of Justice of the European Union and of the European Court of Human Rights The Union therefore recognises the rights, freedoms and principles set out hereafter".

TITLE II FREEDOMS

Article II-68 Protection of personal data

1. Everyone has the right to the protection of personal data concerning him or her.

2. Such data must be processed fairly for specified purposes and on the basis of the consent of the person concerned or some other legitimate basis laid down by law. Everyone has the right of access to data which has been collected concerning him or her, and the right to have it rectified.

3. Compliance with these rules shall be subject to control by an independent authority.

3.1.7 Directorate General Consumer Protection

The increasing importance of consumer policy for the European Commission is also reflected by its decision to found a new Directorate General (DG) with consumer issues as its exclusive objective. Initially, there was just "a consumer unit within DG XI which then covered environment, consumer protection and nuclear safety"[101]. In 1989, three years before the Treaty of Maastricht, which, as analysed before, provided for a legal basis for consumer protection, the Commission formed an independent Consumer Policy Service. The gradual upgrading of consumer policy as an aspect important in policy shaping was starting to provide its first signs. Hence, consumer protection developed as a "finite part of the internal market programme"[102]. "At this time, the Commission considered that the weight of consumer policy had increased so much that it was no longer wise to let it remain within the structure of another DG, where it formed only a smart part of other activities. So, the consumer department was

---

[101] Kendall Vivienne, EC Consumer Law, Wiley Chancery, London, 1994, p 13.
[102] The same.

constituted as an independent authority, although not yet with a DG status"[103]. However, in 1995 and only two years before the establishment of consumer policy as an important aspect in the EU agenda by the Treaty of Amsterdam, the European Commission creates a separate DG for Consumer Affairs (DG XIV). With an independent DG on consumer protection and a constitutional legal basis on which initiatives can be directly adopted "the somewhat chequered history of EC Consumer policy"[104] has finally reached a point where policy and target independence has been achieved.

---

[103] Maier Lothar, Institutional Consumer Representation in the European Community, Journal of Consumer Policy 16, Kluwer Academic Publishers, 1993, p360. Also available in Reich Norbert, Woodroffe Geoffrey, European Consumer Policy after Maastricht, Kluwer Academic Publishers, London, 1994, p78.
[104] Oughton David, Lowry John, Consumer Law, Blackstone Press Limited, London, 2000, p62.

4. The Conceptual Framework

4.1 Introduction

The subject of this book is to describe the new conditions prevailing in the market of the new economy and focus on the new challenges that are subsequently created. Today's legal tools have been sufficiently equipped to deal with the problems and confusions stemming from traditional types of commercial and economic activities. Consumer Protection however, is an issue whose content and nature is very much depending on the nature of transactions that consumers engage in. Recently, it has been widely accepted that the traditional framework within which the consumers developed their activities has been radically altered. The shift in the way part of international commercial activities has been carried had a profound effect on the level of protection that consumers used to enjoy. The notion of protection is tightly bound with the concept of consumer "confidence", which is an issue of vital importance for both government and industry. The rationale behind these concerns did not flow from a genuine sense of protecting the weaker part in a transaction but rather from the commonly accepted principle that commerce and even more intensively electronic commerce cannot flourish if solid confidence on behalf of the consumers is not established. A sense of insecurity will render them unwilling to participate in any form of electronic transaction. This principle stands at the core of the Union's concerns and is now able to direct its policies towards a more protective role. As it will be analysed later e-commerce is accompanied by a lot of advantages for the consumers but also brings along new dangers and new challenges for the existing legal framework. The EU has been effective in trying to adjust to the new landscape and adopt legislative measures to foster consumer confidence and along with it internal market growth. As the EU transforms from a community of western European nations to a Union of a large market comprising more than 500 million consumers its weight on the international stage is significantly heavier. The EU directives related to the subject will be thoroughly analysed and the role played by the EU in the direction of consolidating a more stable regime in world trade in the new framework will be evaluated.

It is claimed "that we are moving from being an industrial to an information society"[105]. Thus, the most fundamental question is "what impact will this have on the law's development?"[106]. As Lionel Costes has put it "each technological progress regularly leads to the same questions concerning the legitimacy of applying classical legal rules"[107]. Thus, regulating electronic commerce must take into account its unique fundamental characteristics such as its international character and mainly "the extremely rapid evolution of techniques and strategies"[108] that consequently creates a new framework in trade imposing new challenges to both consumers and industry. Kallel detects the principal challenge as "achieving a conciliation between the principles of the freedom of commerce and the need to facilitate electronic commerce"[109].

The new situation had been acknowledged by various organisations, countries and industry bodies that have assumed the initiative to shape a strategy on the particular issue. On behalf of the EU, the European Commission in its Communication in July 1996[110] included consumer protection in the list of its main priorities, while identifying the setting up of an appropriate legal environment founded on the new knowledge-based economy as an element essential for the smooth adjustment of the EU policies to the digital challenges. The European Parliament in its Resolution in May 1998[111] adopted a more radical view stating that a high level of consumer protection "constitutes a fundamental right of the European citizens". Finally, the Council in its Resolution in January 1999[112] recognised "the profound impact of new technologies in society in general"[113] and the possible risk imposed on consumers' interests. Therefore,

---

[105] Brownsword Roger, Howells Geraint, Consumer Protection on the Internet: The impact of the information society on law, Institute for Commercial Law Studies, University of Sheffield, available at http://jsis.artsci.washington.edu/programs/europe/Netconference/HowellsPaper.htm Accessed on 5/2/2002.
[106] The same.
[107] "Chaque avancee technologique donne lieu avec regularite aux memes interrogations liees au bien-fonde de l'application des regles juridiques classiques", Kallel Sami, Arbitrage at Commerce Electronique, Revue de droit des affaires internationales, number 1, 2001, p14.
[108] "La regulation du commerce electronique doit tenir compte...de l'evolution extremement rapides des techniques et des strategies de ses auteurs, Ibid at page 14.
[109] "Il s'agira de proceder a une conciliation entre les principes de la liberte du commerce et la necessite de faciliter le commerce electronique". Kallel, ibid at page 15.
[110] Communication from the Commission to the Council, the European Parliament, the Economic and Social committee and the Committee of the regions, Implications of the Information Society on EU policies: Preparing the next steps, COM (96) 395final, July 24th 1996.
[111] European Parliament Resolution on "A European Initiative on Electronic Commerce", COM97 (157).
[112] Council Resolution of 19 January 1999 on the consumer dimension of the information society, OJ C 023, 28/1/99, p1-3, available also at: http://europa.eu.int/eur-lex/en/lif/dat/1999/en_399Y0128_01.html
[113] See Recital Number 1.

it concluded in inviting the Commission to "identify possible loopholes in related legislation"[114]. The Commission had already passed or was about to propose a variety of directives on e-commerce[115], distance contracts[116], misleading and comparative advertising[117] and of course data protection[118].

4.2 New Commerce. New opportunities. New Dangers
4.2.1 The Advantages

As it is easily understood the advent of new technologies and the emergence of internet as an important means of conducting transactions offered a variety of advantages to consumers. The latter are now in a position to obtain cheap access to a variety of products at international level. The consumers are able to make their choices from products meeting their requirements "from virtually any part of the globe while shifting onto the seller the burden of executing the most far reaching delivery, cost and freight and insurance terms only undertaken for businesses in international trade"[119].

It is also cost effective and quite efficient as technologies evolve on a daily basis. Since, this type of software was aiming at appealing to a particularly wide range of customers its manufacturers made sure that the technological equipment in question would be easy to use for the average consumer. Thus, consumers can engage in electronic activities of a commercial nature without the need to possess any special

---

[114] The Council invites the Commission. See number 1.
[115] Directive 2000/31/EC of the European Parliament and the Council of 8 June 2000 on certain legal aspects of information society services, in particular electronic commerce, in the internal market, available at
http://europa.eu.int/smartapi/cgi/sga_doc?smartapi!celexapi!prod!CELEXnumdoc&lg=EN&numdoc=32 000L0031&model=guichett
[116]Directive 97/7/EC of the European Parliament and of the Council of 20 May 1997 on the protection of consumers in respect of distance contracts, supra note 72.
[117] Directive 97/55/EC of European Parliament and of the Council of 6 October 1997 amending Directive 84/450/EEC concerning misleading advertising so as to include comparative advertising, supra note 73.
[118] Directive 95/46EC of the European Parliament and of the Council of 24 October 1995 on the protection of individuals with regard to the processing of personal data and on the free movement of such data, OJ 281, 23/11/1995, p31-50, available at
http://europa.eu.int/smartapi/cgi/sga_doc?smartapi!celexapi!prod!CELEXnumdoc&lg=EN&numdoc=31 995L0046&model=guichett and Directive 2002/58 of the EP and of the Council of 12 July 2002 concerning the processing of personal data and the protection of privacy in the electronic communications sector, OJ L201, 31/07/2002, p37-47, available at
http://europa.eu.int/smartapi/cgi/sga_doc?smartapi!celexapi!prod!CELEXnumdoc&lg=EN&numdoc=32 002L0058&model=guichett
[119] Endeshaw Assafa, Consumer Protection in Cyberspace: Back to Caveat Emptor?, Consumer Law Journal, Andover, Sweet & Maxwell, Volume 7, Number 1, p159.

knowledge on computers. Moreover, advertising strategies and marketing practices have been radically altered and are now shaped on a more personal basis due to the information that the consumers provide, voluntarily or not, while navigating on the net. In this case of course problems related to the legitimacy of such methods arise but this is a subject of concern that will be analysed thoroughly later. For example the newspaper industry has particularly benefited from these methods. Newspaper sites and portals usually ask for a free or low charge subscription on behalf of their on line readers. Thus, they can "obtain precise information about their subscribers' patterns of consumption"[120] by detecting their choice of articles or the advertisements they clicked on. This is considered an effective way to create personal profiles for the site users that will be proven very useful to the marketing industry.

However, the most important advantage offered by internet concerning the consumer remains the low or at least much lower cost of internet conducted transactions. "A funds transfer in a bank costs approximately £1 over the counter, 10p over the phone and 1p over the internet"[121]. Furthermore, the IT industry is rapidly developing and is moving towards the direction of enabling access to internet for growing parts of the population by providing internet linking services to products that used to be irrelevant with on line activities such as mobile telephones. In this manner larger numbers of consumers obtain access to a new market marked by an unprecedented variety in terms of products, manufacturers and quality.

"If there is a place where liberty of choice can be expressed, then this is Internet. It offers great possibilities to be better informed, to ask for more information, to negotiate and to decide having complete knowledge of the reason behind the choice"[122]. Moreover, sellers can benefit by the lack of physical contact with the consumers and therefore have the ability to invest the money saved from maintaining a shop with all its functional and employee costs in innovation or amelioration of the quality of products offered or the services available in general. The open character of

---

[120] The European Commission, On-line services and data protection and the protection of privacy, Volume I, Annex to the Annual Report 1998 (XV D/504/98) of the Working Party established by Article 29 of directive 95/46/EC, Directorate General Internal Market and Financial Services, 1999, p49.

[121] Targett David, B2B or not B2B? Scenarios for the future of e-commerce, European Business journal, 2001, volume 13, number 1, p8.

[122] "S'il y a un espace ou la liberte de choix trouve a s'exprimer, c'est bien sur Internet. Internet offre de grandes possibilites d'etre mieux informe, de demander plus d'informations, de negocier et de decider en toute connaissance de cause", Vallelersundi Ana Palacio, Le commerce electronique, le juge, le consommateur, l'entreprise et le Marche Interieur: nouvelle equation pour le droit communautaire, Revue du droit de l'Union Europeenne, Number 1, 2001, p19.

the internet and the ability to access a variety of services on line along with its borderless character constitute "the strengths of the internet which are often the same as its weaknesses"[123]. The exact elements which turned internet into a unique tool to conduct business and receive services are the same with those of its aspects which can as it will be analysed thoroughly later form the basis for on line insecurity.

4.3 The New Dangers
4.3.1 Consumer Confidence

Notwithstanding, its advantages and the benefits it can bring to consumers Internet brought with it a row of new challenges for both consumers and of course the current state of legal order. As the use of the new technologies became widely applied it was observed that the consumer protection regime that was designed to safeguard consumers' interests in the framework of traditional commerce was insufficient to deal with some novel issues emerging from electronic transactions. It was rapidly anticipated that the existing protection experienced in out of net trade was eroded in the internet context. The impact of this statement on both consumers and the industry itself was profound as this mounting insecurity emerged as the principal obstacle in the way of the further development of e-commerce. The concept of "consumer confidence" has therefore acquired a central position in the designing and planning of policies on behalf of governments and businesses. The consumers fully understood the personal benefits they can enjoy from conducting their commercial activities in an electronic manner but simultaneously felt insecure due to a variety of reasons related mainly to data protection, security of transactions and engaging in distance contracts. Thus, the achievement of a level of protection sufficient enough to ensure consumer confidence in the new means of transaction became an objective of massive importance for the relevant policy makers of the EU. The most important pieces of the Union's legislation regarded the issues from which consumer insecurity was stated to stem: mainly data protection and security of transactions. David Byrne, the European Commissioner for Health and Consumer Protection issues during that period insisted that "we are

---

[123] Valerie Steeves in Steven Hick, Edward F. Halpin, Eric Hoskins, Human rights and the Internet, Macmillan Press Ltd, London, 2000, page 187.

confronted with what I certainly call the e-confidence barrier"[124]. He admitted that "the e-economy creates a new type of relationship between customers and suppliers"[125] and he specifically named the areas of "privacy and confidentiality of data"[126] as the most fundamental concerns of consumers when making use of e-commerce facilities. In his speech at the European Parliament he underlined the importance of safeguarding the interests of the citizens "notably in data protection, crime prevention and safe use of internet"[127]. He tried to alleviate fears and concerns that the EU is not focusing on the notion of consumer confidence by providing the assurance that "fostering consumer confidence in e-commerce is central e-commerce strategy"[128]. He concluded by accepting that the "key worries concern security and confidentiality"[129].

4.3.2 Border Elimination

A person connected to internet is capable of obtaining access to a universal market. He has the ability to engage in a transaction with a supplier located in another country, continent and of course jurisdiction. This aspect of the new technologies may present various advantages to consumers but at the very same time hide risks for the consumers. "Where physical characteristics are used as the starting point for the applicability of law, jurisdiction and enforcement these delimitations will become increasingly controversial"[130]. It is therefore evident that various complicated problems are linked with the blurring of geographical borders and distances. The first is directly related to the choice of jurisdiction, the enforcement of laws and dispute resolution. In cases where a commercial transaction falls into the ambit of more legal orders delicate

[124] Speech by David Byrne, European Commissioner for Health and Consumer Protection, The e-confidence barrier – New regulatory models - Conference on the e-Economy in Europe – European Parliament,Brussels, 2 March 2001, available at
http://www.europa.eu.int/comm/dgs/health_consumer/library/speeches/speech86_en.html
[125] The same
[126] The same
[127] Speech by David Byrne, European Commissioner for Health and Consumer Protection "Cyberspace and Consumer Confidence", Annual Conference of the Kangaroo Group of MEP's, 19 September 2000, available at
http://www.europa.eu.int/comm/dgs/health_consumer/library/speeches/speech55_en.html
[128] The same
[129] The same
[130] Madeleine de Cock Buning, Marc de Vries, Ewoud Hondius, Corien Prins, Consumer@ Protection.EU. An analysis of European Consumer Legislation in the Information Society, Journal of Consumer Policy 24, Kluwer Academic Publishers, 2001, p290.

issues arise that cannot certainly be envisaged by the average consumer. The question over which law applies and maybe more fundamentally how it can apply in a situation where the relevant legal order is not even discernable can be answered with difficulty. The notion of legal certainty is weakened, as it is not clear whether protection can be sought or not.

The lack of borders can have further repercussions on consumer protection not envisaged in the traditional trade context. As consumers act on their own without any contact with other consumers or the supplier himself in case of any problem they can not resort to any consumer protection organisation or group because the latter tend to develop their activities at a national level. Creating consumer organisations with an international ambit of intervention has proved a challenging issue. The internationalisation of issues concerning the general public has been dealt with either by treaties between nations or agreements in the framework of international organisations. Thus, issues that nations in the past tended to view as falling into their domestic legal order have now acquired an international dimension. The protection of environment, human rights and intellectual property provide us with some examples. However, at least up to now there has been no complete world wide initiative of binding nature to deal with the current consumer protection challenges.

4.3.3 Security of Transactions

The rapid development of internet and its sudden emergence as a commercial tool of international appeal has changed the pre-existing landscape in world trade so radically that at least at the initial stage national regulators or the relevant competent organisations could not offer the necessary legal framework for the protection of consumers. Uncertainty over engaging in electronic agreements, concluding electronic contracts or over the ability to bind oneself with digital signatures was prevailing. Uncertainty over the regulatory framework of internet and the ability to actually carry on transactions of high value has contributed at a high level to what was explained to be the lack of "consumer confidence". Consumers could not be aware of the conditions under which a contract formed and signed on internet could be valid producing the same effects that are already familiar to them from more traditional forms of trade.

The lack of confidence also flowed from the inability to know the other party to the transaction. Consumers felt insecure as "in theory once they receive their payment, sellers can disappear without any chance of the buyer being able to trace them or even if he succeeds in doing so without being able to obtain refund"[131]. Hence, the fear of fraud is stronger when buying on line rather in the context of out of the net transaction where physical contact and knowledge of all details of the other party affords a sense of security over the actual performance of the contract on the one hand or the relevant authorities to resort to and the relevant procedure to be followed in case of fraudulent behaviour on the other.

4.3.4 Misleading types of advertising

Internet allows for "unprecedented commercial communications, in terms of intensity, targeting and reach"[132]. The massive advertising campaigns aiming at alluring large number of consumers in the real world does not apply to internet. The marketing and advertising industry have resorted to more personal and individually designed techniques. On internet there is a blurring distinction of what constitutes a part of a marketing scheme and what an article including information about a product. Consumers can easily confuse on line advertisements with sites that aim at informing them about an issue. Although, the body of European law on the subject is not particularly wide the EU has sought to regulate on the necessity to promote goods or services in a manner that clearly constitutes a part of a marketing campaign. The principle underlying the Union's policy on the matter is the need to have consumers who are cognizant of the nature of information they receive. Whether it forms a part of an advertisement or it expresses the views of a source alien to the product. The issue is deemed of major importance and has been dealt under the Electronic Commerce Directive[133] and the Directive on Distance Contracts[134]. However, the issue will not be further analysed at this point.

---

[131] Endeshaw Assafe, supra note 120 at p163.
[132] Madeleine de Cock Buning, Marc de Vries, Ewoud Hondius, Corien Prins, supra note 131 at page 292.
[133] See article 6a on the "clearly identifiable" character of the commercial communication. Available at http://europa.eu.int/smartapi/cgi/sga_doc?smartapi!celexapi!prod!CELEXnumdoc&lg=EN&numdoc=32 000L0031&model=guichett .
[134] See article 4 (2) of the Directive on "clearly" stated commercial purpose of information. Available at http://europa.eu.int/smartapi/cgi/sga_doc?smartapi!celexapi!prod!CELEXnumdoc&lg=EN&numdoc=31 997L0007&model=guichett

4.3.5 Data Protection

> "Many people surf the web under the illusion that their actions are private and anonymous. Unfortunately, there is more information collected about you than you might think. Every time you visit a site you leave a calling card that reveals where you are coming from, what kind of computer you have, and many other details. Most sites keep logs of all visitors"[135].

This statement reflects the magnitude of the real challenge stemming from the expansion of the use of internet today. The relevant challenge is directly linked with the nature of the web, which "is nothing more than a method of transporting digital information"[136]. As analysed in the first part the internet started as a means of exchanging information between universities and evolved into a medium of mass transmission of data founding a new type of marketing industry that is based on the elaboration of the personal information of the users. Information is being collected in order to create a profile of each user so as to direct the adequate advertisements to him according to his specific preferences as the latter are revealed by his on line moves and choices. However, privacy as a notion is not only linked to economic concepts such as the "efficient function of e-commerce" but much more intensively is related to the cultural patterns to which a large part of the consumers adhere to. It constitutes an integral part of the cultural and legal heritage of several nations. The Data Protection Directive will be analysed in the next part along with the place that privacy has assumed in European culture and the way it evolved in the legal order of European nations. As David Asch observes "our decisions as consumers are not made in a vacuum. Consumer purchases are highly influenced by a range of factors including the cultural, social, personal and psychological"[137]. This particular statement reinforces the importance of dealing with the privacy issue in an effective manner because it is not just a matter related to consumer on line behaviour but it has deeper roots stemming from the idea of respect of a fundamental right inherent in the culture of the European citizens. Thus, the threats to privacy imposed by internet are viewed as "the most

---

[135] Angus Hamilton, Rosemary Jay, Data Protection, Law and Practice, Sweet & Maxwell, London, 1999, p464.
[136] Reed Christopher, Internet Law: Text and Materials, Butterworths, London, 2000, p3.
[137] Asch David, Wolfe Brian, New Economy- New Competition, The Rise of the Consumer?, Palgrave, New York, 2001, p22.

significant public policy concern spawned by internet"[138]. In the US a definition widely used in the literature stems from a phrase of the judge Thomas Colley that described privacy as "the right to be let alone"[139]. It is perceived as a right with a strong social meaning as it embodies the ability to have control over the sphere of one's personal affairs. The particular right possesses a content that includes the demand of consumers to have their strictly personal data treated in a manner respectful of their personal life and sense of freedom. As Hetcher observes "the social meaning of personal data collection has changed from a morally neutral to a morally charged status"[140]. Wide spread fears over the treatment of pieces of personal information in combination with the usually high media coverage that the relevant subject entails has pushed privacy to the top of the consumer list of fears and insecurities concerning Internet. "There isn't a day that goes by in the US where you don't pick up a newspaper and see an article on privacy"[141]. Consumers have demonstrated a great sensitivity towards this issue and have refrained from using the web extensively due to fears of privacy abuse. The information age "like the age of science from which it is directly descended...at once secures a more optimal weight of utilities...while simultaneously creating new dangers several of which fall under the privacy rubric"[142]. "Privacy is more important today than it was fifty years ago because now it is so much easier to collect and process information in massive quantities"[143]. The impact of the particular issue was also felt on the industry that had to promote a sort of safety net for consumer privacy as "a precondition for the development of what has come to be known as electronic commerce"[144]. "In today's brand-conscious business world - particularly in an on line environment – a company's reputation on a sensitive matter like privacy can have sweeping consequences. If we have a privacy policy that doesn't match up the

---

[138] Hetcher Steven, Changing the Social Meaning of Privacy in Cyberspace, Harvard Journal of Law and Technology, Harvard Law School, 2001, p149.

[139] Cooley M. Thomas, Cooley on Torts 29 (second edition 1888). See also Gormley Ken, One hundred years of Privacy, Wis. Law Review, 1992, p1335 and Samuel D. Warren & Louis D. Brandeis, The right to Privacy, 4 Harvard Law Review 193, in 1890.

[140] Hetcher Steven, supra note 139 at page 153.

[141] Dr Michael Rozen, chief privacy officer and consumer affairs vice president at WellMed in Portland Oregon, Private Investigations, Data Privacy and the challenge to business, An e-briefing from the Economist Intelligence Unit, Written in Co-operation with Baker & Makenzie, October 2001, p2.

[142] Paul Fairfield, Public/Private, Rowman & Littlefield Publishers Inc, New York, 2005, page 38.

[143] Binns Susan, Internal Market Director at the European Commission in Brussels, An e-briefing from the Economist Intelligence Unit, Written in Co-operation with Baker & Makenzie, October 2001, p2.

[144] Bejot Michel, European Treatment of Internet Privacy issues, Journal of Internet Law, p1. Available at http://www.gcwf.com/articles/journal/jil_jan01_1.html accessed on 5/02/2002.

consumer clicks away"[145]. The initiatives assumed at industry level highlight the magnitude of the change having occurred in the privacy area. In the fifties and sixties the fears for privacy concerned mainly the government activities and policies. "It was this informational aspect of privacy that was most profoundly affected by the rapid developments in information technology during the sixties"[146]. The citizens were concerned about the creation of national databases and demanded protection from government or other public bodies' abuse of their personal information. Now, they resort to the government and national legislators to alleviate fears of privacy invasion on behalf of private companies and individuals. The shift in the trend has been radical and has prompted mainly the EU to initiate the European Directive on Data Protection that has changed the landscape in the relevant field. The causal connection between the abuse of personal data and the function of commercial –mainly but not exclusively- sites has provided the basis for a wide debate which included consumer organisations, national governments, parliaments, international organisations, industry representatives and the recently appeared privacy organisations. The latter are organisations formed by individuals aiming at observing closely the industry in order to detect and bring into media attention cases of privacy misuse. The Electronic Privacy Information Centre (EPIC)[147], The Centre for Democracy and Technology[148] both based in Washington and Statewatch[149] based in London are the most prominent ones and are scrutinising the EU developments on the field.

The foundation of the aforementioned bodies and the launching of the relevant initiatives have been prompted by the very nature of internet. "Publication of information on a web site renders the material, by default, immediately available for transfer to a user in any country in the world"[150]. On line activities of both individuals and companies are fundamentally based on the use of extensive databases of personal information. Therefore, the need to create a balance between the ability of on line economic world to function and the right to safeguard privacy is compelling. It has been stated that "e-commerce highlights the more general societal uncertainty and

---

[145] Swift Zeke, director of global privacy at Procter & Gamble, An e-briefing from the Economist Intelligence Unit, supra note 136 at page 6.
[146] Warren Adam, Sources of Literature on Data Protection and Human Rights, 2001 (2) The Journal of Information, Law and Technology, p3. Available at http://elj.warwick.ac.uk/jilt/01-2/warren.html
[147] www.epic.org
[148] www.cdt.org
[149] www.statewatch.org
[150] Smith J H Graham, Internet Law and Regulation, Third Edition, Sweet & Maxwell, London, 2002, p367.

debate over fair information practices"[151]. There is a delicate situation marked by conflicting legal interests. "Identifying consumers on the internet poses a significant threat to their privacy. On the other hand businesses have a justified interest in authenticating the identity of their counterpart"[152]. If a reasonable solution to reconcile the conflicting interests is not shaped then this will serve as a decisive blow to the further development of electronic commerce. It will considerably hamper consumer confidence and discourage further consumer involvement in on line activities. The EU with its directives (to be examined in next part) has tried to establish a legislative framework, which notwithstanding its shortcomings is at least realistic. The fundamental difference that internet made, which is detected not only "in the ease with which data can be gathered and compiled electronically but also in the ease with which it can be manipulated and used"[153] must find its legislative answer. Due to the international dimension of the web it "needs to be tackled on an international scale"[154] but the EU due to its enlarged internal market comprising more than 450 million consumers can and has played a very significant role in providing the incentive and impetus necessary for the international community to assume initiatives in this field.

4.3.5.1 The focus of the book. The New Landscape in Consumer Privacy and the Nature of the Data Protection Issue. Why is it important?

"There was of course no way of knowing whether you were being watched at any given moment. It was even conceivable that they watched everybody all the time...day by day and almost minute by minute the past was brought up to date"[155]

---

[151] Reidenberg R. Joel, E-Commerce and Privacy Institute for Intellectual Property & Information Law Symposium: E-Commerce and Trans Atlantic Privacy, Houston Law Review, 2001, p718.
[152] Madeleine de Cock Buning, Marc de Vries, Ewoud Hondius, Corien Prins, supra note 131 at page 311.
[153] L'Hoest Raphael, The European Dimension of the digital Economy, Intereconomics, January/February 2001, p49.
[154] Asfaw Tesfaye, Karunanayake Kanishka, Mehta Manish, Parnaik Amol, Shah Aarti, Targett David, Imperial College Management School, London, E-Commerce progress: International Comparisons, European Business Journal, 2001, p95.
[155] Orwell George, 1984, published in 1949. Available on line at http://www.online-literature.com/orwell/1984/ , accessed on August 1st 2003.

Although, with a sense of exaggeration inherent in its essence the aforementioned extract from Orwell's famous book "1984" describes an aspect of the information technology not envisaged at its initial stage that has nowadays assumed massive importance. The new developments in technology had a profound impact on the means of data collection as they changed radically the way and speed with which data can now be accessed and disseminated. The lack of control over private life linked information has been ranked as the principal rationale behind the consumers' continuous unwillingness to make full use of the capacities of electronic commerce. The reason is the very same foundation of e-commerce strategies, which is based on the collection of information. "Data mining – gathering, collating and organising information concerning one's customers and trading partners – is of fundamental importance to all forms of e-commerce"[156]. Thus, collecting of all shorts of personal information is a function inherent in the plans for enhancing the efficiency of commercial web sites. It enables the creation of a particular profile for each consumer linked to the site and the further elaboration of a marketing strategy shaped to meet the demands of the particular consumer it appeals to. Therefore, the profile in question contains private information linked to a personally identifiable consumer. Thus, this sort of data mining "is a form of intrusion into one's privacy in cyberspace"[157]. "Instead of merely collecting bits of isolated information, businesses are now analyzing correlations and amalgamations of seemingly unrelated data attained from various collectors and databases"[158]. The importance of data mining lies in its ability to "transform large volumes of random data into meaningful interpretable information, which enables customer service"[159]. The identification of the preferences of specific consumers leads to the design of a sales policy on a more efficient and individual basis. Businesses are perfectly aware of the trends of consumer choices thus, their profit making is facilitated. A practical example from the marketing industry itself is provided by Martin Evans[160]. A gardening company aiming at promoting its products will

---

[156] Fitzgerald L. Peter, Hidden Dangers in the E-Commerce Data Mine: Governmental Customer and Trading Partner Screening Requirements, The International Lawyer, Spring 2001, Volume 35, No1, American Bar Association, Chicago, Illinois, page 48.

[157] Azmi Madieha Ida, E-Commerce and Privacy Issues: An analysis of the personal data protection bill, Computer and Telecommunications Law Review, Sweet & Maxwell, 2002, p206.

[158] Teh Jeanette, Privacy Wars in Cyberspace: An examination of the Legal and business tensions in information privacy, Yale Journal of Law & Technology, 2001/2002, p24.

[159] The same.

[160] Martin Evans in Susanne Lace, The Glass Consumer, Life in a Surveillance Society, National Consumer Council, The Policy Press, University of Bristol, 2005, page 100.

usually target the primetime slots between 7pm and 9pm whose audience might comprise five million households. The "30 second advertisement might cost £50,000 for nationwide coverage and if there are three repeated exposures per evening for a month, costs would be around £4,5 million plus production and payment for celebrity opinion formers...total costs would be...around £5 million"[161]. Instead of spending such an amount of capital for addressing an audience whose devotion to gardening is somehow uncertain the company in question can alternatively resort to rent a database containing names of consumers who have visited gardening sites or are subscribers to on or off line gardening magazines or newsletters. A list of 500,000 names can be rented at £80 per thousand names amounting to £40,000. If we include production and mailing costs of £300 per thousand recipients the total amount will raise to £190,000. This means that the company would have spent 3,8% of the money it would need to invest to a TV orientated marketing campaign. And since the nature of the product is rather focused on a very specific audience, unleashing an intense campaign appealing to everyone would have limited results at least in relation to the capital spent. In contrast to that the internet campaign would specifically target the audience already acknowledged as interested in the relevant activities. The fragmentation of the consumer audience to smaller pieces on the basis of the collected personal data suits the marketing efforts of most companies as it enables them to focus more effectively on the appropriate market. The benefits enjoyed by the companies involved from data sharing and the use of databases containing personal data with no particular limits are easy to perceive.

Thus, it is clear that the legal world is faced with a new reality that is shaped by the rapid development of computer technology and use, which should not escape its attention. It is true that privacy abuses in an on line environment are not as tangible as in real life but important legal initiatives have already been assumed in this field. Non internet trade had avoided the data protection issues mainly via party consent, a concept whose on line use has appeared increasingly challenging. It is true that consumer concerns relating to respect of "traffic data are relatively low in comparison to those things which require a search warrant to seize"[162] but as people have become more

---

[161] The same.
[162] Jason M. Young, Surfing while muslim: Privacy, Freedom of Expression & the Unintended Consequences of Cybercrime Legislation: A Critical Analysis of the Council of Europe Convention on Cyber Crime & the Canadian Lawful Access Proposal, 9 International Journal of Communications Law and Policy 9, 2004/2005.

accustomed to the nature of internet these conceptions have dramatically changed. The radical changes in technology "will change many relations between individuals, business and the state"[163]. From this very sentence the importance of the issue is well revealed. At the beginning of the new century the issue of privacy has emerged at the centre of a debate of massive importance because it touches upon the interests of the individuals having a direct impact on their rights. It is closely related to the nature of the economy an individual country would like to structure, whether it would be a type of economy where the state can move towards the regulation of important fields of the market or whether the central choice would be to promote the ability of the markets to actually set their own rules and regulate themselves having as an ultimate goal the achievement of what the economists call "maximum efficiency". Thus, since the issue is closely related to the triangle "state-enterprises-citizens" it is evident why it has become the centre of attention of both legislators and the business world. It is in the "context of the development of electronic commerce where personal data have gained their greatest value"[164], which proves the urgent need to regulate effectively an area that has very recently taken shape, whose main challenges are still left to be examined.

The book will focus on the analysis of the EU data protection law and the central choices that underlie its adoption. It will examine the philosophical and historical developments that have led the Union to adopt such a regulative initiative placing the concept of "privacy" as a fundamental human right at the centre of the discussions. This stance will be compared and contrasted to the attitude adopted on the other side of the Atlantic, where historical developments and different constitutional priorities have shaped a divergent agenda on the issue. Data protection rules nowadays are of high relevance both for the examination and the analysis of the legal culture of a country and for more practical issues such as the way companies in a given jurisdiction are conducting their activities. In the framework of a world economy, where the free flow of information has been described as "its life blood[165]", any divergence in the manner personal data are treated can have "crucial implications for any company doing business internationally, and this means virtually every company[166]" and at the same

---

[163] Perri 6, Briscoe Ivan, On the Cards, Privacy, Identity and trust in the age of smart technologies, Demos, London, 1996, page 52.
[164] Iglezakis Ioannis, The Protection of Personal Data on the Internet, National and EU Law Regulations, Commercial Law Review, Sakkoulas Publications, Thessaloniki, 2002, Greece, page 682.
[165] Kuner Christopher, European Data Privacy Law and Online Business, Oxford University Press, Oxford, 2003, page 1.
[166] The same.

time provide vital information on the legal traditions and distinctive cultures from which they spring. This book focuses on the analysis of the regulatory systems adopted in the EU and the USA not only because they constitute the parties of the most advanced commercial relationship of the planet, but also because the different ways they dealt with the issue reveals distinctive cultural approaches. After all the discussion on where the line between the financial benefits of the processing of personal data and the threats on individual freedoms inherent in its function should be drawn, is not only economic but also deeply political and philosophical. It touches upon sensitivities of historic or constitutional nature that are impossible to neglect. The latter are going to be thoroughly presented in order to lead to a further conclusion over which is the approach that can deal with the issue in a more efficient manner. Furthermore, suggestions will be made aiming at adjusting the current legislative regime to the electronic challenges on our privacy.

While, in Europe there is "a broad consensus within the legislative institutions that most of the rationales of the consumer protection instruments apply equally to electronic commerce situations"[167], in the US "not surprisingly the question has been raised whether we may expect any privacy in the information society"[168]. The different approaches assumed by different jurisdictions confirm the complexity of the issue, which is not and cannot be "the unique preserve of lawyers…as its significance in contributing to a rounded and complete social existence"[169] places it at the centre of the attention of a variety of parties within a society including the legislators, human rights organisations, company managers who have to comply with the new rules and of course the individuals irrespective of their capacity as citizens or consumers. The latter are directly involved in the debate as the advent of the new technologies has not only "provided endless sources of information to the general public, but it also provided members of the public the opportunity to become a source of information themselves"[170]. Thus, regulating the particular field either by introducing legislative

---

[167] Kaufman Winn Jane, Haubold Jens, Electronic Promises: contract law reform and electronic commerce in comparative perspective, 27 European Law Review, August 2002, Sweet & Maxwell, London, page 572.
[168] Bergkamp Lucas, EU Data Protection Policy, The Privacy Fallacy: Adverse Effects of Europe's Data Protection Policy in an Information driven Economy, Computer Law and Security Report, Volume 18, number 1, 2002, page 32.
[169] Hull John, Privacy as an Aspect of Public Law: Reflections on R v Broadcasting Complaints, Entertainment Law Review, Sweet & Maxwell, London, 1995, 283.
[170] Stiles Allison, Everyone's a Critic: Defamation and Anonymity on the Internet, 2002 Duke Law & Technology Review, page 4.

measures following the European pattern or by promoting self regulation initiatives driven by market forces in accordance with the practice in the US appears compelling. The regulation of data collection, which creates rights for the consumers and "ensures that these rights are respected"[171] is the actual object of the debate. Although, in the US the prevailing views coincide with the conclusion that when it comes to such a rapidly evolving field as the internet "government attempts to regulate it are likely to be outmoded by the time they are finally enacted"[172], this exactly appears to be the choice made at the EU level. The promotion of Directive 95/46, which constitutes the main relevant legal text on which the book is based, constituted the vivid expression of the Union's conscious choice to intervene and regulate the protection of the personal data of the European citizens. The adoption of the latter came as a natural result of the legislative and historical developments on the continent during the last decades that are to be examined later. However, due to the fact that "any regulatory framework may embody the seeds of its own obsolescence"[173] the EU has moved towards the adoption of yet another directive aiming towards protecting the electronic communications (directive 2002/58) that promotes solutions to issues left uncovered by the central directive. The relevant provisions of the latter are also going to be evaluated in this book. However, at this point the contrast between the European insistence in regulating the protection of data and the choice of the US authorities to endorse a "hands-off"[174] policy towards Internet has already been illuminated. The American policy was clearly explained at the highest possible political level by the former president of the US himself, who insisted on the "the private sector leading the development of electronic commerce and avoiding undue restrictions"[175]. It is interesting to note the basis on which the two parties founded their choices on how to keep their policies updated and in concert with the new technological developments. As in Europe the foundations lay on state regulation, it is clearly indicated that "the history of privacy protection is the history of the effort to regulate the design of technology by means of public institutions.

---

[171] Iglezakis Ioannis, Consumers' Access to Justice in the European Union, Revue Hellenique De Droit International, L'Institut Hellenique de Droit International et Etranger, Sakkoulas Editions, Thessaloniki, page 307.
[172] Du Pont George F., The Criminalisation of True Anonymity in Cyberspace, 7 Michigan Telecommunications Technology Review 191, 2001, accessed via LEXIS NEXIS.
[173] Walden Ian, Regulating Electronic Commerce: Europe in the Global Economy, European Law Review, Sweet & Maxwell, 2001, page 546.
[174] See President Clinton's position at http://www.pbs.org/newshour/cyberspace/
[175] See the Working Paper "A Framework for Global Electronic Commerce" at http://www.technology.gov/digeconomy/framewrk.htm#5.%20PRIVACY accessed on August 6th 2004.

This effort has always been predicated on the belief that architecture is not pre-determined, that it can be subject to reason, public debate and the rule of law"[176]. The impetus for such regulatory efforts "has come from the particular vulnerability to which such data has been exposed by technological advances"[177]. As Froomkin notes "we are still in the early days of data mining, consumer profiling, and DNA databasing, to name only a few. The cumulative effect of these developments has the potential to transform modern life in all industrialised countries. Unless something happens to counter these developments it seems likely that all…may live in the informational equivalent of a goldfish bowl"[178].

The close examination of the issue of data protection can provide the grounds for useful remarks and observations on the different perceptions of the notion of privacy in important jurisdictions. The whole issue can only be viewed in a comparative perspective because information, as explained above, forms the commodity of a new economy that appears to respect no physical borders. Information technology as a science and the trading of personal information that stands at the core of the electronic commerce activities, play a significant role in the framework of the globalised international economy. This observation is further supported by the analysis of the relevant provisions in the Directive referring to the transfer of data to non-EEA (European Economic Area) countries that is thoroughly analysed in the relevant chapter. The significance of the global reach of electronic trade in conjunction with the nature of the commodity in question, which is knowledge and information, highlights the importance of the subject of the book. Thus, it is essential to shape an efficient regulatory regime within which flows of information can sustain global trade while respecting fundamental human rights, as privacy at least at European level is now accepted to be. In the light of this statement the relevant legal texts of the EU are going to be analysed and evaluated. The book aims at contributing to the shaping of a realistic and workable solution that however takes full account of the compelling need to respect human rights. "Science and technology contribute to transform social relations and

---

[176] Rotenberg Marc, Fair Information Practices, Stanford Technology Law Review 1, 2001, accessed via LEXIS NEXIS.
[177] McBride Jeremy, Disclosure of Crime Prevention Data: Specific European and International Standards, European Law Review, 2001, Sweet & Maxwell, page 86.
[178] Froomkin Michael A, Symposium: Cyberspace and Privacy: A New Legal Paradigm? The Death of Privacy?, 52 Stanford Law Review, May 2000, page 1465.

cultural processes in a radical and constant manner"[179]. Thus, the rapid advances of information technology rendered large parts of the existing law simply irrelevant as they radically changed the nature of the legal relations that formed their object. However, it has to be noted that technology is "neither deterministic nor inevitable; the development of science and techniques historically result from human decisions in economic, political and social arenas. What seems as technological imperative is often a self interested choice imposed on others"[180]. Thus, it has to be accepted as a basic initial point of consideration that the objectives of Information Technology as a science have to be of dual nature: the research and innovation techniques that can lead to new inventions on the one hand and the promotion of the human prosperity on the other. As far as the first objective is concerned it obviously falls in the ambit of the natural sciences. However, the promotion of human prosperity can effectively be realised with the close cooperation also with representatives of the social sciences. At this point the role of the legislative, judiciary, academic and other public institutions to contribute to the forming of an effective institutional framework, which will provide for an updated layer of protection, is essentially important. The relevant legislative initiatives shall aim at responding to the new threats on personal freedoms, which emerge as society and along with it technology evolve. "Societies may be seen as both making a range of choices available and limiting them by rules…and the structure of its prevailing beliefs"[181]. Thus, social scientists and legislators also bear the obligation to respect the delicate balance between protecting individual freedoms on the one hand and facilitating further technological advances that are deemed to benefit the general public on the other. Thus, it I argued that the regulation of this sensitive area should take full account of the sometimes contrasting interests of the further development of technology and its impact on the protection of personal data and the protection of human rights that forms one of the fundamental pillars in modern societies. Based on this premise, it is supported that the adoption of the relevant EU Directive with all its deficiencies, which will be presented later, is in the right direction. It assumes the initiative to deal with an issue closely related to human rights in a manner that does not obstruct the smooth

---

[179] Hugo Rojas, La, Culture and Society: Lancrit Theory and Transdisciplinary Approaches: Law, Land and Labour: Constructions of Property and Status in Local and Global Contexts: Labour Law and Genetic Discrimination on Chile, 16 Florida Journal of International Law, 2004, page 561.

[180] René Laperrière in Colin J. Bennett and Rebecca Grant, Visions of Privacy, Policy Choices for the Digital Age, University of Toronto Press, Toronto, 1999, page 186.

[181] W. L. Weinstein in J. Roland Pennock and John W. Chapman, Privacy, NOMOS XIII Yearbook of the American Society for Political and Legal Philosophy, Atherton Press, New York, 1971, page 53.

operation of information flows and subsequently of trade. The importance of the European initiative is further illustrated by the fact that the Commission chose to regulate this field in the framework of its internal market programme that revealed the realistic obligation to take full account of commercial reality.

Thus, the book will shed light on the threats that internet poses to the level of the protection that citizens in their capacity as consumers enjoy in an era when an increasing number of commercial and other private activities take place on line. The focus will be placed on what is the most important aspect of the traditional set of rights which are in peril in the framework of the introduction of technology in every day commercial use: the right to privacy. The evolution of the latter in the European and American legal orders is analysed, compared and contrasted with the aim to detect the origins of contemporary privacy law. Although, privacy is a far reaching area encompassing a great range of fields the focus will mainly remain on the area of data protection as this is the aspect of privacy more closely linked to technological evolution, the development of electronic commerce and the processing of personal data for several commercial or non purposes. Since, an absolute separation of the two concepts is not possible, other aspects of the right to privacy will be analysed and presented as well in the course of an effort to approach the issue of data protection as thoroughly as possible.

4.3.5.2 Defining Privacy

Producing a specific and clear definition of privacy will provide the solid ground on which further analysis will be based. Although, it might seem rational to use a definition of the relevant concept commonly accepted at the literature or business level, it comes as a surprise that the issue in question has been difficult to deal with and has created a new round of dispute mainly in the academic context. The very fact of the existence of a debate on the exact scope of the definition of "privacy" indicates in an illuminating manner the controversy that has accompanied the formation of privacy policies in both sides of the Atlantic. Policies are designed in accordance with the content of the concepts in question, thus difficulties in defining them has obvious repercussions on the aims of the policies or the list of priorities that each policy maker shapes.

According to the Oxford Dictionary Thesaurus, privacy is defined as "the state in which one is not watched or disturbed by others"[182]. Furthermore, the definition for "private" reads "not sharing thoughts or feelings with others" in addition to "where one will not be disturbed"[183]. As far as the origin of the word is concerned, we are informed that it stems from the Latin word "privatus", which means "withdrawn from public life"[184].

Having established this definition as a basis, at least from a linguistic point of view, of the relevant discussion, it is important to note that privacy is "a condition, which is almost universally valued but once the attempt is made to turn the debate from the most general and abstract level, discussion inevitably becomes lost in a quagmire of competing claims and expectations and differing social and cultural experiences"[185]. Lloyd insists that "in terms perhaps more appropriate for the information society, this might be classed as a right not to be subject to surveillance"[186]. Judith Jarvis Thomson argues that "perhaps the most striking thing about the right to privacy is that nobody seems to have any very clear idea what it is"[187]. This statement seems a bit exaggerated now, but if it is to be taken into account that the article in question was published in 1975, it serves as an indication of the difficulties faced by literature even at that stage to provide a specific definition of the right to privacy. Parent noted that "the absence of a clear precise and persuasive definition of privacy is particularly shocking and inexcusable"[188] and proposed that "privacy be defined as the condition of not having undocumented personal information about oneself known by others"[189]. Richard Posner argues that "the concept of privacy is elusive and ill defined...I will...simply note that one aspect of privacy is the withholding or concealment of information"[190]. The focus of the article of Posner on the concealment and on the nature of privacy as a social good to be balanced with the demand for private information was enlightening at this stage and "made a significant contribution to our understanding of one aspect of privacy"[191].

---

[182] Compact Oxford Dictionary Thesaurus, Oxford University Press, p704.
[183] The same
[184] The same
[185] Lloyd Ian, Legal Aspects of the Information Society, Butterworths, London, 2000, page 41.
[186] The same.
[187] Thomson Jarvis Judith, The Right to Privacy, Philosophy and Public Affairs, 4, 1975, page 295.
[188] Parent W. A., A New Definition of Privacy for the Law, Law and Philosophy, 2, 1983, page 305.
[189] Ibid at page 306.
[190] Posner A. Richard, The Right of Privacy, Georgia Law Review, 12, 1978, page 393.
[191] Bloustein J. Edward, Privacy is dear at any price: A Response to professor Posner's economic theory, Georgia Law Review, 12, 1978, page 439.

The most famous definition of the right to privacy was found in the seminal article of Warren and Brandeis as early as in1890[192]. Their article analysed "the right to be let alone" and remained in history as probably the most influential piece of work on the subject. Representatives of the academic community shed lots of ink to express their agreement or disagreement with the content of the article. The latter revived the debate on the issue and provided the grounds for further research. Their arguments rested on the premise that "that the individual shall have full protection in person and in property is a principle as old as the common law", thus "political, social and economic changes entail the recognition of new rights...to meet the demands of society"[193]. The threats to privacy 115 years ago amounted to the increasing interference of the press, especially of that of what we would call tabloid nowadays, to the private lives and activities of some esteemed people of the American society at the end of the nineteenth century. Under the continuous articles on aspects of life that were deemed by the authors to fall into the ambit of private life to be kept away from the public spotlight, they insisted that in an era marked by the "recognition of man's spiritual nature, of his feelings and his intellect...the scope of these legal rights broadened and now the right to life has come to mean the right to enjoy life...and the term property has grown to comprise every form of possession intangible as well as tangible"[194]. Thus, privacy is linked to the "right to enjoy life" after having been let alone, in order to engage in activities performed in the context of a strictly defined personal life.

James Michael also agrees that "of all the human rights in the international catalogue, privacy is perhaps the most difficult to circumscribe and define"[195]. He adds that "in its narrowest sense, some might think of it as no more than a luxury for the better-off in developed countries"[196]. Matthew Finkin agrees with this statement as he notes that "the word privacy did not come into common English usage until the sixteenth century, a time of enormous economic development internationally, both

---

[192] Samuel D. Warren and Louis D. Brandeis, The Right to Privacy, Harvard Law Review, 4, 1890, page 195.
[193] Ibid at page 193.
[194] The same.
[195] Michael James, Privacy and Human Rights, An International and Comparative Study, with special reference to developments in Information Technology, Unesco Publishing, Dartmouth, Paris, France, 1994.
[196] The same.

commercial...and of urbanization. The two may not be unrelated"[197]. Economic development, which came along with technological advances, brought threats to individual privacy that was now seen from a different perspective as people poured into the cities creating a new model of urban life that created a novel need of citizens for some private space. Furthermore, Schoeman has argued that "the practice of privacy evolves only where there is a high degree of economic and social specialisation, when this specialisation liberates individuals from dependence on any group"[198]. The perceptions of privacy may differ, however it has to be agreed that an element of individual culture is certainly inherent in the particular notion. Apart from generally accepted areas of a strictly personal nature, such as health records, the cultural element can be quite influential in determining whether an area or an aspect of one's life and activities can be deemed as strictly private or falling within the open social aspect of somebody's life. Perri 6 has claimed that the inability to reach a common definition stems also from the fact that "as a society we do not and cannot agree on what it is about privacy and private life that we value"[199]. "Even in small agricultural communities, the boundaries of physical space which is private are quite sharply defined"[200]. The desire for privacy does not flow only from one's natural need to "avoid embarrassment from disclosures of certain behaviours that in any given culture"[201] would traumatise someone, but also from the natural urge of an individual "to retreat from the conformist pressures of social norms"[202] to a space totally belonging to oneself. Thus, privacy is directly linked with "the right of the individual to be protected against intrusion into his personal life and affairs, or those of his family, by direct physical means or by publication of information"[203]. "Physical intrusion into private spaces...can place a risk to dignity as a result...of the absence of anonymity or

---

[197] Finkin W. Matthew, Information Technology and Workers' Privacy: A Comparative Study: Part IV: The Comparative Historical and Philosophical Context: Menschenbild: The Conception of the employee as a person in Western Law, 23 Comparative Labour Law & Policy Journal, 2002, page 590.
[198] Schoeman Ferdinard in Finkin W. Matthew, ibid at page 590.
[199] Perri 6, The future of Privacy Volume 1: Private Life and Public Policy, Demos, London, 1998, page 23.
[200] Michael James, supra note 196, at page 2.
[201] Kang Jerry, Information Privacy in Cyberspace Transactions, 50 Stanford Law Review, 1998, page 1212.
[202] Craig D.R. John, Invasion of Privacy and Charter Values: The Common Law Tort Awakens, 42 McGill Law Journal, 1997, 355.
[203] Breslin John, Privacy – The Civil Liberties Issue, 14 Dickinson Journal of international Law, 1996, page 455.

unjustified disclosure of personal information without consent"[204]. As Jeremy deBeer insists there are "zones or realms of privacy, which include rights involving territorial or spatial aspects, rights related to the person, and rights that arise in an information context"[205]. "The first man who, having enclosed a piece of ground bethought himself of saying "this is mine" and found people simple enough to believe him, was the real founder of civil society"[206]. In this context "a person's right to privacy protects the person's personal autonomy...from intrusive behaviour that...causes personal distress"[207]. Jack Hirshleifer supports that "the central domain of what we mean by privacy is a concept...described as autonomy within society"[208]. Ruth Gavison adds that "we desire a society in which individuals can grow, maintain their mental health and autonomy...and lead meaningful lives. Privacy is also essential to democratic government because it fosters and encourages the moral autonomy of the citizen, a central requirement for a democracy...thus, to the extent that privacy is important for autonomy, it is important for democracy as well"[209]. At this point Stanley Benn argues that "the independently minded individual...is the one whose actions are governed by principles that are his own" in the sense that "these principles are subject to critical review"[210]. In this context privacy is seen as "a safeguard against conformism as we act differently if we are being observed...all our actions will be altered and our character will change"[211]. Foucault insisted that "he who is subjected to a field of visibility...becomes the principle of his own subjection"[212]. Hence, as Alan Westin notes, "privacy is at the heart of freedom in the modern state"[213] and is "essential for the well being of the individual"[214]. McCloskey adds that "privacy is a value or ideal in

---

[204] Rowland Diane, Macdonald Elizabeth, Information Technology Law Second Edition, Cavendish Publishing Limited, London, 2000, page 342.

[205] Jeremy deBeer, Employee Privacy: The Need for Comprehensive Protection, 66 Saskatchewan Law Review, 2003, page 386.

[206] Rousseau, Discourse on the Origin of Inequality, taken from Hirshleifer Jack, Privacy: Its Origin, Function, and Future, The Journal of Legal Studies, 9, 1980, page 649.

[207] Catanzariti Therese, Swimmers, surfers, and Sue Smith, Personality Rights in Australia, Entertainment Law Review, 13 (7), 2002, 135.

[208] Hirshleifer Jack, supra note 207, page 649. But see also Epstein Richard A., A Taste for Privacy? Evolution and the Emergence of a Naturalistic Ethic, The Journal of Legal Studies, 9, 1980, for an opposite opinion.

[209] Gavison Ruth, Privacy and the Limits of Law, The Yale Law Journal, 89, 1980, page 455.

[210] Benn Stanley, Privacy, Freedom and Respect for Persons, Nomos, XIII, 1971, page 24.

[211] Humphrey Hubert, extract taken from Benn Stanley, supra note 211.

[212] Michel Foucault in Jeffrey Reiman in Beate Rössler, Privacies, Philosophical Evaluations, Stanford University Press, California, 2004, page 195.

[213] Westin Alan, Privacy and Freedom, Bodley Head, London, 1970, page 350.

[214] See US case: R v Dyment, [1988] 2SCR 417, at 427-428.

our society in the Western World, and in liberal thought generally"[215]. Kalven insists that "privacy is one of the truly profound values for a civilised society"[216]. However, since "societies may be seen as both making a range of choices available and limiting them by rules"[217], the right to privacy is not absolute, "there must be very good reasons for overriding this right, for invading privacy"[218], something that as a principle can be reflected and confirmed by the regulated derogations found in European legislation. As Zimmerman notes "even the most enthusiastic advocates of a right to privacy including Warren and Brandeis recognised that any absolute protection of such an interest would intolerably hamper human discourse"[219]. However, even at this level "the right of privacy has everything to do with delineating the legitimate limits of governmental power...as it may on certain occasions render intolerable a law that violates no express constitutional guarantee"[220].

Thus, privacy is directly related to the notion of "intimacy", which is necessary "to create social relationships that go beyond basic respect due all human beings"[221]. Intimacy as a concept refers to "personal information, which can be defined as those facts, communications or opinions, which relate to the individual and which it would be reasonable to expect him to regard as intimate or confidential and therefore to want to withhold or at least restrict their circulation"[222]. Tom Gerety believes that privacy can be defined as "an autonomy or control over the intimacies of personal identity...intimacy is the chief restricting concept in the definition of privacy"[223]. Apart from "intimacy", privacy has been linked also with "ends and relations of the most fundamental sort: respect, love, friendship and trust...without privacy they are simply inconceivable"[224]. This aspect of privacy is of fundamental importance as according to Charles Fried the aforementioned concepts "depend on the more general notions of morality and respect"[225] and thus, they "each build on a common conception of

---

[215] Mc Closkey H.J., The Political Ideal of Privacy, Philosophical Quarterly, 21, 1971, page 303.
[216] Kalven Harry Jr, Privacy in tort Law: Were Warren and Brandeis Wrong?, Law and Contemporary Problems, 31, 1966, page 326.
[217] Weinstein W.L., The Private and the Free: A Conceptual Inquiry, Nomos, XIII, 1971,page 53.
[218] Mc Closkey supra note 216 at page 303.
[219] Zimmerman L. Diane, Requiem for a Heavyweight: A Farewell to Warren and Brandeis Privacy Tort, Cornell Law Review, 68, 1983, page 293.
[220] Rubenfeld Jed, The Right of Privacy, Harvard Law Review, 102, 1989, page 737.
[221] Kang Jerry, supra note 202, page 1213.
[222] Wacks Reymond, The Poverty of Privacy, The Law Quarterly Review, 96, 1980, page 89.
[223] Gerety Tom, Redefining Privacy, Harvard Civil Rights, Civil Liberties Law Review, 12, 1977, pages 236 and 263.
[224] Fried Charles, Privacy, The Yale Law Journal, 77, 1968, page 477.
[225] Ibid at page 478.

personality and its entitlements"[226]. Privacy contributes to the establishment "of the equal liberty of each person to define and pursue his values free from undesired impingements by others"[227]. The values of morality and respect and the role privacy plays in the shaping of the personality of an individual along with the fact that it can provide the citizens with the space necessary to develop their own set of values underlines in the most emphatic manner the importance of the issue. Hyman Gross builds upon this perception by arguing that "concern about privacy is concern about conditions of life and it is so in the law as it is elsewhere"[228]. He suggested that "privacy is the condition of human life in which acquaintance with a person or with affairs of his life which are personal to him is limited"[229]. Weinstein observes that "privacy, like alienation, loneliness…and isolation is a condition of being apart from others. However, alienation is suffered, loneliness is dreaded, isolation is borne with resignation or panic, while privacy is sought after"[230]. Schwartz adds that "the very fact of placing a barrier between oneself and others is self-defining, for withdrawal entails a separation a role and…from an identity imposed upon oneself by others"[231]. Privacy cannot be understood "independently from society…he need for privacy is a socially created need. Without society there would be no need for privacy"[232]. Emerson states that "privacy is clearly a vital element in any system of individual rights…it is designed to support the individual…in the relations to the collective society. As such it is designed to mark out a sphere or zone in which the collective may not intrude upon the individual will. It, thus, differs from time to time and from society to society depending on where the line is drawn between individual autonomy and collective obligation"[233]. However, there were also different opinions stated such as that of Robert Post, who supported that "privacy rests upon an individualist concept of society and that the enemies of privacy in our time is Community"[234].

---

[226] The same.
[227] Ibid at page 479.
[228] Gross Hyman, The Concept of Privacy, New York University Law Review, 42, 1967, page 34.
[229] Ibid at page 36.
[230] Weinstein Michael, The Uses of Privacy in the Good Life, Nomos, XIII, 1971, page 88.
[231] Schwartz Barry, The Social Psychology of Privacy, found in Weinstein Michael, supra note 231, at page 97.
[232] Barrington Moore in Daniel J. Solove, A Taxonomy of Privacy, 154 University of Pennsylvania Law Review, 2006, page 484.
[233] Emerson Thomas I., The Riht of Privacy and the Freedom of the Press, Harvard Civil Rights, Civil Liberties Law Review, 14, 1979, page 337.
[234] Post Robert, The Social Foundations of Privacy: Community and self in the common Law tort, California Law Review, 77, 1989, page 958.

In considering the issue of privacy "it is of some importance to recall whether one is discussing a state or condition, a desire, a claim or a right"[235]. The "state" as a situation is easily describable as it refers to the solitude that someone wants to achieve in order to create some space for oneself. However, it is a different issue if he is entitled to a claim to achieve this or if he can base his claim on a solid right. Wagner argues that "privacy is an umbrella term for a wide variety of interests"[236]. If "a claim is an argument that someone deserves something, then a right is a justified claim...I shall refer to privacy as an interest, which...it would be a good thing to have, leaving open how extensively it ought to be protected"[237]. However, as Gavison insists we should "reject attempts to describe privacy as a claim"[238]. The book supports that privacy has to be viewed as a right and even more emphatically a right of fundamental nature. A right draws its institutional authority from constitutional and cultural principles deeply embedded in a national legal order. A right can be limited by the need to exercise effectively other rights but it cannot be bought, sold or abandoned. And certainly it cannot be exchanged with a commodity or another value. A right in democratic legal orders is protected by the relevant judicial authorities and finds its place in national legislation. This is the choice made by the EU, as will be explained later, which has enacted specific legislation aiming at protecting private data and as an indication of the status granted to privacy, it has included such a right in the rejected Constitutional Treaty at the part where the Charter of Fundamental Rights were incorporated[239]. Rotenberg also insists that "in the parlance of...government agencies privacy is a value than a right, in public discourse values don't carry the weight that rights do"[240]. His comment is related to the situation in the US, which is thoroughly going to be viewed at a later stage. At this point it is also necessary to refer to "information privacy" as one particular aspect of privacy. The area of information privacy is more specific relating to "the individual's control over the processing, acquisition, disclosure, use of personal information"[241]. It relates to the ability of people to "control the circulation of

---

[235] Michael James, supra note 196, page 2.
[236] Wagner DeCew Judith, The Scope of Privacy in Law and Ethics, Law and Philosophy, 5, 1986, page 145.
[237] The same, at page 147.
[238] Gavison Ruth, supra note 210, at page 425.
[239] See the Constitutional Treaty, Part II, Artilce II-8. See http://europa.eu.int/eur-lex/pri/en/oj/dat/2003/c_169/c_16920030718en00010105.pdf
[240] Rotenberg Marc, Agre E. Philip, Technology and Privacy: the new Landscape, 11 Harvard Journal of Law & Technology 871, 1998.
[241] Kang Jerry, supra note 202, page 1203.

information related to him"[242]. This is the aspect of privacy, on which this book will place emphasis, since it is the area that is most heavily affected by the introduction of new technological techniques in electronic and other transactions.

4.3.5.2.1 Privacy and Data Protection

It is essential for the purposes of this book to distinguish between the two related concepts of privacy and data protection. Discerning the differences between privacy and data protection has proved to amount to a challenging task. In literature and in academic sources the two terms are frequently used in the same spirit and in certain jurisdictions the terms in question represent an entirely or partly identical legal meaning. An indication of this is the USA jurisdiction and legal theory which instead of the term "data protection" prefer to use the term "informational privacy" or sometimes even "privacy" itself further blurring the already delicate borderline between the two. On the contrary in Europe the term "data protection" seems to have been established as a term rather autonomous from privacy. Privacy appears to be constructed at four levels: "firstly, territorial privacy"[243], which concerns the setting of limits on intrusion into the domestic and other environments such as the workplace...it includes searches, video surveillance and ID checks, secondly bodily privacy, which concerns the protection of people's physical selves against invasive procedures such as genetic tests..., thirdly privacy of communications, which covers the security and privacy of mail, telephones, e-mail...and finally information privacy, which involves the establishment of rules governing the collection and handling of personal data such as credit information, and medical and government records. It is also known as data protection"[244]. Thus, data protection is just an aspect of the concept of privacy and more specifically the control over the gathering and further use of personal data which aims at safeguarding our privacy. It is therefore, evident that privacy as a concept is broader than data protection as the latter is linked mainly to the processing and treatment of our personal data, while the former although it encompasses such an

---

[242] Arthur Miller in Michael James, supra note 196, page 3.
[243] Rosenberg in Simone Fischer Hübner, in Cybercrime, Law Enforcement, security and surveillance in the information age, Douglas Thomas and Brian D. Loader, Routledge, London and New York, 2000 page 174.
[244] Electronic Privacy Information Centre, Privacy & Human rights, An International Survey of Privacy Laws and Developments in association with Privacy International, Washington and London, 2003, page 3.

aspect, further extends to cover all areas of our life and personal activities which should be left without interference from third parties. The intrusion into one's home and abusive media publicity do fall within the ambit of privacy but not data protection. In addition to that, it is possible that the violation of a data protection principle will not entail a privacy abuse. For example the use of a data subject's inaccurate and false personal data in order to grant an insurance will lead to the infringement of the data protection legislation since its basic principle over the accuracy of data has been infringed but it might not necessarily be an infringement of privacy if the information concerned is not strictly personal. "On the one hand, the concept of personal data protection is narrower than privacy since privacy encompasses more than personal data. On the other hand it encompasses a wider area, since personal data are protected not only to enhance the privacy of the subject but also to guarantee other fundamental rights such as the right not to be discriminated"[245].

Although, it can be initially argued that a clear distinction between privacy and data protection can be drawn, further analysis renders such a conclusion less convincing. As it is evident throughout this book it is very difficult to separate the two areas as they are integrally connected. The term personal data refers to information linked with all parts of private life and the emergence of internet has created additional difficulties in the efforts to deal with the two terms on an individual and separate basis. In this sense I argue that data protection can be viewed as the modern tool to deal with the recently emerging and technology related challenges to privacy. In the framework of an information based and technology driven economy this aspect assumes an ever growing importance. Today's risks to privacy are radically different than the respective ones twenty or thirty years earlier. In the post war West threats to privacy mainly stemmed from the State interferences in private life which especially in Europe were to a great degree still a legacy of the undemocratic regimes largely in place in the pre war continent. Before the latest technological developments "privacy was effectively synonymous with…physically protecting one's property"[246] but nowadays, the basic threats to privacy originate from the widespread use of new technologies principally by private actors and the lack of control over the collected personal data. "It is a feature of

---

[245] European Data Protection Supervisor, Public Access to Documents and Data Protection, Background Paper Series, July 2005, No 1, page 15.
http://www.edps.eu.int/publications/policy_papers/Public_access_data_protection_EN.pdf accessed on July 10th 2006.

European data protection law that the private and public sectors were...eventually treated equally for the purposes of data protection law"[247]. In this sense data protection is not just an aspect of privacy but maybe the way to deal with the privacy threats of the new era. Since "control pf privacy is increasingly a matter of controlling electronic data acquired by others...it can accordingly be argued that data protection law is already the main avenue for protecting privacy; it may in time become the only one"[248].

Furthermore, alienating data protection from the rest of the privacy area and limiting it into the processing of data stripped from its human rights background can be controversial as well. It can also shed light on the divergence between the US and the European approach on the issue. If for the USA privacy is the concept comprising all aspects of private life and space such as our personal relations and choices along with our home and data protection is just an aspect of it related to the processing of personal data for the continental European legal tradition the landscape is dramatically different. As will be thoroughly analysed later, in accordance with the German jurisprudence, which along with the French one is the most influential in Europe, the right of an individual to determine the use of his personal data forms an integral part of his right of informational self-determination which constitutes a fundamental human right directly linked to universal values such as dignity. In this sense privacy and data protection are closely connected since "the protection of privacy serves a large range of other values and interests, the safeguarding of which must accordingly form part of the rationale and agenda of data protection law. Important examples of such values are personal autonomy, integrity and dignity"[249]. Therefore, data protection is closely related to the exercise of one of our basic human rights, which is the determination of the extent of the disclosure of our personal data and the terms under which this can take place. In this sense it becomes so similar to the notion of privacy that even international organisations treat them in the same or confusingly similar manner. This conclusion can be deduced from the wording used in important data protection legislation texts in

---

[246] Tracey DiLascio, How safe is the Safe Harbour? US and EU Data Privacy Law and the Enforcement of the FTC's Safe Harbour Programme, 22 Boston University International Law Journal, 2004, page 402.
[247] Jeremy Warner, The Right to Oblivion: Data Retention from Canada to Europe on three Backward Steps, 2 University of Ottawa Law & Technology Journal, 2005, page 83.
[248] Steve Hadley, The Law of Electronic Commerce and the Internet in the UK and Ireland, Cavendish Publishing Limited, London, 2006, page 81.

[249] Lee A Bygrave, The Place Of Privacy In Data Protection Law, University of NSW Law Journal, [2001] UNSWLJ 6, accessed at http://www.austlii.edu.au/au/journals/UNSWLJ/2001/6.html on July 10th 2006.

Europe[250] and internationally[251], which in the light of the new technological developments enabling threats to privacy through the collection of personal data increasingly bind the two concepts together. This can indicate that "it is axiomatic that data protection regulation is required to protect the privacy of individual data subjects suggesting that the central issue is merely the problem of reaching agreement on the method of achieving this result"[252].

This analysis aiming at highlighting the substantial convergence between the two concepts does not intend to conclude that the two terms coincide completely. A difference can be detected in the exact definition of the aims of the two rights. "A data protection law should be different from that of a law on privacy: rather than establishing rights, it should provide a framework for finding a balance between the interests of the individual, the data user and the community at large"[253]. The shaping of such a balance stands at the core of the European Data Protection Directive. As insisted before, data protection legislation is founded on the widely recognised ideal of addressing the threats emerging from the new technologies to our privacy while assuring the smooth flow of trade in an era when information is the most valuable asset. Thus, it is a reconciliation between our fundamental right to exercise control over the use of our personal data by third parties and the recognition that after an acceptable

---

[250] See article 1 and recital 10 of the *Directive 95/46* which expressly recognises Article 8 of the European Convention for the Protection of Human Rights and Freedoms *on the right of privacy* as the basis of the EU's cornerstone of data protection legislation.
See also the *Council of Europe*, Convention for the Protection of Individuals with regard to Automatic Processing of Personal Data, Article 1 – Object and purpose: The purpose of this convention is to secure in the territory of each Party for every individual, whatever his nationality or residence, respect for his rights and fundamental freedoms, and *in particular his right to privacy, with regard to automatic processing of personal data relating to him ("data protection")*. Site accessed on July 10th 2006: http://conventions.coe.int/Treaty/en/Treaties/Html/108.htm
[251] The link between data protection and privacy is further strengthened by the language used in the text of international agreements. In *the OECD Guidelines* on privacy and data protection are basically dealt on exactly the same basis. See OECD Guidelines on the Protection of Privacy and Transborder Flows of Personal Data, "*Privacy* protection laws have been introduced…to prevent what are considered to be *violations of fundamental human rights*, such as the *unlawful storage of personal data*, the storage of inaccurate personal data, or the abuse or unauthorised disclosure of such data"… Thus, it is common practice in continental Europe to talk about "data laws" or "data protection laws" (*lois sur la protection des données*), whereas in English speaking countries they are usually known as "privacy protection laws"…Generally speaking, statutes to *protect privacy* and individual liberties *in relation to personal data* attempt to cover the successive stages of the cycle beginning with the initial collection of data and ending with erasure or similar measures, and to ensure to the greatest possible extent individual awareness, participation and control. Site accessed on July 10th 2006: http://www.oecd.org/document/18/0,2340,en_2649_34255_1815186_1_1_1_1,00.html
[252] Diane Rowland, Elizabeth Macdonald, Information Technology Law, Cavendish Publishing Limited, London, 2005, page 309.
[253] 1978 Lindop Report on Data Protection, in Computer Law, Fifth Edition, Chris Reed, John Angel, Oxford University Press, 2003, page 419.

level of protection is achieved and certain safeguards are met there should be no other obstacle to the free flow of information for trade purposes. Moreover, in the data protection legislation context there is yet another balance to be achieved between the rights of the data subjects to control the quality and accuracy of data related to them on the one hand and the data controllers in processing personal data along with the legitimate interests of other administrative bodies to legally process information for other always legitimate ends on the other. Therefore, data protection law does not confer an absolute right. Privacy legislation does not confer an absolute right either since in most jurisdictions for example the authorities can still enter one's home but only after a warrant issued by the relevant authority, but this overwhelming need for shaping a balance with other crucial societal rights and needs as it is the rationale behind the passing of the relevant data protection legislation does not exist.

Apart from the substantive differences between the two concepts the system introduced at the EU level by the leads to further differences this time of procedural nature. "An assertion of privacy, as a right is generally made before a court which is required to exercise its discretion often …taking into consideration principles such as proportionality, by contrast data protection laws, whilst granting individual specific rights, are generally enforced through the intervention of a regulatory authority"[254]. I partly agree with this argument. It is true that privacy abuses will find their way to courts, the European Court of Human Rights has been really active in this field, but data protection claims can also become the subject of intervention on behalf of the judiciary. The system introduced by the Directive with the Data Protection Authorities established in all member states which can impose fines in cases of abuse does limit the resort to courts but this possibility is widely open for the interested parties. The European Court of Justice has recently produced its first couple of judgements related to the Directive which are analysed at the relevant part of the book and serve as a useful interpretation of the provisions of the Directive. Therefore, although clearly the role of bodies such as the Data Protection Authorities and Data Protection Supervisors is significant in the area of data protection, the courts are still left with an important role to play.

4.3.5.3 Profile Advertising and Direct Marketing

---

[254] Chris Reed and John Angel, ibid at page 420.

As already mentioned before profile advertising and direct marketing are industries whose emergence was prompted by the appearance of internet as a significant commercial tool. "Modern information technology has changed not only how commercial transactions occur, but, more fundamentally, the subject matter of commerce itself"[255]. In the framework of traditional out of the net trade, the collection of information constituted only a means for the attainment of an objective on behalf of enterprises. Now however it has emerged as the centrepiece of the activities of a whole new business whose primary objective is the collection of personally attributable and identifiable information. Databases were used in order to classify consumers into categories and keep basic data about one's customers. Now, databases themselves have been the object of a rapidly emerging industry. An industry whose principal focus is the creation of personal profiles, an asset of high value for the marketing world. Ordinary databases and "super massive databases that aggregate scores of individual databases into a searchable whole"[256] are the new object of commercial activity and the trade and exchange of information has been established as the most valuable commodity of the new era. In this particular framework the need of companies to collect personal data from the consumers assumes a compelling character. It becomes an essential element that can assist their efforts to acquire or preserve a competitive position in a highly challenging international market.

"Indeed, the activities of an individual on the internet offer significant opportunities for direct marketing that requires the seller to select a particular group of potential customers identify their needs and develop a specific message, which stands a better chance of getting across than mere mass marketing the so called one to one strategy"[257]. The consumer profiling industry, created on the basis of the new digital reality that affords to traditional businesses and industries a new array of potential marketing abilities, has founded its activities on a new process called "data mining". The term has been used in order to reflect the scanning of all databases available in order to shape a profile for a given consumer that can reveal patterns of behaviour,

---

[255] Bohlmal Erick, Privacy in the age of information, Journal of Information, Law and Technology, 2002, accessible at http://elj.warwick.ac.uk/jilt/02-2/bohlman.html, page1.
[256] Joseph T Thai, The Jurisprudence of Justice Stevens: Panel I: Criminal Justice: Is Data Mining ever a search under Justice Steven's Fourth Amendment?, 74 Fordham Law Review, 2006, page 1737.
[257] Szafran Emmanuel, Overstraeten Van Tanguy, Data Protection and Privacy on the Internet: Technical Considerations and European Legal Framework, Computer and Telecommunications Law Review, 2001, Sweet & Maxwell, p59.

specific preferences and choices made on line. The objective aimed at by such a process is to obtain the ability to make reliable evaluations of the behaviour of a consumer and predict his future needs. In this way an efficient company strategy can be effectively designed. These databases are viewed as a highly valued asset of a given company. "Make no mistake about it. Your customer database is your company's most valuable information asset"[258] seems to be a principle now widely accepted by industry and academics, leading figures of which support that customer information is "one of the most important weapons"[259] a company possesses[260]. Data mining companies such as "Acxiom" have developed an impressive capacity to monitor and analyse customer information concerning millions of households at least in the USA. As the company reveals in its website "there are over thirty million households experiencing a change in life stage every year" so, if companies register to "Acxiom's" services, the latter will reveal to them their target customers. The Company employs "household level segmentation system that places each U.S. household into one of 70 segments based on its specific consumer behaviour and demographic characteristics" that "also has the ability to show the migration of consumers from one cluster to another through the unique life stage methodology"[261]. Thus, all American households are being categorised in certain groups according to their size, the geographical area they are situated, their financial capacity and of course their previous consumer behaviour. As we are informed by the website "all the internal and external customer information in the world isn't very valuable without the technology to bring it together"[262] so, "Acxiom" can provide the methods to "deliver extensive knowledge about customers' purchasing behaviour and interests" and is very "skilled in building privacy components into marketing solutions"[263]. In order to comprehend the scale of the problem it is impressive to read that the company has in its disposal "more than 123 million telephone and address listings throughout the United States and 16 million

---

[258] McClurg J. Andrew, A Thousand Words are worth a Picture: A Privacy Tort Response to consumer Data Profiling, 98 Northwestern University Law Review, 2003, page 72.
[259] See Mena Jesus, Data Mining Your Website 8 (1999), in McClurg supra note 259 at page 72.
[260] And not only the companies. There is widespread use of such methods also by Government Agencies at least in the USA. For relevant information see the Report of the US General Accounting Office at: http://www.gao.gov/new.items/d04548.pdf accessed on august 9th.
[261] See the site of the company at: http://www.acxiom.com/default.aspx?ID=2548&Country_Code=USA&Top_Mind=T accessed on August 9th.
[262] See: http://www.acxiom.com/default.aspx?ID=1842&Country_Code=USA accessed on August 9th.
[263] See the relevant site: http://www.acxiom.com/default.aspx?ID=1844&Country_Code=USA accessed on Auegst 9th.

Canadian listings"[264] along with further "160 million US and Canadian residential and business listings"[265]. Another data mining company "R.L. Polk & Company" "allows you to identify households which meet pre-determined credit criteria that have a wide range of vehicle purchasing characteristics"[266]. In Polk they "collect, compile, and interpret state vehicle registrations and title information, and supply demographic, lifestyle, and other information about consumers" and more importantly they "know what automotive consumers buy, where and when they buy it, and what they are likely to buy next"[267]. Consumers' personal data have been effectively transformed from a means to achieve greater results in trade in services to an object of trade. Nowadays, there is also evidence of cooperation between companies focused on collecting personal data. For example the Royal Bank of Scotland, the Direct Marketing Association and the Institute of Direct Marketing have founded a consortium operating in financial services called TANK![268]. Nectar Consortium includes BP, Debenhams, Barclaycard, Sainsbury's, First Quench, Ford, Vodafone and EDF Energy[269]. Thus, databases of big commercial entities with activities as diverse as energy, telecommunications, banking, clothing, retailing and the car industry have joined forces in sharing the personal data of their consumers. The matching of data from the various databases can easily lead to the creation of personal profiles for every single consumer including details of all his personal choices, bank and retail records.

The methods of obtaining information for marketing and advertising purposes however, have proved highly controversial. The most prominent demonstration of such controversy has been the DoubleClick affair in the USA. DoubleClick is the largest advertising company in the internet and was the first to become the centre of a public dispute after its merger with Abacus Direct in 1999. "Abacus had collected detailed data about the catalogue shopping habits of approximately 90% of Americans, 99 million names and addresses in a database of two billion consumer catalogue transactions, most of which were collected almost entirely without consumer content"[270]. DoubleClick acquires the information it aims at for marketing purposes by

---

[264] See: http://www.acxiom.com/default.aspx?ID=1763&Country_Code=USA accessed on August 9th 2004.

[265] See: http://www.acxiom.com/default.aspx?ID=1762&Country_Code=USA accesed on August 9th.

[266] See: http://www.polk.com/products/polkone.asp accessed on August 9th.

[267] See: http://www.polk.com/news/features/ai.asp accessed on August 9th.

[268] Martin Evans supra note 159 at page 109.

[269] The same.

[270] Teh Jeanette, supra note 159 at page 26.

using cookies and other technologically advanced devices that cannot be detected by the simple user. When a user visited the sites of the companies taking advantage of the services offered by DoubleClick, "a request for the DoubleClick cookie is triggered"[271]. The commercial website of the companies subscribed to DoubleClick sends the ID of its visitors to DoubleClick requiring "all available information about that user, to whom specially targeted material is then sent"[272]. Thus, a whole network of information that was disseminated in a limitless manner had been set up. It was based on the ability of the companies' sites to track the identity of their users and then divulge this piece of information to DoubleClick, which provided the companies subscribed to it with a personal profile of each of the consumers involved. The latter subsequently became the subjects of individually tailored marketing techniques. After the acquisition of Abacus[273] there were openly expressed fears that DoubleClick would obtain access to a vast amount of personal information with the ability to combine the data possessed by both companies. The possibility of matching its already existing organised consumer profiles with additional information concerning the consumers' personal addresses and other pieces of information was perceived as a major threat to privacy. "The merger would yield intrusive or abusive Internet marketing practices"[274]. After the public uproar initiated by privacy safeguarding organisations such as the Centre for Democracy and Technology and the Electronic Privacy Information Centre, in a press statement released on March 2nd 2000, the company clarified that it never had the intention to implement this plan and "and has never associated names, or any other personally identifiable information, with anonymous user activity across Web sites"[275]. It also ensured the public that the company is going to comply with the privacy standards that are going to be set after discussions between industry and the relevant authorities.

"It will not move forward on its plans to tie personally identifiable information to Internet users' online surfing habits until government and industry have reached a

---

[271] Szafran Emmanuel, Overstraeten Van Tanguy, supra note 258 at page 59.
[272] The same.
[273] "The Abacus Alliance database contains transactional data with detailed information on consumer and business-to-business purchasing and spending behaviour", see DoubleClick site at http://www.doubleclick.com/us/product/database/default.asp?asp_object_1=& accessed on August 1st 2003.
[274] Tedeschi Bob, Net Companies Look Offline for Consumer Data, July 21st 1999, The New York Times, available at http://www.nytimes.com/library/tech/99/06/cyber/commerce/21commerce.html .
[275] See the statement at http://www.cdt.org/privacy/000302doubleclick.shtml

consensus on privacy rules for the Internet"[276]. Although, DoubleClick still "uses information about the user's browser and Web surfing to determine which ads to show to him"[277] it has now initiated a privacy policy based mainly on the ability of the consumer to "opt out of the DoubleClick ad-serving cookie, so that no unique information or number is associated with his computer's browser"[278]. Now, the previous consent of the consumer regarding the receipt of the marketing products will serve as a prerequisite for companies that want to make use of DoubleClick's technology and services. The publicity that the DoubleClick issue has caused and the controversy that led to its change of policy serve as clear indicators of the importance of data protection for the public on one hand and the clearly adverse effect that particular marketing methods can have on the protection of privacy on the other.

The DoubleClick case might have demonstrated in a clear manner the magnitude of the problem, but the truth is even more alarming. Consumer profiling and data mining are not activities assumed exclusively by companies that specialise in data collection such as DoubleClick, but constitute now a widely spread technique in the commercial world. "On line booksellers profile customers by tracking the products they view or buy on line, telephone companies...based on when, how often and what numbers they call, supermarkets...by recording and analysing purchasing information collected through discount or loyalty club cards, banks and other financial institutions...based on personal financial data"[279]. Thus, the "most important concern about consumer marketing information...is the operator's ability to link this information with identifying information the consumer has supplied"[280]. It becomes apparent that in the framework of a market where strong competition between companies prevails, the enterprises involved will move towards the direction of taking full advantage of the personal data they possess, in order to form tailored marketing strategies, develop their product policies accordingly to the needs of their consumers and consolidate their presence in the relevant markets in question. The universality of the spread of personal data use places a further burden on the efforts to tackle the

---

[276] See the announcement of the Centre of Democracy and Technology at
http://www.cdt.org/action/doubleclick.shtml
[277] Privacy statement at
http://www.doubleclick.com/us/corporate/privacy/privacy/default.asp?asp_object_1=&
[278] The same.
[279] McClurg J. Andrew, A Thousand Words are worth a Picture: A Privacy Tort Response to consumer Data Profiling, 98 Northwestern University Law Review, 2003, page 66.
[280] Ribstein E. Larry, Kobayashi H. Bruce, State Regulation of Electronic Commerce, 51 Emory Law Journal 1, 2002.

problem effectively. And the developments in information technology do not contribute to this end. Although, "current technology makes it difficult for unrelated businesses to share customer information with other businesses, as their computer systems speak different languages, that obstacle may be eliminated by a technology industry initiative known as Consumer Profile Exchange (CPEX)"[281]. This system will enable the sharing of consumer information gathered by various industries "with the ease of pressing the "enter" button, as it creates standardised XML computer markup language tags that can identify discreet types of personal data"[282].

Thus, the ambiguity of the privacy landscape is further complicated by the new forms of commercial activity and marketing that have been introduced after the emergence of internet as a privileged area of advertising. The ability to track down and note all the choices made on behalf of consumers on the net has profoundly enhanced the scope of performance of new marketing techniques. Traditionally, advertising was aiming at large audiences and did not pose any threat to either anonymity or privacy. Now, every move on the web can be tracked down, stored in personal file along with additional personally identifiable information and comprise a detailed and updated report on someone's preferences, needs, ideas or even on issues of more personal nature like one's family situation. As EPIC specifically stated on the issue "consumers are more at risk today...the profiling is more extensive and the marketing techniques are more intrusive"[283]. It concludes by marking that "anonymity, which remains crucial to privacy on the internet, is being squeezed out by the rise of electronic commerce"[284], as now "every message can be intercepted at any site through which it passes and then traced, forged, suppressed or delayed"[285].

These observations are further supported by the novel strategies adopted by many enterprises aimed at obtaining at any cost to the consumers' privacy, information on their patterns of on line behaviour along with information indicative of aspects of their personality. The latter can prove very useful at the stage of designing a marketing campaign based on the characteristics and preferences of specific individually defined consumers. These methods applied on behalf of many companies have led

---

[281] Ibid at page 67.
[282] The same
[283] Electronic Privacy Information Centre, Surfer Beware III: Privacy Policies without Privacy Protection, 2000, available at www.epic.org/reports/surfer-beware3.html
[284] The same.
[285] Chissick Michael, Data Protection in the Electronic Commerce Era, Computer and Telecommunications Law Review, Sweet & Maxwell, London, 1999, page 109.

distinguished commentators to talk about "a privacy horror show"[286]. The most preoccupying of these techniques is related to "spyware". It is computer software that "gathers and reports information about a computer user without the user's knowledge or consent"[287]. This term is used to describe certain computer programmes and software acquired by an individual user to be installed in his personal computer. There are several children educational programmes, encyclopaedias or financial planning programmes, which "automatically forward to manufacturers, via the Internet, information about the consumers such as details of web surfing habits or identifying personal information"[288] for purposes of generating targeted advertising or "creating customer lists"[289]. "It is more than a nuisance: such software is in effect hijacking the PC, monitoring one's internet use…it harvests personal information personal information, such as one's e-mail address and location or even one's credit card details"[290]. Valuable pieces of personal information that happened to be stored at an individual's computer are transferred via the net without not only the consent but even the knowledge of the user, who is completely unsuspicious over the ongoing process related to the dissemination of his private data. This information is further being processed and structured in lists containing people with "particular characteristics…such as ethnicity, political views and sexual orientation"[291].

4.3.5.4 Providing information "voluntarily"

Web pages and internet companies use a variety of technologies in order to gather information both about their customers and about their simple users and potential clients. The information gathered can be distinguished in two categories based on the existence of consent on the part of the user or his ignorance about the collection of personal information concerning oneself. Users usually tend to voluntarily provide

---

[286] Schwartz Paul, in Sovern Jeff, Protecting Privacy with Deceptive Trade Practices Legislation, 69 Fordham Law Review, 2001, page 1307.

[287] Matthew Bierlein and Gregory Smith, 2004 Privacy Year in Review Annual Update: Internet: Growing Problems with Spyware and Phishing, Judicial and Legislative Developments in Internet Governance and the Impacts on Privacy, 1 Journal of Law and Policy for the Information Society, 2005, page 280.

[288] Sovern Jeff, supra note 287, page 1307.

[289] Jordan M Blanke, Robust Notice and Informed Consent: The Keys to Successful Spyware Legislation, 7 Columbia Science and Technology Law Review 2, 2006.

[290] Spyware, A Hidden Menace, The Economist, June 5th 2004.

[291] See also Privacy On-Line: A Report to the Congress, Federal Trade Commission, 1998, available at http://www.ftc.gov/reports/privacy3/toc.htm , accessed on August 9th 2004.

personal information when they apply on line for a job or a commercial offer, when they subscribe to an on line newspaper or portal or even when they register in order to access their personal e-mail accounts. Although, someone might think that voluntarily afforded information does not pose serious problems to the legislator, the reality is quite different. Consumers with their capacity as simple users or subscribers tend to believe that the information they provide is going to be specifically and solely used for the limited purposes mentioned at the respective part of the web page. However, as was presented in the previous part of the book, personally identifiable data are stored in files that can be later on distributed to other parties with a vivid interest in obtaining personal information about potential customers. Obtaining information in a voluntary manner has many positive effects. Apart from removing the moral argument of collecting personal data in an illegitimate manner, since the consent of the consumers and the fact that they actually assume this initiative removes the responsibility away from the commercial sites and enterprises, providing data voluntarily brings more practical benefits for the commercial world. "Consumer information acquired in such a manner costs firms virtually nothing after the appropriate software has been deployed, when consumers and web site visitors click some buttons on their keyboards, consumer information is collected, stored and categorised virtually without any expenditure of labour once the initial configuration costs have been incurred"[292].

This issue can also be viewed from a different angle. Many companies do encourage the assignment of information on a voluntary basis on behalf of consumers. The most usual method is for a retailer to ask for the personal data of the consumer in order to provide him with a "club card" that guarantees him some sort of preferential treatment usually in the form of some additional credit given to the consumer after he has surpassed a certain level of transactions. In the airline industry it can take the form of "golden mile" programmes, which gather the data of individuals again on a voluntary basis in return for some extra miles of travel this time for free. The issue in question does not only concern the obvious impact that these techniques have on privacy but produces also a highly symbolic side effect. These practices "shift privacy from a right to a commodity and reduce the social expectation of privacy" and equal to "an illusion of voluntariness as where all producers in a given market require an

---

[292] Baumer L. David, Brande Earp Julia, Evers S. Pamela, Tit for Tat in Cyberspace: Consumer and Website Responses to Anarchy in the Market for Personal Information, 4 North Carolina Journal of Law & Technology 217, 2003.

intrusive quality of personal data, as with banks, the data subject is asked to choose between giving consent and losing advantages, privileges, rights or benefits, some of which may be essential to the subject in a given situation"[293].

4.3.5.5 Privacy threatening Technologies
The use of cookies
4.3.5.5.1 Impact on privacy

"A cookie is a computer data storage programme which enables a web site to record, using information on a visitor's hard drive, his or her on line activities"[294]. More specifically, they are "small files transmitted from a web site or a third party advertising company that are saved on the user's computer and retrieved and read by the host website or advertising company when the user returns to the site or views other advertisements on the web placed by the same advertiser"[295]. In essence, "the contents of the cookie file are attached to every subsequent request back to the server for a different web page"[296]. Thus, Cookies are used as the principal technological tool in order to detect, monitor and store the precise route that each consumer follows while navigating on the net. Cookies function at a double stage process: during the first cookies, which means small text files are sent and stored at the computer of the user without his initial consent. The user cannot possibly be aware of the particular process that constitutes a function integral in the operation of the internet. "During the second stage, the cookie is clandestinely and automatically transferred from the user's machine to a Web server"[297]. Whenever, a user tries to obtain access to a particular web page "the browser will, without the user's knowledge, transmit the cookie containing personal information to the Web server"[298]. "To put it more plainly, a cookie is a mechanism that allows a web site to record your comings and goings, usually without

---

[293] Rotenber Marc, Agre Philip, supra note 241 at page 877.
[294] Chissick Michael, Kelman Alistair, Electronic Commerce, Law and Practice, Third Edition, Sweet & Maxwell, London, 2002, p221.
[295] Scherzer H. Dov, EU Regulation of Processing of Personal Data by wholly non Europe based websites, European Intellectual Property Law Review, 2003, Sweet & Maxwell, p294.
[296] Siebecker R. Michael, Cookies and The Common Law: Are Internet Advertisers Trespassing on our Computers?, 76 Southern California Law Review, 2003, page 898.
[297] Viktor Mayer-Schoenberger, 1 West Virginia Journal of Law and Technology 1.1, 1997, available at http://www.wvu.edu/%7Ewvjolt/Arch/Mayer/Mayer.htm, accessed on 22/06/2003.
[298] The same.

your knowledge or consent"[299]. It has also "the ability to determine the exact location of the computer being used"[300] as the latter becomes "uniquely identified and tracked over a session or multiple visits"[301]. It contributes to the creation of a highly detailed profile over one's personality. The latter can be achieved by the close monitoring of one's on line behaviour. The name of the newspaper one reads, the nature of the articles one chooses, the on line purchases one did or the sites he visited in order to be better informed about particular products that thus are of interest to him. Piece by piece a visitor's profile is shaped. Anonymity as an element inherent in the interpretation of privacy as defined in the context of the net is gradually abolished in the light of the new mechanisms used to foster trade and marketing activities.

4.3.5.5.2 A Positive Aspect of the use of Cookies

Various parties argue that cookies can be beneficial because "they enable custom tailoring of content, advertising, speed ordering and product suggestions"[302]. Moreover, they facilitate the access of consumers to register demanding sites as they render "typing in all your personal information and password"[303] unnecessary. Hence, the web site can identify the particular user after his or her first visit and does not require further registering but enables immediate access to its content. It has also stored the number and nature of products purchased so it can show to the particular consumer a set of advertisements based on his already identified interests or a row of offers concerning products that fall into his or her preferences as the latter are openly demonstrated by the choices already made by the consumer in question. The storage of previous browsing activity can lead to a certain degree of facilitation regarding the function of the commercial sites but have led to serious repercussions on consumers' privacy that cannot be by any chance underestimated.

---

[299] Electronic Privacy Information Centre, Report on the use of Cookies, available at: http://www.epic.org/privacy/internet/cookies/
[300] Schiller C. Julia, Information Privacy v The Commercial speech Doctrine: Can the Gramm Leach Bliley Act Provide Adequate Privacy Protection?, 11 CommLaw Conspectus, 2003, page 352.
[301] MacDonnell John, Exporting Trust: Does E-Commerce Need a Canadian Privacy Seal of Approval?, 39 The Alberta Law Review 346, 2001.
[302] Teh Jeanette, supra note 159 at page 26.
[303] A Study on practical consumer experiences with electronic commerce, Consumers International with the financial support of the DG Health and Consumer Protection of the European Commission, http://europa.eu.int/comm/dgs/health_consumer/library/surveys/sur12_en.html , accessed on 23/01/2002.

4.3.5.6. Exchange of data between a user's computer and a web site

It has to be mentioned that data are also disseminated due to a process that actually underlies the whole function of internet as an operational system. The form in which web pages can become available on line is known as "HTTP"[304]. The latter constitutes a request from the computer of the user to the service provider of the particular web site to whom access is purported, for the transferring of a file to the personal computer. As a prerequisite for the aforementioned file transfer, the computer of the user provides the server provider with its Internet Protocol (IP), which has to be emphasised, is afforded exclusively to each terminal and is of unique nature. Its revelation is necessary in order for the Internet Service Provider to know the particular address meaning the particular computer, to which the data requested should be sent. Along with the IP protocol additional information concerning the particular user can be collected by the service provider. The type of service requested, the sites visited, the transactions conducted, the software installed, the language or other settings preferred, the special characteristics of the particular user's connection and the location of some of his files comprise pieces of very important information that can be revealed automatically. Thus, both the service provider and the web site can have a list with the consumer's moves and web site visits during his search on the net. A great part of his privacy has already been revealed and come to public eye from the very first stages of his connection to the net. "Technically, each visit to the internet can be traced and data collected"[305]. Moreover, even the route that an e-mail follows can be traced and stored as the operator is instantly aware of the sender and the recipient, while the content of the mail itself since it is transmitted via several operators can be "intercepted and read by third people"[306]. Thus, "clickstream data" can be easily tracked down as a matter of a routine function of the net. Clickstream data is "the generic name given to the information a web site can know about a user simply because the user has browsed the

---

[304] Hyper Text Transfer Protocol.
[305] Overstraeten Van Tanguy, Szafran Emmanuel, supra note 258 at page 57.
[306] Tanus Daniel Gustavo, Alguien te esta mirando, Information Technology, Mind Opener SA, Edicion Number 50, Noviembre 2000, Buenos Aires, p144. Also available at www.protecciondedatos.com.ar/doc6.htm accessed on 1/7/2003.

site"[307]. It constitutes the picture of a "detailed browsing activity, such as the order of the web pages visited and the time spent at each one"[308]. This information is easily obtained by a web site due to the disclosure of the unique IP address that as explained above constitutes a prerequisite for the function of internet as it is necessary in order to enable a computer to access a web site. The revelation of such information is a serious threat to privacy as "there are several ways it can be traced to an identifiable individual"[309].

The challenges to privacy inherent in the process, which is technically necessary for the function of internet, have led important academics to talk about internet as an "alternate universe, a computer constructed world, a virtual reality, where you are invisibly stamped with a bar code as soon as you venture outside your home"[310]. As the consumer explores the on line world and searches for beneficial commercial opportunities or just information in commercial or non commercial websites about a product or any issue that he is interested in, he gets tracked "through invisible scanners focused on his bar code"[311]. The web sites visited, the choices made, the order web pages were viewed, the actual time spent in each page or newspaper article and the addresses to which e-mails were sent, are all automatically revealed, processed and linked to a specifically defined and traced individual. More specifically, they constitute the material on which the creation of detailed personal profiles is based. As Stan Karas puts it "the real effects of consumer information gathering are best framed as an exercise of power through surveillance"[312]. The latter can unfortunately concern all aspects of private life, even those considered the most intimate like health issues. Pharmaceutical companies used to collect data with difficulty from research conducted by health institutions and conducted campaigns for the promotion of their products. As technology evolves "times change and old orthodoxies quickly morph into discredited doctrine"[313]. Nowadays, a widespread way for pharmaceutical companies to collect health information via internet is "through the keywords individuals use when visiting

---

[307] Lin Elbert, Prioritising Privacy: A Consitutional Response to Internet, 17 Berkeley Technology Law Journal, Summer 2002, p1092.
[308] The same.
[309] The same.
[310] Kang Jerry, supra note 202, at page 1198.
[311] The same.
[312] Karas Stan, Enhancing the Privacy Discourse: Consumer Information Gathering as Surveillance, Journal of Technology Law & Policy, 2002, Volume 7, Issue 1, page 30.
[313] Diane Leenheer Zimmerman, Is there a Right to have Something to say? One View of the Public Domain, 73 Fordham aw Review, 2004, page 305.

search engine sites"[314]. As analysed above, DoubleClick sold certain keywords to respective companies. This tactic informs companies of the requests and interest of the users. Thus, when a medical or pharmaceutical company "owns a specific keyword like "depression" that company's banner ads will appear on the search results page when the phrase or word is used"[315]. One can easily estimate the implications of the revelation of information of such nature. They range from natural nuisance or embarrassment stemming from the divulgence of sensitive personal information to serious consequences including health insurance coverage and employment discrimination. The factor that further complicates the shaping of efficient policies to combat threats to privacy while navigating on line, is the fact that the "very technology that makes cyberspace possible also makes detailed, cumulative, invisible observation of ourselves possible"[316].

The collection of personal data and the creation of detailed profiles linked to individually identifiable consumers have given rise to fears over potential threats to individual freedoms stemming not only from the private sector as already explained before, but also from government agencies and organisations. Clickstream data can assist the investigation of law enforcement agencies in providing useful information over the ideas, thoughts, opinions and interests of a given citizen, who at a specific time is under investigation. Surfers, who have accessed sites with information concerning criminal activities, explosives or drugs, can be easily detected and related to accusations or files of reports made against them. "In addition, law enforcement agents could mine clickstream data to create psychological profiles for use as trial to establish intent or motive"[317], a development that forms a significant challenge for the whole system of justice as we know it at least up to now. Clickstream data could "compile a dossier of a defendant's online behaviour replete with potentially incriminating "evidence""[318]. For example, "a defendant accused of murdering his wife to inherit her assets might be condemned by a clickstream that recorded recent research into manslaughter inheritance statutes or intestacy schemes"[319]. Viewing sites of anti

---

[314] Kao C. Audiey, Linden Ozanne Erica, Direct to Consumer advertising and the Internet: Informational Privacy, Product Liability and Organisational Responsibility, Saint Louis University Law Journal, Volume 46, Number 1, 2002, page 162.
[315] Ibid at page 163.
[316] Kang Jerry, supra note 202 at page 1199.
[317] Skok Gavin, Establishing a Legitimate Expectation of Privacy in Clickstream Data, 6 Michigan Telecommunication Technology Law Review 61, 2000.
[318] The same.
[319] The same

governmental groups can provide the evidence for an individual's alleged participation in a plan to organise a violent demonstration against the government or even to plant a bomb in a government building or service. In the climate of fear and mistrust that prevails especially in the US society after the 9/11 terrorist attacks these methods can assume a central position in efforts of national authorities to tackle organised crime and deal with the new forms of terrorism.

The attack against the Twin Towers has certainly contributed significantly at least in the US to the shifting of the balance to security rather than privacy. "What was once denounced as Orwellian was suddenly embraced as reasonable"[320]. In this context in the US "the temptation will be more and more especially in a polarised society whether it is the red scare in the fifties or terrorism in this century to use those databanks…irrespective of whether they are private or public at some point they will be used by the government to determine who is a good American and who is a bad American. Not determined through prosecution and trial but based on what came up on someone's computer screen"[321]. Thus, internet seems to impose new and serious challenges even to areas of law that seemed unaffected at the early stage of its development such as the area of criminal law and procedure. It is important at this stage to note that "ethical challenges to information gathering are particularly difficult because human beings, with their morals and scruples, are virtually absent from the process"[322]. The ability to collect such a huge range of crime related information can alter the landscape in the area of law enforcement. However, at this stage "the assumptions of imperfect detection, the need for deterrence and the reliance on police and prosecutorial discretion on which our legal system is based will come under severe strain"[323]. Even more chilling is the hypothetical scenario expressed by various academics that "the government or others will attempt to use the ability to construct personal profiles in order to predict dangerous or antisocial activities before they happen"[324]. People, whose profiles correspond to the criteria used by enforcement authorities, will be viewed as suspicious or prone to commit certain criminal activities and can be the subject to increased surveillance or discrimination. Such a profiling

---

[320] Max Guirguis, Electronic Visual Surveillance and the Reasonable Expectation of Privacy, Journal of Technology, Law and Policy, Vol 9, December 2004, Issue 2, page 143.
[321] Douglas J. Sylvester and Sharon Lohr, The Security of Our Secrets: A History of Privacy and Confidentiality in Law and Statistical Practice, 83 Denver University Law Review, 2005, page 206.
[322] Karas Stan, supra note 313, page 47.
[323] Froomkin A. Michael, supra note 179 at page 1471.
[324] The same.

system is currently in use in the USA as a part of an enhanced security system for the country's airports. Its target is to identify any passengers, who have reserved their tickets through the usual process that present any possible risk of being a terrorist. The automated system called CAPS "scores passengers according to a set of weighted criteria to determine which should be subjected to additional security measures"[325]. The criteria for the shaping of the "terrorist profiles are built using a passenger's last name, whether the ticket was purchased with cash, how long before departure it was bought, the type of traveling companions, whether a rental car is waiting, the destination of the flight and passenger, and whether the ticket is one-way or round-trip"[326]. According to the relevant officials "to determine whether a passenger should be selected, the airline reservation computer identifies the factors that the passenger has hit upon and totals the positive and negative scores; those passengers who score below the FAA-prescribed cutoff are selectees"[327]. Although, Janet Reno, the Attorney General, insisted that the criteria will not be determined by elements such as race, religion or ethnic origin it is widely feared that "a profile that uses past travel to a terrorist-list country to identify people who will be selected for heightened scrutiny is guaranteed to discriminate against people who trace their ancestry to those countries and visit their grandparents there"[328]. It seems that we have entered an era when data matching "linking individuals with data about them"[329] and data mining "identifying people who fit a designated computer generated profile"[330], therefore a process of "looking for new knowledge in existing data"[331], are increasingly viewed as acceptable methods to check the creditworthiness of a potential client or to predict a future terrorist attack. The data mining systems usually make use of certain features such as race, ethnicity, gender, age and behaviour linking individuals to the specific characteristics of the chosen profile. It makes use of patterns of behaviours or characteristics and attempts to produce predictive judgements. Thus, by definition since its nature is basically predictive it is prone to mistakes and misjudgements. An additional factor to be taken into account is

---

[325] Declan McCullagh, You? A Terrorist? Yes! see: http://www.wired.com/news/politics/0,1283,19218-2,00.html?tw=wn_story_page_next1 accessed on August 9th.
[326] The same.
[327] The same.
[328] The same.
[329] Daniel J. Steinbock, Data Matching, Data Mining and Due Process, 40 Georgia Law Review, 2005, page 4.
[330] The same.
[331] K.A. Taipale, Data Mining and Domestic Security: Connecting the Dots to Make Sense of Data, 5 Columbia Science and Technology Law Review 2, 2004.

that the collected information usually of commercial nature can reveal several aspects of one's personality, needs and personal trends enabling the classification of individuals into certain socioeconomic marketing categories however, "the complexity of the very identity cannot be captured in the electronic bits and bytes of a marketing profile"[332]. Each one of us possesses a multidimensional personality, which is so complex that it cannot be fully comprehended in all its aspects and parameters from the reading and analysis of commercial choices. In addition to that a commercial entity or a market industry would be interested to analyse the personal data and identify what a consumer is doing and which are his exact choices. Their interest will be fixed on the nature of choices made on the part of the consumers which will reveal their habits and buying patterns very likely to be repeated in the future. In contrast to that an investigative authority would be mainly interested in the rationale behind those choices, in the motive behind the decisions. A marketing company will be interested to be aware of the actual fact that a certain consumer usually buys one way airline tickets in order to effectively design the respective advertising towards him or her. Security services however, will have to see the rationale behind such a decision which in the vast majority of cases would be wholly disconnected from any criminal or terrorist motive. It has to be noted that the use of commercial data for such purposes can be challenging for an additional reason. This is no other than the actual quality and accuracy of the data. A study in the US has indicated that "seventy percent of credit reports have some mistakes, and almost one third have such serious errors that they affect whether the individual is denied credit...identity theft for example adds erroneous data to commercial data bases"[333]. Thus, attempting to predict future behavioural patters on the basis of data collected by commercial sites on the internet can prove controversial or even futile. One can easily imagine the pain, the embarrassment and the problems created in the personal and professional life of a citizen who has been found to fit into the algorithm's profile as a terrorist or even as a person prone to insurance fraud. The existence of databases with individually identifiable information and the incentive given by the urgent need to prevent further terrorist attacks in combination with the

---

[332] David A DeMarco, Understanding Consumer Information Privacy in the Realm of Internet Commerce: Personhood and Pragmatism, Pop Tarts and Six Packs, 84 Texas Law Review, 2006, page 1028.
[333] James X Dempsey & Lara M. Flint, The Future of Internet Surveillance Law: A Symposium to discuss Interne Surveillance, Privacy & the USA Patriot Act: Surveillance, Records & Computers: commercial Data and National Security, 72 The George Washington Law Review, 2004, page 1470.

demonstration of a certain degree of tolerance on behalf of the public mainly in the US[334] in fear of new attacks have rendered this method very popular to the investigative authorities especially in the US.

The dangers hidden in the widespread use of such equipment and techniques based on automated process of profiles in order to determine whether an individual would prefer a specific product over another, will choose a given newspaper due to his political affiliations, will be interested in a trip to Rome to visit Vaticano due to his already known religious beliefs or even more grave would be susceptible to commit a certain crime due to indications from his profile or engage in terrorist activities, are very serious. They constitute a challenge to prevailing legal principles and impose a threat to our legal culture.

4.3.5.7 Data Retention

The landscape in this area is still transforming since it is still experiencing continuous reform and change. The directive initially dealing with issues related to data retention was Directive 97/66 which was repealed and replaced by Directive 2002/58 on privacy and electronic communications[335]. Although, the latter established a certain regime on data retention based on specific parameters it was quickly amended by yet another directive in this area which passed urgently and under the extreme pressure of the bombing of the Madrid trains in March 2004 and the attacks against the London metro in July 2005; directive 2006/24/EC of the European Parliament and of the Council on the retention of data generated or processed in connection with the provision of publicly available electronic communication services or of public communication networks and amending directive 2002/58/EC[336]. The innovative element of the 2002/58 directive is to be found in article 15. The latter allowed member states to adopt data retention measures if necessary for national security, defence,

---

[334] See the USA Patriot Act 2001 at: http://www.epic.org/privacy/terrorism/hr3162.html which came into force almost a month after the 9/11 attack. The Act granted law enforcement authorities wide powers of phone and internet surveillance and access to highly personal data with limited judicial oversight. Section 215 grants the FBI the authority to obtain all sorts of business records including library, medical, bookstore or travel records.
[335] See the directive at:
http://europa.eu.int/smartapi/cgi/sga_doc?smartapi!celexapi!prod!CELEXnumdoc&lg=en&numdoc=320 02L0058&model=guichett July 24th 2006.
[336] See the Directive at: http://www.ispai.ie/DR%20as%20published%20OJ%2013-04-06.pdf July 24th 2006.

public security and the detection and prosecution of criminal offences. These measures could have been introduced for a limited period and in full compliance with the principles of proportionality and respect for human rights[337]. However, if there was no ground for the invocation of article 15 of the Directive the relevant article to apply was article 6[338] which effectively provided for the erasure of traffic data after a period in which its maintenance was necessary for the functions of the service providers. After the transmission of the communication the relevant data should be deleted. Article 5 (1) of the Directive introduced the principle of confidentiality of the relevant data with the exception of the reasons enshrined in article 15 (1). According to that "member States shall ensure the confidentiality of communications and the related traffic data by means of a public communications network and publicly available electronic communications services, through national legislation". Thus, the new regime was based on two parameters. Traffic data should be kept only for the period during which they were absolutely necessary for the function of electronic communications and after that the service providers had the duty to destroy it. In case a member state could invoke one of the grounds stated in article 15 (1), it could introduce data retention measures but only for a limited time and in compliance with the democratic principles mentioned above. As far as the location data were concerned article 9 provided clearly for their processing only "when they are made anonymous, or with the consent of the users or subscribers to the extent and for the duration necessary for the provision of a value added service". An exception to this rule is found in article 10 where it is stated that absence of consent of a user for the processing of location data is permitted when "dealing with emergency calls and recognised as such by a Member State, including law enforcement agencies, ambulance services and fire brigades, for the purpose of responding to such calls". Recital 2 of the directive stated that "this Directive seeks to

---

[337] Article 15 (1) of the Directive: Member States may adopt legislative measures to restrict the scope of the rights and obligations provided for in Article 5, Article 6, Article 8(1), (2), (3) and (4), and Article 9 of this Directive when such restriction constitutes a necessary, appropriate and proportionate measure within a democratic society to safeguard national security (i.e. State security), defence, public security, and the prevention, investigation, detection and prosecution of criminal offences or of unauthorised use of the electronic communication system, as referred to in Article 13(1) of Directive 95/46/EC. To this end, Member States may, inter alia, adopt legislative measures providing for the retention of data for a limited period justified on the grounds laid down in this paragraph. All the measures referred to in this paragraph shall be in accordance with the general principles of Community law, including those referred to in Article 6(1) and (2) of the Treaty on European Union.

[338] Article 6 of the Directive: Traffic data relating to subscribers and users processed and stored by the provider of a public communications network or publicly available electronic communications service must be erased or made anonymous when it is no longer needed for the purpose of the transmission of a communication without prejudice to paragraphs 2, 3 and 5 of this Article and Article 15(1).

respect the fundamental rights and observes the principles recognised in particular by the Charter of fundamental rights of the European Union. In particular, this Directive seeks to ensure full respect for the rights set out in Articles 7 and 8 of that Charter". This appears to be quite significant since the directive should be interpreted in the light of the aforementioned principles. Articles 7 and 8 of the Charter refer to the right to privacy and data protection respectively therefore, albeit innovative in its aims of relaxing the restrictions on data retention, the relevant directive remained on the path previously shaped by the landmark directive 95/46. The Charter is not binding in its nature (unless it is to be incorporated in a future "Reform" or "Constitutional" Treaty which is then effectively ratified by all member states) but it always serves as influential guidance for the shaping of national legislative measures on the one hand and the judgements of the ECJ on the other. The directive in question was heavily criticised because of its departure from the previous regime of the prohibition of data retention. Although, the rules on data retention were relaxed and the road was paved for the much more retention friendly directive 2006/24/EC, it was significant that at least a common harmonised data retention legislative framework was established throughout Europe. Since, the retention of data was deemed necessary only on the basis of certain predetermined grounds and for a limited period, it was right to regulate at European level. Otherwise, the countries which were willing to move towards such direction would have introduced an even more all encompassing legislation allowing for an extensive retention of personal data. Now, a compromise was reached and common rules were to be introduced. This led to the introduction of data retention in the European legal order but under strict requirements. And that's the essence of the European approach towards the issue of data protection.

In March 2006 the passing of Directive 2006/24/EC signalled a radical shift in the way data retention is perceived and regulated at European level. The Directive applies to traffic and location data on both legal entities and natural persons to the related data necessary to identify the subscriber or registered user[339]. But in accordance with article 1 (2) it does not apply to "the content of electronic communications". It has been explained in other parts of this book that excluding the content of the

---

[339] See Press Release 2709th Council Meeting, Justice and Home Affairs, Brussels 21 February 2006. See: http://ue.eu.int/uedocs/cmsUpload/88467_06EN.pdf July 24th 2006. See also the Press Releae of September 21st 2005 at:
http://europa.eu.int/rapid/pressReleasesAction.do?reference=MEMO/05/328&format=HTML&aged=1&l anguage=EN&guiLanguage=en July 24th 2006.

communication especially in relation to internet is rather futile as the actual web sites accessed by the user are enough to reveal everything aimed at by the relevant investigation. When it comes to phone calls the provision is again problematic if not dangerous. If for example the person investigated is a criminal and his phone calls' record is given by the telecommunications organisation to the relevant authorities and they detect a phone call to a third person what will be the position of the latter? Will he be considered as a suspect? Will the fact that he received a phone call by a person under investigation lead to him placed under investigation or prosecuted as well? How can the authorities make such a decision without knowing the content of the conversation in question especially if there is a huge possibility that the phone call could have been of purely personal nature unrelated to any crime or unlawful act? In this case it means that the next natural step to take would be to put all our communications under scrutiny. This however, would lead to the dismantling of the democratic state at least in the form we were accustomed to it up to now.

It is clear that the directive was seen as an essential tool in the fight against crime and more specifically terrorism. According to article 1 (1) the directive aims at ensuring "that the data are available for the purpose of the investigation, detection and prosecution of serious crime, as defined by each Member State in its national law". It is obvious from its wording that the scope left for national implementation, the deadline for which is September 2007, is quite wide and this can amount to a loophole weakening the level of data protection. The data can be retained for the investigation of serious crimes as the latter are defined by national law. Therefore, it is for the member states to define the scope of activities which would justify data retention. This provides the ability to overextend data retention to cover areas not initially perceived to fall within the directive. Of course we will have better guidance next year when the directive will be introduced in national legal orders. The type of data the directive covers can be found in article 5 and include all possible information related to the use of internet or telephone lines. All on and off line traces left by users while surfing on the net or using their landline or mobile fall within the ambit of the directive. Therefore, article 3 provides that "by way of derogation from Articles 5, 6 and 9 of directive 2002/58/EC, member states shall adopt measures to ensure that the data specified in Article 5 of this directive are retained". Article 4 is important since it obliges the member states to adopt measures to ensure that the retained data "are provided only to the competent national authorities in specific cases and in accordance with national law". Although, this provision is of massive importance since it significantly limits the circulation of such data only to the competent authorities, only on the basis of the specific cases investigated and in accordance with the national legislation in force it is still to be seen how this provision will be implemented in national legal orders. The implementation of this provision in my opinion will determine the nature of this directive either as a legislative tool which although it permits extensive data retention at least strictly regulates the use of the relevant data therefore guaranteeing a level of privacy or as a legal measure from which a serious blow to the data protection regime in Europe will originate. If the use of such extensive databases is free for companies or states to access, then privacy protection as it was perceived up to now will have come if not to an end at least to a point critical enough to be considered as of no return. It is not reassuring to read that in the Vienna High Level meeting on freedom, security and justice of March 2nd and 3rd 2006 between the EU and US respective representatives, the US delegation indicated that "it was considering approaching each EU member state to ensure that the data collected on the basis of the recently adopted directive on data retention be accessible to them"[340]. Even more alarming was the comment on behalf of the Austrian Presidency that these data "were accessible like any other data on the basis of the existing...agreements"[341]. Under current agreements if the FBI is interested in EU citizens under investigation it can appeal to the relevant member state prosecutor who can request telephone operators and internet service providers for the relevant information which is subsequently passed to the other side of the Atlantic. The EU representatives added that the Commission will deal with this issue in an expert meeting, thus it is relatively early to draw conclusions. However, if article 4 is notinterpreted and implemented strictly then, the EU data protection edifice will literally collapse. It is encouraging that Franco Frattini Vice-President of the Commission and the EU Commissioner responsible for Justice, Freedom and Security insisted in an interview that "selling traffic data is prohibited. Traffic data should be retained only for reasons of investigating serious crimes and terrorism. They shall be transferred only after a official mandate from the relevant authorities. Otherwise, the company in question is committing a crime and shall be prosecuted"[342]. If this is the

---

[340] Euobserver article, Helena Spongenberg, US Could Access EU Data Retention Information, 12 May 2006.
[341] The same
[342] Interview of the EU Commissioner responsible for Justice, Freedom and Security at the Greek newspaper Eleftherotypia on March 12th 2006.

interpretation which will eventually be given to article 4 then, the directive will at least sustain the level of data protection at satisfactory levels[343].

According to article 6 member states can retain the data for a period between six and twenty four months. Although, this provision seems clear enough, article 12 of the directive expressly allows member states which face "particular circumstances" to extend data retention for at least six months increasing effectively the period of retention to thirty months or more. It provides "a carte blanche to member states to retain other data, or data for less serious crime or crime prevention purposes as they wish"[344]. This provision is unacceptable since it introduces an exception to article 6 by the back door as it allows an extension of the retention period under the bizarre and rather ambiguous condition of facing "particular circumstances". There is no enlightenment over which exactly are those particular circumstances. Do they amount to a terrorist attack which already took place? Do they amount to a terrorist attack which is rumoured to take place in the future? If this is the case, then societies can be held alert for unlimited period of time with the personal data of their citizens retained indefinitely under the obscure and undefined threat of a terrorist attack some time in the near or very distant future. Or do they amount to the commission of a certain yet still undefined crime? Member states are given enormous scope to regulate and introduce loopholes in the purported protection to such extent as to wholly undermine its aims. Article 7 recalls some of the principles of directive 95/46 which apply here as well such as data quality. Article 9 makes the important provision that the relevant data protection authorities, usually the independent authorities set up by the directive 95/46, shall monitor the security of the stored data. This is a provision safeguarding the rights of the European citizens as the relevant authorities albeit recently founded has proved a useful institutional tool in guaranteeing the application of national data protection law. It would have been useful to extend their competence under this directive to cover the demands for the transfer of data to the authorities requesting them. The national data protection authorities have acquired the necessary know-how to deal with privacy abuses and should be encouraged to monitor the process under which personal retained data are transferred to authorities for further use.

---

[343] See also recital 17.
[344] Steve Peers, The European Parliament and Data Retention: Chronicle of a "sell out" foretold?, Statewatch Analysis, page 8, accessed at:
http://www.statewatch.org/news/2005/dec/sp_dataret_dec05.pdf on July 15th 2006.

The Commission has expressed the view that "fundamental rights aspects have been carefully weighed in the preparation of the proposal, and solid data protection rules will be applicable, given that the general and specific data protection provisions established under Directives 95/46/EC and 2002/58/EC will apply. The processing of such data will be under the full supervisory powers of the data protection authorities established in all Member States. The Directive is also fully in line with the European policy on consumer protection"[345]. However, the truth is slightly different. If the data protection authorities are allowed to play a decisive role in this process this will definitely provide further safeguards which will mitigate the rather negative overall effect of the directive. Reasons for concern would still exist. One major concern is the dramatic shift that the directive introduces to the way criminal investigations are evolving. Usually, the investigative authorities chose the people who for some reasons were considered as suspects and after judicial or other legitimate authorisation monitored their activities. These activities naturally fell not only within the legitimate interests of a society but were also compatible with the way Western democracies were structured to function. This piece of legislation embodies the new perception that now all citizens are deemed a priori suspects. All their activities are monitored and scrutinised and their personal data are to be processed in order to discern which of them have the tendency or the plan to become criminals. The directive may transform the basic principle "everybody is deemed innocent until proven guilty" into "everybody is a suspect until he proves he is innocent". Now, monitoring precedes suspicion and the law assumes a purely pre-emptive character, which is not in its nature at least in a democratic society. The vague provisions of the directive over the length of retention create legal uncertainty and fail to provide a convincing explanation over the rationale behind such a long period of data retention, which is yet set to be indefinitely prolonged Apart from the evident threats to human rights and fundamental freedom the directive does not serve the aim of enhancing consumer confidence in internet and subsequently in e-commerce either. The consumers are now aware that whatever they do online can be used against them at some point in the future since their data depending on how the directive will be implemented might end up being possessed by a variety of authorities.

---

[345] See the Press Release at:
http://europa.eu.int/rapid/pressReleasesAction.do?reference=IP/05/1167&format=HTML&aged=0&language=EN&guiLanguage=en July 24th 2006.

For these reasons the directive is not the right step towards the direction of establishing a functional balance between protecting privacy and ensuring security.

4.3.5.8 Examples of Abuse and Public Reaction

There are quite a few cases where IT companies tried to introduce systems that would enable the collection of clickstream data so as to have the precise image of a person's internet activities. Intel Corporation had announced in 1999 its new Pentium III chips for the authentication of documents. Public attention had been stimulated after the warnings of privacy advocates that the system "could be used to identify a computer to prying software or to allow companies or agencies to track a person's movements over the internet"[346]. Although, Intel refused to withdraw its system from the market, it agreed to "allow computer makers to hide it behind digital fig leaf, software that some say has already been compromised"[347]. As a further example the decision of Amazon.com in 1999 to introduce "a new marketing tactic that uses personal data about its 10.7 million customers to compile online lists of books and music that people…are buying"[348] can be provided. The plan proved to be highly controversial, thus Amazon was led to "adjust the programme by letting customers request that their buying habits not be included"[349] in the relevant lists. Another issue that drew a lot of publicity and came under the media spotlight was the disclosure of the fact that Comcast, the third biggest Internet Service Provider (ISP) in the USA, was tracking for six weeks the web sites that its subscribers were visiting. It was blasted by privacy advocates "for its decision to record the web surfing activities of its customers without their knowledge"[350]. Comcast replied that the tracking down of such information had been done for the purposes of ameliorating the performances of its network but the reaction were still strong. After the issue received newspaper headlines the company announced its decision to "immediately stop storing this individual customer information in order

---

[346] Caruso Denise, Exploiting and Protecting Personal Information, The New York Times, March 1st 1999, available at www.nytimes.com/library/tech/99/03/biztech/articles/01digi.html
[347] The same.
[348] Gallagher David F., Amazon Tries to Ease Privacy Worries, August 30th 1999, available at http://www.nytimes.com/library/tech/99/08/biztech/articles/30amaz.html
[349] The same.
[350] See: Comcast Angers Privacy Groups But For What?, February 13th 2002, available at http://www.internetnews.com/bus-news/article.php/974451 accessed on 5/7/2003.

to completely reassure the customers that the privacy of their information is secure"[351]. Microsoft had also become the centre of attention for its decision to introduce a new programme to the market that tracks the habits of the users. "As part of downloading the information about songs and movies from the Web site, the programme also transmits an identifier number unique to each user on the computer. That creates the possibility that user habits could be tracked and sold for marketing purposes"[352]. Microsoft ruled out any intention of abusing its clients' privacy rights and Bill Gates concluded by stating that "users should be in control of how their data is used"[353]. The impact of data protection abuse issues on a company's image in relation to the wide public has provided the incentive for a wide range of companies to introduce a new type of policy on this issue. IBM Corporation, one of the biggest enterprises in the field and the second greatest advertiser on the internet has made public its intention to "pull its ads from Web sites that lacked clear privacy policies"[354]. It added that it would advertise only on sites with a specific privacy policy. The aforementioned initiative was positively perceived by both the industry and consumers community as a pivotal step on behalf of one of the market leaders towards the direction of consolidating a more effective privacy protection policy. This statement is particularly important if viewed in the context of the market self regulation attitude that the USA government has chosen as the adequate policy for dealing with the relevant issues. This aspect of the data protection policy will be further analysed in the relevant section.

---

[351] The same.
[352] D. Ian Hopper, Associated Press writer, Microsoft tracks habits of users, available at http://www.s-t.com/daily/02-02/02-24-02/c03bu090.htm accessed on 21/02/2002.
[353] The same.
[354] Clausing Jeri, IBM takes stand for Consumer Privacy on the Web, April 1st 1999, available at http://www.nytimes.com/library/tech/99/04/cyber/articles/01ibm-ad-column.html   accessed   on 4/08/2003.

5. The evolution of Data Protection in the European Union

"Privacy can be defined as a fundamental, though not absolute, right"[355]. The actual existence of "privacy" as an independent concept can be traced back into classical Greece and ancient China. It is interesting that even in antiquity cultural affiliations played a massive role in the status that privacy enjoyed in a given society. In Ancient Greece "public" was known as "demos" which basically means having to do with people. In a society whose principal characteristic was the active participation of its citizens in public life based on a concept of direct democracy there was not much room left for respecting those who chose to withdraw from what was perceived to be a social as well as moral duty; the participation in public affairs. The word for private was "idios" meaning private or personal. As an indication of the negative appeal of that term stands the fact that this word constitutes the origin "from which comes the English word idiot"[356]. "Idios" or even closer "idiotis" in modern Greek was the person who chose to abstain from public affairs, "a simple form of apolitical yearning...a desire to be left in peace"[357]; a term which although presents certain similarities with today's definition of privacy had evident negative connotations. The public sphere was that of "individuality and excellence" while the private of individual survival and the continuity of the species...the only refuge from the public life which necessarily encouraged shallowness since in public one had to watch oneself as one was scrutinised by others"[358]. The Roman view of privacy was very close to that of Ancient Greece. The Latin roots of the term privacy are "privatus" and "privare". The former meaning "withdrawn from public life" and the latter "to bereave or deprive"[359]. Within this framework, "private life...could only serve as a temporary respite from the demands of the public"[360]. In ancient China the thinkers by third century BC used "the character for private to express the idea of self-centeredness and combined the elements for "private"

[355] Banisar David, Davies Simon from Privacy International, Global Trends In Privacy Protection: An International Survey of Privacy, Data Protection, and Surveillance Laws and Developments, 18 The John Marshall Law School, The John Marshall Journal of Computer and Information Law, accessed via LEXIS-NEXIS, p5.
[356] Barrington Moore JR, Privacy, Studies in Social and Cultural History, M.E. Sharp Inc, New York, 1984, page 82.
[357] The same, page 118.
[358] Lubor C. Velecky in John B . Young, Privacy, John Wiley & Sons, New York, 1978, page 16.
[359] Paul De Hert in C. Nicoll, J.E.J Prins, M.J.M. van Dallen, Digital anonymity and the Law, Tensions and Dimenions, T.M.C. Asser Press, The Hague, 2003, page 56
[360] The same.

and "opposed to" to form the character for public…public and private are mutually opposed"[361]. Thus, it is proved that privacy assumes its content and social value in accordance with the prevailing ideals at a certain society in a given historical moment. Although, some elements of the modern concept of privacy can be traced back in the civilisations which determinedly influenced the contemporary Western beliefs and ideals, its modern shape evolved in conjunction with the consolidation of human rights as a superior value in modern societies and the appreciation of the repercussions of certain aspects of technological evolution. Societies are now organised in a fundamentally different manner as nations "charge a few individuals to do what they…do not wish to do themselves"[362]; the essence of representative democracy. Along with a different social organisation our liberty needed to be regulated and safeguarded on a different basis too. Modern citizens initially required the necessary space free from state intervention to fully develop their personality and at a later stage due to technological progress they expressed their concerns over the collection of their personal data by other individuals and commercial entities. In this context, privacy gradually evolved into a highly valued right of fundamental importance for modern societies. The evolution of technology and the rapid development of several fields of law such as human rights law, constitutional law or even of some aspects of law related to telecommunications and the regulation of the new media, placed privacy at the centre of attention. It has become the subject of regulation by the modern European societies both at national and at the EU level. The rationale behind this can be embodied by the fact that "in one sense all human rights are aspects of the right to privacy"[363]. The significance afforded to privacy as a right standing at the core of human rights protection dictated its inclusion as a protected right in almost all European Constitutions drafted in the last century. Privacy has been viewed as an element necessary for the full development of a democracy and further consolidation of a civil society. As mentioned before the right to privacy can be defined as the right "to be let alone"[364]. That used to mean the right for an individual to have his own space without any intrusion from the state where he can freely develop his personality contributing to the further development of the society as a whole. In the information society context the

---

[361] Barrington Moore JR, supra note 357, page 221.
[362] Thomas Nagel, Concealment and Exposure, And Other Essays, Oxford University Press, Oxford, 2002, page 16.
[363] Banisar David, Davies Simon from Privacy International, supra note 356 at page 4.
[364] See footnote 138.

"right to be let alone" has a slightly different sense comprising the ability of an individual to exercise some short of control over information concerning oneself. The control should be extended to both the nature of information concerning oneself and the direction towards which it can flow. The main difference introduced by the rapid development of technology that took place mainly the second half of the last century is that now there is a delicate and important balance that has to be carefully safeguarded in the context of a modern technologically depending democratic society. This is a balance "between the right to be let alone and the legitimate interests of a society"[365]. The latter is struck by the exemptions that "all data protection regulations provide from the principle that the subject has to give consent to processing of data about the subject person"[366]. The nature and the ambit of application of the relevant exemptions are serving as the criteria upon which the data protection regulation can be judged as sufficiently or insufficiently protective.

5.1 The European Experience

The Europeans (in contrast to Americans as analysed later) regard privacy as a substantial fundamental right. This flows from their experience from as early as the Second World War. The latest European history has provided the basic grounds for the evolution of privacy into a matter of primary concern for the European nations. In the 1960s the government of one of the German federal states, Hesse, expressed its intention to implement its plan to extend the application of information technology to a state project that would enable the better function of certain governmental services and policies with further repercussions on the life of the citizens. In order to realise this plan it was perceived from the very beginning that a large concentration of personal data of the citizens in the hands of state institutions was entailed. There were widely expressed concerns on behalf of the public on the basis of the appalling worries for "the reoccurrence of population control"[367] policies "similar to those exercised by the

---

[365] Wuermeling U. Ulrich, Harmonisation of European Union Privacy Law, 14 John Marshall Journal of Computer & Information Law, Spring 1996, accessed by LEXIS-NEXIS, p412.
[366] Ibid at page 413.
[367] Loring B. Tracie, An Analysis of the Informational Privacy Protection Afforded by the European Union and the United States, University of Texas at Austin School of Law Publications, 37 Texas International Law Journal, Spring 2002, accessed via LEXIS-NEXIS, at page 423.

Nazis"[368] that led to the drafting and establishment of the first Data Protection legislation in the world. It also led to the orientation of Europe towards an approach of regulating data protection at a constitutional, highly centralised level with the important assistance of administrative measures and institutions. Sweden was the second country to follow as early as 1973. France and Germany passed their general data protection laws by the end of that decade. The road had been paved.

5.2 International Organisations

5.2.1 The Organisation for Economic Cooperation and Development

The OECD has been quite active on the particular issue. It issued guidelines on "the protection of privacy and transborder flows of personal data"[369] on September 23rd 1980. The main objective was said to be "harmonisation of national privacy legislation and, while upholding such human rights, to prevent at the same time interruptions in international flows of data"[370]. Although, the guidelines shaped by the organisation constituted a balanced consensus between industry, consumer organisations and member states, the focus of the attention as stated by the OECD was not so much the protection of privacy as the safeguarding of the unimpeded flow of data necessary for international trade. Moreover, the fact that the guidelines do not constitute an effective legally binding tool but only an arrow of recommendations that place no obligations on national governments had undermined their success since their introduction. However, their adoption is considered a very significant event in the way of institutionalising data protection as it raised this issue at the level of negotiations between the main industrialised members of the organisation and most importantly laid down seven basic principles that were to influence other pieces of relevant legislation worldwide. These were:

a) Openness

b) Data Quality Principle

c) Purpose Specification

---

[368] The same.
[369] See the guidelines on line at: http://www1.oecd.org/publications/e-book/9302011E.PDF
[370] Singleton Susan, Data Protection, Butterworths Tolley, 2001, p 263.

d) Use limitation Principle

e) Security Safeguards Principle

f) Individual Participation Principle

g) Accountability Principle[371]

According to point 6 of the guidelines "these Guidelines should be regarded as minimum standards which are capable of being supplemented by additional measures for the protection of privacy and individual liberties"[372]. Thus, the guidelines even if implemented fully by member states would only provide for a minimum level of protection. Furthermore, point 18, which states that "member countries should avoid developing laws, policies and practices in the name of the protection of privacy and individual liberties, which would create obstacles to transborder flows of personal data that would exceed requirements for such protection"[373] made it clear that the main subject of protection as far as the OECD was concerned was the elimination of any burdens that can appear on the way of trade flows. "In this respect the OECD guidelines seem to be a free data flow regulation rather than a data protection regulation"[374].

On December 9th 1999, the OECD published other "Guidelines for Consumer Protection in the Context of Electronic Commerce"[375]. However, the OECD's intention to provide only for "a minimum set of standards in business to consumer electronic commerce in a variety of different areas including...privacy"[376] was confirmed. In section VII dedicated to privacy the OECD states that the relevant issues should be viewed "in accordance with the privacy principles set out in the 1980 guidelines"[377] which as mentioned before initiated only a minimum level of protection. Both the actual part of the text dedicated to privacy and its references are indicative of the importance of data protection for OECD but only as a means of facilitating free of barrier trade.

---

[371] See the OECD Guidelines at:
http://europa.eu.int/comm/internal_market/privacy/instruments/ocdeguideline_en.htm
[372] The same. See point 6.
[373] Look at point 18.
[374] Wuermeling U. Ulrich, supra note 366 at page 414.
[375] Guidelines for Consumer Protection in the Context of Electronic Commerce. See:
http://www1.oecd.org/publications/e-book/9300023E.PDF
[376] Steele K. Betty, Privacy, Confidentiality and Consumer Protection on the Internet, accessed at
www.tntech.edu/www/acad/mayberry/2000N-BettySteele.htm , accessed on 11/02/2002.
[377] See Section VII of the Guidelines.

5.2.2 The Council of Europe

"In January 1968, the Consultative Assembly of the Council of Europe adopted recommendation 509 regarding the interplay of human rights with scientific and technological development"[378]. The Assembly aimed at investigating whether the protection afforded by the European Convention on Human Rights concerning privacy was still effective albeit the new development at the forefront of technology. It is easily observed that the concern of the Council of Europe was orientated towards the protection of human rights rather than any concern of a commercial nature. Here stands the main difference between the approach adopted by OECD and the policy line implemented by the COE. It should be mentioned that the European Convention for the Protection of Human Rights provides for the basis for the protection of personal data in the EU. Its article 8 reads:

"Everyone has the right to respect for his private and family life, his home and his correspondence.

There shall be no interference by a public authority with the exercise of this right except such as is in accordance with the law and is necessary in a democratic society in the interests of national security, public safety or the economic well-being of the country, for the prevention of disorder or crime, for the protection of health or morals, or for the protection of the rights and freedoms of others"[379].

However, "although the threat to personal privacy was recognised by the Human Rights Convention in 1950, the concern for the protection of privacy was heightened by the expansion of computer use and the associated shift from an industrial to an information economy"[380]. As a result of this concern the Council of Europe adopted the Convention for the Protection of Individuals with regard to Automatic Processing of Personal Data[381]. Important instruments that prompted the adoption of the Treaty were the recommendation of the Committee of Ministers in 1973[382] concerning privacy rights in

---

[378] Martin Craig, Mailing Lists, Mailboxes, and the Invasion of Privacy: Finding A Contractual Solution to a transnational Problem, 35 Houston Law Review, Fall 1998, p803. Accessed by LEXIS-NEXIS.
[379] See article 8 of ECHR at: http://www.echr.coe.int/Convention/webConvenENG.pdf
[380] Heydrich W. Michael, A brave new world: Complying with the European Union Directive on personal privacy through the power of contract, 25 Brooklyn Journal of International Law, 1999, p411. Accessed via LEXIS-NEXIS.
[381] See the Convention at: http://conventions.coe.int/Treaty/EN/Treaties/Html/108.htm
[382] Recommendation (73)22 of the Committee of Ministers.

100

the private sector and privately operated databases. In 1974[383] there was another recommendation on behalf of the Committee on the protection of privacy now extended to the public sector with special references to sensitive data issues. As the impetus for further action was provided, it was perfectly clear that initiatives with no compulsory status will not be particularly effective in terms of adoption by the governments of the member states concerned. Thus, the adoption of a Convention whose provisions had to be adhered to by the member states of the Council of Europe had been chosen as the ideal solution. The Convention followed the pattern set by the OECD guidelines "but provided extra safeguards for several sensitive data categories"[384]. However, the actual effectiveness of the Convention was limited due to the fact "that it was not self-executing"[385] thus, "it had no direct legal effect on the law or jurisdiction of the member states"[386]. The signatory countries to the Convention were required to "take the necessary measures in their domestic law to give effect to the basic principles for data protection set out in this chapter"[387]. Although, this obligation had been generally met, the actual flexibility afforded to the member states involved rendered the establishment of a commonly accepted standard of data protection an obscure goal. The member states failed to implement the Convention in an harmonised manner leading to divergent legislative measures and levels of protection[388]. For example "Spain ratified the Convention in January 1984 but did not bring into force any domestic legislation until 1993"[389]. Greece, on the other hand, ratified the Convention in august 1995 and enacted its first data protection legislation in 1997. This was viewed however as a piece of legislation implementing the EU Data Protection Directive (95/46) and not as a law aligning the country's policy with the mandates of the Convention.

---

[383] Recommendation (74)29 of the Committee of Ministers.
[384] Gladstone Julia, The impact of e-commerce on the laws of nations. The US privacy balance and the European Privacy Directive: Reflections on the United States privacy policy, Willamette Journal of International Law and dispute Resolution, Volume 7, 2000, p6. Accessed via LEXIS-NEXIS.
[385] Loring B. Tracie, supra note 368, at page 424.
[386] Wuermeling U. Ulrich, supra note 366 at page 416.
[387] See article 4(1) of the Convention supra note 379.
[388] In 1999 the Committee of Ministers of the Council of Europe issued a recommendation (No R (99) 5) concerning the protection of privacy on the internet. See: http://www.coe.fr/cm/ta/rec/1999/99r5.htm#02 . The recommendation offered non-binding guidelines on the protection of individuals with regard to the processing of their personal data on internet.
Moreover, in 2001 the COE proceeded to amend the Convention in order to allow to European Communities to accede. See:
http://www.coe.int/T/E/Legal_affairs/Legal_co-operation/Data_protection/Documents/International_legal_instruments/Amendements%20to%20the%20Convention%20108.asp#TopOfPage
[389] Bainbridge David, EC Data Protection Directive, Butterworths, London, 1996, p17.

5.2.3 The United Nations

The United Nations were also concerned about the potential abuse of the right to privacy and have assumed several initiatives aimed at combating this phenomenon. Article 12 of the Universal Declaration of Human Rights reads:

> "No one shall be subjected to arbitrary interference with his privacy, family, home or correspondence, nor to attacks upon his honour and reputation. Everyone has the right to the protection of the law against such interference or attacks"[390].

Furthermore, in the International Covenant on Civil and Political Rights of December 16th 1966 article 17 reads:

> "No one shall be subjected to arbitrary or unlawful interference with his privacy, family, home or correspondence, nor to unlawful attacks on his honour and reputation. Everyone has the right to the protection of the law against such interference or attacks"[391].

The office of the High Commissioner for Human Rights has commented on the application of the relevant article that: "In order to have the most effective protection of his private life, every individual should have the right to ascertain in an intelligible form, whether, and if so, what personal data is stored in automatic data files, and for what purposes"[392]. It has to be noted that the Declaration in question is a declaration of principles. It has "no direct legal consequences and no force of law…it cannot be invoked before civil and administrative courts"[393].

Finally, guidelines for "for the Regulation of Computerised Personal Data Files" were issued at the UN level on December 14th 1990[394]. It provided for minimum guarantees that should be introduced in national legislations but they had no particular impact on national legal order since they were not of binding nature.

---

[390] See article 12 at: http://www.un.org/Overview/rights.html
[391] See article 17 at:
http://domino.un.org/unispal.nsf/0/dda106bf303c3cee85256368005960a0?OpenDocument
[392] See the High Commissioner's statement at:
http://www.unhchr.ch/tbs/doc.nsf/(symbol)/CCPR+General+comment+16.En?OpenDocument
[393] Rik Torfs, On the Permissible Scope of Legal Limitations on the Freedom of Religion or Belief in: Belgium, 19 Emory International Law Review 2005, page 638
[394] See the Guidelines for the Regulation of Computerised Personal Data Files at
http://www.unhchr.ch/html/menu3/b/71.htm .

5.3 The EU developments before the adoption of the landmark Directive 95/46

The truth is that "historically the European Commission has not concerned itself with data protection"[395]. As it has already been explained the European Commission had counted on other institutions to implement their policy in the relevant area. However, the Convention ratified at the level of the Council of Europe although very important in the sense of establishing the data protection issue as a matter that needs international attention and legislative initiatives at the level of a multi national organisation, did not have the results aspired to initially. As explained before, it did not lead to a harmonisation or at least to a complete harmonisation of the data protection patterns all over Europe. Apart from the burden that this realisation imposed on the protection of human rights as a whole in the EU, it had a considerable impact also in the process of completing the internal market and enabling the unimpeded flow of data within the EU, which served as a prerequisite for the smooth operation of the internal unified market. Thus, the Commission realised the necessity of assuming an initiative at community level in order to introduce harmonised levels of effective data protection in all member states. The relevant legislative measure would be introduced in the framework of its internal market programme, which serves as the clearest indication of the dual objective of the Commission. Both goals had to be equally and effectively served. An effective protection of a fundamental right of the European citizens and the facilitation of trans-border flow of information that constitutes the basis for the development of trade within the context of the single internal market. The legal basis for its initiatives at this stage was found in Article 8 of the European Convention for the protection of Human Rights and Fundamental Freedoms. The Convention rights "are regarded as being a part of fundamental community law and thus may be used to assist the interpretation of the directive itself"[396]. And additionally, in Article 6, Title I concerning the Common Provisions, of the Treaty on the European Union. The Article reads:

---

[395] Stokes Simon, Data Protection, European Intellectual Property Review, Sweet & Maxwell, 1995, 17 (7), p215.
[396] Jay Rosemary, Hamilton Angus, Data Protection, Law and Practice, Sweet & Maxwell, London, 2003, page 72.

1. The Union is founded on the principles of liberty, democracy, respect for human rights and fundamental freedoms, and the rule of law, principles which are common to the Member States.

2. The Union shall respect fundamental rights, as guaranteed by the European Convention for the Protection of Human Rights and Fundamental Freedoms signed in Rome on 4 November 1950 and as they result from the constitutional traditions common to the Member States, as general principles of Community law.

3. The Union shall respect the national identities of its Member States.

4. The Union shall provide itself with the means necessary to attain its objectives and carry through its policies.[397]

Thus, the adoption of the directive had a solid legal basis of constitutional status. It is based on the article of the Treaty on the European Union; it embodies the safeguarding of rights enshrined in the ECHR and concludes in functioning at the same time as a factor enabling commercial activities within the context of the internal market. The variety of the directive's objectives and the scope of regulation it covers underline its importance for the EU legal order. It is a compromise between the protection of rights, which have been granted the status of "general principles of law" with "overriding constitutional importance within the legal order of the Community"[398] and the assurance of the smooth operation of what has been known as one of the most basic pillars of EU activities: the common market. The directive aimed at fostering "transparency in electronic operations…and harmonisation of national legislation in order to lift the legal obstacles that place a burden on the free movement rules and the electronic commerce services"[399].

"This is the first time that a Community measure is issued specifically to protect the human rights of individual citizens of the Union, in the context of the development of the internal market. As various preambles make clear the Directive seeks to ensure that the further development of this internal market (which requires the free movement of data, including personal data) does protect those rights, as far as the

---

[397] See the article at: http://www.europa.eu.int/eur-lex/en/treaties/dat/C_2002325EN.000501.html
[398] Korff Douwe, EC Study on Implementation of Data Protection Directive, Comparative Summary of National Laws, Cambridge, September 2002, p6.
[399] De Bottini Renaud Par, La Directive "Commerce Electronique du 8 Juin 2000, La Revue du Marche Commun et de l'Union Europeenne, 2001, Paris, page 369.

processing of personal data is concerned"[400]. Furthermore, the Commission in its communication to the Council and the European Parliament had stretched the importance of introducing "additional harmonisation measures...appropriate in areas with significant consumer protection considerations"[401]. The importance of the data protection issues for European consumers had already become clear. Thus, the Commission in its Green Paper on Consumer Protection was presenting the debate over the "central choice around the type of method needed to achieve greater harmonisation...the adoption of a series of further directives...or a mixed approach of a comprehensive framework directive, supplemented by targeted directives, where necessary"[402]. The argument behind this approach is that "if all member states adhere to the minimum standard of protection, there should be no barriers to the movement of personal data within the Community"[403]. Apart from the other fundamental aspects of the relevant issue the consumer protection one was also included in the agenda.

However, it should be noted that there were voices that challenged the inclusion of the directive in the list of minimum harmonisation measures. The directive was indeed passed under the umbrella provision of article 100a of the Treaty, which allows the promotion of measures for the approximation of laws regarding the establishment and functioning of the internal market and requires as it has been demonstrated before a "high level of protection" with regard to issues concerning the consumers. Thus, "the directive cannot be regarded as a pure minimum harmonisation directive since it provides a high level of protection"[404]. Furthermore, since the directive does not set an array of rigid criteria to be strictly followed by the member states, it cannot be viewed as a measure of maximum harmonisation, since it clearly leaves plenty of scope to the national legislator concerning its implementation. The member states have to adopt measures in accordance with the minimum protection afforded by the directive, they can regulate data protection in a stricter manner than the directive, but they cannot resort to over regulation that would endanger the flows of data between member states.

---

[400] The European Commission, Final Report by Douwe Korff (contractor), The feasibility of a seamless system of data protection rules for the European Union, Directorate General XV, Internal Market and Financial Services, 1998, Luxembourg.
[401] Communication from the Commission to the Council and the European Parliament: An Internal Market Strategy for Services: COM (2000) 888.
[402] Commission of the European Communities, Green Paper on European Union Consumer Protection, Brussels, 2.10.2001, COM (2001) 531 final, p10.
[403] Bainbridge David, Computer Law, Fourth Edition, Longman, London, 2000, p363.
[404] Kuner Christopher, European Data Privacy Law and Online Business, Oxford University Press, Oxford, 2003, page 29.

Thus, we have provisions of minimum harmonisation that allow flexibility to the national legislator, whose only limit is the unimpeded flow of data in the EU. Based on this premise, it is argued that the directive embodies "a mixture of maximum and minimum harmonisation approaches"[405].

It should be mentioned that the first important steps were taken by the European Commission under the presidency of Jacques Delors. In December 1993 the Commission published the White Paper on Growth, Competitiveness and Employment[406] and emphasised the importance of "laying the foundations for the information society"[407] because the changes "will also affect consumption patterns...and us as citizens"[408]. Therefore, "one priority...is to protect privacy and ensure the security of information and communication systems"[409]. The White Paper and the support of its main objectives by the European Commission curbed the objections of the opponents of the directive, mainly among the representatives of certain industries that were anxious for the impact of any limitation on the flow of data on their business such as the banking industry, and opened the way for its adoption. The latter, however, provoked negative comments from some academics, whose personal opinion on the issue coincided with that of the aforementioned industries. They found no reason for the adoption of such directive as they insisted that "data protection restricts consumer choice and freedom and results in consumers receiving outdated, lower quality products and services at higher prices"[410]. It was viewed as an "emotional, rather than rational reaction to feelings of discomfort with expanding data flows"[411]. These views represent in a clear manner the philosophical debate that hides behind the adoption of the directive and leads to the fundamental question of whether personal data should be judged on the basis of a human rights approach or having as an ultimate goal the achievement of economic efficiency always presuming that the former comes in contrast with the latter a claim which is not endorsed by this book as will be analysed in the final part of it. It was already demonstrated in this book that the EU

---

[405] Ibid at page 29.
[406] White Paper on Growth, Competitiveness and Employment, The challenges and ways forward into the 21st Century, COM (93) 700 final, Brussels December 5th 1993, see: http://www.gencat.es/csi/pdf/eng/soc_info/basic/WP_growth.pdf
[407] Ibid at page 16.
[408] The same at page 17.
[409] The same at page 19.
[410] Bergkamp Lucas, supra note 169 at page 31.
[411] The same.

chose to include the right to protect personal data in its list of fundamental rights and freedoms. The US on the other hand followed a more economically orientated approach to the whole issue that fuelled a wild debate with social, historical, cultural, financial and philosophical dimensions that is going to be presented at a later stage in a thorough manner. At this point, it is argued that the approach of the EU on the issue, with all its deficiencies and shortcomings has been appropriate as it regulates a commercial field, which can hide very serious threats to individual freedoms. On the other hand as the directive will be presented, it is going to be clear that financial and economic considerations were not just taken into account but constituted one of the two stated objectives of the directive. Thus, the EU assumed a legislative initiative to deal with an existing phenomenon in a realistic manner in the context of its commercial policies. At the EU level, it was realised at an early stage that along with basic individual freedoms, the very competitiveness of European enterprises was at stake since "divergences in data protection legislation and the way it is applied in the member states are creating problems in the free movement of data"[412], an element essential for the function of businesses nowadays, that "is best achieved by providing a common and trustworthy legal infrastructure for business and consumers within the Internal Market"[413]. Hence, the directive was adopted. Another factor of determining importance for the passing of the directive was the special position that the principle in question already enjoyed in the legal traditions of many European countries as is to be demonstrated later. Thus, although sometimes harmonisation initiatives are criticised for "disregarding the rich and deep historical roots of the national laws that are subjected to its influence"[414], it seems that in this case the directive had just confirmed and further entrenched the importance of the principle in question in the European legal world.

---

[412] Rees Christopher, Brimsted Kate, The twelve stages of data protection, IT Law Today, December 2002, p24.
[413] Ramberg Hultmark Christina, The E-Commerce Directive and formation of a contract in a comparative perspective, 2001, 26 European Law Review, Sweet & Maxwell, page 429.
[414] Stephen Weatherill, in Takis Tridimas and Paolisa Nebbia, European Union Law for the Twenty-First Century, Rethinking the New Legal Order, Volume 2, Internal Market and Free movement Community Policies, Hart Publishing, Oxford and Portland Oregon, 2004, page 13.

6. The European Directive on the Protection of Personal Data

6.1 The Object of the Directive

The dual nature of the objective of the Directive is demonstrated in a clear manner in the very first article of it. It is stated that the object of the directive is "the protection of fundamental rights and freedoms of natural persons, and in particular their right to privacy with respect to the processing of personal data"[415] *and* "the free flow of personal data between member states"[416]. It was explained before that the directive aimed at protecting a basic fundamental right of the European citizens in the framework of ensuring the smooth operation of the internal market. Thus, the directive constitutes the product of a process that touched upon and had to reconcile "complex political decisions involving conflicting economic, social and cultural interests as well as fundamental communications and data protection rights"[417]. Recital 11 of the Directive explains that "the principles of the protection of the rights and freedoms of individuals, notably the right to privacy give substance to and amplify those contained in the Council of Europe Convention of 28 January 1981 for the Protection of Individuals with regard to Automatic Processing of Personal Data"[418]. Thus, when the member states have enacted the relevant legislation to comply with the Directive and divergences are eliminated then there should be no limit or prohibition on the free flow of data in the EU. The problem was detected in the fact that several member states with considerable market size and power such as Germany and France, the two biggest markets and economies in the EU, were considering a ban on data transfer to countries with "less rigorous data protection laws"[419] such as Greece and Italy. France and Germany enjoyed a tighter regime of data protection and they were not willing to allow the transfer of their citizens' data to countries that had not promulgated laws establishing the same level of protection. Moreover, since they constituted the two main players at the single market stage they shared a deep interest in the smooth operation of

---

[415] Article 1(1) of Directive 95/46EC of the European Parliament and of the Council of 24 October 1995 on the protection of individuals with regard to the processing of personal data and on the free movement of such data, OJ 281, 23/11/1995, p31-50, available at http://europa.eu.int/smartapi/cgi/sga_doc?smartapi!celexapi!prod!CELEXnumdoc&lg=EN&numdoc=31995L0046&model=guichett

[416] Article 1(2).

[417] Scherer Joachim, European Telecommunications Law: The Framework of the Treaty (of Rome), European Law, Review, Sweet & Maxwell, 1987, 12 (5), 354.

[418] See Recital 11 of the Directive.

[419] Loring B. Tracie, supra note 368 at page 429. Accessed via LEXIS-NEXIS.

the market and thus, provided the impetus of compromising the two objectives with a new directive[420].

6.2 Definitions provided

6.2.1 Personal Data

The definition of all concepts relevant to the Directive is provided in the framework of Article 2. "The function of the definitions is not only to repeat the general understanding of the words but to regulate their legal effect"[421]. Personal data is defined as "any information relating to an identified or identifiable natural person"[422], the data subject. The exact meaning of the "identifiable person" is a person "who can be identified, directly or indirectly, in particular by reference to an identification number or to one or more factors specific to his physical, physiological, mental, economic, cultural or social identity"[423]. The Directive therefore adopted a wide definition of "personal data". Data leading to a direct or an indirect identification of a person falls into the scope of the definition. Thus, when examining whether a certain category of data fulfils the "personal data" criterion, it shall be initially presumed that they do, unless proven that they could not be possibly linked to an identifiable individual. Reference not only to his name but also to other features of even technical nature such as an identification number is included as an element inherent in the ambit of the definition. Thus, reference to national insurance number or to a bank account number can be deemed to fall into the meaning and wording of Article 2(a) of the Directive. "As a result of this broad definition only truly depersonalised data fall outside the scope of application of the Directive"[424]. An example of the scope of the provision is provided by the Article 29 Working Party paper that clarifies certain issues emerging from the directive's interpretation. As it was written above, IP addresses are given by Internet Access Providers to users in order to enable their connection with the net. "Internet Access Providers can, using reasonable means, identify internet users to whom they have attributed the IP addresses as they normally systematically log in a file

---

[420] See also Recitals 5 and 7 of the Directive.
[421] Wuermeling U. Ulrich, supra note 366 at page 424. Accessed via LEXIS-NEXIS.
[422] See Article 2 (a).
[423] The same.
[424] Overstraeten Van Tanguy, Szafran Emmanuel, supra note 258, page 60, accessed via LEXIS-NEXIS.

the date, the time, duration and dynamic IP address given to the internet user…in these cases there is no doubt about the fact that one can talk about personal data in the sense of article 2a of the directive"[425]. The directive provides for an extensive application of the definition over what can fall into the category of personal data. This forms an essential initial step on which the whole construction of EU data protection law can be efficiently shaped. By covering all data that could be linked to an "identifiable individual" EU law extends its application to forms of technical data that would otherwise have remained unregulated such as an IP address that can be at the very end linked to a private individual by the companies concerned. As it was thoroughly explained in the previous chapter, the data mining industry applies advanced methods to loot data from a personal computer, taking advantage of the clickstream data that are stored in a terminal. Privacy is put in peril, as it was demonstrated, when those data are linked to a certain individual. The directive extends its application to such technical characteristics crucial for the safeguarding of an individual's privacy.

This observation assumes a greater importance if viewed in the light of the forthcoming technological developments that may put additional pressure on both individual privacy and on the legal regime that aims at supporting it. The relevant EU law has to proved flexible enough to cover the new technological advances and the subsequent challenges to privacy. A good example of imminent technological steps is presented by the Internet Protocol Version 6 (IPv6). The Working Party has been concerned with the potential consequences of such an application and had already produced its opinion. "The new internet protocol has been elaborated with a view to facilitate connection to the network using multiple equipment such as mobile phones…and has been designed…like a global unique identifier…that leads to increased risks of profiling…as all communications of the user can be linked together much easier, than using cookies…and as the type of terminals connected to the network using the same communication protocol will multiply (heating, light, alarms etc)"[426].

---

[425] Article 29 Data Protection Working Party, Privacy on the Internet, An Integrated EU Approach to On-line Data Protection, 21st November 2000, WP37, see:
http://europa.eu.int/comm/internal_market/privacy/docs/wpdocs/2000/wp37en.pdf accessed on August 10th.

[426] Article 29 Data Protection Working Party, Opinion 2/2002 on the use of unique identifiers in telecommunication terminal equipments: the example of IPV6, 30 May 2002, WP 58, see at:
http://europa.eu.int/comm/internal_market/privacy/docs/wpdocs/2002/wp58_en.pdf accessed on August 10th.

Moreover, IPv6 would make the identification "of the physical location of an internet user a rather trivial task"[427]. The Working Party believes that "security and confidentiality aspects are at stake here...so, the protection of the fundamental right of privacy against such risk of profiling must prevail"[428]. The principle endorsed by the Working Party is that data protection law should apply to the new innovative methods as well. This principle is basically right, but apart from interpreting the relevant provisions in the light of the new developments, so as to be able to cover them, it is absolutely necessary to examine the new landscape after their introduction and consider the potential of adjusting the law to the new reality. We shall wait and see the impact of IPv6 on privacy and implement new measures to adapt the data protection law to the new challenges.

A matter of high importance is also the fact that the directive limits the notion of protection to data related "only to natural persons"[429] excluding from its scope of protection any legal person. It can apply to a case concerning the data of a company or another entity with legal personality but solely to the extent that personal data of a natural person closely related with the legal person in question is involved. The latter can be an employee or a director of a company. However, some additional clarifications should have been given as problems arise, when for instance the legal person in question is a small family business ran by one person. In this case the limits for distinguishing whether the data refer to the natural or the legal person can appear a bit blurred. Usually, where an ambiguity is detected in EU law, we tend to observe divergence in its application in national legal orders. Thus, four member states, Austria, Denmark, Italy and Luxembourg chose to apply their data protection laws also to legal persons[430]. Furthermore, in the electronic telecommunications directive (2002/58), the "legitimate interests of the legal persons"[431] are to be protected when it comes to privacy issues. Korff Douwe argues that "human rights do not extend to public

---

[427] Da Jerker B. Svantesson, Geo Location Technologies and other Means of Placing Borders on the borderless Internet, 23 John Marshall Journal of Computer & Information Law, 2004, page 119.
[428] The same.
[429] Carlin M Fiona, The Data Protection Directive: The Introduction of Common Privacy Standards, European Law Review, 1996, 21 (1), Sweet & Maxwell, page 65.
[430] See: http://europa.eu.int/comm/internal_market/privacy/studies/legal_en.htm accessed on August 10th 2004.
[431] Recital 7 of Directive 2002/58.

bodies...the applicability of data protection to legal persons is ambiguous to say the least"[432].

The Directive also provides us with the information that "sound and image data relating to natural persons"[433] do fall in the ambit of the directive provided that the processing of such data is "automated or if they are contained in a filing system...so as to permit easy access to the personal data in question"[434]. However, if such processing aims at safeguarding goals of "public security, defence, national security or criminal law"[435] nature, then it falls out of the directive's ambit. This is another demonstration of the balance between protecting the fundamental right of privacy and at the same time providing for space for the safeguarding of other legitimate interests.

6.2.2 Processing of Personal Data

Article 2 (b) of the Directive provides for an extremely broad definition of processing. The Commission "chose several phrases to describe processing in order to provide a preventive effect...the meaning of these phrases overlap in order to avoid gaps in the regulation"[436]. The list of activities that article 2 (b) contains is not exhaustive. It is an indicative list of an explanatory nature aiming at clarifying the phrase "any operation or set of operations which is performed upon personal data". In order to fully understand the content and objectives of the particular article it is important to note that it should be viewed in close conjunction with article 6 (1). The latter provides for a list of necessary conditions that determine the lawfulness of the processing in question. Thus, if data are processed "fairly and lawfully"[437], "for specified, explicit and legitimate purposes"[438], in a manner "adequate, relevant and not

---

[432] Korff Douwe, Study on the protection of the rights and interests of legal persons with regard to the processing of personal data relating to such persons, page 17, see: http://europa.eu.int/comm/internal_market/privacy/docs/studies/legal_en.pdf , accessed on August 10, 2004.

[433] See Recital 14 of the Directive.
[434] See Recital 15 of the Directive.
[435] See Recital 16 of the Directive.
[436] Wuermeling U. Ulrich, supra note 366 at page 425, accessed via LEXIS-NEXIS.
[437] See Article 6 (1) (a).
[438] See Article 6 (1) (b).

excessive"[439], "accurately"[440] and for a period "no longer than is necessary for the purposes of collection"[441] then the processing involved is of no concern to the European Commission. The Commission has further emphasised the importance of assuming "appropriate technical and organisational measures…in order to maintain security and thereby to prevent any unauthorised processing"[442]. The processing can take place if one of the requirements listed in Article 7 is met. The latter function as the legitimising requirements of the data processing.

6.2.3 Personal Data Filing System

Article 2 (c) provides the definition of a personal data filing system. The definition is of relevance when examining whether a manual file falls in or out of the scope of the Directive. The rationale behind the debate is the fact that manual files are less likely to give rise to privacy threats due to the effort and money involved in order for such files to be disseminated. As the Commission stated "the progress made in information technology is making the processing and exchange of such data considerably easier"[443]. However, traditionally the concept of "privacy" as the latter evolved in European legal tradition, included all sorts of files that could provide the grounds for an intrusion so the Commission chose to include manual data files in the scope of the Directive's protections if some conditions are fulfilled. In Recital 27 it is stated that "the protection of individuals must apply as much as to automatic processing of data as to manual processing…nonetheless as regards manual processing this Directive covers only filing systems, not unstructured files". It is further explained that "files or set of files which are not structured according to specific criteria shall under no circumstances fall within the scope of this Directive"[444]. Thus, the Directive covers manual data if they are part of a structured file "accessible according to specific criteria, whether centralised, decentralised or dispersed"[445]. Moreover, Article 3 (1) extends the scope of the Directive to "the processing otherwise than by automatic means".

---

[439] See Article 6 (1) (c).
[440] See Article 6 (1) (d).
[441] See Article 6 (1) (e).
[442] See Recital 46.
[443] See Recital 4 of the Directive.
[444] See Recital 27 of the Directive.
[445] See Article 2 (c).

6.2.4 The Controller and the Processor

The Controller can be "the natural or legal person, public authority or agency which determines the purposes and means of the processing of personal data"[446]. The processor is "the natural or legal person, public authority or agency which processes personal data on behalf of the controller"[447]. Thus, a distinction is made between the person that appears responsible for the processing and the person that actually carries it out on his behalf. According to article 6 (2) the controller is the party responsible for ensuring that the conditions allowing for lawful processing enshrined in article 6 (1) are complied with. Additionally, he has the obligation to "implement appropriate technical and organisational measures to protect data against accidental or unlawful destruction, loss, alteration or disclosure"[448]. In this context sufficient guarantees must be provided by the processor to the controller "where processing is carried out on his behalf"[449]. Furthermore, the carrying out of the processing "must be governed by a contract or legal act binding the processor to the controller stipulating that the processor shall act only on instructions from the controller"[450]. It should be noted that if the controller is established in one member state it shall comply with the national provisions of the relevant state, but if he is "established on the territory of several member states he must take the necessary measures to…comply with the national law"[451] of all states involves.

The distinction between the "controller" and the "processor" constitutes one of the most distinctive features of the directive. It is fundamentally important to be able to distinguish whether an agency, a company department or any other entity falls within the definition of a controller or a processor. The rationale behind this is the fact that the controller appears to be the factor principally responsible for applying the directive provisions. He is the one being found liable as a result of an unlawful processing operation (article 23 of the directive) and bearing the obligation to comply with specific national legislation according to the place of his "establishment"[452]. Problems can be created especially at the level of big multinational companies, with branches in several countries and different departments handling data from different sources. There will be

---

[446] See article 2 (d).
[447] See article 2 (e).
[448] See article 17 (1).
[449] See article 17 (2).
[450] See article 17 (3).
[451] See article 4 (1) (a).
[452] See Recital 19 of the Directive.

a personnel section dealing with employee data and also a marketing department with data from various other sources. The determination of the "controller" in this case will be a more complex issue that has, however, to be clarified immediately in order to specify the distinction of the roles and the subsequent relevant national rules to be followed in each case. Thus, the guidelines of the directive or the body of the text itself should have provided us with more information about the relevant issue.

6.2.5 Third Parties and Recipients

A third party is "any natural or legal person...other than the data subject, the controller, the processor, and the persons who under the direct authority of the controller or the processor, are authorised to process the data"[453]. Thus, a third party does not perform any of the activities enshrined for either a processor or a controller and is not a data subject. It can be a person, natural or legal, coming in contact with the data involved without the intention of processing them. The most obvious example of a third party that can be presented at this point is the case of service providers, which receive data as a part of a network and retransmit them to the relevant party. Moreover, "if the Commission were to disclose personal data to the police or another official body with respect to a particular enquiry, then such a disclosure would be to a third party"[454].

A recipient is "any natural or legal person to whom the data are disclosed"[455]. The controller "must provide a data subject from whom data related to himself are collected information about the recipients or categories of recipients of the data"[456] both in cases of collection of data from the data subject and in cases when the data have been obtained from elsewhere[457]. "In specific circumstances normally defined in legislation, like a public official who has the legal authority to pursue an investigation"[458], the relevant party involved is not deemed to be a recipient.

---

[453] See article 2 (f).
[454] The European Commission, Directorate General Internal Market, IDA Projects: A Guide to Data Protection Compliance, Final Report, 1998, Annex to the annual Report of Article 29 Working Party, page 13.
[455] See article 2 (g).
[456] See article 10 (c).
[457] See article 11 (1) (c).
[458] The European Commission, supra note 263 at page 13.

6.2.6 The data subject's consent

The interpretation of what constitutes consent on behalf of the data subject is an issue of great significance for the application of the Directive. Its importance lies in the central position that the data subject's consent assumes in the directive's provisions. It is equivalent to a criterion for making data processing legitimate[459] or even a necessary precondition that enables the processing of the so-called categories of sensitive data[460]. As it is deduced from the definition of "consent" in article 2 (h) it comprises as integral concepts the elements of a consent given "freely", "specifically" and after the provision of "information" basically from the controller as mentioned before[461]. Thus, the consent in order to be valid must be "freely given", which means without any physical or psychological pressure or any threat of any other nature and "specific" a concept relating to the exact purpose for which consent is required. These must be the basic characteristics of the subject's "indication of his wishes". The choice on behalf of the Commission of the particular wording means that no contract is required. When such contract serves as a precondition for the purposes of the directive it is stated clearly[462]. However, it has to be noted that the term "indication" has contributed to some short of vagueness as to what is its exact ambit and what is the precise nature of behaviour falling in its rather ambiguously stated definition. The main issue that should have been clearly defined is whether "consent must be opt in or opt out"[463]. This lack of clarity once again leads to the conclusion that a wide scope of implementation and interpretation is afforded to national jurisdictions that will decide the issue in question. This ambiguity should have been avoided as it paved the way for member states to regulate for the adoption of "opt out" solutions instead of the more privacy friendly "opt in". Nevertheless, in article 14(b) the directive specifically provides for an opt out solution, when it comes to direct marketing and the use for consumer data for such purposes.

---

[459] See article 7 (a).
[460] See article 8 (2) (a).
[461] See articles 10 and 11 mentioned in the analysis of the "recipient" definition.
[462] See article 17 (3).
[463] Kuner Christopher, supra note 166, page 68. See also Vilasau Monica, The Right to Privacy and to Personal Data Protection in Spanish Legislation, Computer and Telecommunications Law Review, Sweet & Maxwell, 2003, 9 (7), 196.

6.3 The scope of the Directive

The scope of the Directive is regulated by article 3. The issue of whether manual files and processing fall within its scope of application has already been dealt before. It is important to mention that the Directive does not apply to "activities that fall outside the scope of community law"[464] and "in any case in activities concerning public security, defence and state security"[465]. It is also added that the Directive does not apply to processing performed "by a natural person in the course of a purely personal or household activity"[466]. The latter concerns mainly cases of private individuals compiling files with addresses of personal friends, or phone numbers and other information used solely for personal purposes.

6.4 National Law Applicable

The central principle promoted by the directive is expressed in article 4 (1). "Each member state shall apply the national provisions it adopts pursuant to this directive to the processing of personal data". The Commission's choice was to encourage the application of the national law of the member states, which of course is shaped in accordance with the provisions of the directive and in compliance with the general guidelines that form the policy choices of the EU on this issue. According to the relevant article the issue of selection of law is based on the place of the establishment of the controller. As recital 18 explains "any processing of personal data must be carried out in accordance with the law of one of the member states; whereas in this connection processing carried out under the responsibility of a controller who is established in a member state must be governed by the law of that state". As far as the precise meaning of the word "establishment" in the particular context is concerned recital 19 points out that "establishment on the territory of a member state implies the effective and real exercise of activity through stable arrangements". If for example a controller established in France "transmits personal data to Germany for processing"[467]

---

[464] Titles V and VI of the Treaty on European Union, mainly common foreign and security policy and police and judicial cooperation in criminal matters
[465] Article 3 (2).
[466] The same.
[467] See the example presented by the European Commission, Directorate General, Internal Market and Financial Services, 1998, Handbook on cost effective compliance with Directive 95/46/EC, p17.

then the applicable national data protection law is the law of France, where the controller is established. The potential interference of many legal orders and consequently of a variety of national laws, although harmonised, could lead to confusion as to the exact scope of competence of each authority and the precise ambit of application of the relevant national laws. Therefore, the directive provides for the ability of each supervisory authority to "be competent whatever is the national law applicable to the processing in question, to exercise on the territory of its own member state the powers conferred on it in accordance with paragraph 3. Each authority may be requested to exercise its powers by an authority of another member state"[468]. Thus, in the example presented before with the controller installed in France and transmitting data to Germany for processing, the applicable law would be the French one, however, the Supervisory Authority provided for by German data protection law would also be involved since the processing is taking place in the territory of Germany.

There is also the case of a data controller established in one member state with subsidiaries established in other member states. In this case according to article 4 (1) (a) and recital 19 the "legal form of such an establishment, whether simply branch or a subsidiary with a legal personality, is not a determining factor...each of the establishments must fulfil the obligations imposed by the national law applicable to its activities".

The framework of protection is further clarified by recital 20, which emphasises that "the fact that the processing of data is carried out by a person established in a *third* country must not stand in the way of protection of individuals provided for in this directive...in these cases the processing should be governed by the law of the member states in which the means used are located". The latter is referring to article 4 (c), which embodies an effort to provide for protection even in case of an out of the Union established controller. According to article 4 (2) in this case "the controller must designate a representative established in the territory of a member state", where the equipment used is situated. The controller or the representative "must notify the supervisory authority referred to in article 28 before carrying out any processing"[469] and also inform the data subjects both in cases of data collection directly from them[470]

---

[468] Article 28 (6) of the Directive.
[469] See article 18 (1).
[470] See article 10 (a).

or from third sources[471]. Therefore, the national laws of the countries, which host the equipment used for processing are going to apply.

The main question at this stage is what exactly constitutes a "use of equipment". Since the directive remains silent on this issue it would be useful to note that the most usual use of equipment when it comes to on line activities is the actual use and function of website servers. The latter are used by a website operator because they host the files that comprise a particular website. It is possible that a website operator is located in a different country than the website server. Hence, according to the wording of article 4 (1) (c) if a website operator is located outside the EU but it is conducting its activities and transfers data with the use of its website server or servers that are established within the territory of the Union then the relevant national law of the member state or states involved applies.

A loophole in the scope of the relevant provision's application was observed. The question referred to what happened in case of data transfer that violated EU data protection law, when both the controller and equipment used are established outside the territory of the EU. The Working Party introduced under article 29 of the directive provided an answer by including in the definition of equipment the personal computers of the users, "which may be used for nearly all kind of processing operation"[472]. As it specifically stated "the user's PC can be viewed as equipment in the sense of Article 4(1) (c) of the Directive"[473]. "The controller decided to use this equipment for the purpose of processing personal data...and this equipment is not used only for purposes of transit through Community territory"[474]. Thus, the Working Party concludes that even in case of cookies sent by a website operating out of the geographical territory of the EU to the hard disc of a user's computer within the EU "the national law of the member state where this user's computer is located applies..."[475].

The particular provisions do not apply when "such equipment is used only for purposes of transit through the territory of the Community"[476]. However, the non-

---

[471] See article 11 (1) (a).
[472] Article 29 Data Protection Working Party, Working document on determining the International Application of EU Data Protection Law to Personal Data Processing on the Internet by non-EU based websites, Adopted on May 30th 2002, 5035/01/EN/Final, WP56, European Commission, Internal Market DG, Brussels, page 9.
[473] Ibid at page 11.
[474] The same.
[475] The same.
[476] Article 4 (1) (c).

application of the directive in the particular case "does not absolve the controller from designating a representative established in the member state"[477].

Two very important elements concerning the directive and its application were highlighted by the Working Party document analysed above. The first concerned the actual geographical scope of the directive's application, which also comprises the countries of European Economic Area (EEA). As the document states "the reference to the European union should be understood as referring also to EEA"[478]. This is of obvious importance when having to determine whether the controller is established within or outside of the limits of the EU. The area of the EEA countries is deemed as the area to which the protection afforded applies. The second important point included in the same document concerns the identity of the data subjects. "It is not necessary for the individual to be an EU citizen or to be physically present or a resident of the EU. Thus, in the cases discussed above the individual could be a US or a Chinese national"[479].

At this point, I have to note that the particular article can also create problems with its uncertainty. I am referring mainly to the provision enshrined in article 4 (1) (c) that creates a rule for jurisdiction determination, whose main characteristics remain vague. The intentions of the European legislators have been good, but the result is problematic. The relevant provision is drafted with the use of wording that extends the application of EU law virtually to the whole planet. Every multinational company, which maintains some sort of contacts with Europe will fall within the ambit of EU law, just because it is engaged in electronic communications with individuals situated in Europe. This provision might intend to protect at a maximum level European citizens, but it leads to a great degree of uncertainty as it renders itself unenforceable. Bygrave argues that Article 4(1)(c) gives rise to the possibility of "regulatory overreaching in an online environment…where rules are expressed so generally and non discriminatingly that they apply prima facie to a large range of activities without having much of a realistic chance of being enforced"[480]. The problems related to the ignorance   of   European   privacy   standards   and   rules   on   behalf   of

---

[477] The European Commission, Directorate General Internal Market and Financial Services, supra note 275, page 17.
[478] Article 29 Data Protection Working Party, supra note 473, page 2.
[479] Ibid at page 7.
[480] Bygrave Lee, European Data Protection, Determining Applicable Law Pursuant to European Data Protection Legislation, Computer Law and security report, 2000, page 255.

controllers established in other parts of the world, such as south eastern Asia for example, have been largely ignored. Furthermore, distinguishing the exact location where the controller is established would prove very difficult in effect. In an over extending on line world, it is impossible both for individuals and for the data authorities to determine the exact geographical location of the controller's establishment.

Another problematic area is formed by the interpretations the Working Party gave to the term "equipment". The term had been, as analysed above, granted an unrealistically wide scope of application that reflects the challenges emerging from the limitless nature of the net to traditional legal order constructions. If personal computers can be considered equipment for the purposes of this article, then many complicated cases will arise. On which basis can a controller be found to fall within the scope of the article, if a data subject located in the EU has sent him an e-mail? And what exactly is the meaning of "making use" of the equipment? Of great interest is at this point the content of Recital 47 that reads "Whereas where a message containing personal data is transmitted by means of a telecommunications or electronic mail service, the sole purpose of which is the transmission of such messages, the controller in respect of the personal data contained in the message will normally be considered to be the person from whom the message originates, rather than the person offering the transmission services". Thus, in case of a data subject from the EU communicating via electronic mail with a website established out of the EU, it would be the data subject, which would be deemed as the controller. The explanations of the Working Party regarding cookies, which was analysed above, can also lead to problematic situations related to the same reason. The vast over-extension of the EU law applicability may render it simply enforceable. It is not possible to imagine how EU law would apply to all websites that operate worldwide, which send cookies to the PCs of users situated in the EU. These provisions should be reconsidered in order to shape a new set of rules that would deal with the problem on a more realistic basis. To achieve this objective, the EU has to take into serious consideration the international character of internet, so as to try to foster solutions in close cooperation with the rest of the parties at international level. Such   solutions   would   be   more   efficiently   promoted   with   the presence and agreement of the relevant authorities representing at least the most important players of electronic trade internationally. The EU can be quite effective in regulating issues that develop within its own geographical scope and via the use of its massive commercial and economic power to influence others towards the direction of adjusting to its own standards, article 25 serves as a fine indication of this statement, but the borderless character of internet deprives any effort to curb problems such as cookies on a unilateral basis of any chance to succeed.

6.5 General Rules on the lawfulness of the processing of personal data

Articles 5 to 21 deal with the issue of the lawfulness of data processing. Article 5 is a general provision according to which member states do have the scope necessary to provide for in a more detailed manner the precise conditions under which processing can be lawful. Of course the ability of the states to regulate in this field is going to be limited within the context provided by the directive. The latter provides for a layer of regulation that serves as the minimum level of protection that can be afforded at European level. However, the member states are allowed to process forward making their own choices on the particular issue in relation to whether they are going to enact a higher level of protection or not.

6.6 Data Quality

Article 6 provides for five principles serving as conditions that render the processing of data a legitimate activity. According to article 6 (1) (a) the processing must be "fair and lawful"[481]. "This means that the individual may not be deceived or misled about the purpose for which the data are being processed"[482]. This principle is also directly connected with the provisions of articles 10 and 11 that render provision of information to the data subject necessary. The relevant information that has to be passed to the data subject includes the identity of the controller, the purposes of processing and further details such as the names of the data recipients[483]. Furthermore,

---

[481] See also recital 28.
[482] Szafran Emmanuel, Overstraeten Van Tanguy, supra note 258 at page 61.
[483] See articles 10 and 11.

the fairness principle "requires that personal data may only be collected in a transparent way"[484]. The importance of this principle is obvious since it provides the grounds for justifying the illegitimate use of various devices such as the cookies. Since the latter are text files that are sent to the user's hard drive without his knowledge or consent then it becomes clear that the use of cookies for the collection of information is not in accordance with the "transparency" requirement.

Article 6 (1) (b) provides for the necessity to demonstrate a "specified", "explicit", and "legitimate" purpose for the processing concerned and to avoid "further processing" that can be "incompatible" with the aforementioned purposes. Although, the Directive appears to grant to European citizens a high level of protection safeguarded by quite strict rules it has to be mentioned that the particular terms used are vague. "Specified" purpose can be easily interpreted as a "purpose defined before data are collected and in as precise a fashion as possible"[485]. Thus, the obligation to inform the data subjects stands once again at the core of the directive's protection regime (articles 10 and 11). As far as the term "legitimate" is concerned it has to be noted that the exact extent and scope of its meaning cannot be deduced by the wording of the provision. Legitimacy can be assessed on the basis of the particular legislation enacted by the member states for the implementation of the directive and after the consultation of the supervisory authorities introduced at national level[486]. This may lead to a clarification or at least further understanding of what "legitimacy" in the particular context entails but it can also lead to a variety of divergent applications since it is directly depending on the relevant national provisions that may vary in terms of content.

Furthermore, the same article refers to "further processing with incompatible purposes". The term incompatible is not analysed by the article. The lack of any clarification of the terminology selected can potentially lead to divergent application around the EU. "The issue is how the incompatibility of any secondary processing with the primary purpose is to be determined"[487]. In Belgium the law assesses incompatibility on the basis of "reasonable expectations of the data subjects"[488] while

---

[484] European Consumer Law Group, Consumer Transactions on the Internet, ECLG/194/2000, Brussels, 2000, p12.
[485] Wuermeling U. Ulrich, supra note 366, page 431.
[486] See article 28.
[487] Korff Douwe, supra note 399, page 63.
[488] Ibid at page 64.

in the Netherlands the compatibility test "is strictly applied"[489]. Thus, a variety of national provisions appears inevitable.

The same phenomenon of divergence in member states legislation can be observed also in the case of scientific research[490], which is supported by the directive as long as there are appropriate safeguards for the processing of data. The nature or character of the safeguards to be provided for are not specified, thus member states were led towards a variety of regulations. Spain and Italy provide for "no safeguards with regard to secondary processing for research purposes"[491] whereas in Greece, Luxembourg and Portugal "special authorisation of the Data Protection Authority"[492] is required.

The content of article 6 (1) (c) further supplements the purpose requirement of 6 (1) (a). Purpose must also be "adequate, relevant and not excessive". Thus, the nature of the purpose for which data can be lawfully processed is specified.

Paragraph (d) states as an obligation the "accuracy" of data stored and their "up to date" storage. Whether the checking of data on a frequent basis constitutes a realistic scenario is something to be proved. The availability of actual methods to verify the reliability of the data concerned is another issue with which the directive did not deal.

Article 6 (1) (e) was criticised for the contradiction inherent in its content. As a result of this principle "data should be deleted or made anonymous"[493] after the fulfilment of the initial processing purpose. However, that can stand as an impediment for the processing of data for research purposes since anonymous data are usually deemed inappropriate for scientific research that entails detailed databases of the subjects concerned.

As article 6 (2) informs us it is for the controller to "ensure that paragraph one is complied with". This provision is repeated in the text of article 17.

6.7 Criteria for making Data Processing Legitimate

"It is a unique feature of the Directive, among the international data protection instruments, that it adds to the data protection principles a further list of criteria for

---

[489] Ibid at page 65.
[490] See also recital 29.
[491] Korff Douwe, supra note 399, at page 66.
[492] Ibid at page 67.
[493] Overstraeten Van Tanguy, Szafran Emmanuel, supra note 258, page 61.

making data processing legitimate"[494]. Thus, "in order to be lawful the processing of personal data must in addition be carried out with the consent of the data subject"[495]. The meaning of consent has been analysed before in the framework of article 2 (h).

Article 7 (b) leads to the legitimisation of data processing if this "is necessary for the performance of a contract". The wording of the provision in question has also attracted criticism for vagueness as it does not provide any information as to which are the elements that are considered necessary for the performance of a contract. As for the data concerned, they "can only be those of the contractual partner and not of third parties"[496]. The information "prior to the entering of a contract" concerns the information that the one party of the contractual relationship has to reveal to the other in order to achieve the conclusion of the contract. If, however, a contract is finally not concluded then according to the already analysed article 6 (1) (e) the data concerned should be erased.

According to 7 (c) processing is deemed legitimate where it is being performed due to compliance with a legal obligation of the controller. Namely, obligations stemming from the relevant EU law or introduced by national legal orders. Article 7 (d) permits processing for "the protection of the vital interests of the data subject". Recital 31 defines the latter as "interests essential for the data subject's life". If the particular provision is referring to data related to the subject's health then it should be read in conjunction with article 8 that regulates sensitive data.

Article 7 (e) focuses on the case of tasks "carried out in the public interest" or in the "exercise of an official authority". Recital 32 states that national legislation will determine the precise conditions under which a controller can perform such tasks. The ambiguity in the wording of the provision has led to divergence in the way the member states have dealt with this issue. The UK refers to processing that is necessary for "the administration of justice" or for "any other functions of a public nature exercised in the public interest by any person"[497]. However, the law in Austria allows processing only by public authorities and "only insofar as these tasks or functions are specifically laid down by law"[498].

---

[494] Korff Douwe, supra note 399, page 70.
[495] Recital 30.
[496] Wuermeling U. Ulrich, supra note 366, page 434.
[497] Korff Douwe, supra note 399, page 78.
[498] The same.

Finally, article 7 (f) regulates a balance between "the legitimate interests pursued by the controller" and "the fundamental rights and freedoms of the data subject"[499]. Further clarification over the scope of this provision is provided by recital 30 that states the ability of "member states to determine the circumstances in which personal data may be used or disclosed to a third party in the context of the legitimate ordinary activities of companies and other bodies"[500]. It also provides for disclosure of data to a third party "for the purposes of marketing whether carried out commercially or by a charitable organisation"[501].

6.8 The Processing of special Categories of data

One of the central characteristics of the directive is the "establishment of greater scrutiny and protection for certain types of information, specifically those dealing with race, religion, health or political beliefs"[502]. "The creation of special protection is also understood as requiring attention as to...how data will actually be used"[503]. It is interesting to note that the respective member state laws promulgated to implement the directive place an emphasis on the protection of specific fundamental freedoms that are deemed of the highest importance for the corresponding European member states' societies. As a clear indication of this is the fact that "the Spanish law reaffirms a constitutional stipulation that no one may be forced to reveal his religion or beliefs"[504] while the Danish law places a greater weight on processing of data concerning "political affiliations"[505].

Article 8 (1) provides for the basic rule of the protection of sensitive data and article 8 (2) presents a list of derogations from the aforementioned rule. According to recital 33 of the directive, "derogations from this prohibition must be explicitly provided for in respect of specific needs". Thus, only derogations enshrined in the directive or in member state laws implementing the directive can actually apply in a valid manner. "Explicit consent", a concept analysed before can function as a factor

---

[499] See the text of 7 (f).
[500] Recital 30.
[501] The same.
[502] The European Commission, Directorate General Internal Market, Reidenberg R. Joel, Schwartz M. Paul, On-line Services and data protection and privacy, Volume II, Luxembourg, 1998, p9.
[503] The same.
[504] Korff Douwe, supra note 399, at page 86.
[505] The same.

that can legitimise processing of sensitive personal data. However, as the directive provides in article 8 (2) (a), the member states passing their own legislation can prohibit any derogation even when the explicit consent of the data subject has been given. The conditions under which the particular clause will apply will be clarified by the relevant national laws. The member states have moved towards the direction of adopting provisions in accordance with their individual legal culture in the context of the particular article. France, a country that as mentioned before had a history of developed data protection legislation and a country that threw its weight behind the adoption of the directive, enacted a law to implement the directive specifically requiring the data subject consent to have been "expressed in writing"[506]. It has been mentioned before that the directive does not require at any stage that the notion of "explicit consent" entails a written form. Thus, it was a conscious choice on behalf of the French legislator to afford a greater level of protection. Furthermore, in Germany, Italy and Greece the laws "lay down additional formal requirements and stipulate that processing of sensitive data even if it falls within one of the exempted categories may still only take place if a prior authorisation is obtained from the data protection authority"[507].

Article 8 (2) (b) covers the cases of obligations stemming from employment law. It is also necessary, as stated before, that these obligations are clearly provided by national law. Denmark and Finland permit the processing of data on the part of the employers "on trade union membership"[508], while Greece and Belgium forbid the processing of "certain categories of data such as genetic data"[509] on behalf of the employers "even with consent of the data subject"[510].

Article 8 (2) (c) includes the protection of the "vital interests" of the subject as an additional reason on which derogations can be legitimately founded. The concept of "vital interests" has been analysed in the framework of article 7 analysis. As stated before it mainly refers to health issues. Article 8 (2) (d) provides assurances for the smooth function of particular non profit political, philosophical, religious or trade union associations. The latter can process data of their members only for pure operational

---

[506] Ibid at page 87.
[507] Ibid at page 88.
[508] Ibid at page 89.
[509] The same.
[510] The same.

reasons. The directive permits it as long as "the data are not disclosed to a third party without the consent of the data subjects"[511].

Article 8 (2) (e) refers to the cases where the data subject has chosen to openly reveal data that can be taken as sensitive. The data subject reveals information considering himself on his own initiative. Therefore, it cannot be judged as an illegitimate practise. Moreover, sensitive data can be revealed in the case of "establishment of legal claims". This is normally perceived in the framework of a trial during which a part of the sensitive data of one party involved may need to be processed so as for the legal claims to be sufficiently founded.

Article 8 (3) deals with a very serious issue concerning medical data. The derogation in question is justified by the massive importance that the processing of such data can have for the function of hospitals or other medical institutions. The protection of such a sensitive category of data is imperative but at the very same time the function of socially important institutions such as the medical ones appears of great significance also. A further point that can assist in shaping a more balanced relationship between the two fundamentally important aims is "the obligation of secrecy" enshrined in the relevant legislation. Recital 33 further explains that "derogations from this prohibition must be explicitly provided for in respect of specific needs…where the processing of these data is carried out for certain health related purposes by persons subject to a legal obligation of professional secrecy"[512]. The shaping of the appropriate balance appears absolutely necessary due to the nature of medical data and their high personal and societal value. This definitely special value vested in such data has to be safeguarded in the framework of the ability to use linked and automated data bases for other reasons than the recognised as legitimate ones. As Lawrence O. Gostin points out that in the light of interlinked medical databases, the society "must reckon with the potential diminution of privacy. One method of affording some measure of privacy protection to patients would be to furnish rigorous legal safeguards"[513]. The EU with this directive attempted to do just that. There is a delicate balance to be achieved between "human

---

[511] See 8 (2) (d) of the directive.
[512] See recital 33.
[513] Nola M. Ries, Privacy Law: Patient Privacy in a Wired ad Wireless World: Approaches to Consent in the Context of Electronic Health Records, 43 Alberta Law Review, 2006, page 712.

dignity and human rights as against public health, scientific progress and commercial interests in a free market"[514]. It depends on the society and the most essential principles which lie at its foundations to determine the shift of the balance towards a certain end. This doesn't mean that a modern society will opt for the one end precluding the other, as it would rather treat a certain set of principles as the most fundamental and then regulate legitimate exceptions so as to serve sometimes conflicting needs as well. With the directive a conscious choice was made to grant additional protection to sensitive data while the permitted derogations were clearly regulated. This approach can be contrasted with the dominant one in the US where sensitive data such as the genetic one are treated under the angle of a pure market approach. Market efficiency has been upgraded as the principal goal of policy making and it has been found as the main way to lead to the satisfaction of public interests. Since, market efficiency is bound with serving the public interest it has comfortably become the aim of lawmaking. "Lawmakers (in the US) typically associate the public interest with generating and making available the maximum amount of information for medical researcher, prospective employers and insurers, for governmental agencies and others. This view tends to see genetic information as a commodity and leads to the limited and sectoral protection that American law provides for personal genetic information"[515]. The divergence in the terminology used reveals the magnitude of difference between the EU and the US. In the EU when talking about sensitive data, as will be thoroughly analysed later, the term preferred is "fundamental right" while in the US the term "commodity" appears frequently in literature and academia. A wide gap in the societal and philosophical approaches to the issue of privacy and data protection is hidden behind the terminology chosen.

Article 8 (4) provides for a derogation based on the concept of "substantial public interest". Thus, member states can "derogate from the prohibition...when justified by grounds of important public interest...in areas such as public health and social protection...in order to ensure the quality and cost effectiveness of the procedures used...in the health insurance system, scientific research and government statistics; whereas it is incumbent on them to provide specific and suitable safeguards

---

[514] Timothy Caulfield and Nola M. Ries, Consent, Privacy and Confidentiality in Longitudinal, Population Health Research: The Canadian Legal Context, 12 Health Law Journal, 2004, page 10.
[515] Richard Cole, Authentic Democracy: Endowing Citizens with a Human Rig in their Genetic Information, 33 Hofstra Law Review, 2005, page 1242.

so as to protect fundamental rights and the privacy of individuals"[516]. Moreover, official authorities can pursue aims "laid down in constitutional law or international public law"[517]. Finally, "where in the course of electoral activities the operation of the democratic system…requires that political parties compile data on people's political opinion, the processing may be permitted for reasons of important public interest, provided that appropriate safeguards are established"[518]. The problem with the particular provision is the wide scope it leaves for the member states to define what they consider to fulfil "substantial public interest". The Irish law allows processing for the purpose of "collecting any tax or duty or to determine entitlement to social welfare payments"[519], while Belgium has also included a clause allowing processing "by recognised institutions working in the field of sexual crimes"[520] and "for the benefit of human rights organisations"[521]. In France "public security, the fight against terrorism, defence and State security"[522] are deemed substantial enough to justify exemptions.

Article 8 (5) deals with the issue of data concerning criminal offences and the registers of criminal convictions. Article 8 (1) does not include the relevant data in the category of "sensitive data"[523]. However, the laws of "Finland, Greece and the UK include data on criminal offences in the general category of sensitive data"[524]. The direct consequence of this is "that such data can be processed on the basis of any of the exceptions set out in article 8 (2), including the consent of the data subject"[525].

The final provision of article 8 concerns "national identification numbers". These may concern the individual number that somebody may have on his identity card, the number on a driving license or the social security number. The risk lays in the ability of linking the particular data processed to a certain individual.

---

[516] Recital 34.
[517] Recital 35.
[518] Recital 36.
[519] Korff Douwe, supra note 399, page 91.
[520] The same
[521] The same
[522] Ibid at page 93.
[523] See article 8 (1) defining the categories of sensitive data.
[524] Korff Douwe, supra note 399, page 94.
[525] The same.

6.9 Processing of data and the freedom of expression

Article 9 introduces another derogation concerning processing for journalistic or artistic purposes. The derogation is based on the need to shape a balance between the respect of privacy and the freedom of expression "as guaranteed in particular in article 10 of the European Convention for the Protection of Human Rights and Fundamental Freedoms"[526].

6.10 Information to be given to the data subject

Articles 10 and 11 provide for the information that ought to be given to the data subject. The articles contain a minimum level of information that should be provided leaving member states the ability to regulate for more. The scope left for further regulation is specifically enshrined in both articles, which oblige the member states to provide for "at least" the following information. The basic difference between the two articles is that article 10 refers to the cases where data has been collected from the data subject himself[527] and article 11 from third distinctive sources[528]. The identity of the controller and the purposes of the processing form the core of the content of the obligation to provide information. Furthermore, article 11 provides for some exceptions to the rule enshrined in its first paragraph, as it does not require a disclosure of the relevant information in case of processing for scientific or historical research[529]. Article 11 (2), however, places the obligation on member states to "provide appropriate safeguards".

6.11 Right of Access

Article 12 establishes the right of the data subjects to obtain under reasonable terms access to processed data related to them[530]. Thus, member states are required to enact legislation allowing data subjects to obtain "confirmation as to whether or not data are being processed...communication in an intelligible form of the data

---

[526] See recital 37.
[527] See recital 38.
[528] See recital 39.
[529] See recital 40.
[530] See recital 41.

undergoing processing...knowledge of the logic involved in any automatic processing in the case of article 15 (1)"[531]. "The directive does not indicate how often or how quickly the controller must provide the requested information"[532]. It is only stated that the information must be provided in an "intelligible form". Thus, "it will be vital to look to the implementing legislation in each member state for additional guidance"[533]. The right of access regulated by article 12 has to be seen in conjunction with article 11 providing for the obligation of the controller to provide information to the data subject concerning the processing of his data when the latter are obtained from a third party. Otherwise, "the right of access is not helpful where the subject is unaware that his personal data are stored by someone"[534]. The respective rights enshrined in article 12 (b) and (c) serve as natural consequences of the right to access. They safeguard the right of the data subject to rectify, erase or block the data that fail to comply with the directive's provisions and to notify subsequently the recipients of such information for the rectifications occurred. The issue of what constitutes "incomplete or inaccurate nature of the data"[535] remains open and needs to be examined under the light of the analysis of the provisions of the member states implementing laws. "All member states provide for the right of data subjects to receive confirmation of whether data on them are being processed...in Austria and Germany this is implied in the right of access rather than particularly stipulated...while the law in Greece, more significantly, extends the right about whether data have been processed on the data subject in the past"[536].

6.12 Exemptions and Restrictions

Article 13 provides for exemptions in the application of rights concerning data quality (article 6), the right of information (articles 10 and 11), the right of access (article 12) and the publicising of processing operations (article 21)[537]. The grounds underlying the exemptions[538] are national and public security, defence, the prosecution

---

[531] Article 12 (a)
[532] Crutchfield Barbara George, Lynch Patricia, Marsnik F. Susan, US Multinational Employers: Navigating through the Safe Harbour Principles to comply with the EU Directive, 2001, The American business Law Association, 38 American Business Law Journal, accessed by LEXIS-NEXIS, page 744.
[533] The same.
[534] Wuermuling U. Ulrich, supra note 366, page 437.
[535] Article 12 (b).
[536] Korff Douwe, supra note 399, page 107.
[537] See also recital 44.
[538] See also recital 43.

of criminal offences, breaches of ethics for regulated professions, important financial interests of the member states and the rights and freedoms of others. The content of this article merely repeats that of article 3 (2) that contained almost identical limitations. What is more interesting in the particular article amounts to the restriction relating to the "protection of the data subject or of the rights and freedoms of others"[539]. In this case "member states may for example specify that access to medical data may be obtained only through a health professional"[540].

6.13 The Right to Object

Article 14 includes the right of the data subject to object to the processing of his data. It should be noted that the particular right is given in certain cases only. If the processing is motivated "at least"[541] by public (article 7(e)) or legitimate interests (article 7 (f)) then the right to object can exist only "on compelling legitimate grounds"[542]. Apart from this exhaustive list of reasons founding a right to object, member states are not obliged to introduce further cases for which the right of objection could be applied. However, "where otherwise provided by national legislation"[543] they actually do so. The right to object to "processing on legitimate grounds originates in France as it was included in the pre-implementation law in that country adopted in 1978"[544].

Article 14 (b) refers to the direct marketing industry. It provides for the ability of the data subject to object to the processing of his personal data free of charge and when the controller anticipates that the data are going to be processed[545]. Moreover, it provides for a second alternative stating that before the data are disclosed the data subject must be informed about the imminent disclosure "and be offered the right to object free of charge"[546]. The condition of justifying his right to object on "compelling and legitimate"[547] grounds does not exist in the direct marketing context.

---

[539] Article 13 (1) (g).
[540] Recital 42.
[541] Article 14 (a)
[542] Article 14 (a).
[543] The same.
[544] Korff Douwe, supra note 399, page 111.
[545] Article 14 (b).
[546] The same.
[547] Article 14 (a).

6.14 Automated Individual Decisions

Article 15 regulates the issue of automated individual decisions. Here, the "primary formal focus is on the type of decision as opposed to data processing"[548]. "The provision is not based on any international regulation. Only French law has a comparable regulation"[549] founded on the concept that "information technology must serve mankind and should not violate human identity or fundamental rights thus, it is prohibited to take judicial, administrative and private sector decisions on the basis of automated processing of data, which constitute a personality profile"[550]. What the EU tried to deal with is the situation where a decision is made based on pure automatic process without the ability of the subject to object or even obtain knowledge of the actual performance of the particular process. As Wuermeling insists "it deals with the ethical impact of the possibility that computer decisions might replace human decisions"[551]. The directive explains that "member states shall grant the right to every person not to be subject to a decision which produces legal effects concerning him or significantly affects him and which is based *solely* on automated processing of data"[552]. Thus, in order for the provision to apply the decision in question must be "solely" an automated one, based exclusively on an automated process. Hence, "if a company wants to make a decision which is not solely automated it must provide that a human checks the outcome"[553]. The ambiguity of the particular provision is embodied in the absence of any reference as to what exactly it really means as "solely automated decision" and to what extent the participation of a person to the process of its adoption can deprive it of the character of a decision exclusively automated. In any case "it is quite difficult for the subject to prove if somebody has taken part in the decision or not"[554]. The second important element of the provision is the requirement to refer to a decision that has legal effects on the person involved or at least it is "significantly affecting him"[555]. A decision with legal effects on somebody is easily discernable, what amounts to a "significant effect" however, is something that needs to be further

---

[548] Bygrave Lee, Automated Profiling, Minding the Machine: Article 15 of the EC Data Protection directive and Automated Profiling, 17 Computer Law and Security Report, 2001, page 17.
[549] Wuermeling U. Ulrich, supra note 366, page 441.
[550] Korff Douwe, supra note 399, page 119.
[551] Wuermeling U. Ulrich, supra note 366, page 441
[552] Article 15 (1).
[553] Wuermeling U. Ulrich, supra note 366, page 441.
[554] The same.
[555] Article 15 (1)

explained. Since automated decisions assume an increasing role in the way a business functions, for instance we may receive mail due to automated sending of e-mail advertisements to a massive number of people, it was essential for the Commission to distinguish some cases where the need of protection appears imperative. Otherwise, the object of the regulation will end up being a commercial practise with no particular significance for any consumer. Therefore, the directive specifically states that the "automated processing of data must be intended to evaluate certain personal aspects relating to him, such as his performance at work, creditworthiness, reliability, conduct, etc"[556]. Only when aspects of somebody's personal or professional life are violated then the ability to invoke the relevant article is provided. The provision is very important as it concerns an increasing array of activities that are performed without the interference of the human factor. The most important are "creditworthiness, judging performance, reliability or conduct at work"[557]. Computers "are frequently involved in executing assessments that have previously been the preserve of human discretion in the context of determining persons' credit ratings, insurance premiums or social welfare entitlements"[558]. The issues in question are of massive significance since the areas that can be covered by exclusive computer decision making cover significant part of an individual's economic and personal well being. Insurance and loan matters can now be judged on the basis of pre-collected data resting in several databases without any contribution to the whole process on behalf of the interested data subjects. Although the particular provision seems to cover these situations, there should be an independent rule or provision drafted to make sure that there is a remedy when dealing with these situations. When insurance, loans or premiums are based on automated decisions based on pre-collected data compilation, questions are raised over the validity of such judgements since there is no scope for thinking or taking certain conditions into account. This can only happen if the interested parties are directly involved in the process as it was the case in the past. Furthermore, the pre-collected data might be false, forged or simply not updated. The issues at stake are too important to be left to processes with no ambit for human interaction. For these reasons a provision explicitly dealing with these issues should have been inserted in the directive.

---

[556] The same.
[557] Singleton Susan, Data Protection, the New Law, Jordan's, 1998, page 36.
[558] Bygrave Lee, supra note 549, page 18.

Article 15 (2) provides for certainly defined derogations from the rule stated in 15 (1). According to paragraph 2 (a), a person can be subject to an automated decision, when the latter "is taken in the course of the entering into or performance of a contract" even if that entails legal or other significant effects on him. We can be led to that conclusion "provided that the request for the entering into or the performance of the contract, lodged by the data subject, has been satisfied or that there are suitable measures to safeguard his legitimate interests, such as arrangements allowing him to put his point of view"[559]. Another case is enshrined in 15 (2) (b), which states that derogation "is authorized by a law which also lays down measures to safeguard the data subject's legitimate interests".

6.15 Confidentiality and Security of Processing

Articles 16 and 17 rest on the premise that "data protection regulations cover the lawfulness of processing, but they must be assisted by technical measures to protect data against an unlawful processing"[560]. Article 16 places the controller at the centre of the protection system granting him the authority to permit access to personal data to a processor or any other body. The directive imposed a limit on the number of individuals or bodies with an access to the data concerned.

Article 17 must be read in conjunction with Recital 46. They both refer to the necessity of introducing "the appropriate technical and organisational measures...particularly in order to maintain security...and prevent any unauthorised processing...the relevant measures must take into account the state of the art and the costs of their implementation"[561]. The "state of the art" must be defined "on a European level otherwise it could cause different levels of protection in the member states"[562]. Article 17 (3) provides for the obligation of a legally binding act between the controller and the processor in order for the latter to obtain the ability to access and process the data involved. This provision sheds light on the nature of the relationship between the processor and the controller contained in article 2 (e).

---

[559] Article 15 (2) (a)
[560] Wuermeling U. Ulrich, supra note 366, page 441.
[561] Recital 46.
[562] Wuermeling U. Ulrich, supra note 366, page 442.

6.16 Notification of the Supervisory Authority

Article 18 establishes an obligation to notify the supervisory authority, which is established "as the legislator must also secure the monitoring of the processing conditions"[563], before the carrying out of any processing on behalf of the controller or his representative. Recital 48 states that "the procedures for notifying the supervisory authority are designed to ensure disclosure of the purposes and main features of any processing operation for the purpose of verification that the operation is in accordance with the national measures taken under this Directive".

The following paragraphs of the same article regulate the exceptions from the notification rule. "In order to avoid unsuitable administrative formalities, exemptions from the obligation to notify and simplification of the notification required may be provided for by Member States in cases where processing is unlikely adversely to affect the rights and freedoms of data subjects, provided that it is in accordance with a measure taken by a Member State specifying its limits"[564]. The same type of regulation is provided also in the case "where a person appointed by the controller ensures that the processing carried out is not likely adversely to affect the rights and freedoms of data subjects"[565] provided of course that the aforementioned person can exercise his functions "in complete independence"[566].

Articles 18 (3) and (4) provide for exemptions related to registers open to the public or non-profit associations with philosophical or other interests[567].

Article 19 provides only for the necessary elements that need to be included in the notification. The pieces of information that "at least"[568] should form a part of the notification include the name of the controller, the purpose of the processing, the recipients of the data involved and proposed transfer of data to third countries.

---

[563] Lloyd J Ian, Information Technology Law, Third Edition, Butterworths, London, 2000, page 83.
[564] See recital 49.
[565] Recital 49
[566] The same.
[567] See also recital 50.
[568] Article 19 (1)

6.17 Prior Checking and Publicising of Processing Operations

Article 20 (1) promotes the "ex post facto verification by the competent authorities"[569] as a sufficient measure to comply with the directive. Moreover, member states have the ability to define in their domestic legislation "specific risks to the rights and freedoms of data subjects by virtue of their nature, their scope or their purposes, such as that of excluding individuals from a right, benefit or a contract, or by virtue of the specific use of new technologies"[570]. It is emphasised that the supervisory authority after having received the notification "from the controller or the data protection official"[571] should "check such processing prior to it being carried out"[572]. Another measure aimed at enhancing the level of data protection is envisaged in article 21 that places the obligation upon the member states to publicise the processing operations[573]. However, the means of publication are not specified.

6.18 Remedies and Liability

Articles 22 to 24 provide for remedies and damages in case of a breach of the rights conferred on individuals by the directive and its implementing national laws. Member states must provide for the availability of a judicial remedy[574], which applies cumulatively with the administrative remedy before the supervisory authority.

In this case the subject is also entitled to damages[575] unless the controller "proves that he is not responsible for the damage, in particular in cases where he establishes fault on the part of the data subject or in case of force majeure"[576]. If he proves that on his part all appropriate measures to avoid damage were taken then he may escape liability.

Apart from the damages that the data subject is entitled to in case of an unlawful processing of his personal data, the controller who is responsible for such behaviour

---

[569] Recital 52.
[570] Recital 53.
[571] Article 20 (2).
[572] Recital 54.
[573] Article 21 (1)
[574] Article 22.
[575] Article 23
[576] Recital 55 and article 23 (2).

can be subject to sanctions[577]. Such sanctions may be governed by private or public law"[578].

6.19 The Transfer of Data in Third Countries

Article 25 probably constitutes the most highly disputed article of the directive at an international level. It provided the basis for a wide range of debates originated by the fact that it embodied one of the very few occasions where the EU extended its scope of regulation to other legal orders and countries, which do not form a part of the Union. It placed its –especially after the enlargement huge market size and power- behind the enforcement of the directive and declared that it will not exchange and transfer data to third countries if the latter do not offer "an adequate level of protection". This concept is being interpreted in the light of the provisions of the EU law. In simple words if the rest of the trading partners of the EU wish to continue their trading agreements and relations with the EU, they have to comply with the Union's data protection standards. The magnitude of the importance of such extension of the EU regulation ability is enormous and emerged as an issue which was highly criticised especially in the US. The reactions on the other side of the Atlantic and the compromise reached between the world's two biggest trading partners will be presented at the following part of the book.

The directive fully recognises that "cross border flows of personal data are necessary to the expansion of international trade"[579] and concludes that "the protection of individuals guaranteed in the Community by this directive does not stand in the way of transfers of personal data to third countries, which ensure an adequate level of protection"[580]. Thus, the Community places the protection of personal data at a central position in its commercial policy, stating that only countries that can provide for adequate protection of the European citizens personal data can benefit from trading relations with it. As a vivid proof of that the Union clearly stated that "the transfer of personal data to a third country which does not ensure an adequate level of protection must be prohibited"[581] and "in any event transfers to third countries may be effected only in full compliance with the provisions adopted by the member states pursuant to

---

[577] Article 24.
[578] Recital 55.
[579] Recital 56.
[580] The same
[581] Recital 57

this directive and in particular article 8"[582]. This can be seen as an effort of the Union to restrict the transfer of data to countries whose legislation or commercial patterns are not in accordance even with the more upgraded level of protection afforded by article 8 to sensitive data.

Article 25 (1) moves further towards the direction of placing even stricter requirements on third countries interested in receiving data from the EU in the framework of commercial activities as it underlines that member states can permit the transfer of data "without prejudice to compliance with the national provisions adopted pursuant to the other provisions of the directive"[583]. Taking into account the divergences in the national legislation adopted in the light of the directive, the wording is of massive importance since it provides for the ability of the member states to place further restrictions on the transfer of data to third countries. Even if an "adequate level of protection" is actually safeguarded by a third country a member state can prevent transfer of data to it, if certain requirements introduced by its national law are not met. A situation that indicates the previous finding can be illustrated by the following example: "In Austria, Greece, Portugal and Spain the law makes clear that in the absence of a Commission finding, only the national authorities can determine that a particular third country provides for adequate protection."[584] Otherwise, a transfer can take place only "on the basis of one of the specified derogations"[585]. However, "in the other countries it would appear that…individual controllers can make this assessment for themselves, and can therefore decide to transfer data to third countries…if they themselves believe that the laws or regulations in the country in question are adequate"[586]. In any case Article 25 "encourages the creation of a wider forum for the free movement of personal data between EU states and third countries with an adequate protection"[587].

Article 25 (2) does not include a specific definition of adequacy but rather presents a list of factors that can be deemed as indicative of the existence of the latter. Nature of data, duration of the process involved the country of origin and the country of

---

[582] Recital 60
[583] Article 25 (1)
[584] Korff Douwe, supra note 399, page 190.
[585] The same.
[586] The same.
[587] Harris R. Peter, International Developments, European Directive, Implementation Issues with Application of directive 95/46EC to Third Countries, 33 World Data Protection Report, May 2002, page 33.

final destination, the rules in force in the particular country and the security measures that have been assumed in the particular case form the basis of the assessment of "adequacy"[588]. As far as the criterion of the country of origin or final destination is concerned, it has to be noted that it has little importance as irrespective of both factors the directive applies to all processing taking place in the EU. However, it serves as a remainder that if data only "transit through the territory of the Community"[589], then the directive finds no application. It has been argued that "since the EU directive only mandates that the non member state possess an "adequate" as opposed to an "equivalent" level of data protection, it authorises a lower level of data protection for information flowing outside the EU than for information flowing within the EU"[590]. This approach has been criticised as several parties within the EU "find it undesirable that data protection can be lower in third countries"[591] in comparison with the Union. The definition of the term "adequacy" in the article is absent so the Working Party has contributed to the effort of acquiring more concrete criteria for the identification of such a level of protection. According to it adequacy "is almost dependent on whether the jurisdiction has a comprehensive data protection law...when private sector data protection laws require the companies to comply with a range of requirements that generally meet the standards set out in the EU Data Protection Directive"[592].

The member states and the Commission bear the mutual obligation to inform each other of cases relating to judging whether an adequate level of protection is ensured or not[593]. Member states shall "take the measures necessary to prevent" the transfer of data to countries that the Commission, assisted by the Committee of article 31, finds that "they do not ensure an adequate level of protection"[594]. Thus, if both relevant factors discover that there is a case of an insufficient level of protection they ought to inform each other. According to article 25 (4) the Commission will then proceed with its evaluation on the basis of article 31 (2). The problem is that the directive does not define the measures that the member state must take in order to

---

[588] Article 25 (2).
[589] Article 4.
[590] Loring B. Tracie, supra note 368, page 433.
[591] Heydrich W. Michael, supra note 381, page 415.
[592] The European Commission, Directorate General Internal Market, Application of a Methodology designed to Access the Adequacy of the Level of Protection of Individuals with regard to Processing Personal Data: Test of the Method on Several Categories of Transfer, Final Report, September 1998, Luxembourg, p165.
[593] Article 25 (3).
[594] Article 25 (4).

prevent the transfer of data. If these are going to be of administrative or legal nature or sanctions imposed on the bodies that at the very end transferred data to countries with an inadequate protection level this remains to be seen. However, the potential "risk of an information embargo and the extra jurisdictional effects of the EU directive…and the effort of the EU to transform the EU directive into a global standard of data protection"[595] has been the subject of a debate mainly between the EU and the US. The criticism has been based on the extra territorial effect of the EU directive. However, there were different views stated by other third countries also affected by the implementation of the EU directive and especially the provisions on the transfer of data. According to a view coming from New Zealand "since sanctions can be imposed upon the organisation *within* a member state of the EU that makes transfers to countries like New Zealand *if* the member state regulator determines that there is inadequate protection for the personal information transferred, then the relevant provisions of the EU directive do not have extraterritorial effect"[596]. The reason behind this argument is that "it will not be the recipient New Zealand organisation that is liable but the EU organisation, which initiated the transfer"[597]. Thus, the importance of the EU directive lies in the fact that the EU body will probably decide to "simply freeze all transfers of data to New Zealand than to worry about the complexities of compliance"[598]. The impact of this effect on the trade relations between an EU company and a third country company will be so essential that cooperation between the two to comply with the directive's standards will be deemed imperative.

Thus, in determining whether a country has an adequate level of protection according to EU standards the Commission has the principal role. The competence vested in it stems from Article 25 (6) that provides in conjunction with article 31 (2) process to be followed in such case. The procedure entails the following:

A proposal from the Commission,

An opinion of the group of the national data protection commissioners (Article 29 working party)

---

[595] Loring B. Tracie, supra note 368, page 436.
[596] Legorburu Bruce, Doing Business between the EU and New Zealand: What do you have to do to protect Personal Information these days, Computer and Telecommunications Law Review, 2000, Sweet & Maxwell, accessed via LEXIS-NEXIS, page 96.
[597] The same.
[598] The same.

An opinion of the Article 31 Management committee delivered by a qualified majority of Member States.

A thirty-day right of scrutiny for the European Parliament, to check if the Commission has used its executing powers correctly. The EP may, if it considers it appropriate, issue a recommendation.

The adoption of the decision by the College of Commissioners[599].

"The effect of such a decision is that personal data can flow from the fifteen EU Member States and three EEA member countries (Norway, Liechtenstein and Iceland) to that third country without any further safeguard being necessary. The Commission has so far recognized Switzerland, Hungary and the US Department of Commerce's Safe Harbour Privacy Principles as providing adequate protection"[600].

6.20 Derogations

Article 26 provides for exemptions to the article 25 rule. It includes the circumstances under which a transfer to a country with inadequate data protection regime can take place. The main grounds justifying an exemption include the unambiguous consent of the subject[601], the performance of a contract[602], public interest or defence of legal claims[603], the vital interests of the data subject[604], registers open to the public[605]. Article 26 (2) provides for the ability of the member states to authorise a

---

[599] The European Commission, DG Internal Market, Commission decisions on the adequacy of the protection of personal data in third countries, available at: http://europa.eu.int/comm/internal_market/privacy/adequacy_en.htm

[600] The same.
[601] Article 26 (1) (a). This concept has been analysed at earlier stage. See also article 2 (h).
[602] Article 26 (1) (b), (c). see also recital 58.
[603] Article 26 (1) (d). The concept of "public interest has been analysed before. See also article 7 (e), see also recital 58.
[604] Article 26 (1) (e). This concept has been analysed before. See also article 7(d).
[605] Article 26 (1) (f). See also recital 58.

transfer of data to a country which lacks of accordance with EU standards when the controller can give "adequate safeguards with respect to privacy and fundamental rights...such as appropriate contractual clauses"[606]. In such case the member state must inform the Commission that "can object on justified grounds"[607] or decide that "certain contractual clauses offer sufficient safeguards"[608]. Member states have to comply with this decision. However, particular measures may be taken to compensate for the lack of protection in a third country in cases where the controller offers appropriate safeguards"[609]. It has to be noted that in all cases concerning the transfer of data to a third country the Commission has given the green light. The countries examined were Switzerland[610], Hungary[611], Canada[612], most recently Argentina[613] and the USA with the highly controversial "Safe Harbour" agreement that "generated a heated debate"[614] and will be analysed at the final part of the book.

A question that emerges after the first reading of the article is whether the issues of "consent" on behalf of the data subject is related to the "opt in" or the "opt out"

---

[606] Article 26 (2).
[607] Article 26 (3).
[608] Article 26 (4).
[609] Recital 59.
[610] Commission Decision 2000/518/EC of 26.7.2000, O. J. L 215/1 of 25.8.2000, also available at:
http://europa.eu.int/smartapi/cgi/sga_doc?smartapi!celexapi!prod!CELEXnumdoc&lg=en&numdoc=320 00D0518&model=guichett
See also Opinion 5/99 of the Art. 29 Data Protection Working Party, available at:
http://europa.eu.int/comm/internal_market/privacy/docs/wpdocs/1999/wp22en.pdf
[611]Commission Decision 2000/519/EC of 26.7.2000, O.J. L 215/4 of 25.8.2000, available at:
http://europa.eu.int/smartapi/cgi/sga_doc?smartapi!celexapi!prod!CELEXnumdoc&lg=en&numdoc=320 00D0519&model=guichett
See also: Opinion 6/99 of the Art. 29 Data Protection Working Party, available at:
http://europa.eu.int/comm/internal_market/privacy/docs/wpdocs/1999/wp24en.pdf
[612] See: Commission Decision 2002/2/EC of 20.12.2001 on the adequate protection of personal data provided by the Canadian Personal Information Protection and Electronic Documents Act, O.J. L 2/13 of 4.1.2002, also available at:
http://europa.eu.int/smartapi/cgi/sga_doc?smartapi!celexapi!prod!CELEXnumdoc&lg=en&numdoc=320 02D0002&model=guichett
See also: Frequently Asked Questions on the Commission's adequacy finding on the Canadian Personal Information Protection and Electronic Documents Act (March 2002), available at:
http://europa.eu.int/comm/internal_market/privacy/adequacy/adequacy-faq_en.htm
See also: Opinion 2/2001 of the Art. 29 Data Protection Working Party, available at:
http://europa.eu.int/comm/internal_market/privacy/docs/wpdocs/2001/wp39en.pdf
The Commission Staff Working Paper on the adequate protection provided by the Canadian PIPEDA:
http://ec.europa.eu/justice_home/fsj/privacy/docs/adequacy/canada_st15644_06_en.pdf
[613] Commission Decision C (2003) 1731 of 30 June 2003, available at:
http://europa.eu.int/comm/internal_market/privacy/docs/adequacy/decision-c2003-1731/decision-argentine_en.pdf
See also: Opinion 4/2002 of the Art. 29 Working Party, available at:
http://europa.eu.int/comm/internal_market/privacy/docs/wpdocs/2002/wp63_en.pdf

144

solution. Since, this article serves as the derogatory basis for article 25, the highlight of the directive, it is presumed that "opt in" is preferred. However, as at many instances while examining the directive, this issue shall be determined more effectively at member state level. It is very important that this provision is inserted in the article providing European citizens with the ability to determine the destination of their own data. Since this comes in an era, when there is an increased awareness and sensitivity over this issue, the matter of individual consent can act as an effective safeguard to the dissemination of personal data to countries whose legal order does not provide any adequate protection for personal data.

Another interesting feature of the article is that it allows the transfer of data based on a contractual agreement. This can take the shape of an "ad hoc contract" enshrined in article 26(2). "Essentially, the contract identifies a group of data that is being transferred and the purposes for such transmission, and sets forth in detail the rights and obligations of both parties in relation to such data"[615]. Thus, if "a multinational company wants to transfer both human resources data and client related data…it could enter into a contract for each database"[616]. In this case, the national data protection authorities in each member state involved will have to check and approve the contract in order to decide on whether its content fulfils the criteria set by the directive and the guidelines of the Commission for transmitting data in a framework of adequate protection. Apart from the "ad hoc contract" there is also the ability to sign the "standard contractual clauses"[617] (a set of model clauses for controller to controller transfers and a set for controller to processor transfers) enshrined in article 26(4) and adopted by the Commission[618]. In this case the national Data Protection Authorities will have to be notified but are not obliged to afford their approval as in the case of the "ad hoc" contracts, as the clauses are already approved by the Commission, which drafted them in the first place. The latter is a much safer means to transfer data, since it constitutes a document drafted in an almost identical manner at pan-European level and

---

[614] Bejot Michel, European Treatment of Internet Privacy Issues, Journal of Internet Law, GrayCary, available at: www.gcwf.com/articles/journal/jil_jan01_1.html , accessed on 5/02/2002.
[615] Barcelo Rosa, Seeking Suitable Options for importing Data from the European Union, 36 The International Lawyer, Number 3, 2002, page 996.
[616] The same.
[617] See: http://europa.eu.int/comm/internal_market/privacy/modelcontracts_en.htm accessed on August 10th 2004.
[618] See: http://www.europa.eu.int/eur-lex/pri/en/oj/dat/2001/l_181/l_18120010704en00190031.pdf , Commission Decision 2001/497/EC of 15 June 2001 under the Directive 95/46/EC - O.J. L 181/19 of 4.7.2001

therefore, offers to all the parties involved the necessary sense of security, transparency and certainty. Moreover, as the Commission notes "parties are free to agree to add other clauses as long as they do not contradict, directly or indirectly, the standard contractual clauses approved by the Commission or prejudice fundamental rights or freedoms of the data subjects. It is possible, for example, to include additional guarantees or procedural safeguards for the individuals (e.g. on-line procedures or relevant provisions contained in a privacy policy, etc.). All these other clauses that parties may decide to add would not be covered by the third party beneficiary rights and would benefit from confidentiality rights where appropriate"[619]. It is also important to note that the standard contractual clauses include provisions on joint and several liability, which "means that, when data subjects have suffered damage as a consequence of the violation of the rights conferred on them by the contract, they are entitled to obtain compensation from either the Data Exporter or the Data Importer or both"[620]. Therefore, the effectiveness of their application is seriously supported by the specific regulation of liability issues.

Both articles 25 and 26 constitute valuable tools in the hands of the Commission in its effort to create safeguards for the privacy of the EU citizens. As analysed before, the trans-national character of internet does not allow governments to assume initiatives on their own and if they do, it severely undermines their effectiveness. On this basis, I criticised the provision found in article 4(1)(c) of the directive. However, I support that the provision of article 25 formed a necessary aspect of the directive. If the EU constructed a regime that guaranteed relative safety of personal data for the EU citizens but left transfers of their data in the framework of a globalised economy ran basically by electronic means of payment, unregulated then the whole system of internal protection would seem rather futile and pointless. Companies would transfer their data to unregulated "data heavens" and would render the directive an ineffective legislative tool left without a role. Moreover, the Commission demonstrated the necessary realism by allowing the transfer of data to countries with "adequate protection" and not to countries with "equivalent protection". Although, this choice has become the object of severe criticism by many respectable parties within the EU, such as the European Parliament, which used serious legal arguments against this policy, it has to be always

---

[619] See the FAQs issued by the Commission at:
http://europa.eu.int/rapid/pressReleasesAction.do?reference=MEMO/01/228&format=HTML&aged=1&language=EN&guiLanguage=en acceseed on August 10th 2004.
[620] The same.

kept in mind that this directive has a dual objective. It provides for the protection of personal data, protecting the fundamental right of the Europeans to enjoy their privacy, but also aims at allowing the uninhibited operation of the internal market and the external trade relations of the EU. As long as adequate safeguards are provided, trade shall operate smoothly. The Commission drafted the standard contractual clauses to harmonise the contractual standards across the continent, which was necessary to deal with the insecurity and the uncertainty created to both business and lawyers by a relatively new and widely unexplored field. The EU balanced the two rights on a realistic basis and came up with the directive that with all its shortcomings appears to be a reliable means to deal with the issue. In a perfect world the absolute protection of data will have rendered the transfer feasible only in cases of full compliance with the EU privacy model, but the Commission and the member states had to design their policies on more realistic parameters. As it will be demonstrated later, the EU model has proven to be hugely influential in countries with cultures and legal orders that share few common elements with the EU. Legislation has been enacted in countries such as Hong Kong, New Zealand and Canada aiming at "achieving alignment with the EU…as an important bridge towards increased economic opportunities with the lucrative European marketplace"[621]. In Canada the new privacy act "represents a shift away from an industry self regulation model for protecting privacy towards a more regulatory approach…based on the possible imposition of data flow restrictions by the EU as a result of the EU Directive on data protection"[622]. In this sense the EU directive "represents a dramatic increase in the reach and importance of data protection laws"[623]. Thus, it is obvious that the Directive had a very positive impact on the issue examined in this book. One of the most important contributions of this directive is that it elevated the issue into a matter of international importance as it placed it as a criterion for its commercial relations. This remark proves the effectiveness of making the choice to protect a fundamental human right with evident economic side effects in the framework of the Union's economic policies. It elevated this right to a criterion that everyone had to fulfil. As analysed before, several articles of the directive were

---

[621] Ritter B Jeffrey, Hayes S Benjamin, Judy L Henry, Emerging Trends in International Privacy Law, 15 Emory International Law Review, 2001, page 103.
[622] Sookman Barry, Legal Framework for E-Commerce Transactions, Computer and Telecommunications Law Review, 7 (4), 2001, page 88.
[623] Swire P Peter, Litan Robert, None of Your Business: World Data Flows, electronic Commerce, and the European Privacy Directive, 12 Harvard Journal of Law and Technology, 1999, page 683.

vague and lacking clarity and detail. At that point it was noted that this has obvious repercussions on legal certainty. However, while examining the national laws of member states, as they were presented during the analysis of the directive, it became clear that the lack of clarity produced also some positive effects. It left a wide scope for national legislators to regulate the relevant field. And it proved to be an effective method in the sense that the measures adopted at national legal order level were usually stricter than the provisions of the directive as they were further adapted to the legal cultures of the individual states. Therefore, the directive managed to harmonise national legislations in an effective manner and had a very positive contribution in consolidating a data protection culture in Europe and promoting privacy in the top of the agenda internationally.

The directive was heavily influenced by the humanistic traditions of certain European countries. Some of the elements that form these traditions were already presented before, while the legal history of mainly Germany and France that led to the adoption of the directive will be extensively analysed in the next chapter and compared with the distinctive and divergent historical view of the US. Even the term "data protection" constitutes a translation of the German term "datenschutz"[624] betraying the sources of the directive's influences. Concluding, it is emphasised that the directive despite its deficiencies and its potential need for adjustments, a feature of all pieces of legislation that regulate an area rapidly evolving, had a clear overall positive effect on the reinforcing of data protection standards in Europe with already obvious international implications.

6.21 Codes of Conduct

The adoption of codes of conduct is encouraged to support the implementation of the national provisions introduced after the adoption of the directive. The main duty of the member states as enshrined in article 27 is to ensure that the relevant codes of trade associations or other bodies are drafted "in accordance with the national provisions pursuant to the directive"[625] and the "specific characteristics of the

---

[624] Murray J Patrick, The Adequacy standard under Directive 95/46: Does US Data Protection meet this Standard?, 21 Fordham International Law journal, 1998, page 943.
[625] Article 27 (2).

processing carried out in certain sectors"[626]. The importance of the codes is limited by the fact that they do not have a binding effect. They serve mainly as guidelines for the industry. Therefore, their effectiveness is rather doubted.

6.22 The Supervisory Authority

The establishment in member states of authorities aiming at "monitoring the application within their territory"[627] of the directive provisions "is an essential component of the protection of individuals with regard to the processing of personal data"[628]. The basic requirement concerning the nature of the authority that stems from the directive is the necessary independent status of the authority in question[629]. The main duties of such authorities include consultation of national governments[630] and their competence is applied with a wide range of powers vested to them by the state such as investigative and intervention powers and the power to engage in legal proceedings[631]. Decisions made by the supervisory authority may be appealed against through the courts. Its authority must draft a report "at regular basis"[632] stating its activities that include the hearing of claims "lodged by any person ...concerning the processing of personal data"[633]. As far as the geographical scope of its competence is concerned every supervisory authority is competent "whatever the national law applicable to the processing in question to the exercise on the territory of its own member state the powers conferred on it"[634]. This provision refers back to the issues analysed in the framework of article 4 that promoted the law of the country where the "establishment of the controller" is located as the applicable one[635]. Thus, in the example presented in the framework of article 4 analysis, if a controller established in France transmits personal data to Germany for processing then the applicable national data protection law is the law of France, where the controller is established. According to article 28 (6) however, the Supervisory Authority provided for by German data

---

[626] Recital 61.
[627] See article 28 (1).
[628] Recital 62.
[629] Recital 62 talks about "complete independence".
[630] Article 28 (2).
[631] See srticle 28 (3) and recital 63.
[632] Article 28 (5)
[633] Article 28 (4)
[634] Article 28 (6)
[635] See the analysis of Article 4.

protection law would also be involved since the processing is taking place in the territory of Germany. This system ensures a harmonised level of protection around the EU. The latter is even more enhanced due to the obligation of cooperation between the respective supervisory authorities[636] "so as to ensure that the rules of protection are properly respected throughout the EU"[637].

6.23 The Working Party

The other organ that forms a part of the Union's data protection institutional structure is the Working Party. The latter has "an advisory status"[638] and acts independently. "It must advise the Commission and contribute to the uniform application of the national rules adopted pursuant to the directive"[639]. It is composed by a representative of the national supervisory authority and a representative of the Commission[640]. Its main duties are the analysis of issues emerging from the application of national measures adopted under the directive[641], providing the Commission with opinions on the level of protection in third countries[642], advise it on any proposed amendments[643] and on the codes of conduct adopted at European level[644].

6.24 The Committee

The final organ compiling the system of data protection in the EU is the Committee whose function and competence are enshrined in article 31. Its role has been illustrated before in the framework of article 26 (3) regulating the Commission's response to the authorisation of data transfers granted by member states on the basis of one of the article 26 derogations. It is composed of the representatives of the member states and chaired by the representative of the Commission[645], and provides the

---

[636] The same.
[637] Recital 64.
[638] Article 29 (1)
[639] Recital 65.
[640] Article 29 (2)
[641] Article 30 (1) (a)
[642] Article 30 (1) (b)
[643] Article 30 (1) (c)
[644] Article 30 (1) (d)
[645] Article 31 (1)

Commission with their opinion on the draft of measures proposed by the latter[646]. If the proposed measures are drafted in a manner conflicting with the Committee's opinion then they shall be communicated to the Council, which by qualified majority can take within three months a different decision[647].

6.25. Implementing the Directive

"At the latest at the end of a period of three years of its adoption member states shall bring into force the laws, regulations and administrative provisions necessary to comply with the directive"[648]. The directive entered into effect on 25 October 1998. By the date it should have been implemented in national legal orders, almost all member states had passed the respective legislation[649]. However, five of them (France, Luxembourg, the Netherlands, Germany and Ireland) failed to notify the Commission about the measures necessary to adopt the directive, thus the Commission "took them to Court"[650].

The Commission also emphasised the direct effect of the data protection directive. This was an important step in enhancing the protection afforded to European citizens as it entails the ability to invoke some of the directive's provisions before the national courts even before the actual implementing legislation is passed[651]. Moreover, in some cases private individuals are even in a position to claim damages for a breach of a directive's provision due to their state's inability to implement the directive in its national legal order[652].

---

[646] Article 31 (2)
[647] The same
[648] Article 32 (1)

[649] See also: The European Commission, DG Internal Market, Status of implementation of Directive 95/46 on the Protection of Individuals with regard to the Processing of Personal Data, available at: http://europa.eu.int/comm/internal_market/privacy/law/implementation_en.htm

[650] Data protection: Commission takes five Member States to court, available at: http://europa.eu.int/rapid/start/cgi/guesten.ksh?p_action.gettxt=gt&doc=IP/00/10|0|AGED&lg=EN&displ ay= accessed on 16/8/2003.
[651] See Case 42/74, Van Duyn v Home Office, [1974] ECR 1337 and case C-106/89 Marleasing SA v La Commercial Internacionale de Alimentacion [1990] ECR I-4135 [1992] 1 CMLR 305.
[652] Cases C-6 & 9/90 Francovich & Bunifaci v Italy [1991] ECR I-5357, [1993]2 CMLR66.

151

7. Data Protection in Europe. The Legal and Historical Developments which led to the Directive and related Case Law

7.1 The case of France

"More than 100 years ago, long before the concept of data in its temporary sense was conceived of, the French historian Alexis de Tocquenille postulated that if the private rights of an individual are violated...the manners of a nation are corrupted, jeopardising the entire society"[653]. This view embodies the central ideals that marked the privacy debate in France since the nineteenth century. France along with Germany were the two countries that placed their clear imprint on the Data Protection directive and influenced decisively the ideological debate that accompanied the proposal for the directive at European level. It is going to be demonstrated that the roots of the data protection regime in Europe as it stands now, was the outcome of the philosophical, historical and political developments mainly in these two countries, whose legal cultures remain as two of the most evocative and influential in the continent. It is important to analyse the process that led to the development of the directive in both countries, because in this manner the theoretical background of the directive, the legal premise on which subsequent law was based on and the confrontational debate that spread even at the other part of the Atlantic are going to be better illuminated and understood. Thus, the debate with the US that follows at the next chapter of the book can be viewed and judged in its historical context.

In France the concept of privacy is treated as "a value primarily threatened by two forces: the excesses of the free press and the excesses of the free market"[654]. The elaboration of the concept can be traced back to the nineteenth century and was closely linked to the notion of "honour", a value that stood at the centre of the nobility's ideals at that time. Thus, the honour of the aristocracy in France at the beginning of that century was seen to be threatened mainly by rumours that could be spread unjustifiably by the press and by the side effects of the market economy and the constant commercial

---

[653] Campbell Dennis, Fisher Joy, Data Transmission and Privacy, Martinus Nijhoff Publishers, London, 1994, page 1
[654] Whitman Q James, The Two Western Cultures of Privacy, Dignity versus Liberty, 113 Yale Law Journal, April 2004, page 1171.

transactions that were taking place in Parisian society at that point. French privacy law began to take its shape as a response to these situations that placed unimaginable burdens on the right of the French citizens, and more on the French aristocrats back then, to protect their honour. "Privacy law has been in essence the history of the resistance in the name of honour of two of the most fundamental values of American liberty: the value of free speech and the value of private property as distributed through the market"[655]. This balance was also expressed in the French Constitution of 1791, where the press was afforded a wide array of protection, but at the same time, safeguards were inserted against "private life injuries"[656]. The threats towards privacy at that period stemmed mainly from the press. Here, it has to be noted that with this constitutional provision the right to privacy appeared for the first time in a constitutional document albeit in an indirect manner. It was not an explicit reference to a clearly stated right of privacy, but it was viewed as some sort of limitation imposed upon the freedom of press, so widely defined at that moment. And it is obvious from the context that the right of privacy was still considered to be bound up with nobility as mainly the latter would deal with problems related to press publications. However, since we are talking about a document that regulates the affairs of the whole nation, it is obvious that in an equivalent situation all French citizens irrespective of their social status could benefit. Thus, the protection, although indirect, was extended to the whole of the French society.

Judges have played a very influential role in establishing a right to privacy in France. Although, such a right as analysed above, was not specifically provided for in the Constitution, the Court promoted its existence and shaped its form as early as in 1858. In the *Rachel*[657] case an actress was passing her last moments in her death bed, when her sister hired a photographer to take some photos of her in such a situation. Although, a different agreement was made, the photographs found their way to the public exposure. The Court, based on article 1382 of the Civil Code that restricted publication of private life facts without the consent of the person involved, stated that "the right to oppose this reproduction is absolute, it cannot be ignored without stirring the most intimate sentiments...where the human personality is an issue...and

---

[655] The same.
[656] See Constitution of September 3rd 1791, at: http://www.premier-ministre.gouv.fr/fr/p.cfm?ref=15008 accessed on August 12th.
[657] Tribunal du Premiere Instance de la Seine, 1858, June 16th, DP III 62.

personality rights are inherently inalienable"[658]. Thus, it ordered the seizure of the photos and banned further reproduction. This type of justification shares many similarities with the approach on the other side of the Rhine and is based on the notion of "personality" and the respect that is due to it. The balance struck by the Court here is delicate and in some terms controversial. The seizure of the photographs was deemed to violate the rights of the photographer, who "had a property right, the copyright in the photographs"[659]. Furthermore, as noted before, privacy in *Rachel* was found to be strictly related to the notion of "personality". Indeed, "in the French legal system privacy rights are but one of a bundle of personality rights, as are the moral rights of creators…thus, the personality rights include the moral rights of authors, the right to privacy, the right to control the use of one's image, and the right to protect one's honour and reputation…and just as an author's moral rights give him control over his artistic creation, the other personality rights give individuals the power to control and regulate the use of various attributes of the self"[660]. Thus, inherent in the judgement in *Rachel*, and through this in the law of privacy as it functioned in France, was a conflict between the two personality rights: on the one hand the right of the creator to control his artistic creation and on the other the right of the individual to privacy, which was linked with the notions of reputation, honour and control on the use of one's image. The decision represents the magnitude of importance that the French courts and legal order was about to afford to the protection of private life, even in cases of conflict with other rights also linked with the concept of personality. The discussions taking place today over the balance between the self regulation of internet as the cornerstone of on line freedom, and the regulation of restrictions to protect privacy even by placing some limits on some on line functions finds its roots in the continental legal tradition.

The same balance and the conflict behind it were demonstrated in *Dumas*[661]. In this case Dumas sued for the publication of photos, whose rights he had sold. Although, the photographer had "a property right, the copyright in the photographs… and this was the mid nineteenth century and property rights were regarded as something closed to sacred in the legal cosmos of the day…the Court found a countervailing right to

---

[658] Hauch M Jeanne, Protecting Private Facts in France: the Warren & Brandeis Tort is Alive and Well and Flourishing in Paris, 68 Tulane Law Review, 1994, pages 1233 and 1234.
[659] Whitman James, supra note 655, page 1176.
[660] Hauch M Jeanne, supra note 659, pages 1228 and 1229.
[661] Dumas, Appeals Court, Paris, May 25th 1867.

property: the right to privacy...which qualified the absolute claims of the law of property"[662]. The Court ruled that "even if a person had tacitly consented to the publication of embarrassing photos, that person must retain the right to withdraw his consent...because...he has forgotten to take care of his dignity"[663]. Even more importantly, the Court stated that "privacy must be allowed to trump property...because privacy as an aspect of one's honour was not a market commodity that could simply be definitely sold...any such sale by a person who had forgotten his dignity had to remain effectively voidable"[664]. Thus, the right to privacy is closely linked not only with the notion of "personality" but also with that of "human dignity". In other words privacy is found to be bound to two of the most fundamental values of mankind protected at the highest possible level by all national constitutions and international treaties as they form the hard core of human rights and values. That's the place reserved by the French legal culture to privacy. At the centre of the basic humanistic values. This statement will be shown to be reflected in the ideals of the German legal tradition as well. On the contrary the situation and the evaluations on the other side of the Atlantic are significantly divergent.

Under this light, in the press law of 1868, publishing "a fact of a person's private life"[665] could be fined, a provision that was found controversial, highly exaggerated and finally removed in the following 1881 law. However remained indicative of the centrality of the right to privacy in the French legal order. Throughout the nineteenth century the right to privacy was shaped through judicial decisions. Case law remained the main source of indication over the reinforced status of the relevant right in France. Although, it was judicially articulated as early as in 1858, its expansion and enaction came almost a hundred years later and more specifically in 1970. The Privacy Act of 1970 "provides for the general mechanism of protection of private life...and article 22 of the Act was incorporated in the Civil Code under Article 9"[666]. It reads "everybody has the right to require respect of his private life"[667]. In France "the

[662] Whitman Q James, supra note 655, page 1176.
[663] The same.
[664] The same.
[665] Baker R Wallace, deFontbressin Patrick, The French Refere Procedure and Conflicts of Human Rights, 25 Syracuse Journal of International Law and Commerce, Spring 1998, page 79.
[666] Dupre Catherine, The Protection of Private Life Against Freedom of Expression in French Law, European Human Rights Law Review, 6, 2000, page 627.
[667] Chacun a droit au respect de sa vie privée. Les juges peuvent, sans préjudice de la réparation du dommage subi, prescrire toutes mesures, telles que séquestre, saisie et autres, propres à empêcher ou faire cesser une atteinte à l'intimité de la vie privée; ces

right of privacy extends to all aspects of an individual's spiritual and individual being…each person has the exclusive power to define the boundaries of his private life and the circumstances under which private information may be divulged publicly"[668]. "The right is meant to provide each individual with the security that he will be free from unwarranted intrusions so that he may enjoy a certain liberty as he lives his private life in a free society"[669]. Thus, the right to privacy is also connected with personal liberty apart from dignity and personality. Its character assumes a universality, which underlines its significance. At this point the French legal theory and practise make another step closer to the German approach, which also focuses on the link between privacy, liberty, human dignity and personality standing at the centre of an individual's life in a free democratic society. The Act of 1970 introduced the requirement of a "breach of intimate private life…which was clearly understood as meaning a more restrictive dimension of private life"[670], that has to be defended[671] "against the onslaught of electronic technology designed to capture and communicate an ever expanding array of sensory data concerning human life"[672]. Although, specialised legislation focused on privacy rendered France a pioneer on the issue the Constitution of the French Republic of 1958 does not include an explicit right to privacy. The Constitutional Court of France asserted with its rulings that such a right is implicit in the French Constitution[673].

---

mesures peuvent, si il y a urgence, être ordonnées en référé. See: http://www.rabenou.org/code/civil/L1T1.htm accessed on August 12th 2004.

[668] Gigante Alexander, Ice Patch on the Information superhighway: Foreign Liability for Domestically Created Content, 14 Cardozo Arts & Entertainment Law Journal, 1996, page 543.

[669] Hauch M Jeanne, supra note 659, page 1222.

[670] Dupre Catherine, supra note 667 at page 645.

[671] Here, the issue is the area of an individual's life that can be deemed as most intimate. This remark, once again, bears great similarities with the German theories of the "personality spheres". As it had been the case of Germany, the same definitional problems of the "intimacy area" were detected also on the French theory. However, in practice this most intimate part of personal life has been found to comprise health, sexual and family life. As it will be explained later in the German context, this space usually refers to the activities that are included in article 8 of the directive as "sensitive personal data". Data that due to their more intimate nature require a priori a greater level of protection irrespective of other requirements. However, apart from some generally accepted areas, the member states have also enacted additional categories of sensitive data in accordance with their distinctive national cultures.

[672] Hauch M Jeanne, supra note 659, page 1223.

[673] Décision 94-352 du Conseil Constitutionnel du 18 Janvier 1995.

7.1.1 The directive in the French legal order

In France in September 2000 CNIL (Commission Nationale de L'Informatique et Libertes) gave its opinion "on a preliminary draft law concerning the protection of individuals with regard to the processing of personal data and amending law 78-17 of 6 January 1978 on data processing, files and freedoms"[674]. In July 2001 the minister of Justice presented the draft law to the Council of Ministers and in January 2002 the National Assembly adopted the new law on personal data protection. As recently as in April 2003 the Senate adopted the implementation law and thus France finally transposed the directive into its national legal order[675]. The implementation of the directive in the French legal order came as a natural evolution of the already existing data protection legislation of 1978[676] and the legislation of "17 July 1971, tending to reinforce the guarantee of individual rights of citizens that established the right of the respect of privacy as an entitlement of individual rights"[677]. The 78-17 of 1978 law, which applied to automated data processing and to all lists computer based or not[678] provided for a similar array of rights related to on line privacy abuses with that of the subsequent directive. According to that, "computer technology must be available to every citizen and may not undermine human dignity, human rights, privacy or individual and public liberties"[679]. The influence of the spirit of the 1978 French data protection law on the EU directive is laid bare. CNIL has been quite active in

---

[674] The European Commission, DG Internal Market, Fifth Annual Report on the Situation regarding the Protection of Individuals with regard to the Processing of Personal Data and Privacy in the European Union and in third Countries, Covering the year 2000, Part II, Adopted on March 6th 2002, Luxembourg, page 8.
[675] See the chronological progress of the adoption of the implementing legislation at the site of CNIL: http://www.cnil.fr/frame.htm?http://www.cnil.fr/textes/directiv.htm
The legislative act in question can be accessed at: http://www.cnil.fr/textes/docs/CNIL-Loi78-17_modSenat1-VI.pdf

[676] See the law at: http://www.cnil.fr/index.php?id=301#Article1 July 14th 2006.
[677] Charles de Haas, in Michael Henry, International Privacy, Publicity & Personality Laws, Butterworths, 2001 Décision 94-352 du Conseil Constitutionnel du 18 Janvier 1995 Décision 94-352 du Conseil Constitutionnel du 18 Janvier 19951, page 133.
[678] Article 2: La présente loi s'applique aux traitements automatisés de données à caractère personnel, ainsi qu'aux traitements non automatisés de données à caractère personnel contenues ou appelées à figurer dans des fichiers, à l'exception des traitements mis en oeuvre pour l'exercice d'activités exclusivement personnelles
[679] Sophie Nerbonne, in Frank Hendrickx, Employment Privacy Law in the European Union: Surveillance and Monitoring, Intersentia, Antwerpen , Oxford , New York, 2002, page 91. Original text of Article 1: L'informatique doit être au service de chaque citoyen. Son développement doit s'opérer dans le cadre de la coopération internationale. Elle ne doit porter atteinte ni à l'identité humaine, ni aux droits de l'homme, ni à la vie privée, ni aux libertés individuelles ou publiques.

highlighting the dangers rising from the use of internet for consumers and has presented detailed reports on on-line privacy issues[680].

7.2 The case of Germany

Germany has played an essential and important role in fostering data protection in Europe as it is a country with strong legal tradition in the particular field. "Germans take data protection very seriously and this is reflected partly in the extensive amount of...case law and public discussion...devoted specifically to privacy"[681]. "Data protection is firmly rooted in the Constitution in particular through the seminal 1983 *Census* judgement"[682]. The Census judgement, which will be further analysed, is deemed of major importance for Germany and the whole of the EU as well as it was a decision of the Constitutional Court that introduced "a new constitutional right: the right of informational self-determination"[683]. It embodies the right "of each individual to decide by himself the communication and the use of the information related to him"[684].

German cultural and historical developments are of high importance as the evolution of this debate in Germany provided the theoretical basis and the legal framework, within which EU data protection law shaped and evolved. German case law and academics contributed to the debate by offering solid arguments, which influenced data protection issues at European level. In Germany it was not the rapid developments of technology that fuelled the relevant discussions but some rather painful historical experiences that marked German and European history throughout the twentieth century. The latter are related to the rise of Nazism in the country and everything that it brought to humanity. "Nazi Germany was a society in which privacy was for all practical purposes nonexistent. When the individual was not actually under

---

[680] See: http://www.cnil.fr/traces/traces.htm
[681] Bygrave in Philippa Webb, A Comparative Analysis of Data Protection Laws in Germany and Australia, (2) Journal of Information, Law and Technology, 15 December 2003, (JILT).
[682] The European Commission, DG Internal Market, Existing case law on compliance with data protection laws and principles in the Member States of the European Union, Korff Douwe, Annex to the Annual Report 1998, of the Working Party established by article 29 of the Directive 95/46EC, Luxembourg, page 30.
[683] Le Senat, La Protection des Donnees Personnelles, Les Principaux Textes, Allemagne, accessed at: www.senat.fr/lc/lc62/lc621.html on 30/06/2003.
[684] The same.

surveillance, he was always possessed by the fear that he might be"[685]. Degradation of human values and contempt for the basic guarantees of human existence shed its shadow not only on the German legal world but also on the society as a whole, which developed certain sensitivities and fears. It has to be added that Germany had been the place where philosophical ideals that emphasised the value of human beings and the absolute obligation for respect of human personality had flourished the previous century. Kant had elaborated the concept of human dignity in his influential "Foundations of the Metaphysics of Morals"[686], where he argued that "all moral agents should develop their talents to the maximum extent compatible with the freedom of others". From Kant's theoretical principles, it can be deduced that philosophical debates in Germany concentrated on the issue of individual freedoms, the ability of man to develop his personality to the fullest capacity and the limits that are placed on this process by the demands and the needs of the organised industrial society, where collective objectives have to be equally served. The balance between the two ends continues to be at the centre of constitutional debates worldwide even today. Thus, it is worth noting that Germany became a fertile land where fundamentally conflicting ideals related both to the respect of human rights and their absolute degradation, happened to evolve steadily. It has to be noted that a very significant role in the process of consolidating a strong legal regime that could safeguard human rights values was effectively played by the Federal Constitutional Court of Germany, whose case law remains highly influential not only for the domestic but also for foreign legal orders.

The German constitution, or rather the Basic Law, was adopted in 1949, only four years after the end of the World War II. The adoption of the constitutional text was seen as the means to smash the links with the recent decadent past and re-found the German constitutional landscape this time with vivid references to the human dignity ideals envisaged by Kant. Thus, the Basic Law is a "value orientated constitution that obligates the state to realise a set of objectively realised principles rooted in justice and equality that are designed to restore the centrality of humanity to the social order and thereby secure a stable democratic society on this basis"[687]. More significantly, the

---

[685] Senator Edward V. Long, The Intruders, The Invasion of Privacy by Government and Industry, Frederick A. Praeger, New York, Washington, London, 1967, page 22.
[686] Groundwork of the Metaphysics of Morals. Edited by Mary Gregor, Cambridge University Press, New York, 1998 .
[687] Eberle J Edward, Human Dignity, Privacy and Personality in German and American Constitutional Law, Utah Law Review, 1997, page 967.

Kantian concept of the organisation of state, where the rule of law would prevail, initiatives on behalf of the state would be based on a clearly defined legal basis and would comply totally with the fundamental principle of proportionality[688], was regulated at a constitutional level. Furthermore, "it included a body of fundamental rights...with articles of most significance for the issue of privacy"[689]. "German privacy law grew in large part out of an effort to create a richer German alternative...especially to English ideas of liberty"[690]. The distinctive feature of "the protection of privacy in the German tradition is regarded as an aspect of the protection of...personality, a characteristically dense German concept, with roots in the philosophy of Kant, Humboldt and Hegel"[691]. The "personality right, which is jointly created by the two first articles of the Basic Law, constitutes the basis for the protection of the individual"[692] and comprises the right to personal dignity. This array of constitutional protection afforded at the highest possible institutional level has been interpreted by the Federal Constitutional Court to include as a basic element the protection of personal data. Articles 1 and 2 of the German Constitution read:

Article 1 [Human dignity]

(1) Human dignity shall be inviolable. To respect and protect it shall be the duty of all state authority.

(2) The German people therefore acknowledge inviolable and inalienable human rights as the basis of every community, of peace and of justice in the world.

(3) The following basic rights shall bind the legislature, the executive, and the judiciary as directly applicable law.

Article 2 [Personal freedoms]

(1) Every person shall have the right to free development of his personality insofar as he does not violate the rights of others or offend against the constitutional order or the moral law.

---

[688] See Groundwork of the Metaphysics of Morals, supra note 683 for further analysis.
[689] Craig John DR, Nolte Nico, Privacy and Free Speech in Germany and Canada: Lessons for an English Privacy Tort, 2 European Human Rights Law Review, 1998, Sweet & Maxwell, 162.
[690] Whitman Q. James, The Two western Cultures of Privacy: Dignity versus Liberty, 113 Yale Law Journal, April2004, page 1180.
[691] The same.
[692] Thwaite J Gregory, Brehm Wolfgang, German Privacy and Defamation Law: The Right to Publish in the shadow of the Right to Human Dignity, 16 (8) European Intellectual Property Law Review, 1994, page 337.

(2) Every person shall have the right to life and physical integrity. Freedom of the person shall be inviolable. These rights may be interfered with only pursuant to a law.

Article 10 (Privacy of letters, posts, and telecommunications). (amended 24 June 1968)[693]

1. Privacy of letters, posts, and telecommunications shall be inviolable.

2. Restrictions may only be ordered pursuant to a statute. Where a restriction serves to protect the free democratic basic order or the existence or security of the Federation, the statute may stipulate that the person affected shall not be informed of such restriction and that recourse to the courts shall be replaced by a review of the case by bodies and auxiliary bodies appointed by Parliament.

The codification of a catalogue of human rights with human dignity at the top, in the text of the constitution signalled a much needed change in the approach of the country towards basic human values. The "inviolability" of human dignity renders it "the highest legal value in Germany of the free person"[694]. The right to human dignity is inherent in the personality right, which is enshrined in articles 1 and 2 of the Basic Law. It is heavily related to the right to the "free development of personality" as provided for in Article 2. Personality is a concept that "Germans invoke when Americans would invoke liberty, and like liberty it does involve a kind of freedom"[695]. Only for Americans "liberty" is translated into freedom from state control and ability to participate independently in the market process, while for Germans it embodies their thirst to "be left alone"[696] to "give full expression of their capacities and powers"[697]. In *Elfes*[698], the Court provided one of the most clarifying indications on the scope it affords to the right of personality. Elfes[699], who was a political activist, requested a visa to travel abroad so as to participate in yet another political event. He was denied the visa on the grounds that his activities were threatening national security. He argued that

---

[693] Cf Bundesgerichtshof Betriebs Berater 1990, 739. The Federal Supreme Court held in February 1990 that this article is addressed as well o individuals regulating their personal relations with other citizens. The opening of a letter is a violation of the right of the personality of the sender and the addressee.
[694] Eberle J Edward, supra note 688, page 973.
[695] Whitman Q James, supra note 655, page 1181.
[696] Thwaite and Brehm, supra note 693, page 337.
[697] Whitman, supra note 655, page 1181.
[698] 6 BVerGE 32, 1957.
[699] See: http://www.iuscomp.org/gla/ accessed on August 11th 2004.

the denial on behalf of the authorities to issue him a visa was against his right of personality. The Court agreed by illustrating the "catch-all function of article 2 personality rights, which capture claims not protected by the more specific guarantees in the catalogue of personal rights"[700]. Personality rights were now connected to a general "freedom of action", which could be limited only by constitutionally provided limitations or rights of third parties[701]. This ruling is of major significance as the right to privacy is not specifically provided for in the Constitution in an independent manner but, it has been interpreted by the Court to fall within the ambit of the right to human dignity and personality that as analysed above constitute the most high ranking values in the catalogue of constitutionally protected human rights in the German legal order. Thus, the case law shed light over the application of these fundamental principles of the German legal order on situations concerning the violation of privacy. In *Census* the Court determined that "personality rights include protection of informational privacy"[702].

7.2.1 Case Law on Privacy

7.2.1.1 Mikrozensus Case

The *Mikrozensus*[703] in 1969 case was a seminal one in the privacy context. It provided the Court with the chance to start developing its jurisprudence on the issue. The judgements were meant to influence the way the whole European data protection construction was about to be shaped. The object of the case was a questionnaire distributed by federal authorities to citizens enquiring about some of their habits such as their standard of living. The questionnaire was aiming at forming a profile of the population according to which more efficient policies could be designed at federal level. The intrusion into what was later defined as "spheres of personal life" provoked overt reactions on behalf of the public opinion, which remained sensitive on this issue due to the painful experiences of the recent past. In its decision the Constitutional Court insisted on the limits imposed upon the ability of the state to collect information for

---

[700] Eberle, supra note 688, page 981.
[701] See article 2 (1) of the Basic Law.
[702] Census Case, 65 BVerfGE 1, 64, 1983.
[703] BVerGE 27,1.

statistical purposes and emphasises its judgement that the compulsory collection of such data, which the state purports to keep in its own files even if these are held anonymously, is in direct contrast with the principle of human dignity. The treatment of the citizens was not one that revealed respect of mankind as the latter becomes the object of control on behalf of the state. Since personal information was required the case fell in the scope of article 2 of the constitution. Thus, the Constitutional Court ruled that "the state could not take any measure, enact any law, which would violate or infringe the essence of personal freedom as encompassed within the limits of article 2"[704]. Protecting personal data as an aspect of the right to personality, was found to be the barrier beyond which the state cannot move as simply as that. Otherwise, the state would infringe the right of human dignity bestowed on every citizen and that would bring it within the jurisdiction of the Court. The level of protection afforded by the Court is impressive. Protection of privacy forms an integral part of the hard core of the German institutional order. As the Court concluded in this case, "the Basic Law guarantees individuals an inviolable area of personal freedom in which one can freely develop his life (and personality) and thus, all state interference should be removed from this space"[705]. The Court recognises the creation of a "personal sphere", an "inner realm" (Innenraum), where the individual can expect to remain intact from intrusions. And subsequently every collection of data for statistical purposes is not found to infringe the personality right unless it touches upon data that fall within this intimate space[706]. The Court underlines that the judgement is consistent with the principles of human dignity and autonomy and reserves man "at root in the Basic Law"[707]. The influence of Kant with his emphasis on providing the space for the unfolding of human capacity is decisive.

However, the distinction the Court made on the basis of three types of personal spheres provided the basis of a wide debate between the Court and academics, who argued that such a distinction creates uncertainties over the precise limits of the aforementioned spheres. The first sphere is the "social", which "concerns the public, economic and professional appearance of the individual"[708], the second is the "intimate

---

[704] Mikrozensus 27 BVerGE at 6.
[705] The same.
[706] Mikrozensus at 7.
[707] Mikrozensus at 6.
[708] Craig DR John, supra note 690, page 174.

sphere", which "covers the inner world of thoughts and feelings" and the final one is the "private"[709] one that "offers an intermediate level of protection to personal matters, which are not by their very nature of public interest"[710]. This conflict although, it appears to be purely theoretical has a special significance since it affects the status of "sensitive personal data", which were analysed above. It supports that the classification of data as simply personal or sensitive, to which a greater degree of protection is afforded, is based on the nature of the data in question and not on the dangers inherent in their processing. Thus, the focus for the distinction is on the data and not on the nature of the processing. Accordingly, the protection granted to data is to be shaped at a different level corresponding with the sphere that the data in question falls to. If we are talking about data that falls into the "intimate sphere", the protection has to be absolute, in sharp contrast to data included in the other two spheres that can be subject to limitations. This theory, which assumed a principal position in the theoretical background of the privacy debate, can lead to confusion and uncertainty over the exact scope of protection. Recognising that some categories of data such as the ones concerning health, have some speciality since they really fall into the absolute intimate scope of an individual's personality, is a necessary point for the debate to depart from. This is heavily supported by the character of the specific data that can cause embarrassment to an individual and have an impact on his relations with other individuals or on his employment and insurance arrangements. However, as in almost all areas of law there are no absolute distinctions. The complete separation between the nature of data and the processing can cause interpretational difficulties. The processing of health data by the individual's personal doctor is valuable for the patient as it creates a history on which prescriptions and medications are based. Nobody would object to that. However, processing of such data by a pharmaceutical company for its marketing campaign or on behalf of an insurance company or a trade union create a completely different situation. Thus, although we should distinguish some part of our personal life that has more intimate characteristics, and that is exactly the choice made by the directive, it is futile to ignore the specific conditions of the processing in question. The whole construction by the court of the three spheres is a bit vague as it would be difficult to definitely discover the exact classification of information. It has some purely legalistic characteristics that blur the borderline between the categories proposed. It

---

[709] The same

164

fails to take into account all the dimensions of the issue. In any case apart from specific types of data that can be universally accepted as "intimate" and strictly personal, and these are the ones that justifiably form the object of article 8 of the directive, the relevant classification is heavily influenced by distinctive cultural patterns. Hence, the book argues for the separation of some of the data solely because their content and character necessitates a greater degree of protection, but cannot support this complicated theoretical construction that fails to consider other crucial parameters such as the reasons and the nature of processing. An example of this, are the different interpretations afforded to article 8 on sensitive data protection of the directive by the different member states, which included in the relevant list divergent categories of data that in their respective societies are deemed to demand stricter protection. For example in the French law implementing article 8 of the directive, information about the individual's private and family life is not included in the list of sensitive data, in sharp contrast with the Scandinavian countries, where such inclusion was made.

7.2.1.2 Zensus Case

The Zensus[711] case constitutes another landmark case that although judged at federal German level had a decisive impact on data protection at pan-European level. The Federal Census Act of 1983 provided the grounds for a new round of controversy. The Act was passed in order to regulate and enable the collection of data of social and demographic nature on behalf of the citizens. The data was necessary for the planning and the design of government policies on a more effective basis. The data required, did not only concern the obvious areas of names, addresses and gender, but extended to more personal types of information such as the declaration of religious affiliations[712]. The most alarming fact was that the Act permitted the sharing of the relevant information with local governments that could consequently use the data for the shaping of their own policies. The case was brought to the Court following the uproar of public opinion reflected also in the national press. The Court suspended the on going

---

[710] The same
[711] BVerfGE 65, 1983.
[712] Zensus, ibid at 4-7 and 12-13.

census, until it could reach a decision on its constitutionality. What was at stake here was the privacy of millions of citizens, which could be heavily invaded by the creation of extensive profiles with the characteristics of the widest possible range of the population. Thus, the controversy touches upon, for the first time, the new technology that could now facilitate such plans for the creation of collective profiles. The Court observed that the threats against human liberty are now advanced "due to the advent of new computer technology"[713]. And it concluded that since the principle of human dignity and value stand at the core of the constitutional protection along with the right of self determination of an individual as a member of a democratic society, these principles must continue to be firmly respected "in the light of new developments and the threats they entail to human personality"[714]. In its effort to adapt the human dignity principle to the changing economic parameters, it introduced what will remain in history as the "right of informational self determination". As the technological developments enable advanced processing of personal data that can now be linked easily with the data subject, new challenges are posed to human autonomy[715]. The individual's personal development and along with it the well being of the society would be seriously impaired, if the individuals lack knowledge over what is being communicated about them. Thus, they may refrain from exercising certain of their rights especially those related to freedom of religion, expression and political affiliation[716]. The function of a democratic society would be subsequently undermined as its citizens' willingness to participate would have received a decisive blow. Thus, the citizens must be protected through the establishment of a right of informational self determination that would allow at least up to an extent control over one's own personal data.

However, the Court places a limit upon the right of informational self determination, and therefore, departs from its previous position of "personal spheres" that determined the protection of the data concerned. The protection afforded was in respect of the sphere in which the data in question was classified. Focus was on the content of data irrespective of other factors. In *Zensus* the Court marks a shift in its approach. After arguing that there is "a social dimension to personal data…related to

---

[713] Zensus, at 17 and 42.
[714] Zensus at 41.
[715] Zensus at 43.
[716] The same.

the needs of public authorities to design policies to serve the public interest"[717], "citizens must accept certain limitations to their right to informational self determination on over ridding public interest grounds"[718]. These limitations as stated above, can flow from the obligation to consider another individuals rights. This principle of a pure Kantian nature, has a constitutional basis on article 2 (1), and provides that "the protection of one person's personality and privacy when clashing, for example, with another person's freedom of expression the competing values will have to be balanced"[719]. Especially, since a range of rights, such as the right of expression (article 5 (1)) are also enshrined in the constitution. Such a balancing test between human dignity and privacy on the one hand and the right of expression on the other, was applied by the Court in *Mephisto*[720] and *Lebach*[721], where, however, it concluded that due to factual arguments and the application of the principle of proportionality the right of expression had to be limited. The important point is that the two rights were being put in a balancing process. The limitation of the right of informational self determination can also stem from a law enacted by the parliament on a solid legal basis that therefore forms a part of the constitutional order of the country as demanded again by article 2 (1). By this law limitations can be introduced provided of course that the latter are in compliance with the principle of proportionality that discourages excessive measures as means to achieve an end. Hence, the Court ruled that the collection of data for a national census on which national policies are to be based, is legitimate[722]. In order to reach this conclusion the Court examined the nature of the information, the method of collection and its stated uses[723]. The reasoning and the criteria used to legitimise the data collection can reveal the source of influence on the European directive that has great similarities with the regulatory conclusions of the presented German cases. The German legal culture definitely had a massive impact on the rationale behind the directive, its theoretical background and the historical premise on which it was promoted.

---

[717] Zensus at 44.
[718] The same.
[719] Amelung Ulrich Tilman, Damage Awards for Infringement of Privacy, The German Approach, 14 Tulane European and Civil Law forum, 1999, page 37.
[720] Mephisto 30 BVerfGE 30, 173, 1971. See also: http://www.iuscomp.org/gla/ accessed on August 11th 2004.
[721] Lebach 35 BVerfGE 202, 1973.
[722] Zensus, at 47.
[723] Zensus at 46.

At this point I have to comment upon the new approach adopted by the Court. In the light of the new developments the Court abandoned the determination of the degree of sensitivity of data in accordance with their nature, which was to be determined by the sphere they fall into. Now, the new technological abilities entail a new approach concentrated more on the objective of the processing. If this is provided by law, concerns the serving of the public interest, satisfies the criterion of proportionality and is adequately scrutinised by the relevant authorities, the informational self determination right can be limited. The critical factor for the protection of data is not the vague definition of the sphere they belong to, but the ability to be processed in close relation to its objective. This approach is more realistic and has a positive effect as it enables clarity and focuses on the real risks. The directive was built on these parameters, something that proved the prevailing part of the debate, which however continues up to now on whether sensitive data should form a separate category or not. This issue has already been thoroughly analysed in this book.

7.2.1.3 Tagebuch Case

The *Tagebuch* case[724] (Diary case) concerned the ability of the Court to use or not the diary of a man as a piece of evidence in the framework of a trial. The man was accused of murder and kept a diary after consultation with his therapist, who urged him to write down his thoughts. His insecurities, private thoughts and inability to have a relationship with women were all demonstrated with detail. In addition to all this, the acts he described presented some similarities with the murder he was accused of committing. The dispute erupted when the diary was proposed to be brought in the trial as a part of the evidence. The court expressed its belief that the presentation of the diary, which includes personal thoughts and feelings of the individual, will constitute a violation of his personality right enshrined in the constitution. The personal space he has to structure and express his thoughts and consequently his ability to develop his personality will be infringed[725].However, the diary, albeit a part of his personal life, had to be presented to the Court as the "general public interest" demanded so[726]. The Court

---

[724] See Tagebuch, BVerfGE 80, 367, 1989.
[725] Tagesbuch, at 368 and 369.
[726] The same.

confirmed its adherence to informational self determination right but declared at the same time that "the overriding public interest element will serve as the limitation imposed upon it"[727]. The use of a diary in the context of criminal case "touched the private sphere and was consequently subject to a balancing test…the prevailing public interest in the efficient administration of criminal justice and crime prevention was a sufficient reason for allowing their taking it into evidence"[728].

The interesting point in this case, was that the Court attempted to reconcile the two approaches it had adopted in the *Mikrozensus* and the *Zensus* cases. In its effort, however, it fostered an approach that was marked by contradictions and revealed the difficulties emerging from the spheres theory when it comes to defining the limits of protection. While allowing the presentation of the diary, it concluded that "even overriding public interest might not justify the intrusion into the most intimate sphere"[729] to which the diary with all the personal thoughts that contained was presumed to belong. Thus, according to the Court, the right of informational determination and personality can be limited when the outcomes of the balancing test with overriding public interest allow so, but still there is "a hard core of personality from which all official entry is prohibited"[730]. However, after admitting the existence of such a hard core of personality that remains inviolable even against public interest, it resorted to actually balancing the "inviolable" part of personality with the need to promote justice and concluded that the promotion of the needs of justice prevails. The approach of the Court reveals a serious inability to provide a certain clear definition of its previously stated theory of the spheres. The ruling in *Tagebuch* proves that the specific theory has serious definitional problems and is very difficult to be applied in court due to its vagueness. The balancing test, which the Court promoted in this case can certainly promote the needs of justice, while protecting the interests of the subject if it is found that his personality and privacy rights supersede the trial needs. But, basing a ruling on the theoretical and hard to comprehend, heavily legalistic, greatly inflexible and difficult to interpret sphere construction can only lead to confusion as this case proves.

---

[727] Tagesbuch, at 373.
[728] Rehm Gebhard, 32 University of West Los Angeles Law Review, 2001, page 288.
[729] Tagesbuch at 373.

7.2.1.4 Regulatory Developments in Germany

The system of data protection in Germany is quite complex. It is based on the federal law of 1990 on the protection of personal data of natural persons, on various sectoral federal laws "that apply specifically to certain categories of data"[731] and finally on data protection laws adopted at the level of the German federal states (Laender) applying mainly in the public sector activities. The federal law of 1990 had replaced the respective law of 1977, which turned Germany into "the first country to possess a general law in the particular field"[732]. Thus, legislation was in place "when problems did begin to manifest themselves albeit the emerging law did not sufficiently foresee the different threats consequent on internet technology and the legacy is legislation which is arguably more relevant to a previous technological era"[733]. The main characteristic of the German data protection law was that it dealt with the public and private sectors in a different manner. The protection started "at the moment of the collection of the data in question"[734] and extended to all sorts of files and documents. On the contrary as far as the private sector was concerned the scope of protection was limited only to automatic or manual files. In March 1999, however the minister of Internal Affaires presented a draft law on data protection. In March 2001 the Federal Data Protection Act was adopted[735]. The new law applies to both "federal authorities and businesses"[736]. Furthermore, all federal states (Laender) "apart from Sachsen and Bremen adopted new data protection laws to implement the directive. These acts apply to the public sector of the respective Laender"[737]. The integration of the Data Protection Directive in the German legal order contributed to a great degree to the harmonisation of data protection within Germany. "The implementation of the EU directive into German law will regulate nearly all e-commerce related aspects of the processing and use of personal data of natural persons"[738]. Furthermore, it extended the protection

---

[730] The same.

[731] Le Senat, supra note 684.

[732] Le Senat, La Protection des Donnees Personnelles, Note de Synthese, accessed at: www.senat.fr/lc/lc62/lc620.html , accessed on 30/6/2003.

[733] Diane Rowland, Data Retention and the War against Terrorism – A Considered and Proportionate Response? 2004 (3) The Journal of Information, Law and Technology (JILT).

[734] Le Senat, supra note 684.

[735] Access it at: http://www.bfd.bund.de/information/bdsg_eng.pdf

[736] Drews Ludwig Hans, Data Privacy Protection in German, The Effects of the German Federal Protection Act from the perspective of Siemens AG, updated special reprint, February 2003, page2. Available at Siemens intranet at: http://dsb.siemens.de/dspages/InfoSchulung.htm

[737] See http://europa.eu.int/comm/internal_market/privacy/law/implementation_en.htm#germany

[738] Baker & McKenzie, Doing E-Commerce in Europe, A Report, 2001, page 91.

previously afforded by the federal laws to new fields of data that remained out of the ambit of protection. Although, the concept of "sensitive data" was absent from the text of the 1977 federal law, after the transposition of the directive "all the legal texts currently in force contain similar guarantees with those of the directive"[739].

7.3 The case of the United Kingdom

The case of the UK is quite interesting, because its case resembles more the situation and legal arguments raised in the US context rather than the respective ones expressed in Europe. The UK, however, presents interest also from another aspect. It is a country, where its legal system based on "English common law knows no general right of privacy and Parliament had been reluctant to introduce one"[740]. The relevant discussions on privacy in the UK had "traditionally concentrated on the actions of the press and other media"[741] and it was only until the case of *R v Brown*[742] that the spotlight was put on the threats stemming from information technology. In *Brown* it was stated that "English common law does not know a general right of privacy but...there has been some legislation to deal with particular aspects of the problem. The Data Protection Act 1984...is one such statute"[743]. "That the individual shall have full protection in person and in property is a principle as old as the common law; but it has been found necessary from time to time to define anew the exact nature and extent of such protection"[744]. Based on this premise, the need to introduce a right to privacy was becoming apparent[745]. In courts the privacy cases were dealt on the basis of the law of confidence whose roots "lie in equity"[746]. The law "would protect what might reasonably be called a right of privacy, although the name accorded to it would be

---

[739] Le Senat, supra note 684.
[740] Morton Jeremy, Data Protection and Privacy, European Intellectual Property Review, 18 (10), 1996, Sweet & Maxwell, 558-561.
[741] The same.
[742] *R v Brown* [1996] 1 All ER 545.
[743] *R v Brown* [1996] 1 All ER 545 at 555.
[744] Azmi Madieha Ida, E-Commerce and Privacy Issues: An analysis of the Personal Data Protection Bill, 8(8), Computer and Telecommunications Law Review, 2002, 206-212.
[745] See also Kaye v Robertson [1991] FSR 62, where it was clearly stated that a right of privacy did not exist in the UK legal order. However, an element of a right to privacy was indeed recognised in *Morris v Beardmore* [1980] 2 All ER 753. Lord Scarman described the right to privacy as fundamental.
[746] David Bainbridge, Introduction to Computer Law, Fifth Edition, Pearson Longman, London, 2004, page 100.

breach of confidence"[747]. At that point "the emergence of an independent right of privacy from the common law was a distinct possibility"[748]. Viewing privacy within the context of a breach of confidence[749] was problematic from many aspects. In *Guardian Newspapers*[750] the House of Lords "discarded the requirement of a confidential information. Under the force of Lord Goff of Chieveley's criticism of that requirement as illogical where an obviously confidential document came into the hands of someone with whom the injured party had no confidential relationship"[751] the House of Lords explicitly acknowledged that the concept of confidence had already acquired two forms: The first is related to trade secrets which are accompanied by a duty of confidence flowing from "a transaction or a relationship between parties"[752] and the second linked to privacy where a breach of privacy "would be preconditioned upon circumstances where a relationship, whether of confidence or otherwise existed"[753]. In landmark *Douglas v Hello* the court stated that "what a concept of privacy does is accord recognition to the fact that the law has to protect not only those people whose trust has been abused, but those who simply find themselves subject to an unwanted intrusion into their personal lives. The law no longer needs to construct an artificial relationship of confidentiality between the intruder and victim: it can recognise privacy itself as a legal principle drawn from the fundamental value of personal autonomy"[754]. It was argued that "the information must be confidential in nature but it is now recognised that a pre-existing duty of confidence is not necessary if it is plain that the information is confidential and for the adjective confidential one can substitute the word private"[755]. Lord Hoffmann in *Campbell v MGN* stated that "what human rights law did was to identify private information as something worth protecting as an aspect

---

[747] See *Hellewell v Chief Constable of Derbyshire* [1995] 1 WLR 804 and *R v Department of Health, ex parte Source Informatics Ltd* [2001] QB 424.
[748] Loon Wee, Emergence of a Right to Privacy from within the Law of confidence?, 18(5) European Intellectual Property Rights Review, 1996, page 312.
[749] See also *Coco v AN Clark*, [1969] RPC 41, where the three requirements for an action of breach of confidence were spelled out. McGarry J stated that the information must have the necessary quality of confidence about it…that information must have been communicated in circumstances importing an obligation of confidence…there must be an unauthorised use of the information to the detriment of the party communicating it.
[750] [1990] 1 A.C. 109 (H.L.) *A.G. v Guardian Newspapers Ltd* (No2).
[751] Russel Brown, Privacy Law: Article: Rethinking Privacy: Exclusivity, Private Relation and Tort Law, 43 Alberta Law Review, 2006, page 597.
[752] *Guardian Newspapers* supra note 751 at 281.
[753] Russel Brown supra note 752, page 597.
[754] Sedley LJ, in *Douglas v Hello Ltd*, 2 WLR, 2001, 992 at paragraph 126.
[755] *Douglas* paragraph 83.

of human autonomy and dignity"[756]. Thus, the developments mainly at the level of case law "to protect privacy within the existing framework of the common law may well have been in response to government indecision over the recent decades on the issue of privacy"[757]. The problem was that "the UK lacked experience in applying fundamental human rights in the constitutional context"[758]. In *Malone* the court rejected a claim that a telephone tapping contravened the right to privacy by arguing that "it is no function of the courts to legislate in a new field. The extension of the existing laws and principles is one thing, the creation of an altogether new right is another...only parliament can create such a right"[759]. The right to privacy as analysed above was included in the European Convention on Human Rights, but the latter was not incorporated in the UK law but in 1998 with the Human Rights Act[760], with which "the right to privacy...acquired binding legal force"[761] requiring "public authorities to respect privacy rights"[762]. Thus, before the enaction of the 1998 Act it was "well known that in English law there was no right to privacy, and accordingly there was no action for a breach of a person's privacy"[763] as "the right of privacy was first ignored and then expressly disavowed by the judiciary in England and Wales...so long...that it can be recognised now only by the legislature"[764]. As Lord Denning had argued "we have as yet no general remedy for infringement of privacy; the reason given being that on the balance it is not in the public interest that there should be one"[765]. Although, English law has been keen to cover with its protections aspects of the private life of individuals and has a rich tradition[766] in the protection of personal autonomy, an attitude that reached its peak as early as in 1604, when in "Semayne's case it was stated that the

---

[756] Rebecca Wong, in Mathias Klang and Andrew Murray, Human Rights in the Digital Age, Glasshouse Press, London, 2005, page 155.

[757] Mackenzie P. Andrew, Privacy – A new Right in UK Law, 12 Scots Law Times, 2002, 98-101.

[758] Craig DR John, Nolte Nico, supra note 690, 162.

[759] *Malone v Meropolitan Police Commissioner[1979] Ch 344, 372*

[760] It has to be noted however that the 1998 Human Rights Act refers to the relationship between the individual and the public authorities while the Data Protection Act 1998 covers the relationships between individuals as well.

[761] Emanuel Gross, The Struggle of a Democracy against Terrorism, Protection of Human Rights: The Right to Privacy versus the National Interest – The Proper Balance, 37 Cornell International Law Journal, 2004, page 82.

[762] Richard Clayton, Hugh Tomlinson, Privacy and Freedom of Expression, Oxford University Press, 2001, page 64.

[763] Singh Rabinder, Strachan James, The Right To Privacy in English Law, 2 European Human Rights Law Review, 2002, 129.

[764] The same.

[765] *Re X* (1974), [1975] 1 All ER 697 (CA) at 704.

[766] See: Lord Gordon Slynn, The Development of Human Rights in the United Kingdom, 28 Fordham International Law Journal 477, 2005.

house of everyone is to him as his castle and fortress"[767], the right of privacy "is just in its infancy"[768]. This statement is quite astonishing if we take into account that English law has its roots "back to the Magna Carta, which placed individual liberties above all others except communal rights, a concept adopted by British common law in the thirteenth century"[769]. In 1361 the "English Justices of the Peace Act provided for the arrest of peeping toms and eavesdroppers. From the beginning the intent to protect an individual from the government was clear: the poorest man may in his cottage bid defiance to all force of the Crown. It may be frail; its roof may shake; the wind may blow through it; the storms may enter; the rain may enter; but the King of England cannot enter"[770]. This position places the UK at the forefront of nations protecting personal liberties at a very early stage in history, however, as far as the right in question is concerned recognised protection came much later and specifically after the incorporation of the ECHR.

Thus, the important step was taken with the introduction of the ECHR to the UK law, "until the passage of which the concept of privacy was one that neither parliament nor the courts had taken the initiative to develop[771]". Before that, although "the ECHR guaranteed a right of privacy to individual citizens against the governments of signatory states, which included Britain...because Parliament had refused to give the ECHR domestic effect, British courts did not vindicate the individual autonomy rights recognised under the ECHR"[772]. The ECHR signals towards the direction that the state "will be subject to positive as well as negative obligations...not only must public authorities not disclose private information, but they must also not make laws which invade the privacy of the individual"[773]. This over extended application of the relevant article was not received with much ease by various parties within the UK and it was argued that the best solution would be to "develop the common law by relying on existing domestic principles in the laws of trespass, nuisance, copyright, confidence and

---

[767] Singh Rabinder supra note 764.
[768] Singh R, Privacy and the Media after the Human Rights Act, 1998, 712.
[769] Bale B. Robert, Informed Lending Decision v Privacy Interests in Great Britain, 10 Transnational Lawyer 77, 1997.
[770] Cardonsky B Lauren, Towards a Meaningful Right to Privacy in the United Kingdom, 20 Boston University International Law Journal, 2002, page 396.
[771] Taylor Nick, Policing, Privacy and Proportionality, European Human Rights Law Review, 2003, 86-100.
[772] Krotosnynski J Ronald, Autonomy, Community and Traditions of Liberty: The Contrast of British and American Privacy Law, 1990 Duke Law Journal, page 1417.
[773] Coad Jonathan, Privacy – Article 8. Who needs it?, Entertainment Law Review, 2001,12 (8), 226-233.

the like to fashion a common law right of privacy"[774] instead of incorporating and applying the new regime introduced by the Convention.

There was even a greater sense of unease with the passing of the Directive. The passing of such comprehensive legislation on data protection that provided for a list of rights for the data subject was not received warmly in the UK as it was not consistent with the legal tradition of the country as analysed above. "The Home Office intends only to satisfy the minimum requirements of the Directive"[775]. The UK government "opposed the directive arguing that it would impose burdensome obligations on companies"[776], because "banks and financial institutions, especially those with international connections, are probably more affected by data protection legislation than any other type of organisation"[777]. Those industries are of primary importance for the UK economy. In order to transpose the directive the UK passed in 1998 a new Data Protection Act regulating one of the most important aspects of privacy[778]. The Data Protection Registrar stated in his 1994 report that "data protection legislation is about the protection of individuals rather than the regulation of industry It is civil rights legislation rather than technical business legislation"[779]. The new 1998 Act[780] has a wider scope of application in the sense that it covers also specific manual files[781] that are structured with particular reference to individuals or manual files accessible to the public, in contrast to the 1984 Act that covered only files operating automatically[782]. "Responsibility for enforcing UK data protection rules rests now primarily with a government regulator, the Information Commissioner, formerly known as the Data Protection Commissioner"[783]. The implementation of the directive in the British legal order also led to the extension of protection to "sensitive data". "The law of 1984 did

---

[774] Lord Irvine LC in Coad Jonathan, ibid.
[775] Morton Jeremy, supra note 741, 558.
[776] Carlin M Fiona, The Data Protection Directive,: The Introduction of Common Privacy Standards, European Law Review, 1996, 21 (1), 65.
[777] Moakes Jonathan, Data Protection in Europe – Part 1, Journal of International Banking Law, 1986, 1(2), 77.
[778] Access it at: http://www.hmso.gov.uk/acts/acts1998/19980029.htm
[779] Tenth Annual Report of the Data Protection Registrar, 1994, London, HMSO.
[780] See Durie Robyn, An Overview of the Data Protection Act 1998, Computer and Telecommunications Law Review, 2000, 6 (4), 88-93.
[781] Jabbour Vivianne, Rowe Heather, The Proposed Data Protection Directive and the Data Protection Act 1984, Computer and Telecommunications Law Review, 1 (2), 1995, 38-46.
[782] See Rebeiro Michael, A Glancing Blow to Computer Privacy, Computer and Telecommunications Law Review, 2(3), 1996, 122-124.
[783] Mullen Kenneth, UK Developments: Data Protection and on line Privacy, Cyberspace Lawyer, Volume 6, Number 7, 1998, page 24, accessed via LEXIS-NEXIS.

not explicitly define the concept of sensitive data"[784]. It provided only for the ability of the Minister of Internal Affaires to assume regulatory measures concerning particular categories of data such as data related to health, or opinions of political nature[785]. "It is due to the transposition of the EU directive into the UK legal order that the concept of sensitive data was introduced into English law"[786]. Furthermore, and "most significantly the Registrar has emphasised that the Directive introduces into English law a right to informational privacy, which is effective since 1998"[787]. "The rights introduced…incorporate concepts, which are entirely new to English law. The rights do not depend on whether the data subject would have rights under the existing law of confidentiality or other branches of law"[788]. As Ian Lloyd puts it, we are now "effectively moved from a situation where the data controller can process personal data unless otherwise prevented by law, to one where an individual can claim what is almost proprietary right to prevent processing unless the controller can show cause why this should be permitted"[789].

Thus, the introduction of both the ECHR and the Directive to the UK law, have brought a significant shift in the way the issue in question was viewed by both the courts and literature. A right to privacy does exist now in the UK legal order, which is brought much closer to the continental point of view on the issue. Although, there were similarities between the approach taken by the UK and the US on the issue of privacy, now the former deals with the issue in a manner more consistent with the rest of its EU partners.

7.4 The case of Greece

The case of Greece serves as a clear indication of the importance of the directive since it led to the adoption of the first data protection law in the country. The previous efforts to introduce data protection legislation in Europe were as stated before unsuccessful due to the usual non-binding nature of the recommendations concerned. After the adoption of the directive the enforcement of implementing legislation even in

---

[784] Le Senat, supra note 684.
[785] The same.
[786] The same.
[787] Saltzman Ilana, Cassidy Joanna, The Data Protection Directive: How is UK Data Protection Law Affected, International Company and Commercial Law Review, 1996, 7(3), 110-114.
[788] White Antony, Data Protection and the Media, European Human Rights Law Review, 2003, 25-36.
[789] Lloyd Ian in White Antony ibid.

countries with no previous experience in the field[790] became compelling. Greece adopted the law on the protection of individuals with regard to the processing of personal data in 1997[791]. The law is considered to include provisions of stricter character than the requirements of the Directive leading to a tighter regime of protection. Infringement of the legislation entails civil, administrative and penal liability. Furthermore, the creation of an independent authority, the Hellenic Data Protection Authority, with the main task of scrutinising aspects of public activities and legislative initiatives to detect any abuse in the processing of personal data, fostered more effective norms of protection. The issue of vital importance is that as a direct consequence of the Directive the protection of personal data assumed a constitutional status, with the relevant article being inserted in Part II of the Hellenic Constitution on "Individual and Social Rights". It "therefore creates an individual civil right and at the same time a social right guaranteed *erga omnes*, without any discrimination. Even if the State totally ignores its obligations arising from the above mentioned article, this constitutional provision remains at all times active, developing a direct effect that should be applied not only by the courts but also by the administration"[792]. Therefore, a country that did not implement any data protection legislation before the Directive introduced protection of personal data at constitutional level inspired by the Directive. There can be no clearer indication of the influence of the Directive in national legal orders.

More specifically, the network of articles provided by the Constitution itself creates an array of protection, with foundations and parameters that can be viewed as identical to those in the German legal order. "The protection of privacy in Greece has traditionally been considered a fundamental human right. Greek law, jurisprudence, and legal theory traditionally accept that the right to privacy is a derivative of a broader right to personality. The latter is an autonomous, non transferable "composite" or "framework right" since it also includes several particular dependent rights such as the right to respect of honour, reputation, personal integrity and professional image"[793]. Article 2 paragraph 1 places "the value of the human being" as one of the primary obligations of the State. In article 5 paragraph 1, the "right to develop freely one's

---

[790] Greece and Italy were the only countries in the EU-15 with no specific data protection legislation.
[791] See the law at: http://www.dpa.gr/legal_eng.htm
[792] Koussoulis Stelios, Regulating Electronic Commerce, Revue Hellenique de Droit International, L'Institut Hellenique De Droit International et Etranger, Thessaloniki, Greece, 2002, page 355.

177

personality" stands at the core of the Constitutional protection, Article 7 paragraph 2 protects human dignity, while article 19 states that the "secrecy of all forms of communication shall be absolutely inviolable". A new article 5A paragraph 2 confirms that "everyone has a right to participate in information society...with the guarantees of articles 9, 9A and 19 (on privacy and data protection)". These articles along with article 9 paragraph 1 clarifying that "the private and family life of the individual is inviolable" and of course the new 9A on the right to be protected by electronic processing of personal data, create a new landscape for data protection that not only is in complete accordance with the standards of the directive but goes well beyond it. The (revised in 2001) Constitution included in article 9A the right of the individual to protect his personal data from any collection, processing and use especially by electronic means. In the explanatory part it was stated "that the constitutional right of protection against collection, storage or processing of personal data by electronic or other means constitutes the confirmation of the harmonisation of the Hellenic legal order with the Council of Europe Convention and Directive 95/46"[794]. Thus, article 9 creates a constitutional right of privacy and article 9A a constitutional right of data protection which therefore assumes a constitutional recognition of its status as one of the most significant aspects of privacy in legal, social and cultural terms. Of absolute importance is the provision of article 25 paragraph 1, that states that "the rights of man as an individual and as a member of the society...also apply to relations between private individuals to which they pertain", thus horizontal effect of the relevant protection is constitutionally guaranteed. It follows the patterns set by the German legal tradition and assures protection at constitutional level. In addition to that, the aforementioned constitutional principles have been widely reflected in the text of other significant pieces of legislation such as the Hellenic Civil Code which in articles 57 – 60 includes the general rules for the protection of personality, provisions which can be invoked in cases of privacy abuses. According to article 57 a person who has suffered from such an offence has the right to claim the cessation of such an offence and its non recurrence in the future. A further claim for damages based on the provisions regulating unlawful acts completes his bundle of rights.

---

[793] Leonidas Kanellos in Frank Hendrickx supra note 680 page 131.
[794] Hellenic Constitution, article 9A, http://confinder.richmond.edu/greek_2001.html

This legal development was very much needed as the phenomenon of the creation of databases containing personal and often sensitive data was proved to be quite widespread in the country. The sector having a leading role in this development is the private sector. The most significant example of the situation described was the programme known under name "Tiresias", which was created in 1997 by several banking organisations and contained various sorts of information about citizens who have received a loan, owe money to services of the public sector or had in the past problems to cover the cheques they had issued[795]. There was a "black list", where the names of people with financial problems were included. The issue monopolised the headlines when it was announced that almost 1,300,000 people were registered in the database, a number that is equal to the one fifth of the active population of the country. If one's name was included in the list the possible consequences may have included the refusal on behalf of the bank to issue a loan, provide guarantees or other banking services. Thus, the repercussions of having one's profile included in such a database or having stored information about an individual that was inaccurate or lacked update, were too serious to be ignored.

7.5 The jurisprudence of the European Court of Justice on the Data Protection Directive

It is very important to see the related case law produced by Europe's two most influential Courts in order to draw conclusions over the exact scope of the contemporary right of privacy at the level of the common European institutions. The European Court of Justice (ECJ) and the European Court of Human Rights (ECHR) are the two basic pillars of the European Union legal order. Although, the latter is not institutionally bound to the Union but to the Council of Europe its rulings are highly significant for the EU member states as they are binding. All the member states of the EU are members of the Council of Europe and the respect of human rights and fundamental freedoms stands at the very core of the Union's functions and existence. The two courts "are in relationship of cooperation and not one of confrontation...the development of the ECJ case law shows a tendency towards convergence (with ECHR)"[796]. The European construction is based on "a system of protection of

---

[795] See newspaper "Ta Nea", 15/6/2000.
[796] Takis Tridimas, The General Principles of EU Law, Second Edition, Oxford University Press, 2006, page 343.

fundamental rights that recognises the universality of human rights and emphasises non discrimination"[797]. Article 6 of the Treaty explicitly states that: "The Union is founded on the principles of liberty, democracy, respect for human rights and fundamental freedoms, and the rule of law, principles which are common to the Member States. The Union shall respect fundamental rights, as guaranteed by the European Convention for the Protection of Human Rights and Fundamental Freedoms signed in Rome on 4 November 1950 and as they result from the constitutional traditions common to the Member States, as general principles of Community law". Therefore, the rights enshrined in the European Convention among which is the right to privacy and the subsequent rulings of the ECHR play a pivotal role guaranteed by the Treaty itself. As far as data protection and the related directive are concerned, the ECJ has provided us only with a couple of rulings which shed light on the actual provisions of the directive and the appropriate way to interpret its content. The incorporation of the directive in the national legal orders has taken place fairly recently and therefore there is not a particularly rich ECJ jurisprudence on this issue. However, as the national legislations on data protection further entrench themselves in national legal orders more preliminary questions will be made on behalf of the national courts to the ECJ, which will produce a great range of rulings on the specific topic.

The most recent ECJ ruling was that of May 2006 related to the agreement between the European Council and the US in regard to the transfer of passengers' personal data to the United States Bureau of Customs and Border Protection[798]. The agreement demanded that within 15 minutes of take-off for the United States, a European airline must send the US authorities 34 items of personal information about the passengers on board The European Parliament sought the annulment of that decision (Council Decision 2004/496/EC of 17 May 2004)[799] along with the annulment of the Commission (Decision 2004/535/EC of 14 May 2004) on the adequate protection of personal data contained in the Passenger Name Record of air passengers transferred to the United States Bureau of Customs and Border Protection. Following the terrorist

---

[797] Sophie Robin Olivier, Immigration Law and Human Rights: Legal Line Drawing Post September 11: Symposium Article: Citizens and non Citizens in Europe: European Union Measures against Terrorism after September 11, 25 Boston College Third World Law Journal, 2005, page 200.
[798] See the ruling at: http://curia.europa.eu/jurisp/cgi-bin/form.pl?lang=EN&Submit=rechercher&numaff=C-317/04 Joined Cases C-317/04 and C-318/04 July 16th 2006
[799] See the 2004/496/EC decision at:
http://ec.europa.eu/justice_home/fsj/privacy/docs/adequacy/pnr/2004-05-28-agreement_en.pdf

attacks of 11 September 2001, the United States passed legislation in November 2001 providing that air carriers operating flights to or from the United States or across United States territory had to provide the United States customs authorities with electronic access to the data contained in their automated reservation and departure control systems, referred to as 'Passenger Name Records' ('PNR data'). On 13 June 2003 the Working Party on the Protection of Individuals with regard to the Processing of Personal Data, set up by Article 29 of the Directive, delivered an opinion[800] in which it expressed doubts regarding the level of data protection guaranteed by those undertakings for the processing operations envisaged. It reiterated those doubts in an opinion of 29 January 2004. On 31 March 2004 the Parliament adopted a resolution considering that the draft decision on adequacy exceeded the powers conferred on the Commission by Article 25 of the Directive. It called for the conclusion of an appropriate international agreement respecting fundamental rights that would cover a number of points set out in detail in the resolution, and asked the Commission to submit a new draft decision to it. It also reserved the right to refer the matter to the Court for review of the legality of the projected international agreement and, in particular, of its compatibility with protection of the right to privacy[801]. The Court stated that "article 3(2) of the Directive excludes from the Directive's scope the processing of personal data in the course of an activity which falls outside the scope of Community law, such as activities provided for by Titles V and VI of the Treaty on the European Union, and in any case processing operations concerning public security, defence, State security and the activities of the State in areas of criminal law"[802]. "While the view may rightly be taken that PNR data are initially collected by airlines in the course of an activity which falls within the scope of Community law, namely sale of an aeroplane ticket which provides entitlement to a supply of services, the data processing which is taken into account in the decision on adequacy is, however, quite different in nature. That decision concerns not data processing necessary for a supply of services, but data processing regarded as necessary for safeguarding public security and for law-enforcement purposes"[803]. The transfer falls within a framework established by the public authorities that relates to public security. The decision on adequacy concerns

---

[800] See it at: http://ec.europa.eu/justice_home/fsj/privacy/docs/wpdocs/2004/wp87_en.pdf
[801] Paragraphs 33 to 38 of the ruling.
[802] Paragraph 54.
[803] Paragraph 57.

processing of personal data as referred to in the first indent of Article 3(2) of the Directive. That decision therefore does not fall within the scope of the Directive.[804] The decision on adequacy ((Decision 2004/535/EC of 14 May 2004) must consequently be annulled and it is not necessary to consider the other limbs of the first plea or the other pleas relied upon by the Parliament[805].

Concerning the Council Decision (2004/496/EC of 17 May 2004) to transfer the passenger data to the US authorities per se the Court noted that "article 95 EC does not constitute an appropriate legal basis for Decision 2004/496. The decision does not have as its objective and subject-matter the establishment and functioning of the internal market by contributing to the removal of obstacles to the freedom to provide services and it does not contain provisions designed to achieve such an objective. Its purpose is to make lawful the processing of personal data that is required by United States legislation. Nor can Article 95 EC justify Community competence to conclude the Agreement, because the Agreement relates to data processing operations which are excluded from the scope of the Directive"[806]. The Court concluded by arguing that "the Agreement relates to the same transfer of data as the decision on adequacy and therefore to data processing operations which, as has been stated above, are excluded from the scope of the Directive. Consequently, Decision 2004/496 cannot have been validly adopted on the basis of Article 95 EC"[807]. Therefore both decisions were annulled as none was founded on the appropriate legal basis as handing over information for public security and law enforcement purposes falls within the ambit of the member states' criminal law powers and not within the EU scope of competence. EU data protection rules do not cover processing operations concerning public security, defence, state security and the activities of the State in areas of criminal law. Thus, the Court's ruling was based on a purely legal argument over the scope of the EU data protection legislation and it refrained from considering the privacy argument raised by the Parliament. However, the Court gave the Commission 90 days to reshape the agreement and resubmit it for further scrutiny.

---

[804] Paragraph 59
[805] Paragraph 61
[806] Paragraph 63
[807] Paragraphs 68 and 69

In *Bodil Lindqvist* Case C-101/01[808] the Court ruled for the first time on the scope of the data protection directive and freedom of movement for such data on the internet. Mrs Lindqvist was involved in preparing people for Communion in the parish of Alseda (Sweden). At the end of 1998 she created a web page on her personal computer at home to enable parishioners preparing for Confirmation to obtain easily the information they were likely to need. Those pages contained information on Mrs Lindqvist and 18 of her colleagues in the parish, including their first names and occasionally their full names. She also provided details such as the nature of work done by her colleagues and their hobbies. She had also included on her website information concerning their family circumstances and their telephone numbers. She also incorporated information about one of her colleagues injuring her foot and working part-time due to medical reasons.

Mrs Lindqvist was fined SEK 4 000 for processing personal data by automatic means without notifying the Swedish supervisory authority for the protection of electronically transmitted data in writing, for transferring data to third countries without authorisation and for processing sensitive personal data related to the foot injury and the medical reasons due to which her colleague chose to work part time. She appealed against that decision to the Swedish Court of Appeal, which asked the ECJ whether the activities with which Mrs Lindqvist is charged are contrary to the provisions of the data protection directive which is intended to ensure the same level of protection in all the Member States for the rights and freedoms of individuals in that regard. The ECJ clearly explained "that the act of referring, on an internet page, to various persons and identifying them by name or by other means giving their telephone number or information about their working conditions and hobbies *constitutes* the processing of personal data wholly or partly by automatic means within the meaning of article 3 (1) of the directive"[809]. Therefore, the Court afforded the widest possible scope to the relevant provision which is to cover all information and data which can lead to the identification of a certain individual. And posting such data on a self made internet home page was found to constitute such an act, an act of processing data by automatic

---

[808] See: http://curia.europa.eu/jurisp/cgi-bin/gettext.pl?lang=en&num=79968893C19010101&doc=T&ouvert=T&seance=ARRET&where=()
July 16th 2006. Judgment of 06/11/2003, Lindqvist (Rec.2003,p.I-12971)
[809] See: http://europa.eu.int/eur-lex/pri/en/oj/dat/2004/c_007/c_00720040110en00030004.pdf July 16th 2006.

means. Thus, by definition an internet page falls within the ambit of the directive and of article 3 (1). Furthermore, the Court explicitly stated that article 3(2) which provided the grounds on which derogations for paragraph 1 are introduced did not apply in this case. "Such processing of personal data does not fall within the category of activities for the purposes of public security nor within the category of purely personal or domestic activities, which are outside the scope of the directive". Hence, the Court asserted that creating a web page at home and posting personal data on it is not a purely personal or household activity which justifies invoking the exception to the article 3 (1) rule. Especially, this part of the ruling reveals the over reaching effect of the directive since it catches not only the publication of personal data for commercial use or purposes but even that in the framework of a personal hobby.

Lindqvist insisted that her actions were justified by her freedom of expression and that the activities she engaged into were "in the course of a non-profit-making or leisure activity and are not carrying out an economic activity and are thus not subject to Community law"[810]. The Court found the activities in question "essentially not economic but charitable and religious"[811]. It also insisted that the exception of article 3 (2) is interpreted strictly and therefore "charitable or religious activities such as those carried out by Mrs Lindqvist cannot be considered equivalent to the activities listed in the first indent of Article 3(2) of Directive 95/46 and are thus not covered by that exception"[812]. The exception covers only "the processing of data carried out by a natural person in the exercise of activities which are exclusively personal or domestic, correspondence and the holding of records of addresses...relating only to activities which are carried out in the course of private or family life of individuals, which is clearly not the case with the processing of personal data consisting in publication on the internet so that those data are made accessible to an indefinite number of people"[813].

Finally, the Court concluded that the inclusion of information over the foot injury and the choice to work part time for medical reasons constituted processing of data concerning health within the meaning of article 8 (1) of the directive on the processing of sensitive personal data. The court clarified that "the expression data concerning health used in Article 8(1) thereof must be given a wide interpretation so as

---

[810] Paragraph 30 of the judgement.
[811] Paragraph 39 of the judgement.
[812] Paragraph 45 of the judgement.

184

to include information concerning all aspects, both physical and mental, of the health of an individual"[814]. Taking into account that "Mrs. Lindqvist had not informed her colleagues of the existence of those pages or obtained their consent, nor did she notify the Datainspektionen (supervisory authority for the protection of electronically transmitted data) of her activity. She removed the pages in question as soon as she became aware that they were not appreciated by some of her colleagues"[815], it is obvious that she didn't satisfy the requirement of article 8(2) of the directive. The latter legitimises the use of sensitive personal data such as those related to health when explicit consent on behalf of the data subject has been expressed. This was not the case here.

Furthermore, the Court stated that there is *no* transfer of data to a third country in the sense of article 25 of the directive where an individual in a member state loads personal data onto an internet page which is loaded on an internet site on which the page can be consulted and which is hosted by a natural or legal person who is established in that member state or in another member state, thereby making those data accessible to anyone who connects to the internet, including people from a third country[816]. The Court stated that "one cannot presume that the Community legislature intended the expression transfer [of data] to a third country to cover the loading, by an individual in Mrs Lindqvist's position, of data onto an internet page, even if those data are thereby made accessible to persons in third countries with the technical means to access them"[817] and so "it must be concluded that Article 25 of Directive 95/46 is to be interpreted as meaning that operations such as those carried out by Mrs Lindqvist do not as such constitute a transfer [of data] to a third country. It is thus unnecessary to investigate whether an individual from a third country has accessed the internet page concerned or whether the server of that hosting service is physically in a third country"[818]. This part of the judgement constitutes a rational approach to the reality of internet as if the court afforded to article 25 such a great scope then the creation of websites even for the most trivial reasons would have been rendered literally impossible. And the Court concluded by insisting that "the provisions of the directive

---

[813] Paragraph 46 and 47 of the judgement.
[814] Paragraph 50 of the judgement.
[815] Paragraph 14 of the judgement.
[816]http://europa.eu.int/eur-lex/pri/en/oj/dat/2004/c_007/c_00720040110en00030004.pdf   Lindqvist Ruling.
[817] Paragraph 68 of the judgement

do not in themselves entail a restriction contrary to the principle of freedom of expression or other fundamental rights. It is for the national authorities and courts responsible for applying the national legislation implementing the directive to ensure a fair balance between the rights and interests in question, including those fundamental rights"[819].

The third case on the area of data protection which shed light on the interpretation of the directive was *Rechnungshof (C-465/00)*[820], which concerned the applicability of the directive and its potential direct effect. Under Austrian law, bodies subject to control by the Rechnungshof (Court of Audit) are obliged to transmit to it the salaries and pensions exceeding a certain threshold paid to their employees and pensioners. The disclosure of the names of the persons concerned is not expressly mentioned in the Austrian legislation, but it follows from the doctrine adopted by the Rechnungshof. The Rechnungshof collects the data in an annual report which is submitted to the Nationalrat (lower house of Parliament), the Bundesrat (upper house of Parliament) and the Landtage (provincial parliaments). It is also made available to the public. Certain organisations, including ÖRF and other public undertakings, regional and local authorities and a statutory professional representative body, did not submit the relevant data or did communicate it but devoid of the names of the employees. The basis for excluding such data was the data protection directive of 1995. The Rechnungshof applied to the Verfassungsgerichtshof (Constitutional Court of Austria) to settle the difference of opinion *(C-465/00)*. Two employees of ÖRF, Ms Neukomm and Mr Lauermann, brought proceedings to prevent ÖRF from complying with the Rechnungshof's request to communicate the data. They appealed against the dismissal of that application to the Oberster Gerichtshof (Supreme Court) (C-138/01 and C-139/01). The two Austrian courts put questions to the Court of Justice on two points: is the Austrian legislation compatible with Community law and are the provisions of

---

[818] Paragraph 70 of the judgement
[819] http://curia.europa.eu/en/actu/communiques/cp03/aff/cp0396en.htm Lindqvist Ruling.
[820] See the ruling at: http://www.curia.europa.eu/jurisp/cgi-bin/gettext.pl?lang=en&num=79969479C19000465&doc=T&ouvert=T&seance=ARRET&where= July 16th 2006.

Community law directly applicable, in that they may be relied on to block the application of national rules which are contrary to them.[821]

The Verfassungsgerichtshof argued that "comprehensive information for the public, as intended by the national legislature with respect to the income of employees of bodies subject to control by the Rechnungshof whose annual remuneration exceeds a certain threshold has to be regarded as an interference with private life, which can be justified under Article 8(2) of the Convention only if that information contributes to the economic well-being of the country. An interference with fundamental rights cannot be justified by the existence of a mere public interest in information. The court doubts that the disclosure, by means of the Report, of data on personal income promotes the economic well-being of the country. In any event, it constitutes a disproportionate interference with private life. The audit carried out by the Rechnungshof is indubitably sufficient to ensure the proper use of public funds"[822]. The Austrian Government noted that "when reviewing proportionality, the extent to which the data affects private life must be taken into account. Data relating to personal intimacy, health, family life or sexuality must therefore be protected more strongly than data relating to income and taxes, which, while also personal, concern personal identity to a lesser extent and are thereby less sensitive"[823]. On the contrary the Court argued that "the data at issue in the main proceedings, which relate both to the monies paid by certain bodies and the recipients, constitute personal data within the meaning of Article 2(a) of Directive 95/46, being information relating to an identified or identifiable natural person. Their recording and use by the body concerned, and their transmission to the Rechnungshof and inclusion by the latter in a report intended to be communicated to various political institutions and widely diffused, constitute processing of personal data within the meaning of Article 2(b) of the directive"[824]. The data must be collected for specified, explicit and legitimate purposes (Article 6(1)(b) of Directive 95/46) and must be adequate, relevant and not excessive in relation to those purposes (Article 6(1)(c)). In addition, under Article 7(c) and (e) of the directive respectively, the processing of personal data is permissible only if it is necessary for compliance with a legal obligation to which the controller is subject or is necessary for the performance of a

---

[821] See the Press Release and a summary at:
http://curia.europa.eu/en/actu/communiques/cp03/aff/cp0341en.htm July 16th 2006.
[822] Paragraph 21 of the judgement.
[823] Paragraph 52 of the judgement.
[824] Paragraph 64 of the judgement.

task carried out in the public interest or in the exercise of official authority vested in the controller ... to whom the data are disclosed[825]. However, according to article 13(e) and (f) of the directive, the Member States may derogate *inter alia* from article 6(1) where this is necessary to safeguard respectively an important economic or financial interest of a Member State or of the European Union, including monetary, budgetary and taxation matters or a monitoring, inspection or regulatory function connected, even occasionally, with the exercise of official authority in particular cases including that referred to in subparagraph (e)"[826]. Even Article 8 of the Convention on privacy, while stating in paragraph 1 the principle that the public authorities must not interfere with the right to respect for private life, accepts in paragraph 2 that such an interference is possible where it is in accordance with the law and is necessary in a democratic society in the interests of national security, public safety or the economic well-being of the country[827]. It necessarily follows that, while the mere recording by an employer of data by name relating to the remuneration paid to his employees cannot as such constitute an interference with private life, the communication of that data to third parties, in the present case a public authority, infringes the right of the persons concerned to respect for private life, whatever the subsequent use of the information thus communicated, and constitutes an interference within the meaning of Article 8 of the Convention[828].The Austrian Government observes, more generally, that the interference provided for by that provision is intended to guarantee the thrifty and appropriate use of public funds by the administration. Such an objective constitutes a legitimate aim within the meaning both of Article 8(2) of the Convention, which mentions the economic well-being of the country, and Article 6(1)(b) of Directive 95/46, which refers to specified, explicit and legitimate purposes[829]. The interest of the Republic of Austria in ensuring the best use of public funds, and in particular keeping salaries within reasonable limits, must be balanced against the seriousness of the interference with the right of the persons concerned to respect for their private life[830]. The Court concluded that the publication "of the names of the recipients of that income is both necessary for and appropriate to the aim of keeping salaries within reasonable limits, that being a matter for the national

---

[825] Paragraph 66 of the judgement.
[826] Paragraph 67 of the judgement.
[827] Paragraph 71 of the judgement
[828] Paragraph 74 of the judgement
[829] See paragraph 81 of the judgement
[830] See paragraph 84 of the judgement

courts to examine"[831]. "The answer to the first question must be that Articles 6(1)(c) and 7(c) and (e) of Directive 95/46 do not preclude national legislation such as that at issue in the main proceedings, provided that it is shown that the wide disclosure not merely of the amounts of the annual income above a certain threshold of persons employed by the bodies subject to control by the Rechnungshof but also of the names of the recipients of that income is *necessary* for and *appropriate* to the objective of proper management of public funds pursued by the legislature, that being for the national courts to ascertain"[832]. As far as the second question was concerned the Court ruled that "Articles 6(1)(c) and 7(c) and (e) of Directive 95/46 *are* directly applicable, in that they may be relied on by an individual before the national courts to oust the application of rules of national law which are contrary to those provisions".

7.6 The jurisprudence of the European Court of Human Rights on Privacy

In contrast with the limited ECJ case law on the application and interpretation of the directive the ECHR can present a rich case law on privacy which is enshrined in article 8 of the ECHR. Its cases highlight the parameters of the right to privacy and demonstrate its importance in the European legal order. Before presenting the cases indicative of the Court's stance towards privacy it should be stated that one of the interpretational tools of the Court is dynamic interpretation. In accordance with this principle the ECHR interprets the Convention dynamically, which means "as a living instrument in which the meaning of terms may change over time depending on societal values...the Court takes into account contemporary realities and attitudes, not the situation prevailing at the time of the drafting of the Convention in 1949-1959"[833]. This statement is of high importance since threats to privacy have significantly evolved over the years as a result of technological development. Therefore, it is crucial to note that the content of the right to privacy has evolved to include challenges unknown at the

---

[831] Paragraph 90 of the judgement.
[832] Paragraph 94.
[833] H. Tomas Gomez Arostegui, Defining Private Life under the European Convention on Human Rights by referring to Reasonable Expectations, 35 California Western International Journal Law, 2005, page 158.

point of the Convention's drafting. In *Niemietz*[834] the Court gave a very broad definition to the right to privacy linking it "with notions of personal autonomy and development"[835]. It stated that "the Court does not consider it possible or necessary to attempt an exhaustive definition of the notion of "private life". However, it would be too restrictive to limit the notion to an "inner circle" in which the individual may live his own personal life as he chooses and to exclude them entirely from the outside world not encompassed within that circle. Respect for private life must also comprise to a certain degree the right to establish and develop relationships with other human beings. There appears, furthermore, to be no reason of principle why this understanding of the notion of "private life" should be taken to exclude activities of a professional or business nature since it is, after all, in the course of their working lives that the majority of people have a significant, if not the greatest, opportunity of developing relationships with the outside world"[836]. Consequently, "whether the retention of traffic data collected on internet relates to private, business, professional or other environments, it falls under the scope of the right to privacy as expressed in article 8 ECHR"[837]. In the light of this principle the Court ruled in *Z v Finland*[838] that the protection of personal data and even more importantly the protection of sensitive data such as medical information "is of fundamental importance to a person's enjoyment of his right to respect of privacy and family life; and that there must be appropriate safeguards to prevent communication or disclosure of personal health data"[839]. The Court found that "that the disclosure of the applicant's identity and medical condition by the Helsinki Court of Appeal constituted a breach of Article 8"[840]. In another case *Lüdi v Switzerland*[841] the Court introduced the concept of "reasonable expectations of privacy". The relevant doctrine assumed essential importance in the privacy framework

---

[834] Niemietz v Germany, ECHR, December 16th 1992. See the judgement at:
http://cmiskp.echr.coe.int/tkp197/view.asp?item=1&portal=hbkm&action=html&highlight=Niemietz&se
ssionid=7862396&skin=hudoc-en July 16th 2006.
[835] Jemima Stratford in Madeleine Colvin, Developing Key Privacy Rights, Hart Publishing, Oxford and Portland, 2002, page 17.
[836] Paragraph 29 of the judgement.
[837] Caroline Goemans and Jos Dumortier in C. Nicoll, J.E.J Prins, M.J.M. van Dallen, Digital anonymity and the Law, Tensions and Dimenions, T.M.C. Asser Press, The Hague, 2003, page 173.
[838] (1997) 25 EHRR 371
[839] Richard Clayton, Hugh Tomlinson, supra note 763, page 39.
[840] See the ruling:
http://cmiskp.echr.coe.int/tkp197/view.asp?item=1&portal=hbkm&action=html&highlight=Z%20%7C%
20v%20%7C%20Finland&sessionid=7791837&skin=hudoc-en July 16th 2006.
[841] See the ruling:
http://cmiskp.echr.coe.int/tkp197/view.asp?item=1&portal=hbkm&action=html&highlight=L%FCdi%20
%7C%20v%20%7C%20Switzerland&sessionid=7791885&skin=hudoc-en July 16th 2006.

and it has to be distinguished from the respective doctrine developed by American courts which is thoroughly analysed later. In *Lüdi* the Court stated that "a person involved in criminal activities is entitled to a lesser expectation of privacy"[842]. The person in question was involved in drug trafficking, and the authorities aimed at better investigating the criminal acts in which he was involved by monitoring his phone calls. The telephone interception was authorised by the Indictments Chamber and was terminated by the investigating judge. An undercover agent was also used to monitor his activities. The Court found that "there is no doubt that the telephone interception was an interference with Mr Lüdi's private life and correspondence. Such an interference is *not* in breach of the Convention if it complies with the requirements of paragraph 2 of Article 8 (art. 8-2)"[843]. Paragraph 2 of article 8 states that a public authority can interfere to the exercise of the right to privacy, provided its actions are performed in accordance with the law and in the interests of national security, public safety or the prevention of disorder or crime among others. The measures adopted in this case were found to be based on Articles 171b and 171c of the Berne Code of Criminal Procedure and to aim at the "prevention of crime", therefore the Court had no doubt whatsoever as to its necessity in a democratic society. The same rationale for the justification of the deployment of an undercover agent to monitor his activities was employed. Interestingly enough, the Court concluded that "Mr Lüdi must therefore have been aware from then on that he was engaged in a criminal act punishable under Article 19 of the Drugs Law and that consequently he was running the risk of encountering an undercover police officer whose task would in fact be to expose him"[844]. No violation if article 8 was detected. The Court had therefore linked the reasonable expectations to privacy with the limits that the Convention sets on the exercise of the right to privacy. If limitations are legitimately imposed on privacy by law or for the prevention of crime or for reasons of national security then the person in question shall assume that he is running the risk of experiencing an interference with his privacy. What distinguishes the notion of reasonable expectations of privacy as it is shaped by the ECHR with the respective doctrine adopted in the other side of the Atlantic is that the ECHR has granted a substantially more limited scope to it. The

---

[842] Sjaak Nouwt, Berend R. de Vries, Roel Loermans, Reasonable Expectations of Privacy, Eleven Country Reports on Camera Surveillance and Workplace Privacy, T.M.C Asser Press, The Hague, 2005, page 334.
[843] Paragraph 39 of the judgement.
[844] Paragraph 40.

reasons for presuming reasonably that one's expectations of privacy might be limited are to be found in the text of the Treaty and constitute the legislated derogations to privacy and are accepted only when they are judged as necessary in a democratic society. The principle of proportionality "inherent in the Convention"[845] forms a criterion to determine the legality of all derogations.

In *Halford v UK*[846] the applicant was at that time the highest ranking female police officer in the UK. She applied for a promotion to become a Deputy Chief Constable but she was refused on the basis of what she complained had been a discriminatory motive. She also accused her colleagues of intercepting the phone calls made from her office phones in order to obtain information to use against her in the discrimination proceedings. The British government explained to the court that her telephone calls fall outside the protection of the Convention because she couldn't have any reasonable expectation of privacy in relation to them[847]. The Court rejected this argument based on two premises. First it invoked previous case law[848] which concluded that telephone calls made from business premises are covered under private life and correspondence rules and secondly it reversed the reasonable expectation of privacy argument made by British government. The Court stated that there was no indication of any warning given to her about any potential monitoring of her phone conversations. "She would, the Court considers, have had a reasonable expectation of privacy for such calls, which expectation was moreover reinforced by a number of factors. As Assistant Chief Constable she had sole use of her office where there were two telephones, one of which was specifically designated for her private use. Furthermore, she had been given the assurance, in response to a memorandum, that she could use her office telephones for the purposes of her sex-discrimination case (see paragraph 16 above)"[849]. The court

---

[845] Nonnie L Shivers, Firing "Immoral" Public Employees: If Article 8 of the European Convention on Human Rights Protects Employee Privacy Rights, then why can't we?, 21 Arizona Journal of International and Comparative Law, 2004, page 635.
[846] See the ruling at:
http://cmiskp.echr.coe.int/tkp197/view.asp?item=1&portal=hbkm&action=html&highlight=Halford%20%7C%20v%20%7C%20UK&sessionid=7791922&skin=hudoc-en July 16th 2006.
[847] Paragraph 43: the Government expressed the view that an employer should in principle, without the prior knowledge of the employee, be able to monitor calls made by the latter on telephones provided by the employer.
[848] See Niemietz v. Germany judgment of 16 December 1992, Series A no. 251-B, Huvig v France Series A no. 176-B, p. 41, para. 8, and p. 52, para. 25 and Klass and Others v.Germany judgment of 6 September 1978, Series A no. 28, p. 21, para. 41, A. v. France judgment of 23 November 1993, Series A no. 277-B).

[849] Paragraph 45.

accepted that intercepting her phone calls constituted an interference by a public authority with her right to privacy. Article 8(2) of the Convention as explained above permits such an interference when it takes place in accordance with law. At this point the Court added a very significant requirement to that. "This expression does not only necessitate compliance with domestic law, but also relates to the quality of that law, requiring it to be compatible with the rule of law"[850]. In the context of secret measures of surveillance or interception of communications by public authorities, because of the lack of public scrutiny and the risk of misuse of power, the domestic law must provide some protection to the individual against arbitrary interference with Article 8 rights (art. 8). Thus, the domestic law must be sufficiently clear in its terms to give citizens an adequate indication as to the circumstances in and conditions on which public authorities are empowered to resort to any such secret measures"[851]. "Such interference was not "in accordance with the law" since domestic law did not provide any regulation of interceptions of calls made on telecommunications systems outside the public network. It cannot therefore be said that the interference was "in accordance with the law" for the purposes of Article 8 paragraph. 2 of the Convention (art. 8-2), since the domestic law did not provide adequate protection to Ms Halford against interference by the police with her right to respect for her private life and correspondence[852]. Therefore, the UK was found to be violating article 8 of the Treaty. This case also underlined the rigorousness of the criteria applied when dealing with the reasonable expectations concept. The lack of clear legislation allowing for a derogation from the right to privacy and the interference of the public authority is deemed as grounds concrete enough to prevent the application of the doctrine and to safeguard the full application of article 8 (1).

In *P.G & J.H v UK*[853] the issue was whether the police may covertly record a conversation between a police officer and a suspect in an actual police station in order to acquire an audio sample of the suspect' voice. "The Government submitted that the use of the listening devices in the cells and when the applicants were being charged did not disclose any interference, as these recordings were not made to obtain any private

---

[850] Paragraph 49.
[851] The same.
[852] Paragraph 51.
[853] See the ruling at:
http://cmiskp.echr.coe.int/tkp197/view.asp?item=1&portal=hbkm&action=html&highlight=P.G.%20%7C%20v%20%7C%20UK&sessionid=7791960&skin=hudoc-en July 16th 2006.

or substantive information (only the voice samples). The aural quality of the applicants' voices was not part of private life but was rather a public, external feature... the applicants could have had no expectation of privacy in that context"[854]. The Court made the choice to judge the issue on the basis of whether and how the information of the applicants was processed. "Private-life considerations may arise, however, once any systematic or permanent record comes into existence of such material from the public domain. It is for this reason that files gathered by security services on a particular individual fall within the scope of Article 8, even where the information has *not* been gathered by any intrusive or covert method"[855]. The Court invoked the Council of Europe's Convention of 28 January 1981 for the protection of individuals with regard to automatic processing of personal data to argue that "while it is generally the case that the recordings were made for the purpose of using the content of the conversations in some way, the Court is not persuaded that recordings taken for use as voice samples can be regarded as falling outside the scope of the protection afforded by Article 8. A permanent record has nonetheless been made of the person's voice and it is subject to a process of analysis directly relevant to identifying that person in the context of other personal data. Though it is true that when being charged the applicants answered formal questions in a place where police officers were listening to them, the recording and analysis of their voices on this occasion must still be regarded as concerning the processing of personal data about the applicants...the Court concludes therefore that the recording of the applicants' voices when being charged and when in their police cell discloses an interference with their right to respect for private life within the meaning of Article 8 § 1 of the Convention"[856]. In this ruling the court related the reasonable expectations of privacy to the processing of personal data. Even if the individuals in question could not have had a reasonable expectation of privacy at a given moment, if their data were to be processed and used in an illegitimate way this could still amount to a violation of article 8. This interpretation of article 8 is very strict and it reveals on the one hand the Court's determination to safeguard the right of privacy and on the other hand its willingness to adjust its content to the new circumstances prevailing at any given moment[857].

---

[854] Paragraph 54.
[855] Paragraph 57.
[856] Paragraph 59 and 60.
[857] Interestingly enough the Supreme Court of the United States had given a completely different answer to a very similar question. In *United States v Dionisio 410 US 1 (1973)*, the Court stated that there can be

194

In *Peck v UK*[858] the city's public surveillance system caught footage from person attempting to commit a suicide publicly in a street using a knife. Because of the surveillance system in place police were ready to intervene and prevent him from putting an end to his life. The images from the incident later appear in the local press and eventually found their way to national TV as they were broadcast in a BBC programme. The government argued that "the incident in question did not form part of his private life given the substance of what was filmed and the location and circumstances of the filming. The applicant's actions were already in the public domain. Disclosure of those actions simply distributed a public event to a wider public and could not change the public quality of the applicant's original conduct and render it more private"[859]. The applicant "was not complaining about being filmed by CCTV (as this saved his life) but took issue with the disclosure by the Council of the CCTV material which resulted in the impugned publications and broadcasts"[860], which made several members of his family and neighbours to recognise him. "As a result, the relevant moment was viewed to an extent which far exceeded any exposure to a passer-by or to security observation and to a degree surpassing that which the applicant could possibly have foreseen when he walked in Brentwood on 20 August 1995... the Court considers that the disclosure by the Council of the relevant footage constituted a serious interference with the applicant's right to respect for his private life"[861]. It concluded that the interference to his private life was disproportionate and unjustified as the passing of the footage to the media was not accompanied by safeguards such as the covering of his face and identity.

In *von Hannover v Germany*[862] Princess Caroline tried to stop the publication of photographs of her along with her boyfriend at a restaurant, shopping and playing tennis. Her efforts were not successful as the German Federal Constitutional Court ruled that she is a public figure and therefore when she is out of her home she is the

---

no reasonable expectation of privacy in the sound of one's voice "any more than he can reasonably expect that his face will be a mystery to the world". Paragraph 14.

[858] See the ruling at:
http://cmiskp.echr.coe.int/tkp197/view.asp?item=2&portal=hbkm&action=html&highlight=Peck%20%7C%20v%20%7C%20UK&sessionid=7792003&skin=hudoc-en July 16th 2006.

[859] Paragraph 53.

[860] Paragraph 54.

[861] Paragraph 62 and 63.

[862] See the ruling at:
http://cmiskp.echr.coe.int/tkp197/view.asp?item=3&portal=hbkm&action=html&highlight=Hannover%20%7C%20v%20%7C%20Germany&sessionid=7792003&skin=hudoc-en July 16th 2006.

subject of photographers' interest unless she withdraws to a place out of public eye where it is evident to everyone that she wants to be left alone. The ECHR on the contrary noted that "there is no doubt that the publication by various German magazines of photos of the applicant in her daily life either on her own or with other people falls within the scope of her private life"[863]. In this case the applicant did not complain against an action of the State but against "the lack of adequate State protection of her private life and her image"[864]. The state may have obligations involving the adoption of measures designed to secure respect for private life even in the sphere of the relations of individuals between themselves[865]. These obligations could include shaping an adequate balance between competing interests such as privacy and the right of expression. "Although freedom of expression also extends to the publication of photos, this is an area in which the protection of the rights and reputation of others takes on particular importance. The present case does not concern the dissemination of "ideas", but of images containing very personal or even intimate "information" about an individual. Furthermore, photos appearing in the tabloid press are often taken in a climate of continual harassment which induces in the person concerned a very strong sense of intrusion into their private life or even of persecution"[866]. In the cases in which the Court has had to balance the protection of private life against freedom of expression, it has always stressed the contribution made by photos or articles in the press to a debate of general interest. However, since in this case the photos show mainly moments of her daily life "the Court considers that the publication of the photos and articles in question, the sole purpose of which was to satisfy the curiosity of a particular readership regarding the details of the applicant's private life, cannot be deemed to contribute to any debate of general interest to society despite the applicant being known to the public"[867]. And in these conditions freedom of expression calls for a narrower interpretation. The Court "reiterates the fundamental importance of protecting private life from the point of view of the development of every human being's personality. That protection extends beyond the private family circle and also includes a social dimension. The Court considers that anyone, even if they are known to the general public, must be able to enjoy a "legitimate expectation"

---

[863] Paragraph 53.
[864] Paragraph 56.
[865] Paragraph 57.
[866] Paragraph 59.
[867] Paragraph 65.

of protection of and respect for their private life"[868]. Furthermore, increased vigilance in protecting private life is necessary to contend with new communication technologies which make it possible to store and reproduce personal data. The court here tried to link again the reasonable expectations of privacy with the conditions of data processing. However, the latter here appears to be complementary to the former. In finding that the German courts did not manage to strike the right balance between the two conflicting rights, the Court concluded that there had been a breach of article 8.

In a very recent case (Copland v. the United Kingdom - 62617/00 [2007] ECHR 253 (3 April 2007) the ECHR provided us with a very important ruling in an issue of massive significance for European citizens; the level of privacy in their employment premises. In this case the applicant's telephone, e-mail and internet usage were subjected to monitoring during her employment, at the Deputy Principal's of the College she had been working at instigation. According to the British Government, this monitoring took place in order to ascertain whether the applicant was making excessive use of the College facilities for personal purposes. The Carmarthenshire College is a statutory body administered by the State. The Government stated that the monitoring of telephone usage consisted of analysis of the college telephone bills showing telephone numbers called, the dates and times of the calls and their length and cost. But, the applicant also believed that there had been detailed and comprehensive logging of the length of calls, the number of calls received and made and the telephone numbers of individuals calling her. The applicant's internet usage was also monitored. The Government accepted that this monitoring took the form of analysing the web sites visited, the times and dates of the visits to the web sites and their duration and that this monitoring took place from October to November 1999. The Government admitted the monitoring but supported that this did not extend to the interception of telephone calls or the analysis of the content of websites visited by her. The monitoring thus amounted to nothing more than the analysis of automatically generated information to determine whether College facilities had been used for personal purposes which, of itself, did not constitute a failure to respect private life or correspondence. Therefore, the case of *P.G. and J.H. v. the United Kingdom*, could be distinguished since there actual interception of telephone calls occurred. Furthermore, there were significant differences from the case of *Halford v. the United Kingdom*, judgment of 25 June 1997, *Reports of*

---

[868] Paragraph 69.

Judgments and Decisions 1997 III, where the applicant's telephone calls were intercepted on a telephone which had been designated for private use and, in particular her litigation against her employer. The Government supported that firstly, it pursued the legitimate aim of protecting the rights and freedoms of others by ensuring that the facilities provided by a publicly funded employer were not abused. Secondly, the interference had a basis in domestic law in that the College, as a statutory body, whose powers enable it to provide further and higher education and to do anything necessary and expedient for those purposes, had the power to take reasonable control of its facilities to ensure that it was able to carry out its statutory functions. It was reasonably foreseeable that the facilities provided by a statutory body out of public funds could not be used excessively for personal purposes and that the College would undertake an analysis of its records to determine if there was any likelihood of personal use which needed to be investigated. The applicant asserted that the conduct of the College was neither necessary nor proportionate. There were reasonable and less intrusive methods that the College could have used such as drafting and publishing a policy dealing with the monitoring of employees' usage of the telephone, internet and e-mail.

According to the Court's case-law, telephone calls from business premises are *prima facie* covered by the notions of "private life" and "correspondence" for the purposes of Article 8 § 1 (see *Halford*). It follows logically that e-mails sent from work should be similarly protected under Article 8, as should information derived from the monitoring of personal internet usage. The applicant in the present case had been given no warning that her calls would be liable to monitoring, therefore she had a reasonable expectation as to the privacy of calls made from her work telephone (see *Halford*, § 45). The same expectation should apply in relation to the applicant's e-mail and internet usage. The Court recalls that the use of information relating to the date and length of telephone conversations and in particular the numbers dialled can give rise to an issue under Article 8 as such information constitutes an "integral element of the communications made by telephone" (see *Malone v. the United Kingdom*, judgment of 2 August 1984 § 84). The mere fact that these data may have been legitimately obtained by the College, in the form of telephone bills, is no bar to finding an interference with rights guaranteed under Article 8. Moreover, storing of personal data relating to the private life of an individual also falls within the application of Article 8 § 1. Thus, it is irrelevant that the data held by the college were not disclosed or used against the applicant in disciplinary or other proceedings. Accordingly, the Court considers that the collection and storage of personal information relating to the applicant's telephone, as well as to her e-mail and internet usage, without her knowledge, amounted to an interference with her right to respect for her private life and correspondence within the meaning of Article 8. The Court recalls that it is well established in the case-law that the term "in accordance with the law" not only requires compliance with domestic law, but also relates to the quality of that law, requiring it to be compatible with the rule of law. As there was no domestic law regulating monitoring at the relevant time, the interference in this case was not "in accordance with the law" as required by Article 8 § 2 of the Convention. The Court would not exclude that the monitoring of an employee's use of a telephone, e-mail or internet at the place of work may be considered "necessary in a democratic society" in certain situations in pursuit of a legitimate aim. However, having regard to its above conclusion, it is not necessary to pronounce on that matter in the instant case. There has therefore been a violation of Article 8 in this regard and the British Government has to pay 10,000 € fine to the applicant. This case has been a very significant step towards laying the framework for a certain level of privacy protection at the work place. The Court laid down the necessary requirements for the protection of employees' privacy at their workplace and accepted that telephone calls and visits to internet site are "prima facie" covered by the notions of "private life" and "correspondence".

8. The EU and USA trade relations after the adoption of the Directive.

8.1 The new landscape

When the EU data protection directive came into force the US "was presented with an economic dilemma it simply could not ignore any longer, one that may force the US to close the privacy gap between its status quo policy of commercial data freedom and the EU's pro-consumer privacy protections"[869]. If it failed to do so, "then the US quite simply could not do business with EU customers"[870] who fall into the scope of the directive's application. The reason behind the initial reactions on behalf of the US was the sudden realisation of the global impact of the EU privacy laws. "Along with US companies many businesses established outside the EU faced potential data disruptions due to the directive's restriction on international transfers of personal data. Nations around the globe are responding to this pressure by adopting the EU privacy model"[871]. Thus, countries with legal systems, commercial values and history as different as Switzerland, Hungary, Hong Kong, Argentina, Canada and New Zealand moved towards the direction of adopting policies and legislative drafts in accordance with the initiatives assumed at EU level. More significantly they decided to align their privacy laws with the laws of a Union of countries they did not belong to. "A decade ago compliance with privacy requirements was a relatively simple manner for US companies"[872]. But now the consequences of the directive on the US were immediately realised and amounted to the "possibility of facing EU style privacy laws across the globe"[873] and in various "increasingly interconnected"[874] jurisdictions. Canada, one of the most important partners of the US, adopted the Personal Information Protection and Electronic Documents Act (PIPEDA) as a response to the EU Directive. "The Canadian

---

[869] Clear Marie, Falling Into the Gap: The European Union's Data Protection Act and Its Impact on US Law and Commerce, 18 John Marshall Journal of Computer and Information Law, 2000, page 981, accessed via LEXIS-NEXIS.
[870] The same.
[871] Glover Rodney, Worlton Amy, Rein Wiley, United States: Trans-National Employers must harmonise conflicting Privacy Rules, World Data Protection Report, November 2002, Volume 2, number 11, page 3.
[872] Michael L. Rustad, Sandra R. Paulsson, Monitoring Employee E-mail and Internet Usage: Avoiding the Omniscient Electronic Sweatshop: Insights from Europe, 7 University of Pennsylvania Journal of Labour and Employment Law, 2005, page 829.
[873] Glover Rodney supra note 872.
[874] Richard W Downing, Shoring Up the Weakest Link: What Lawmakers around the World need to Consider in developing comprehensive laws to combat cybercrime, 43 Columbia Journal of Transnational Law, page 707.

legislature knew that if it failed to enact comparable measures the European privacy laws could act as a non-tariff barrier for Canadians seeking to conduct business with one of the world's strongest trading blocs"[875]. PIPEDA enacted n April 2000, "is now fully extended to cover all private and public organisations that collect, use or disclose personal information"[876]. On 20 December 2001, the European Commission recognised that the Canadian Personal Information Protection and Electronic Documents Act (PIPED Act) provides adequate protection for certain personal data transferred from the EU to Canada[877]. Australia, another common law jurisdiction, has also acted in the direction of harmonising its data protection standards with those of the EU. Australia's Private Sector Privacy Act Agreement (2000 amendment) was passed to deal with the risks of disturbances in its trade flows with the EU. However, this Act[878] exempts small business, those with an annual turnover of less than three million Australian dollars, from its ambit. This "threshold exempts 94% of all Australian businesses which conduct 30% of total business sales"[879]. The Working Party commented that "it is necessary to assume that *all* data transfers to Australian businesses are potentially to a small business operator which is not subject to the law"[880]. The Working Party also noted that the treatment of sensitive data under the Act was not up to the European standards while problems were detected to the right of the European citizens to correct their personal data. Therefore, it concluded that the Australian law could be found adequate "only if appropriate safeguards were introduced to meet the above mentioned concerns". Norway "despite a lack of any constitutional guarantee of privacy and a history of enacting sectoral legislation similar to the US"[881] passed the Personal Data Act of 2000. Chile passed the Law for the Protection of Private Life in 1999. It has 24

---

[875] Leah E. Frazier, Extraterritorial Enforcement of PIPEDA: A multi-tiered Analysis, 36 George Washington, International Law Review, 2004, page 212.
[876] Asim Z. Haque, Mathie H. Le, 2004 Privacy Year in Review Annual Update: International: Privacy Year in Review: Canada's PIPEDA and Japan's Personal Information Protection Act, 1 Journal of Law and Policy for the Information Society, 2005, page 478.
[877] See: http://ec.europa.eu/justice_home/fsj/privacy/thridcountries/adequacy-faq_en.htm#1 and http://europa.eu/rapid/pressReleasesAction.do?reference=IP/02/46&format=HTML&aged=1&language=EN&guiLanguage=en accessed on July 11th 2006.
[878] See: David Lindsay, An Exploration of the Conceptual Basis of Privacy and the Implications for the Future of Australian Privacy Law, 29 Melbourne University Law Review 131, 2005.
[879] Alexandra T. McKay, The Private Sector Amendment to Australia's Privacy Act: A First Step on the Road to Privacy, 14 Pacific Rim Law & Policy Journal, 2005, page 233.
[880] See Working Party Opinion 3/2001 on the level of protection of the Australian Privacy Amendment (Private Sector) Act 2000: http://ec.europa.eu/justice_home/fsj/privacy/docs/wpdocs/2001/wp40en.pdf accessed on July 11th 2006.
[881] Ryan Moshell, And then there was one: the Outlook for a self-regulatory US amidst a Global Trend toward Comprehensive Data Protection, 37 Texas Technology Law Review, 2005, page 390.

articles, covering processing and use of personal data in the public and the private sectors and the rights of individuals (of access, correction, and judicial control)[882]. Japan passed its Data Protection Act in 2003. On May 23, 2003, "the *Diet* passed and enacted the bill (The Personal Data Protection Act) with another package of four information protection bills that comprise two laws that cover private businesses, government organizations and independent administrative agencies"[883]. Ukraine also became active in this field although largely due to its communist past when personal data was treated as an essential tool in the hands of the regime in order to exercise effective control on the local population, it possessed no previous experience in data protection. Its parliament has registered "two bills the Bill on Personal Character Information and the Bill on Protection of Personal Data"[884]. The proposals were seen as a proof of Ukraine's choice to come closer to EU norms and legislation aspiring to participate in European integration in the future. The impact of the directive can be quite important in certain industries such as outsourcing as well. Several businesses around the world have responded to globalisation challenges and international competition by ceding certain of their functions such as data processing to entities based in other jurisdictions usually with low labour costs. Therefore, a bank in the UK can send the data of its clients to India to have them processed. The passing of the directive and the subsequent national legislations had a substantial impact on such an argument. For example "Lloyds TSB Group Union filed suit against Lloyds TSB alleging violations of the Data Protection Act for the bank's decision to outsource work to India"[885]. The argument laid on the premise that India's protection of personal data does not meet the EU's adequacy criterion. In such a case the company in question, which has outsourced the personal data of European citizens can face grave fines along with lawsuits from clients whose personal information such as credit card numbers, account numbers, addresses and telephone numbers have been leaked.

---

[882] See: http://www.privacyinternational.org/article.shtml?cmd%5B347%5D=x-347-83550 July 11th 2006.
[883] See: http://www.privacyinternational.org/survey/phr2003/countries/japan.htm July 11th 2006.
[884] Olena Dmytrenko, Cara D. Cutler, Does Ukraine need a Comprehensive Statute to "control" private data controllers?, 5 Washington University Global Studies Law Review, 2006, page 42.
[885] Justin Kent Holcombe, Solutions for Regulating Offshore Outsourcing in the Service Sector: Using the Law, Market, International Mechanisms, and Collective Organisations as Building Blocks, 7 Univesity of Pennsylvania Journal of Labour and Employment Law, 2005, page 572. See also: Mohd. Salman Waris, Indian law-a semblance of data privacy, Privacy and Data Protection, 2005. Linda S. Spedding, An Overview on Outsourcing, Advising Business: Law & Practice, 2005. Roger K. Baker, Offshore IT Outsourcing and the 8th Data Protection Principle with reference to Financial Services, International Journal of Law and Information Technology, 2006.

Thus, the problem emerging rapidly and unexpectedly for US businesses had three dimensions. The first is more obvious and entails the possibility of data transfer ban from the EU to US with easily predicted consequences on trade between the two partners. The second comprises the already mentioned possibility of dealing with a variety of countries important for US trade that would have adopted laws in compliance with EU standards. The final dimension refers to the "European subsidiaries that must comply with privacy laws in the countries where they have operations, and such foreign privacy laws can be significantly more constraining than their US counterparts"[886]. The radical shift in the way rules at the level of international trade are created brought uproar both in US industry and literature. "With regard to new developments in the law, close attention should be paid to those countries and legal systems, which are most likely to influence others because of their strong position in the global marketplace. The US plays a leading role in a number of economic fields, but its position concerning e-commerce is an astonishingly dominating one"[887]. Moreover, in 2001 just after the EU directive came into force "the European on line industry was approximately one tenth of the size of that of the US"[888]. The EU data protection directive was the first time that the US had to face a situation where rules and guidelines were set by another partner. The EU, a market place of 450 million consumers proved that it had the ability to impose its own standards as one of the most important parties in world trade. "Before the EU became a single economic entity, no European country had as crucial a trading relationship with the US as does the unified EU. Combined into a single trading partner the Union has the kind of trading power that makes it critical to find common ground"[889]. "US companies are unwilling to forego the immense European market and have concluded it is most efficient to adapt their worldwide product and service offerings to EU requirements...sometimes size really does matter"[890]. The issue assumes even more importance if it is taken into account that "in practical terms the dispute and its resolution engaged the world's two most powerful and highly interdependent economic entities. Together the EU and the US account for more than

---

[886] Glover Rodney supra note 872 at page 1.
[887] Ulrich Christian, Consumer Protection in Electronic Commerce Transactions in Germany and in the United States, Part II, GrayCary, Journal of Internet Law, 2000, available at www.gcwf.com/articles/journal/jil_dec00_1.html , accessed on 5/02/2002.
[888] Ah-Wong Jacqueline, Gandhi Puja, Patel Heena, Targett David, Shah Urvi, Tran ToDenh, E-Commerce Progress: inhibitors and the short term future, European Business Journal, 2001, page 100.
[889] Clear Marie, supra note 870, page 984.
[890] Thomas Daemen, Book Review: The United States of Europe: The New Superpower and the End of American Supremacy by T.R Reid, 11 Columbia Journal of European Law 717, 2005.

half of the world GDP"[891]. Moreover, "the relationship between the US and Europe is the engine of the world economy and information flow is the oil that keeps the machinery running"[892]. The importance of US-EU trade relations[893] and the central role acquired by the data protection directive are perfectly highlightened.

8.2 Differences in the way privacy is perceived in Europe and the US

8.2.1 European Values v American Sensitivities

State Regulation v Self Regulation

Americans and European perceive privacy "in fundamentally different ways"[894]. This divergence can be linked with the speciality of the nature of privacy as "the sense of what must be kept private, of what must be hidden before the eyes of others, seems to differ strangely from society to society...this is a point frequently made by citing the literature of ethnography...and a large historical literature"[895]. Thus, the debate between the US and the continental EU countries has to be viewed through this angle as "the conflict reflects unmistakable differences in sensibilities about what ought to be kept private...on the two sides of the Atlantic with the two different cultures of privacy"[896]. It is also an issue of the societal composition as France and Germany are relatively homogeneous in the sense that their history was based from an early stage on the notion of the nation state with common cultural and moral values. US is "extremely heterogeneous...and pluralistic, it is difficult for its population to agree on core values"[897] as its backgrounds can be so different. The differences in the matter of

---

[891] Long J. William, Quek Pang Marc, Personal Data Privacy Protection in an age of globalisation: the US-EU Safe Harbour Compromise, Journal of European Public Policy, June 2002, Taylor & Francis Ltd, page 326.
[892] The same.
[893] See also: Smitherman W Charles, The New Transatlantic Marketplace: A Contemporary Analysis of the US – EU Trade Relations and Possibilities for the Future, 12 Minnesota Journal of Global Trade, 2003, 251.
[894] Fromholz M. Julia, Foreign Law: a) Data Privacy: The European Union Data Privacy Directive, 15 Berkeley Technology Law Journal, 2000, page 466, accessed via LEXIS-NEXIS.
[895] Whitman Q James, supra note 655, page 1153.
[896] Whitman supra note 655 at page 1154 and 1160.
[897] Eberle J Edward, supra note 688, page 1049.

approach are even reflected in the exact terminology the two parties use when referring to the particular issue. "Americans tend to use the word "privacy", while the Europeans discuss "data protection"[898]".

The divergence in the terms used, reveals a deeper philosophical difference over which is and must be the appropriate role of the state in a modern society. This divergence has also been supported by the different set of values and priorities dominant in the legal traditions of the two sides. As analysed extensively before, in the European legal tradition privacy appears directly linked with human dignity and the right to develop freely one's personality. In the US the dominant principle at the top of the country's legislative agenda has traditionally been "liberty" to the pursuance of which the Americans have shaped their legal system. Of course as all legal concepts, liberty has also been shaped in accordance with the history of the US in a way that reflects its distinctive cultural pattern. While in Europe "liberty" means freedom against everyone that can infringe it, in the US it is more narrowly defined to freedom against the State. This reveals "different starting points and different ultimate understandings of what counts as a just society[899]". While, Europeans seem to rely on the state to regulate an ambit of protection of their personal dignity, the Americans feel that the latter will be best protected if the state refrains from regulating any such area. Europeans appear to pursue different political and social ideals founded on the necessity to safeguard their public image that can be impaired by the collection of details related to their personal lives that they would prefer to remain private. On the other hand, Americans pursue freedom as an expression of their ability to develop their activities unobstructed by government interference. Companies in the US can promote policies that are not consistent with sufficient data protection standards, because in any case that makes them more efficient as they save costs. Although, the US consumers give up part of their privacy due to the lack of data protection policies on behalf of the companies, they don't demonstrate any particular sort of resentment, because they enjoy the fruits of the companies' efficiency. "Willingness of exchange suggests that each party receives something they value more highly than the thing they are exchanging, and this is efficient indeed, it lies at the heart of the concept of economic efficiency"[900]. "Markets

---

[898] The same.
[899] Whitman Q James, supra note 655, page 1163.
[900] Martin C. McWilliams, Applicants laid Bare: The Privacy Economics of University Application Files, 34 Hofstra Law Review, 2005, page 193.

tend to achieve maximum economic efficiency with maximum information...a perfectly competitive market achieves highest efficiency but presumes perfect information...sufficient information leads to correct assessment of consumer demand, attracts optimal investment...while strong privacy rights restrict the availability of highly relevant information leading to...inefficient allocation of resources"[901]. For example frequent visits to certain commercial sites reveal the actual preferences or needs of a certain consumer. This data can be included in a personal profile which can be used for the shaping of a personalised marketing strategy which will save the company from forwarding thousands of spam mails to a variety of recipients since it can address that particular user with tailored advertisements taking into account his purchasing habits. Moreover, large commercial sites such as Amazon.com could not be able to effectively deal with demand and allocate their resources in an efficient way with strong data protection legislation in force. If consumers at a certain period prefer a certain title (The Da Vinci Code or the Harry Potter books) Amazon needs to contact the publishers to buy large numbers of those particular titles and not for instance of purely historical books which during that period will have a low demand. The unrestricted use of personal data can indeed lead to the better planning of business strategies on behalf of the business and to a greater abundance of choices for consumers.

On the other hand, European citizens appear to need more than efficiency. They need to feel assured that the choices they make as consumers will not jeopardise their private lives by shedding light on angles of personal life which they would have preferred them to remain private. "The idea that any merchant might have access to the image of your financial history is simply too intuitively distasteful to people brought up in the continental world"[902]. Dignity and protection of privacy supersedes some economic arguments and finds its place at the top of the citizens' agenda. This is clearly reflected in the different perception over the tracking of consumer data on the two sides of the Atlantic. The Americans focus on the benefits from such a practice, which are linked again with the achievement of "efficiency" such as the ability "of the marketers to learn more easily the consumers' preferences and provide them more easily with the

---

[901] Shubhankar Dam, Remedying a Technological Challenge: Individual Privacy and Market Efficiency; Issues and Perspectives on the Law relating to Data Protection, 15 Albany Law Journal of Science & Technology, 2005, page 347.
[902] Whitman, supra note 655, page 1192.

goods and services they seek"[903]. Data Protection legislation like the EU Directive entails a greater control on behalf of the consumers of their personal information, a practice which does not find many supporters in the USA. "We must recognise the costs of granting to citizens too much control over personal data. Such costs include inefficiency…people can conceal unfavourable personal information to the detriment of their business and communication partners"[904]. On the other hand the absence of such legislation in Europe was deemed to allow intrusive practices and violations of the personal individual scope which reveal parts of the behaviour and personality of the people abusing their dignity. "Protecting privacy is an important way of ensuring that individuals receive the respect they deserve, whether or not there is any quantifiable economic benefit that can be set off against efficiency losses or increased regulatory costs"[905]. Apart from that, by addressing the major fears of the Europeans over the treatment of their on line collected personal data with the passing of the relevant legislative initiatives, the EU had also moved towards enhancing the efficiency of its domestic on line industry as well. If we take into account that on line insecurity and an ambiguous landscape over the security of transactions and personal data had discouraged many Europeans to take advantage of the full commercial capacity of internet the passing of the relevant legislation to allay those fears had actually opened new market dimensions to the industry. It is true that some additional costs or procedures are now necessary in order to comply with the requirements of the directive but at least it has attempted to deal with the most basic of the reasons behind the European consumers' reluctance to conduct their transactions on line at least to the extent that Americans do. Although, the directive and the supportive mechanism it established are relatively recent "over 62% of the data controllers surveyed by the European Commission did not believe responding to data requests was a significant resource drain"[906]. Thus, "enhancing protection appears to be just one way to boost business"[907] especially by ensuring a sizeable part of the public which refused to

---

[903] The same.
[904] Jerry Kang & Benedikt Buchner, Privacy in Atlantis, 18 Harvard Journal of Law and Technology, 2004, page 251.
[905] James P. Nehf, Incomparability and the Passive Virtues of ad hoc Privacy Policy, 76 University of Colorado Law Review, 2005, page 3.
[906] Todd A. Nova, The Future Face of the Worldwide Data Privacy Push as a factor affecting Wisconsin Businesses dealing with Consumer Data, 22 Wisconsin International Law Journal, 2004, page 799.
[907] Olena Dmytrenko, Ali Nardali, .NET Passport under the Scrutiny of US and EU Privacy Law: Implications for the Future of Online Authentication, 1 The Ohio State University, Journal of Law and Policy for the Information Society, 2005, page 624.

compromise with conceding part of its privacy on line to engage in e-commerce activities.

In addition to that, the argument over "efficiency" and its presumed undermining in case of setting data protection principles which have to be met appears to be flawed from a historical point of view as well. Data protection law or consumer law were not the only ones which flourished in contrast to such claims over placing hurdles to efficiency. Another established part of law such as environmental law also found its way to international legal prominence albeit statements made on behalf of industry that it would impose costly requirements that certain businesses would have to meet. It is now however internationally accepted that business cannot expand and develop in disrespect to environmental law principles. Societies have therefore traditionally imposed legitimate limits to economic practices in fulfilment of other superior social aims. An additional historical fact could be included in such an analysis. The creation of the European social state was founded on similar principles. If judged from a pure economic point of view it can be supported that it has been proved economically inefficient as it led to the financing of certain social policies which do not attract the approval of business world such as social and unemployment benefits etc. This is the reason that the social state in the form we have experienced it in Europe was not introduced and implemented in the US. However, the governments of most European countries, which are included in the list of the world's most developed nations, have found it imperative to fund such policies in order to limit existing social differences, achieve a certain degree of wealth redistribution and assist the parts of the society in greatest need. Europe took social considerations in account while designing its economic policies and this choice did not prevent it from becoming one of the world's most developed regions where social differences did not become as sharp as in the US. This historical and empirical experience must be used in the e-commerce framework. Human rights considerations should be taken into account while designing internet policies. Data protection should stand at the core of such policies without thoughts of potential risks for efficiency. In any event the latter would be undermined in case of an unregulated internet where the consumers and the citizens feel that their data are left exposed for everyone to illegitimately use them. Europe has proved up to now that respect for human rights in this case privacy, is not only compatible with efficiency but also a requirement for its achievement.

In this context, the on line personal data collection policies of the US enterprises remained an object of self regulation, away from any unpleasant government interference, while in Europe the element of "dignity" shifted the balance from "efficiency" to state regulation of the citizens' privacy, shaped on the basis of consent and limited purpose. In Europe, it was widely supported that efficiency and privacy can be compatible. This compatibility could be constructed on the grounds that underlined the creation of the directive. Privacy was not perceived to be realised with restrictions of data flows, but rather with regulating requirements that can legitimise the collection and processing of the personal data. In the US, even this was found to contrast with market mechanisms that should always be left to function on their own.

Thus, "while the US purports to rely more on market mechanisms, the European Union relies more on state regulation"[908]. The latter also recognises "in a way that the US' sectoral approach to privacy legislation has not, that data once gathered becomes a commodity independent of the industry that collected it"[909]. The US system "an eclectic blend of common law, statutes and contract is in keeping with our (the American) values far more than alternatives found in Europe, which in the data protection area are covered by comprehensive and intrusive public licensing and regulatory bodies"[910]. The difference lies in the premise that "privacy has historically not been an established right in the United States"[911], but also to the "role of the government in private life"[912]. The comparison with the evolution of data protection in Europe throughout the last century, which was analysed thoroughly at a previous part of the book, will offer a clear picture of the existing differences in approach. The adoption of such a stance is not related only to privacy issues but it shares much stronger and deeper roots in the collective American national identity, culture and historical experience. "In child rearing Americans concentrate on teaching the child to be himself and self-dependent preparing

---

[908] Shaffer Gregory, Globalisation and Social Protection: The Impact of EU and International Rules in the Ratcheting Up of US Privacy Standards, 25 The Yale Journal of International Law, 2000, page 3, accessed via LEXIS-NEXIS.
[909] Laura Hildner, Defusing the Threat of RFID: Protecting Consumer Privacy through Technology Specific Legislation at the State Level, 41 Harvard Civil Rights – Civil Liberties Law Review, 2006, page 155.
[910] Finkin W. Matthew, Employee Privacy, American Values and the Law, 72 Chicago Kent Law Review, 1996, page 222.
[911] Winer M. Jonathan, Regulating the Free Flow of Information: A Privacy Czar as the Ultimate Big Brother, 19 John Marshall Journal of Computer and Information Law, 2000, page 38, accessed via LEXIS-NEXIS.

him for his individual struggle in life"[913]. When the United States acquired their independence and drafted their constitution the concept of privacy was defined by American political theory on the basis of certain parameters. "First was the concept of individualism…second was the principle of limited government with its corollaries…the moral primacy of the private over the public sphere of society…third was the central importance of private property and its linkage with the individual's exercise of liberty…to free citizens from…control…exercised over subjects by kings…in the European society"[914]. Thus, the liberty to live without state intervention even in the form of state regulation is an integral part of American identity. If this principle is combined with that of individualism which basically entrusts the individual citizens with a variety of rights and the responsibility to conduct their life with minimal interference or even assistance from the state the reasons behind the American reluctance to adopt the European state centred approach becomes more evident. These principles have led to additional essential differences between the American and continental European societies as the example of the role and development of the social state in the two continents reveals. The third principle on which the American legal and political theories were based is also indicative of the chasm between American and European philosophical approaches. The primacy of private property, which is to be interpreted as conducting private activities without being subject to persistent regulation by a superior authority irrespective of whether this is the king or a government stands at the core of American political beliefs. The popularity in the US legal theory of dealing with privacy from a property right's perspective, which can and should be distributed by its owner in absolute accordance to his wishes determined by the price for giving it away stems from this principle. Hence, it can be easily concluded that "traditionally Americans have been less likely than Europeans to turn to the government to regulate private enterprise, instead relying on the market or new technologies to address public concerns about commercial activities"[915]. In Western Europe there is an expectation on behalf of the public that the government will actively engage in the protection of the rights of its citizens. The role of the government in the

---

[912] Flora J. Garcia, Bodil Lindqvist: A Swedish Churchgoer's Violation of the European Union's Data Protection Directive should be a Warning to US Legislators, 15 Fordham Intellectual Property, Media & Entertainment Law Journal, 2005, page 1206.
[913] Alan F. Westin, Privacy and Freedom, Atheneum, New York, 1967, page 11.
[914] Ibid at page 330.
[915] Fromholz M. Julia, supra note 895, page 467.

European economy and society is overwhelming as the state does fund "extensive social security systems intended to reduce social inequality"[916], while it maintains a central if not the most important role in health and education along with the supervision of economic activities through a number of independent authorities such as the Competition Authority, which are established to ensure that the market respects the existing state regulations. Since, in Europe the role of government in regulating the citizens' rights is not only legitimate but highly desirable the choice for protecting aspects of privacy with the adoption of data protection legislation became clear at an early stage. An example of the impact of the divergence in the approach towards the concepts of "private" and "public" between the US and the EU on privacy is the use of genetic information by employers. In the US where the focus is placed on the individual, the issue is dealt with by "legislation that is predominantly designed to address misuses of genetic information as workplace discrimination"[917]. It views the misuse of such data as a form of discrimination against the employee in question. In this case the employee must prove he was a victim of discrimination caused by the results of the use of his personal data. On the contrary the EU takes a clear data protection approach in accordance to which the employee has a legitimate interest in controlling his sensitive data, which takes precedence over the general interests of the employer unless the latter can effectively use one of the exceptions of article six of the directive on sensitive data and manages to legitimately make use of it. Thus, in Europe "privacy is not a subject you can bargain about as it is considered a fundamental human right"[918]. The EU legal order has shaped a comprehensive framework within which privacy stands as a fundamental human right and adopted a more proactive approach in accordance with post war historical experiences. "The United States, however, has rejected all attempts to legislate any full set of standards...and insisted on a more reactive policy"[919]. Thus, in the framework of the reactive policy context, the "US has

---

[916] Yohei Suda, Monitoring E-mail of Employees in the Private Sector: A Comparison between Western Europe and the United States, 4 Washington University Global Studies Law Review, 2005, page 251.
[917] Nancy J King, Sukanya Pillay, Gail A Lasprogata, Workplace Privacy and Discrimination Issues related to Genetic Data: A Comparative Law Study of the European Union and the United States, 43 American Business Law Journal, 2006, page 159.
[918] Schriver R. Robert, You cheated, you lied: The Safe Harbour Agreement and its Enforcement by the Federal Trade Commission, 70 Fordham Law Review, 2002, page 2778, accessed via LEXIS-NEXIS.
[919] Reidenberg R. Joel, Restoring Americans' Privacy in Electronic Commerce, 14 Berkeley Technology Law Journal, 1999, page 773, accessed via LEXIS-NEXIS.

generally advocated a self regulatory approach to governing electronic commerce"[920]. "Self regulation has obvious attractions…as businesses that participate in voluntary schemes are likely to have more loyalty to these rules than to imposed legal norms"[921]. It is the "least intrusive and most efficient means to ensure fair information practices, given the rapidly evolving nature of the Internet and computer technology"[922]. In addition to that, self regulation appears to be more flexible than legislation as it is relatively easy to adjust it to potentially new circumstances which may in the meantime occur. This assumption is based on the dynamic interaction between technology and the shaping of policy. "Whether policy makers rely on courts, statutes or moral persuasion in an effort to regulate or control how technologies are being developed and used, all of these regulatory levers interact with the technology in a very interesting way. Namely, the technology changes"[923]. The self regulation approach can appear more flexible from a cultural point of view as well especially if it is to be picked up as a "solution which the industry itself has devised and it allows for regional and cultural variation to take into account the different standards of different societies"[924]. In a big divergent country such as the US with a federal system governing fifty states with different approaches and views such a system can produce obvious benefits. Furthermore, self regulation avoids the "one size fits all" effect of state introduced general legislation. The legislative approach might not take into account differences between industries or technologies. "For instance it may be entirely appropriate to differentiate between the regulation of biometric authentication in the banking industry and the video rental industry"[925]. However, it can also create a tension between "consumer legitimate expectations and a more business orientated conception of fair trading"[926].Bergkamp argues that "in market economies business use of personal data would appear to be self

---

[920] Global Information Infrastructure Commission, Consumer Protection in Electronic Commerce, An overview of Current Initiatives, August 1999, available at www.giic.org/focus/ecommerce/ , accessed on 24/06/2003.
[921] Howells Geraint, Wilhelmsson Thomas, supra note 28, page 385.
[922] Pippin Ken, Consumer Privacy on the Internet: It's "Surfer Beware", 47 The Air Force Law Review, 1999, page 125.
[923] Michael A Geist, Doris Estelle Long, Leslie Ann Reis, David E Sorkin and Fred Von Lohmann Copyright and Privacy: Collision or coexistence? Conference Brochure: Copyright & Privacy, Through the Technology Lens, 4 The John Marshall Law School Review of Intellectual Property Law, 2005, page 244.
[924] Conor Foley, Liberating Cyberspace, Civil Liberties, Human Rights and the Internet, edited by Liberty, Pluto Press, London, 1999, page 276.
[925] Gwen Kennedy, Thumbs Up for Biometric Authentication, 8 Computer Law Review & Technology Journal, 2004, page 401.
[926] The same at page 387.

limiting as a result of the market mechanism...legislation involves the state's coercive powers and restricts the liberties of the persons that are subject to its requirements...thus, coercion and legislation is an evil"[927]. This opinion takes for granted that the market mechanisms are in a position to solve every problem and deal effectively with challenges on personal liberties. The book strongly objects to this argument. This argument places an enormous weight behind industry, along with the belief that the interests of the citizens coincide with those of business. There is no question that in many cases, this is achievable, but it is more important to strike a balance between competing or conflicting interests than ignore consumer fears by vesting maximum trust in the market's ability to promote effective policies in all fields. Bergkamp is also against state regulation because "by allowing people to determine the face they want to present to the world, we allow them to deprive others of a competitive or economic advantage...as it restricts the ability to learn about the less attractive side of individuals and to communicate that information to others...and hence increases the risk that people...defraud other people"[928]. There is a loophole in this analysis. It is a matter that falls within the absolute discretion of individuals to decide which parts of their personal life should be communicated to others in complete dependence with the nature or purpose of such communication. This is a basic right related to their ability to live their lives without the sense that the latter lacks private character. Judging this basic need with "competitive" requirements reveals the real grounds of the arguments, which have nothing to do with sensitivities over citizens rights that can be supposedly better dealt with under complete market freedom. As a confirmation of this the Federal Trade Commission "in its 1998 report to Congress, decided that self regulation was not working to protect the privacy of children on line...as 88% of the sites studied collected personal identifying information...by May 2000 the FTC noted improvement but...not enough to ward off a call for legislation"[929]. However, it has to be noted that in 2001 it shifted its position as "it is still too soon to fashion workable legislation"[930]. The US restated its faith in self regulation. An example of the divergence in the level of protection afforded to European and American consumers was provided by the change

---

[927] Bergkamp Lucas, supra note 169, page 35.
[928] Bergkamp, supra note 169, page 36.
[929] MacDonnell, supra note 302, page 361.
[930] Kambas J William, A Safety Net in the E-Marketplace: The Safe Harbour Principles offer comprehensive Privacy Protection without stopping Data Flow, 9 ILSA Journal of International and Comparative Law, 2002, page 150.

of policy in the use of personal data on the part of Amazon.com. In September 2000 Amazon.com announced to its clients that in contrast to its declared policy up to that point it would share its customers' personal data with selected third parties. The customers who objected to the new policy were free to release themselves from their relationship with the company but the lists with their personal data such as their credit card numbers along with their purchasing choices and personal preferences and habits were left in the possession of Amazon.com and subject to its new policy. The important issue was that "nothing in current US law or regulatory policy prevents Amazon from doing so"[931]. In the EU, this issue might have drawn civil or criminal liability especially if sensitive personal data were involved. The data subject should have provided his consent to the use of his data, which should have been used for an end approved by him.

So, it continues to be the case that "in the US context negotiations with private parties, specifically industry, to obtain self regulations instead of binding regulations is often a privileged tool. This, of course, avoids bureaucratic controls…leading to flexible implementation by the private actors, but this transfer of responsibility to business is very worrying"[932]. It is not only very worrying, but also quite ineffective. Moreover, "the FTC's goal has not been to mandate strong consumer friendly information practices only market efficient ones"[933]. The market mechanisms that were presented before can lead to effective self regulation, when there is some sort of pressure brought by one group, in this case the consumers, to the industry. When the group most affected by some market practices pursues its interests in a collective manner that embodies not only its determination but, more importantly in business terms the reputation and the market appeal of the enterprises in question they can be effective. Internet, however, and consequently on line consumers present some particularities that render such market mechanisms if not irrelevant at least non functional. Instead of being able to pursue their interests, consumers "face a collective action problem in seeking as a group to bring about the collective good of more respectful website privacy practices. Groups will stand their best chance of pursuing

---

[931] Richard Hunter, World Without Secrets, Business, Crime and Privacy in the Age of Ubiquitous Comuting, Gartner Press, John Wiley & Sons Inc, page 7.
[932] Catinat Michel, The National Information Infrastructure Initiative in the United States – Policy or Non Policy? Part 1, Computer and Telecommunications Law Review, 1998, 4 (3), page 73.

collective goods when the membership is close knit…this is more likely for groups that are close to one another in geographical space, and for groups that share similar…preferences and histories"[934]. Thus, the character of internet as an international network providing access to an international audience with distinctive cultures, in the framework of which "reacting to industry practices" might be a concept completely unknown, in conjunction with the severe organisational problems one may have to face in order to coordinate the efforts of several thousands of people spread around the globe, render self regulation initiatives in the digital environment an unfortunate choice of tool to balance the interests in question. Furthermore, this diversity inherent in the nature of internet is not only decisive when it comes to the body of consumers, but has a significant impact also on the commercial world. "Even within the group of merchants one is likely to find a heterogeneous structure of social, cultural, economic, moral, and criminal versatility and diversity…this divergence in values will make it difficult for the private sector to establish a common set of norms"[935]. Hence, the lack of uniformity of ideals and objectives is not only the principal characteristic of one of the parties in the digital relationship, but marks at the same degree the enterprise world. The latter can appear to have different business philosophies, divergent management norms, corporate cultures, distinctive moral limitations and thus, difficulties of coordinating. Moreover, appealing to a global audience, as is the case for on line business, provides more incentives to employ every possible method to consolidate one's position in such a lucrative and wide market than ensuring one's position in a market previously confined to national geographic limits. Now, companies have additional reasons to make use of any means available to take advantage of the vast international market and can impinge on the consumers' privacy and data without the ethical reservations of the past. The cost of the opposite would be too high. And let's not forget that the information technology means that facilitated the unprecedented growth of world trade, were the same that actually enabled the collection of data at least with such impressive ease. Thus, in such conditions it would be deeply

---

[933] James P. Nehf, Shopping for Privacy on Line: Consumer Decision Making Strategies ad the Emerging Market for Information Privacy, 2005 University of Illinois Journal of Law, Technology and Policy, page 4.
[934] Hetcher A Steven, The Emergence of Website Privacy Norms, 7 Michigan Telecommunications Technology Law Review, 2001, 1.
[935] Alboukrek Karen, Adapting to a New World of E-Commerce: The Need for Uniform Consumer Protection in the International Electronic Marketplace, 35 George Washington International Law Review, 2003, page 453.

doubtful if not impossible that the "invisible hand" of the free market that Adam Smith described, would be sufficient to alleviate the relevant fears.

Even if convergence of policies is achieved and industry agrees to adhere to specific self regulation norms, there is another important obstacle to be tackled. Self regulation norms fail to prove their value, when they cannot be effectively enforced. In the US "enforcement of the privacy standards occurs through organisational sanctions only. There is no recourse to traditional venues, such as the courts, in the event of non compliance"[936]. "The US may be unique in endorsing self regulation without legal sanctions to incentivise it or enforce it. It is hard to believe that the strategy is anything more than a political device to avoid regulation"[937]. Even if the development of a respectful Alternative Dispute Resolution system can have a beneficial effect on consumer issues, it has to be built on solid bases. The influence of such systems in Europe is at least up to now marginal and their efficacy in the US remains to be seen. Thus, although self regulation policies do have positive aspects as they involve to a greater degree the businesses concerned, the particular nature of the internet requires state intervention. That cannot be interpreted as an effort to heavily regulate an indeed rapidly developing field, but to readjust the existing legislative framework to the new landscape. With close cooperation between government and industry, frequent updates and flexible interpretations of the legal framework, that can be achieved. The fact that the internet is an area marked by its vast size does not mean that it should remain unregulated or governed by instruments that lack the necessary effectiveness. Consumer confidence, a necessary precondition for the success of the net as a commercial field, will be hampered if the net remains a place of anarchy undermining legitimate consumer interests. Many commentators share this view and have reached the conclusion that because "self regulation policy is severely inadequate…governmental is necessary in order to regulate the dissemination of personal information gathered by the web sites"[938].

---

[936] Jeffrey B Ritter, Benjamin S Hayes, Henry L Judy, supra note 622, page 109.
[937] Froomkin Michael, Symposium: Cyberspace and Privacy: A new legal paradigm? The death of privacy?, supra note 179, page 1527.
[938] Kotzker Jason, The Great Cookie Carer: Internet Privacy and Target Marketing At Home and Abroad, 15 Saint Thomas Law Review, 2003, page 730.

8.2.2. EU v US

Human Right v Property Right

For the United States to accept such a view and adopt the corresponding legal framework "would be a jarring change from the current privacy regime"[939]. That is explained by the fact that "the US legal system treats privacy as a personal property right that may be disposed of as one sees best, rather than an unassailable human right"[940]. "American notions of privacy are historically reflected in the concept of "rugged individualism". Privacy has been deemed to be akin to personal property…we can trade our privacy as though it were something we individually own"[941]. Affording our privacy the character of a property right can have some very serious repercussions. Such a choice "does not by itself determine how property rights should be allocated between the individual and the collectors. Why should the individual's claim to her personal information be prior to the claim of collectors?"[942]. According to the "labour desert theory", the rights of collectors must be protected to a greater degree than that of the data subjects, because "a person who invests her labour in a common good acquires a property in it"[943]. Thus, the question raised by some academics is to whom does the data belong? Do they belong to the data subject, to whom they refer to or to the data collector since due to his investment they were able to acquire commercial value and be gathered in the first place? Apart from the ambiguity over the issue of the carrier of such right, there are more issues to consider. Even if it is presumed that a property right covering one's personal data is recognised, then the principal question would be its duration. Normally, property rights do not have a specific period of duration and they can be sold or inherited. However, this potential development will clash with some personal data that need to be shared with other parties, such as the data stored by ISPs as an element necessary in the function of internet or health data used by the doctor or the medical institution in question for medical purposes. It has been suggested that this

---

[939] The same.
[940] Long J. William, Quek Peng Marc, supra note 892, page 332.
[941] Kesan P Jay, Cyber Working or Cyber Shirking?: A First Principles Examination of Electronic Privacy in the Workplace, 54 Florida Law Review, page 306.
[942] Bergelson Vera, It's Personal But is it Mine? Towards Property Rights in Personal Information, 37 University of California Davis Law Review, 2003, page 419.
[943] The same.

property right should be shaped having intellectual property as an icon and "in particular copyright with which personal information has certain similarities"[944]. "Both are about balancing a creator's desire to control a particular set of data with consumers' desires to access and redistribute that data"[945]. However, copyright covers the expression of the ideas in question, but not the content of the ideas themselves. Thus, the traditional notion of copyright is rather difficult to afford a satisfactory level of protection. In addition to that further problems can emerge, as "calling information property will not automatically attract standard criminal sanctions against theft or wrongful misappropriation of property. That's because most theft laws are formulated such that wrongdoer must have an intention to permanently deprive the victim of the property in question"[946]. In the case of personal data the issue is that sensitive information will be communicated to parties it should never have reached, but the data subject is still "in possession" of his data. In law meanings are very precise and unless restated they cannot fully apply to novel situations.

However, even the discussions over the property right reflect the chasm between the two sides. In the EU data protection it is described as a fundamental human right, while in the US it is more viewed as "another good that the consumer might choose either to retain or to barter away"[947]. However, it has to be noted that there are some serious arguments supporting the introduction of such a type of protection mainly because by "recognising a property right in such information would not only give consumers certain privileges, but also would give businesses a legal incentive to pay consumers for the use of their personal information as without such incentive businesses could continue collecting, using and disseminating consumers' information with little regard for their interests"[948]. This argument is very serious and should assume a central place in the debate over adequate possible solutions to the privacy lacuna, but it has to be added that it seems that its focus is on the wrong area. If businesses would be inclined to pay the consumers for the use of their data that would

---

[944] Bergelson, supra note 943, page 437.
[945] Sonia K. Katyal, Privacy v Piracy, 9 International Journal of Communications Law and Policy 7, 2004/2005.
[946] Lipton Jacqueline, Protecting Valuable Commercial Information in the Digital age: Law, Policy and Practice, 6.1 J.Tech.L & Pol'Y2, 2000.
[947] Kramer Chuang Lynn, Private Eyes are Watching You: Consumer On-line Privacy Protection – Lessons from Home and Abroad, 37 Texas International Law Journal, 2002, page 390.
[948] Basho Kalinda, The Licensing of Our Personal Information: Is it a Solution to Internet Privacy?, 88 California Law Review, 2000, page 1526.

definitely be some sort of relief for a great number of them, but the problem is that according to my opinion it still does not address the real issue. The issue is not if a given company pays a consumer an amount of money in return for the use of his sensitive medical data, but the real issue amounts to discovering a formula so that a company will not be able to process such sensitive data at all. The focus must be on the nature of the processing of the data, the objective for which it takes place and of course the consent of the data subject rather than the acquisition of a material return after the dissemination of important personal data. The issue is not getting money in return for the data escaping our control, but being able to control at least the most private of the information that concerns us. On this basis the focus of the property right debate has been misleading. Personal privacy "is a good for every individual that deserves to be protected in its own right on grounds that ought to be differentiated legally and morally from those pertaining to private property or freedom of contract"[949]. An item "is commodified to the extent that we are willing to exchange it for a price in the market"[950]. Thus, the "commodification of personal information will…actually promote the collection and use of personal information"[951] as it will motivate the trading of such data. In relation to that I have to add at this point, that affording a property right value to information presupposes an information and awareness campaign to enlighten the public over its control -or a lack of it- on its personal data, what it means to have them disseminated and the potential repercussions of such dissemination. If the data subjects are not informed with details on the issue, they will accept deals that undermine their privacy in ways they cannot even perceive. Passengers may be willing to reveal every possible detail on their life, because airline companies offer half price tickets, or individuals may fill in all sections of questionnaires drafted by direct marketing companies, because the latter offer them a range of consumer products at great discounts. This danger lurks in the corner. This does not mean that the whole discussion, on whether a property right should be afforded, is not very useful and has not offered important arguments to embark upon. It is a very interesting proposal and should be examined thoroughly as it can contribute to the shaping of an efficient

---

[949] Jean L. Cohen, in Public and Private in Thought and Practice, Perspectives on a Grand Dichotomy, Jeff Weintaub, Krishan Kumar, The University of Chicago Press, Chicago & London, 1997, page 139.
[950] Richard Warner, Surveillance and the Self: Privacy, Identity and Technology, 54 DePaul Law Review, 2005, page 861.
[951] Tal Z. Zrsky, Desperately Seeking Solutions: Using Implementation Based Solutions for the Troubles of Information Privacy in the Age of Data Mining and the Internet Society, 56 Maine Law Review, 2004, page 25.

solution to the problem discussed. However, it should be based on a more adjusted elaboration of already existing legal concepts. However, apart from its practical aspects we should take into account the rich legal and philosophical theory behind this debate. "Unlike proprietary…rights, human dignity…cannot be bartered away or exchanged under traditional notions of…contract law as seen in US law"[952]. This certainly highlights the actual debate founded on the dual character of the communication of information, which can be seen as the exercise of both a human right and in the commercial framework an economic activity. The US have almost exclusively focused on the latter, while the EU have sought a more balanced approach protecting communications as a human right, but with the economic nature very high on the priority agenda. The EU approach as analysed before, embodies a more effective approach both from a practical, albeit with adjustments needed, and a moral point of view.

8.2.3 Regulatory Framework in the USA

"The American legal tradition eschews a powerful state role in society and draws on a deep seated philosophy of limited government. Even in the wake of increases in government regulation following the New Deal and Progressive Eras, US law making rhetoric remained hostile towards the regulation of industry"[953]. There is the fear that even some sort of government regulation will confirm that the "cyberspace has the potential to be the most fully and extensively regulated space that we have ever known, anywhere, at any time in our history. It has the potential to be the antithesis of a space of freedom"[954].

The US uses[955] "a sectoral approach that relies on a mix of legislation,

---

[952] Nancy J King, Sukanya Pillay, Gail A Lasprogata, Regulation of Electronic Employee Monitoring: Identifying Fundamental Principles of Employee Privacy through a Comparative Study of Data Privacy Legislation in the European Union, United States, Canada, 2004 Stanford Technology Law Review 4.
[953] Kesan P Jay, supra note 942, the same.
[954] Lessig in Mailland Julien, Freedom of Speech, the Internet, and the Costs of Control: The French Example, 33 New York University Journal of International Law and Politics, 2001, page 1206.
[955] See also: Myers M Jennifer, Creating Data Protection Legislation in the US: An Examination of the Current Legislation in the EU, Spain, and the United States, 29 Case Western Reserve Journal of International Law, 1997, 109.

regulation and self regulation"[956]. According to literature there are three main characteristics of US privacy law. "It is diverse, decentralised and dynamic"[957]. The diversity element stems from the fact that "the US does not have a unified overarching regime of privacy protection but rather a patchwork of privacy legislation"[958]. The principal reason for that is "the right to privacy is not enumerated in the Constitution, thus the common law has struggled to become the fountain of such right"[959]. Americans have associated their right of privacy with their prerogative to live without any interference on the part of the state. This type of attitude flows from "the unique origination of the US as a group of colonies of individuals who fled the tyranny of a controlling government"[960]. Furthermore, there is an American "obsession with freedom of information that can be characterised as a holdover from the generation that made the nation and thought secrecy in government one of the instruments of Old World tyranny and committed itself to the principle that democracy cannot function unless people are permitted to know what their government is up to"[961]. "Privacy law in the US delivers far less than it promises because it resolves virtually all conflicts in favour of information candour and free speech"[962]. The American idea of privacy is mainly "privacy against the government"[963]. One result of such mentality appears to be that at least in the case of privacy "the fulfilment of the private sector's interests over those of the public"[964], especially if we take into account that as a result of privatisation and deregulation sizeable parts of industry and sectors of economic activity have recently passed from the public to the private sector. This has resulted in personal data "moving between sectors as services previously offered by national governments were devolved to commercial interests"[965]. So, this approach to data protection flowing from "the US philosophy that laws should ensure citizens' access to government, while still

---

[956] Davidson J. Stephen, Andresen A. Katheryn, UCITA and other US Laws in an International EU Perspective, GrayCary, Journal of Internet Law, 2000, available at www.gcwf.com/articles/journal/jil_july00_1.html , accessed on 5/02/2002.
[957] Glancy Dorothy, Symposium on Internet Privacy, At the Intersection of Visible and Invisible, 16 Santa Clara Computer and High Technology Law Journal, May 2000, page 358, accessed via LEXIS-NEXIS.
[958] Schriver R. Robert, supra note 919, page 2786.
[959] Craig Martin, supra note 379, page 807.
[960] Gladstone Julia, supra note 385, page 5.
[961] Swire P Peter, Litan Robert, supra note 624, 683.
[962] David A. Anderson in B.S. Markesinis, Protecting Privacy, 1999, page 140.
[963] The same.
[964] Renée Marlin Bennett , Knowledge Power, Intellectual Property, Information and Privacy, Lynne Rienner Pblishers, Boulder London, 2004, page 246.
[965] David Lyon, Surveillance Society, Monitoring Everyday Life, Open University Press, Buckingham, 2001, page 144.

protecting them from government...this enables the US to regulate the public sector extensively, but generally prevents the federal government from limiting interactions between private citizens"[966]. There is only one federal act protecting informational privacy, the Privacy Act of 1974. Yet it "only applies to data processing conducted by the federal government not by state governments or the private sector"[967]. However, even that Act was accompanied by a certain degree of controversy since it was felt that there was a need to "balance the right of privacy against the right of individuals, the press and others to have assured freedom of access to information"[968]. Therefore, the Privacy Act was succeeded by amendments to the 1966 Freedom of Information Act to endure the maintenance of such a balance. However, after the passing of both Acts "a commission formed under the auspices of the Privacy Act recommended that the policing of informational privacy in the private sector to be left to self regulation and voluntary guidelines...the Congress agreed on setting the precedent for a policy of targeted, largely ineffectual legislation aimed at promoting data privacy in industrial practices"[969].

An additional reason for abandoning a centrally adopted legislative solution was the absence of any explicit privacy right enshrined in the American constitution where the right to privacy is a "watershed of a whole progeny of rights which exist in and through the Constitution for the protection of the privacy of a person"[970]. Thus, the relevant right became the object of regulation only on a pure sectoral basis. In 1998 the Children's Online Privacy Protection Act[971] was passed in order to deal with the sensitivity of the issues related to the collection of personal data belonging to children. One year later the Financial Services Modernisation Act[972] was passed, constituting the first comprehensive legislation in the US in the area of financial services. The Confidential Information Protection and Statistical Efficiency Act (CISPEA) was introduced in 2002[973]. The Act aimed at "protecting the confidentiality of federal

---

[966] Murray Patrick, supra note 625, page 970.
[967] Shaffer Gregory, supra note 909, page 12.
[968] David Lyon & Eli Zureik, Surveillance, computers and Privacy, University of Minnesota Press, Minneapolis/London, 1996, page 157.
[969] Ryan Moshell, supra note 882, page 376.
[970] Alain A. Levasseur, Civil Law, Procedure and Private International Law: The Boundaries of Property Rights: La Notion de Biens, 54 The American Journal of Comparative Law, 2006, page 159.
[971] See also: http://www.ftc.gov/bcp/conline/pubs/buspubs/coppa.htm and
http://www.ftc.gov/privacy/privacyinitiatives/childrens.html accessed on August 17th 2004.
[972] See: http://www.ftc.gov/privacy/glbact/index.html accessed on August 17th 2004.
[973] See: www.eia.doe.gov/oss/CIPSEA.pdf July 12th 2006.

statistical data"[974]. The Cable Communications Policy Act was passed in 1984[975] to protect the privacy of cable subscribers. Disclosure of personal data generally required prior consent, with the two exceptions for business necessity and detection of cable piracy. Disclosure of personal information without consent is also permitted pursuant to a court order. The Video Privacy Protection Act was passed in 1988[976] in reaction to the disclosure of Supreme Court nominee Robert Bork's video rental records in a newspaper. An issue to consider is "is the interaction of the VPPA with the recent Patriot Act, which expanded law enforcement powers to procure information such as library records and individual purchasing records "in the course of an ongoing investigation" a lower standard than the traditional warrant"[977]. The Fair Credit Reporting Act was enacted in 1970 to protect the consumers from the disclosure of inaccurate personal information held by consumer reporting agencies. However, it applies only to the credit industry and its exception, mainly the disclosure of personal data for "legitimate business purposes" is interpreted very widely. The Financial Modernization Act of 1999, otherwise known as the "Gramm-Leach-Bliley Act" or GLB Act, includes provisions to protect consumers' personal financial information held by financial institutions. The GLB "does not cover the transfer of data between affiliates"[978]. "The individual consumer has absolutely no control over this kind of "corporate family" trading of personal information"[979]. It is based on an opt out choice and it lacks a consumer access provision. Therefore, it can be found to contradict even with the principles and provisions of the Safe Harbour agreement between the US and the EU. In general there is an abundance of legislative initiatives regulating several sectors of economic activity with sometimes conflicting provisions, a plethora of exceptions interpreted widely, a regulatory scope which is usually narrow and a lack of an enforcement strategy.

Furthermore, at the level of the federal states there is an absence of federal data protection legislation as the tendency is more towards some sector specific statutes in

---

[974] Douglas J Sylvester, Sharon Lohr, Counting on Confidentiality: Legal and Statistical Approaches to Federal Privacy Law after the USA Privacy Act, 2005 Wisconsin Law Review, page 1072.
[975] See: http://www.buskegroup.com/Conducting_a_Community_Needs_Assessment.pdf July 12th 2006.
[976] See: http://www4.law.cornell.edu/uscode/html/uscode18/usc_sec_18_00002710----000-.html July 12th 2006.
[977] See: http://www.epic.org/privacy/vppa/#cases July 12th 2006.
[978] Kyle Thomas Sammin Any Port in a Storm: Th Safe Harbour, the Gramm Leah Bliley Act and the Problem of Privacy in Financial Services 36 George Washington International Law Review, 2005, page 666.
[979] See: http://www.epic.org/privacy/glba/ July 12th 2006.

force. Although, a number of federal constitutions expressly protect privacy such protection is generally limited to the right of the citizen against the government and do not regulate relations between citizens"[980]. "It may seem odd but in the US the private sector is subject to less regulation over the use of personal information than the public sector"[981]. "The rights of individuals against private parties are primarily found in state tort law"[982]. "There is no comprehensive data protection law in the US. This explains why the EU directive requires only "adequate" protection as opposed to "equivalent" protection, which was the standard in early drafts of the directive"[983]. "The regulation of the private sector has been let to the competence of the market factors. Companies have enough scope to implement their own data protection policies based on an analysis of the market they appeal to and to the degree of interest demonstrated on behalf of the consumers. Privacy protection is seen more as an element inherent in the profile of the company that wants to appear with a pro-consumer image. Market mechanisms are guided to shape a privacy policy because the relative tendency within the American consumers has been detected. It constitutes a response of the industry to growing consumer fears over the destination and use of their private data. Generally, the approach to privacy adopted in the US is "philosophically consistent with the strong tradition of a laissez faire state, which calls for minimal interference of government upon the private sector"[984]. It "seeks to draw a balance between the individual's desire to maintain a level of privacy over his personal information and society's benefit in its use of such information"[985].

8.3 The Safe Harbour Agreement

The Safe Harbour agreement was necessary in order for the requirements of the directive over an "adequate" level of protection offered by third countries to which the data are to be transferred to be satisfied. The directive "in effect forced the US to abide by the EU regulations, to negotiate with it in order to win an interpretation that is more

---

[980] Heydrich W. Michael, supra note 381, page 410.
[981] Ibid at page 14.
[982] Heydrich W. Michael, supra note 381, page 409.
[983] Blanke M. Jordan, Safe Harbour and the European Union's Directive on Data Protection, 11 Albany Law Journal of Science and Technology, 2000, page 64, accessed via LEXIS-NEXIS.
[984] Ibid at page 411.
[985] Castor A. David, Treading Water in the Data Privacy Age: An Analysis of Safe Harbour's first year, 12 Indiana International and Comparative Law Review, page 268, 2002, accessed via LEXIS-NEXIS.

flexible than the words of the directive suggest other than suffer the ill consequences of not being able to transfer data out of the EU"[986]. The eventual conclusion of the agreement had a positive effect on EU policy shaping also as it provided it with the chance to examine thoroughly the directive's application and enforcement. This was quite difficult at the period of time immediately after the directive came into force because "the safe harbour negotiations seemed to occupy the attention of EU regulators that they might have otherwise given to enforcement activities"[987].

The Directive was heavily criticised by various parties in the US, which remained suspicious of the good will on the part of the EU. As analysed before the EU introduced the directive in order to smooth the operation of the common market by enabling the flow of data within it and at the same time to provide the necessary protection to the fundamental right of its citizens to enjoy protection of their personal data and subsequently life. However, in the US the interpretation afforded to the EU motives was not as idealistic as that. The Directive will afford "an economic protectionist advantage against competition from the US and other countries...as a company from the US might find it too expensive to comply with the Directive, thus a European firm might win business that otherwise would have gone to the US firm"[988]. Hence, "it keeps out a number of US competitors...favouring EU companies to the detriment of US ones"[989] and "takes away another competitive tool of internet companies: internet companies could otherwise distinguish themselves from their competitors according to the level of the privacy protection they provide...it will have the effect of levelling the playing field"[990]. Furthermore, the "business that is developing technology to enable users to control the amount of data they reveal may be lost"[991]. That cannot be proved as technology will always evolve, the law will try to catch up, but counter technology will always be necessary for an effective solution. Ira Magaziner, the Clinton administration technology advisor, commented on the

---

[986] Smith Seagrumn, Microsoft and the European Union Face Off over Internet Privacy Concerns, Duke Law and Technology Review, August 2002, page 16, accessed via LEXIS-NEXIS.
[987] Kuner Christopher, Beyond Safe Harbour: European Data Protection Law and electronic Commerce, The International Lawyer, American Bar Association, Chicago, Illinois, Volume 25, number 1, 2001, page 83.
[988] Swire Peter, Litan Robert, supra note 624, 683.
[989] Vitale Angela, The EU Privacy directive and the Resulting Safe Harbour: The Negative Effects on US Legislation concerning Privacy on the Internet, 35 Vanderbilt Journal of Transnational Law, 2002, page 347.
[990] Vitale, ibid at 351.
[991] Ibid page 354.

Directive: "we don't recognise the validity of the EU approach...we would say that the US has equivalent privacy protection. I don't believe it is lesser. I believe it is different"[992]. The "US are favouring deregulation and market forces...they continue to rely heavily on case law developments...the EU in contrast has worked to construct a coherent edifice that balances state control and market forces"[993]. "The US have maintained a regulation averse approach to privacy"[994] because, the "US business lobby is so strong the resulting web of privacy legislation is thin"[995]. But "the individual data subjects have very little bargaining power. Traditionally, this is where government should step in, but to date, the US government has all but refused"[996]. The European Commission did not however, and the outcome of its interference is the object of reactions from the US.

Some representatives of US industry have suggested that the "Directive imposes unfair restrictions on international trade"[997]. Such a non tariff barrier would violate the principles, if not specific provisions, of the General Agreement on Trade and Tariffs"[998]. In the Uruguay Round no decision was reached on the level of restrictions "one country can impose on another to protect the privacy rights of its citizens"[999]. Article 5(d) of the Final Act Embodying the Results of the Uruguay Round, Annex on Telecommunications reads: "a Member may take such measures as are necessary to ensure the security and confidentiality of messages, subject to the requirement that such measures are not applied in a manner which would constitute a means of arbitrary or unjustifiable discrimination or a disguised restriction on trade in services"[1000]. Thus, the question was whether the privacy rules of the EU constitute a disguised discrimination. The issue is whether the rules in question are applied in the same manner to both domestic and foreign companies. The directive when adopted allows all flows within the EU, as a strong regulatory level is already created. As for foreign companies it

---

[992] Ewing Mike, The Perfect Storm: The Safe Harbour and the Directive on Data Protection, 24 Houston Journal of International Law, 2002, page 336.
[993] Haubold Jens, Kaufman Winn Jane, Electronic Promises: Contract Law Reform and E-Commerce in a Comparative Perspective, European Law Review, 2002, 27 (5), page 567.
[994] Monahan Amy, Deconstructing Information Walls: The Impact of the European Data Directive on US Businesses, 29 Law and Policy in International business, 1998, page 278.
[995] Monahan ibid at page 280.
[996] Monahan supra note 995 at 294.
[997] See also: Sookman B. Barry, E-commerce, Internet and the Law – A Survey of the Legal Issues in Canada, Computer and Telecommunications Law Review, 1999, 5(3), 74 and Chissick Michael, Data Protection in the E-Commerce Era, Computer and Telecommunications Law Review, 1999, 5 (4), 109.
[998] Monahan Amy, supra note 995, page 289.
[999] The same.

requires an "adequate" level, which has made it difficult for American companies to claim discrimination. Thus, there were complains over the scope that the Directive left to individual member states to promote stricter requirement in their national law. US companies are basically afraid that the EU member state will try to assist their lagging industries such as the direct marketing one from stark competition over the more advanced US ones. And when the level of protection is deemed inadequate, the EU blocks the data transfer. "Thus, it lowers the standard but strengthens the enforcement mechanism"[1001]. The EU defended export restrictions "on the grounds of protecting the interests of European citizens against exploitation of their data by US interests and encouraging European data sources to find European providers of the kinds of services otherwise being sought in the US"[1002]. Under the GATS the EU must give "national treatment" to non EU countries. "A company should not be put at a disadvantage solely because it is not from the importing nation and should be treated as it was a company of the importing nation"[1003]. Apart from the fact that the EU applies its data protection legislation on equal terms to both domestic and foreign businesses it is supported that "any ban on data transfers would harm EU registered companies as much as"[1004] the non EU registered ones. In addition to that article XVI of the GATS[1005] justifies the introduction of rules aimed at safeguarding the privacy of individuals as long as they are not a form of arbitrary discrimination.

However, there is also the argument that it is not the directive that violated the WTO rules, but the Safe Harbour agreement. "The EU may have violated its commitments under the WTO by holding American companies to substantially different and lower standards when judging the adequacy of the American privacy regime than it does companies from Australia or elsewhere in the world"[1006]. If found

---

[1000] See: http://www.sice.oas.org/Trade/ur_round/UR25DE.asp accessed on August 16th 2004.
[1001] Monahan, supra 995, at 292.
[1002] Jeffey Ritter, supra note 622, page 100.
[1003] O'Quinn John, supra note 565, 683.
[1004] Colin J. Bennett and Charles D. Raab, The Governance of Privacy, Policy Instruments in Global Perspective, Ashgate, 2003, page 88.
[1005] Article XVI of GATS, General Exceptions: Subject to the requirement that such measures are not applied in a manner which would constitute a means of arbitrary or unjustifiable discrimination between countries where like conditions prevail, or a disguised restriction on trade in services, nothing in this Agreement shall be construed to prevent the adoption or enforcement by any Member of measures: (ii) the protection of the privacy of individuals in relation to the processing and dissemination of personal data and the protection of confidentiality of individual records and accounts

[1006] Shapico Eric, All is not fair in the Privacy Trade: The Safe Harbour Agreement and the World Trade Organisation, 71 Fordham Law Review, 2003, page 2781.

that "through the agreement the EU is offering different and more favourable treatment to the US than that offered to other countries, then the Safe Harbour agreement is a violation of GATS by the EU"[1007] as an infringement of the "treatment no less favourable" principle.

In July 2000, the European Commission after almost two years of negotiations with the US Commerce Department finally approved a set of rules known as the Safe Harbour Agreement designed to allow the flow of data from the EU to the US after the adherence of the companies of the latter to some fixed rules. "Although, the EU considers legislation the most appropriate means to protect data privacy, the safe harbour principles represent a negotiated approach to self regulation designed to meet the requirements of the directive"[1008]. The acceptance of the Safe Harbour agreement by the EU was deemed as a "transitory political success in the US"[1009]. However, in Europe open reservations were expressed at the prospect of data being transferred to the US under more relaxed criteria in comparison to the directive. Thus, data protection agencies in Europe "will still have considerable latitude in dealing with the US"[1010] as the agreement represents a "weakening of the European standards"[1011]. The US companies in order to acquire the ability to receive data from the EU need to implement the principles laid in the agreement and to integrate its elements in their company policies. "Decisions by organisations to qualify for the safe harbour are entirely voluntary…and in order to obtain and retain the benefits of the safe harbour they have to publicly declare that they do so"[1012]. Companies that have been qualified in accordance with the safe harbour agreement, as interpreted in accordance with the Frequently Asked Questions issued by the US department of commerce on July 21st 2000, are deemed to offer an "adequate" protection and must certify it on an annual basis at the Commerce Department. The basic criticism regarding the agreement in the US is related to its very narrow ambit of application. It can only apply to organisations

---

[1007] Ibid page 2784.
[1008] Reynolds B. John, European Data Privacy Regulation and its Impact on American Business, Washington Legal Foundation, Contemporary Legal Notes Series, Number 35, September 2000, www.wlf.org , page 5.
[1009] Reidenberg R. Joel, E-Commerce and Trans-Atlantic Privacy, 38 Houston Law Review, Fall 2001, page 730, accessed via LEXIS-NEXIS.
[1010] The same.
[1011] Ibid at page 732.
[1012] Fried Frank Harris Shriver & Jacobson, Data Protection v Privacy: United States and EU come to Terms on a Safe Harbour, Cyberspace Lawyer, May 2000, Volume 5, number 3, page 15, accessed via LEXIS-NEXIS.

and bodies "that fall within the regulatory jurisdiction of the Federal Trade Commission and the Department of Transportation"[1013], thus massively important industries such as the banking and telecommunications fall out of its scope of application as they are not included in the FTC jurisdiction. Furthermore, the authority of the FTC is limited. It can only prosecute companies "that misrepresent their purpose for collecting information. This provides companies with a loophole, because if they do not provide a privacy policy there is no misrepresentation"[1014]. If a company commits itself to compliance "failure to abide to such certification could subject to FTC enforcement action, private law suits (under state common law theories) or in extreme cases in prosecution for criminal false statements"[1015].

It is also interesting to note that the safe harbour agreement regulates the transfer of data from the EU to the US affording the enshrined protection to the respective data flows and is inapplicable to the transfer of data from the US to EU. The fact is that up to now very few companies have adhered to the safe harbour principles "possibly because many companies find it difficult to meet the requirements for compliance at this time...or they find it easier to register and comply directly in the EU"[1016]. With all its shortcomings, the Safe Harbour agreement placed privacy in the everyday policy agenda of the US commercial world and that's an achievement on its own. It did manage to set some standards that although are deemed lower than the respective of the EU, they are certainly more advanced than the ones practiced by US businesses before the agreement. And certainly to some extent it will provide as time passes by the necessary motive for companies to adhere to as it will be received as some sort of enhanced protection, at least for American standards, that American consumers can feel more confident with.

[1013] Reidenberg R. Joel, supra note 920, page 731.
[1014] Vitale Angela, supra 990, page 340.
[1015] Kotzker A Jason, supra note 939, page 755.
[1016] Marsnik F. Susan, Lynch Patricia, George Barbara, supra note 533, page 752.

8.3.1 The Seven Safe Harbour Principles

Notice

In order for a US organisation to be eligible to apply for the safe harbour protection it has to expressly and publicly comply with all seven principles enshrined in its text. An organisation bears the obligation to notify individuals in a clear and conspicuous manner "about the purposes for which it collects and uses information about them, how to contact the organization with any inquiries or complaints, the types of third parties to which it discloses the information, and the choices and means the organization offers individuals for limiting its use and disclosure, where the organization is using or disclosing it for a purpose other than that for which it was originally collected or for a purpose which it was processed by the transferring organization"[1017].

8.3.2 Choice

The system of opting out is selected as the most adequate manner to protect reasonable disclosure of data. The main obligation amounts to informing the individuals about their opting out right in an explicit manner. As far as sensitive information is concerned data subjects must be given an explicit choice (opt-in) to determine whether their data are going to be revealed to third parties or not. Exemptions apply only in relation to respect of the vital interests of the person involved, the establishment of legal claims, medical issues, issues concerning an organisation's obligation in the field of employment law, and already openly manifested data even of such nature and activities of non-profit seeking bodies[1018].

8.3.3 Onward Transfer

"To disclose information to a third party organisations must apply the notice and choice principles"[1019]. If the initial recipient of the data transfers them to a third party, the final recipient must also behave in compliance with the safe harbour principles. This obligation can be assured by written agreement between the recipients of the data. The Working Part of article 29 of the directive found the particular practice

---

[1017] See http://www.ita.doc.gov/td/ecom/Principles1199.htm
[1018] Fried Frank Harris Shriver & Jacobson, supra note 1013, page 16.
[1019] Reynolds B. John, supra note 1009, page 11.

as "inconsistent with the general rules set out for guaranteeing the enforcement and the liability of organisations under the safe harbour system"[1020]. If the original recipient becomes aware of any type of data misuse on behalf of the final recipient then he bears the obligation to prevent him from further abuse, otherwise he may be found liable.

8.3.4 Security

This principle mainly entails the adoption of "every reasonable precaution to protect the data from loss, misuse, unauthorised access, disclosure, alteration and destruction"[1021]. Increased security to protect sensitive data is emphasised. Which precaution measures are considered "reasonable" are not however defined in the particular case.

8.3.5 Data Integrity

The concept central to this principle is "relevance" or "compatibility" of the processing of personal information with the purposes of their collection. An organisation shall take all necessary initiatives to "ensure that data is reliable for its intended use, accurate, complete and current"[1022].

8.3.6 Access

"Consumers have a reasonable, although not an absolute, right to access and validate personal information gathered about them as well as to rectify, alter or omit any erroneous information"[1023]. Access can be impeded if the expenses required to provide it can be deemed as disproportionate to the risks inherent in the use of the relevant data. There is no clear indication of what is considered to be the level of expenses that can prevent the subject from accessing his data. Or what is the exact nature of the risks that fail to justify the respective expenses. The particular point along with the enforcement principle constituted the main fields that provided the ground for dispute between the EU and the US. The European Parliament was the European institution most openly opposed to the principles which at the very end refused to endorse.

[1020] Article 29 Data Protection Working Party, Opinion 4/2000 on the level of protection provided by the "Safe Harbour Principles", adopted on May 16th 2000, CA07/434/00/EN, page 6, available at http://europa.eu.int/comm/internal_market/privacy/docs/wpdocs/2000/wp32en.pdf
[1021] Fried Frank Harris Shriver & Jacopbson, supra note 1013, page 17.
[1022] Blanke M. Jordan, supra note 984, page 73.

8.3.7 Enforcement

Enforcement forms one of the elements necessary for the effectiveness of a regulation. Every organisation that seeks to qualify within the safe harbour context is required to create mechanisms to "guarantee its adherence to the principles, examine and settle the consumer complaints and ensure that the organisation resolves violations of the seven principles"[1024]. Hence, the enforcement procedures and means are mainly associated with the private sector. This provision equates to a serious downgrading of the protection standards introduced by the directive, which specifically provided for the ability to resort to judicial remedies (article 22) and undermines the protection afforded to the European citizens by the directive. The Working Party commented that "the individuals concerned by an alleged violation of the principles would not be assured of the right to stand before an independent instance"[1025]. This is because "although the individuals concerned can complain directly to FTC, there is no guarantee that the FTC will examine their case"[1026]. The Commission on the other hand focused on the fact that "a wide array of sanctions to enforce safe harbour rules existunder dispute resolution mechanisms, but not all such mechanisms have indicated publicly their intention to enforce safe harbour rules and not all have in place privacy practices applicable to themselves that are in conformity with the principles, as requires by safe harbour rules"[1027].

[1023] Loring B. Tracie, supra note 368, page 447.
[1024] Ibid at page 448.
[1025] Article 29 Working Party, supra note 1021, page 7.
[1026] The same.
[1027] Commission Staff Working Paper on the application of Commission Decision 529/2000/EC of July 26th 2000 on the Safe Harbour Privacy Principles and related Frequently Asked Questions issued by the US Department of Commerce, Brussels 13.02.2002, SEC (2002) 196, page 2. See Decision 529/2000/EC at:
http://europa.eu.int/smartapi/cgi/sga_doc?smartapi!celexapi!prod!CELEXnumdoc&lg=en&numdoc=320
00D0520&model=guichett

8.4 Overview of US Constitutional Developments and Case Law

Although, as analysed before, a great number of legislative initiatives[1028] were passed, the main question over the role of the Constitution remained. The latter was interpreted mainly by case law that provided for the framework of the privacy discussions in the US. In its very early case *Hoyt v MacKenzie and Others (1848)[1029]* the court had decided that unauthorised publishing of letters shall remain unpunished when their author cannot found neither a property right on them nor subsequently a privacy right. There is a property right when the letters in question are "literary compositions"[1030]. The Court's argument was based on the principle that since the author of the letter did not consent to its publication, he lost an interest in it as literary property. The letters had no literary value otherwise the author would have published them. "It would therefore be a perversion to…restrain their publication upon the ground that the writers had an interest in them as literary property"[1031]. And the court cannot punish crimes "except so far as they are connected with the rights of property"[1032]. In *James Woolsey v Owen B. Judd (1855)[1033]* the court changed its opinion but in essence the legal basis of its ruling remains identical. This time it finds that the unauthorised publication of a letter is unjustified but again because this time a property right is infringed. The court changes its mind only in its finding that the author now does have a property right in his letter even if this is unpublished. The court believed the author has "the right which every man has to the exclusive possession and control of the products of his own labour"[1034]. Thus, the right to privacy is still bound to a property right. In *Pollard v Photographic Co (1888)[1035]* the court stated that the publication of a photograph of a lady taken by a photographer under ordinary circumstances was a breach of confidence. Many years later in *Griswold v Connecticut[1036]* the Court stated

---

[1028] See also: Driver's Privacy Protection Act 1994, see http://www.accessreports.com/statutes/DPPA1.htm , The Health Insurance Portability and Accountability Act 1996, http://www.healthprivacy.org/usr_doc/34226.pdf .
[1029] Privacy: The Right to be Let Alone, Morris L. Ernst & Alan U. Schwartz, Milestones of Law Series, The MacMillan Company, New York, London, 1962, page 26.
[1030] Ibid page 33.
[1031] Ibid page 28.
[1032] The same.
[1033] Ibid at page 30.
[1034] Ibid at page 32.
[1035] Ibid at page 60.
[1036] 381 US 479 (1965).

that a law prohibiting the use of contraceptives violated what it called a right to "marital privacy". The judges in their analysis of the ruling referred to the First, Third, Fourth and Fifth Amendments as the constitutional basis of their judgement. The issue relies in the nature of the constitutional rights as rights against the state. The privacy rights stemming from the amendments do not constitute an exception to this rule. Even, when "the Supreme Court has addressed citizens' interest in privacy from non governmental intrusion, it almost never identifies the Constitution as the source of that interest"[1037].

The First Amendment "recognises a person's rights to privacy in cases when one person's speech collides with another's freedom of thought and solitude"[1038]. It reads "Congress shall make no law respecting... abridging the freedom of speech, or of the press"[1039]. "Freedom of speech is sacrosanct. We as a culture hold freedom of speech, much higher than other legal systems. We cannot protect the individual privacy without giving up some control over the freedom of speech. Informational privacy is the antithesis of the goal of the First Amendment – to protect the free flow of information"[1040]. In the context of the First Amendment "two rights, though equally important, seem to be mutually exclusive...it protects the privacy of every person to think and express thoughts freely, it also fundamentally blocks the power of the government to restrict expression, even in order to protect the privacy of other individuals"[1041]. Thus, when the battle between privacy and freedom of expression is being fought in the framework of the First Amendment, "the First Amendment has universally triumphed"[1042] and along with it: freedom of expression. In *Talley v California*[1043] and *McIntyre v Ohio Elections Commission*[1044], the issue concerned anonymous speech in conjunction with government regulations that try to place limits upon it. The Court after it underlined the valuable effects from being able to express one's opinions anonymously provided the legal world with some guideline remarks over the interpretation of the Amendment. Thus, it emphasised the value that society

---

[1037] Litan Robert, Cate H. Fred, Constitutional Issues in Information Privacy, 9 Michigan Telecommunication Technology Law Review, 2002, page 40.
[1038] Roch P Michael, Filling the void of Data Protection in the US: Following the European Example, 12 Santa Clara Computer & High Technology Law Journal, page 88.
[1039] See: http://www.law.cornell.edu/constitution/constitution.billofrights.html#amendmentvi
[1040] Kramer Chuang Lynn, supra note 948, 387.
[1041] Crisci L Camrin, All the World is not a Stage: Finding a Right to Privacy in existing and proposed Legislation, 6 NYU Journal of Legislation and Public Policy, 2003, page 211.
[1042] Neil M. Richards, Reconciling Data Privacy and the First Amendment, 52 UCLA Law Review, 205, page 1155.
[1043] 362 US 60, (1960)

can derive from the ability of citizens to express their views without revealing their identities as a means of enabling controversial opinions that can spur debates, which would, in the light of recognition, not have been expressed in fear of criticism or condemnation. "In the process anonymous speech works to limit government power by allowing oppressed groups a voice...and allows ideas to be considered without bias...at the same time the right is not absolute. When it conflicts with...law enforcement, the Court takes into account the value of the speech, the necessity of an identity requirement and whether the latter is the least restrictive alternative"[1045]. Thus, the Court may have focused on the importance of privacy when expressing one's opinions in the First amendment context, but drew a clear line to design its limits. After having defined the internet as "the most participatory marketplace of mass speech that...the world...has yet seen"[1046] Justice Holmes argued that there is a "marketplace of ideas, where the best test of truth is the power of thought to get itself accepted in the competition of the market, which must be free from government regulation. The marketplace must allow all ideas, including those that are repellent to some listeners to circulate freely"[1047]. This statement reveals the importance of freedom of expression for the US legal order and the precedence it therefore enjoys when it is to be weighted against other rights and especially privacy. Thus, the protection afforded by the Amendment to privacy finds a limit that can be quite restrictive as it serves as one of the cornerstones of the American legal traditions. And to paint with even brighter colours the differences in the balancing of rights and ideals with Europe, it is noted that even if "at some unknown future time information technology might get so powerful that the values of individual dignity, integrity, freedom and independence will indeed be threatened by destruction...free speech, whether it is free speech that reveals personal information or speech that communicates socially harmful ideas...ought not to

---

[1044] 514 US 334, (1995)
[1045] Crump Catherine, Data Retention: Privacy, anonymity and Accountability On – Line, 56 Stanford Law review, 2003, page 223.
[1046] Diane Rowland, Griping, Bitching and Speaking your Mind: Defamation and Free Expression on the Internet, 110 Penn State Law Review, 2006, page 519.
[1047] Justice Holmes in Murphy T Caitlin, International Law and the Internet: An Ill Suited Match Case Note on UEJF & LICRA v Yahoo Inc, 25 Hastings International and Comparative Law Review, 2002, 405.

be restricted today merely on the grounds that…such speech might possibly destroy individual dignity"[1048].

An interesting case was that of *Whalen v Roe*[1049] which concerned an Act requiring doctors to fill out forms for potentially harmful prescription drugs. A copy of the form in question was kept by the doctor, while another one was sent to the pharmacy and yet another one to the Department of Health. The forms in question included the name and the type of the drug along with personal information such as the patient's name, address, and age. The rationale behind the adoption of such a measure was related to the efforts made on behalf of the relevant governmental agencies to combat and limit the use of specific drugs whose effects were deeply harmful to human health. The basic question was whether the reporting and record-keeping requirements violated a claim to privacy embraced by the concept of liberty under the Fourteenth Amendment. The decision in question is important as the court stated that "the right of informational privacy is implicit in several constitutional guarantees"[1050]. The court still refrained from recognising any constitutional status to the existence and origination of a right to privacy but asserted its view that such a right is implicit in the spirit and content of constitutional guarantees and liberties. "The constitutional question presented is whether the State of New York may record, in a centralized computer file, the names and addresses of all persons who have obtained, pursuant to a doctor's prescription, certain drugs for which there are both a lawful and an unlawful market"[1051]. The court stated that "it would seem clear that the State's vital interest in controlling the distribution of dangerous drugs would support a decision to experiment with new techniques for control…it follows that the legislature's enactment of the patient-identification requirement was a reasonable exercise of New York's broad police powers. The District Court's finding that the necessity for the requirement had not been proved is not, therefore, a sufficient reason for holding the statutory requirement unconstitutional"[1052]. The court therefore, found that the requirement of keeping records with such information is justified as it is legitimised by the state's vital interest

---

[1048] Volokh Eugene, Symposium: Cyberspace and Privacy: A new legal paradigm? Freedom of Speech and Information Privacy: the Troubling Implications of a Right to stop People from speaking about you, 52 Stanford Law Review, 2000, page 1112.
[1049] *Whalen v Roe* 429 U.S. 589 (1977)
[1050] Natalie Gomez Velez, Internet Access to Court Records, Balancing Public Access and Privacy, 51 Loyola Law Review, 2005, page 387.
[1051] 429 U.S. 589, 591
[1052] 429 U.S. 589, 598

to control the distribution of dangerous drugs. The broad meaning given to the term "vital interest" is of concern since its over extension and the lack of a concrete definition of its content can lead to serious limitations on the extent of the protection in question. So, in order to protect public health it allowed the collection of sensitive information. However, it also argued that the District's Court finding that keeping records was not necessary to attain this end was not related to the constitutionality of such a measure. Although, the court seemed to disassociate the constitutionality of a state policy related to privacy with the principle of proportionality with the same ruling it recognised that "protecting privacy have in fact involved at least two different kinds of interests. One is the individual interest in avoiding disclosure of personal matters and another is the interest in independence in making certain kinds of important decisions"[1053]. The interesting point is not only the recognition by itself of the content of informational privacy but the fact that the latter refers to an "interest in avoiding disclosure" and not a "right" in doing so. The terminology and the wording chosen reveal the intentions of the court. It is still very interesting to note that the court recognised that informational privacy comprised two interests: not to disclose personal matters and having the independence to assume important personal decisions by oneself. The court concluded that "we are persuaded, however, that the New York programme does not, on its face, pose a sufficiently grievous threat to either interest to establish a constitutional violation"[1054] and that "we are not unaware of the threat to privacy implicit in the accumulation of vast amounts of personal information in computerized data banks or other massive government files... The right to collect and use such data for public purposes is typically accompanied by a concomitant statutory or regulatory duty to avoid unwarranted disclosures. Recognising that in some circumstances that duty arguably has its roots in the Constitution..."[1055]. This is the most important part as it marks one of the rare moments where the Supreme Court acknowledges that a duty to avoid unwarranted disclosures of personal data, which basically means a duty to avoid an infringement of the right to informational privacy "has its roots in the Constitution". The wording is again very carefully constructed so as to avoid the clear definition of informational privacy as a constitutional right, however

---

[1053] 429 U.S. 589, 599
[1054] 429 U.S. 589, 600
[1055] 429 U.S. 589, 605

it is the closest the court has ever been in establishing a link between informational privacy and the US Constitution.

The Fourth Amendment is the basis on which a rich jurisprudence has been developed by the Court. It reads "the right of the people to be secure in their persons, houses, papers, and effects, against unreasonable searches and seizures, shall not be violated, and no warrants shall issue, but upon probable cause, supported by oath or affirmation, and particularly describing the place to be searched, and the persons or things to be seized"[1056]. Although, it concerns seizures by the government, the principles developed can be effectively extended to cover other areas where privacy can be viewed as being abused. The landmark case that presents the requirements and reasoning of the Court in the relevant issues is *Katz v United States*[1057]. Katz used a public phone booth to make a phone call, without suspecting that the FBI would intercept and record his conversation with the use of an eavesdropping device planted for this reason. The issue here was governmental surveillance in citizens' life but, also something that was meant to create a breakthrough in US law. As the constitutional text is drafted to include only "persons, houses, papers and effects" the question raised concerned whether government surveillance could be caught only when occurring in these premises or also in places sharing a less strict connection with the individual in question. The Court set out the important rule that the character of a government search as an act caught by the Fourth Amendment will not be determined by the literal interpretation of the legal text by itself, but mainly by "whether a reasonable person would have been justified in assuming privacy"[1058]. Thus, the Court went beyond the actual meaning of the text and extended the protection constitutionally provided for to all places an individual could be justified to presume he is enjoying his privacy. "Once it is recognised that the Fourth Amendment protects people and not simply areas against unreasonable searches an seizures it becomes clear that the reach of that amendment cannot turn upon the presence or absence of a physical intrusion into any given enclosure"[1059]. Hence, the way was paved for the Amendment to catch even cases of electronic surveillance. The requirements placed upon such an interpretative extension were "that a person has exhibited an actual expectation of privacy" and that

---

[1056]See: http://www.law.cornell.edu/constitution/constitution.billofrights.html#amendmentvi
[1057] 389 US 347 (1967).
[1058] Crump Catherine, supra note 1046, page 199.
[1059] Katz at 353.

this expectation must be one "that the society is prepared to recognise as reasonable"[1060]. The test is based on a subjective pillar, the belief of the individual, and an objective one, which is whether this belief can be accepted as reasonable by the society. The terms used created ambiguity as no further guidelines had been given over which are the criteria that render a "privacy expectation" "reasonable". This created an uncertainty that once again was up to the Court to dilute. The only important indication offered by the Court was the controversial statement that "what a person knowingly exposes to the public, even in his own home or office, is not a subject of fourth amendment protection"[1061]. This statement can be viewed as seriously limiting the wider ambit of protection created after the Court's judgement. Information divulged voluntarily cannot be covered by the relevant protection. Thus, the question can be whether consumer data collected on line can be protected. Since, consumers are aware due to the nature of internet that when they surf on line they leave some traces behind and they accept this process could that be taken as "voluntarily offering their personal data" so the latter cannot be viewed as being seized by state or anybody else?

In *Smith v Maryland*[1062] the Court held that there is "no actual expectation of privacy in the phone numbers one dialled, and that, even if one did, the expectation was not legitimate"[1063]. After police request the phone company recorded the incoming and outgoing calls of Smith, who argued that his reasonable expectation of privacy was violated. The reasoning behind this was highly controversial and highlights the negative implications of the *Katz* judgement. The Court insisted that Smith had no reasonable expectation of privacy, because any "person would...typically know that...the telephone company has facilities for recording this information...and in fact it does this for a variety of legitimate business purposes"[1064]. The striking outcome of this reasoning is that "technological possibility determines what one can reasonably expect to be private"[1065]. And if the technological possibility was found advanced enough in the framework of telephone companies to record the numbers used, in the internet context such an acceptance would immediately undermine and annul any basic

---

[1060] Ibid at 361.
[1061] Ibud at 351.
[1062] 442 US 735 (1979)
[1063] The same at 745.
[1064] The same at 743.
[1065] Crump Catherine, supra note 1046, page 201.

expectation of privacy as ISPs have the ability to record all sites visited[1066], the duration of the visit, the mails sent and the destinations of such mails. An ISP "is in a position to see virtually everything a consumer does"[1067]. And all this can well be attributed to the smooth functioning of the net, which would on this basis remove any privacy ambition. The Court also insisted that there was no reasonable expectation of privacy in this case as telephone numbers are not deemed to be "communication content".[1068] According to the Court, keeping a record only of the numbers dialled without intercepting the conversation of the individual does not amount to an abuse of privacy. Thus, the surveillance is justified due to a distinction between the actual content of the conversation and the numbers dialled. I find that the ruling has completely neglected the obvious ability of the telecommunications company or the police in the specific case to link the numbers with particular individuals. But, even of we agree that the numbers themselves do not infringe the private space of someone at least up to the degree that the recording of a conversation would, it has to be noted that the respective consideration at the internet level would be impossible. Such a distinction would be completely futile in the internet context. In internet revealing the sites visited or the names towards which mails were sent is as important as revealing the content of the communications taking place. If a person is found to regularly visit religious or political sites, we don't need to know more in order to form a complete image over his religious or political beliefs. Here, the revelation of the sites visited equals divulgence of the communication content. Furthermore, such a wide interpretation would catch literally all consumer information on line. Both information provided by the consumers voluntarily to register in a site for example and the information that they do not reveal on a voluntary basis, but they presume it is collected such as their traffic data. An acceptance of such a principle would render the whole debate on privacy vastly irrelevant. As "Justice Marshall explained in his dissent in *Smith*, implicit in the concept of assumption of risk is some notion of choice. Application of the assumption of risk principle to involuntary data collection is contrary to the values the Fourth Amendment was intended to protect"[1069].

[1066] See also: *United States v Hambrick*, 55 F.Supp.2d 504, 1999.

[1067] Kramer Chuang Lynn, supra note 948, page 401.

[1068] Crump Catherine, supra note 1046, at 741.

[1069] Skok Gavin, supra note 318, 61.

In *O'Connor v Ortega*[1070], the Court had to deal with a case in which state hospital officials searched the desk of a doctor to find evidence for a sexual harassment enquiry. His personal letters were seized. The Court ruled that when the intrusion is performed by a supervisor and not a state official, this amounts to usual practices in the framework of the workplace that may render some employees' privacy expectations unreasonable. Such expectations "may be reduced by virtue of actual office practices and procedures or by legitimate regulation"[1071]. Thus, in this case the Court moved one step further and elevated workplace practices to the level of yet another legitimate limit on the "reasonable privacy expectations" of the citizens that appear to be increasingly difficult to be founded on a given basis. Since the Fourth Amendment "test does not involve a fixed moral conception of what ought to be private, nor does it involve application of a formal legal test"[1072], the courts can shape the framework in which its freedoms are expressed in a more restrictive manner than envisaged initially.

In *United States v Miller*[1073] the Court held "that a bank depositor had no legitimate expectation of privacy in transactional records compiled and kept by his bank, because he voluntarily conveyed the financial information to his bank, and because the information was exposed to bank employees in the ordinary course of business"[1074]. Even more revealing is the following "the depositor takes the risk…even if the information is revealed on the assumption that it will be used only for a limited purpose and the confidence placed on the third party will not be betrayed"[1075]. Thus, the Court denies complete protection of personal data even on the basis of a breach of confidence relationship. Revealing one's data for reasons absolutely necessary in today's life would amount to a permanent divorce from any protection of such data. Thus, this logic prevents the granting of even minimum protection to almost all types of data related to our daily economic life and activities. In order to allay the fears of the dissemination of our personal data to third parties the only solution appears to be complete abstinence from normal activities inherent in today's lifestyle. We have to provide our data to enjoy the services of the banking, tourist, or information technology

---

[1070] 480 US 709, 1987.
[1071] Ortega at 717.
[1072] Spencer B. Shaun, Reasonable Expectations and the Erosion of Privacy, 39 San Diego Law Review, 2002, page 848.
[1073] 425 US 435 (1976)
[1074] Skok Gavin, supra note 318, paragraph 17, 61.
[1075] Miller at 443.

industry and to reap the benefits of education and health systems. Hence, following such a principle would be highly detrimental to privacy.

In *Reno v ACLU*[1076] the Court recognised several characteristics on which internet activities can be classified such as "spontaneity, exclusivity, interactivity of the communication"[1077]. It asked whether sending an e-mail can be perceived as sending a letter in a sealed envelop or just a postcard[1078]. If the Court decides the standard to be applied is that of the letter, "it may recognise a reasonable expectation of privacy in the content of a mail...but if it views it as a postcard...then it will not"[1079]. The position assumed by the Court is very surprising. The court took a position that undermined the basic guarantees of privacy on internet. The successful development of the latter is basically influenced by the confidence consumers would vest in it as a means of communication firstly and conducting business at a later stage. If they are informed by the Court that even their mail is considered "a postcard", and that as a principle has been vested with the official authority of the Supreme Court, then I cannot imagine how people would be expected to trust the new medium.

The same test was applied in *United States v Simons*[1080], where the Court held that the employee in question did not have a reasonable expectation of privacy, while navigating through internet in his office as employees were warned that all internet activity would be recorded. Again no such expectation could be founded, because Simons should have known that his activities are to be watched. But, the problem on internet is that clickstream data are possible to be monitored by corporations as data mining emerges as an industry with an independent status. Thus, we are going to be increasingly aware of our exposure to on line scrutiny as technology evolves. According to this logic, the public will lose its expectation of privacy and subsequently its ability to enforce such rights, because it should have been aware of the technical abilities inherent in the systems used to be tracked down and recorded. Awareness assumes the bizarre position of limiting one's privacy rights. It is afforded a meaning and a status equal to that of explicit consent and this can be a dangerous practice both for legal certainty and actual safeguarding of individual liberties.

[1076] 521 US 844 (1997).
[1077] Crump Catherine, supra note 1046, page 207.
[1078] See also *United States v Charbonneau*, 979 F.Supp. 1177, (1997)
[1079] Crump Catherine, supra note 1046, page 207
[1080] *United States v Simons*, 206 F.3d 392, 2000.

In *Kyllo v United States*[1081], the ruling was also an astonishing one. Here, the Court stated that the nature of technology can determine the existence of an expectation of privacy. The house of the defendant was scanned by a thermal imaging device, used without a warrant, in order to reveal the places within the house that were "unusually hot"[1082], which was an indication of growing marijuana. The Court ruled that the expectation of privacy was reasonable but the interest lays in the actual justification of the ruling. It relied on the fact that "thermal imaging technology is not in general public use"[1083] in sharp contrast to commonly used technologies such as "airplane and helicopter flight", which have revealed to the public "areas of the house and cartilage that once were private"[1084]. Thus, if the latter surveillance measures were used, which are "commonly used technologies" no privacy expectation could have been justified even into one's house. Furthermore, when the day comes that thermal imaging technology will be widely used by law enforcement authorities, then the public would be deprived of its expectations as this method of surveillance would also be classified in the "commonly used" ones. Here, the Court moves towards the direction of limiting not only the scope afforded to the protection in Katz, but also towards the placement of limits on the literal content of the Fourth amendment, which protects privacy in one's house.

This ruling revealed the striking differences between the interpretation that the ECHR afforded to the "reasonable expectations of privacy" doctrine and the respective one of the US courts. As analysed above the interpretation afforded by the US court is the widest possible, flexible enough to encompass almost all possible cases of privacy abuse unless the issue in question is related to privacy infringements which involve such sophisticated technologies that the victims could not possibly foresee or expect any such intrusion. In simple words the doctrine is constructed in such terms so as to minimise protection in the relevant field as it legitimises all forms of privacy infringement as long as their existence can be somehow presumed or expected by the citizens in question. In sharp contrast to that, the ECHR produced a very different interpretation of the aforementioned concept. As analysed at the relevant part in accordance with the a line of cases the ECHR specifically adjudicated in *Lüdi v*

[1081] Kyllo 533 US 27, 2001.
[1082] Kyllo at 30.
[1083] Kyllo at 34.
[1084] Kyllo at 34.

Switzerland that there is no reasonable expectation of privacy *only* in cases of an infringement of privacy performed in accordance with the law, in the interests of national security, public safety or the prevention of disorder and crime among others. Therefore, the reasonable expectations of privacy in accordance with the Court's reasoning is directly linked with the limits that the Convention itself sets on the exercise of the right to privacy. Thus, only if limitations are legitimately imposed on privacy by law or for the prevention of crime or for reasons of national security then the person in question can assume that he is in risk of experiencing an interference with his privacy. In simple words the scope of application of the relevant doctrine in the European context is significantly more limited as it applies only on the basis of legislated derogations and in line with the judgement that their application is necessary and proportionate in a democratic society. The comparative analysis of the fundamental for privacy doctrine of "reasonable expectations" reveals the magnitude of the differences in judicial approach in the two sides of the Atlantic and underlines the major divergence in views, legal perceptions and philosophical concepts lying in the background. In the European context the *Kyllo* outcome would have been the same but the reasoning behind it would have been wholly different. The monitoring would have been found illegitimate not only because the technology in use was not widespread and therefore anticipated but because its place in use was not performed in accordance with law and was not necessary for other legitimate aims in the framework of a democratic society. The same would have been the ruling in *Smith v Maryland.* The ECHR would have examined whether the requirements of the law for the monitoring of phone calls applied in this case. If it did and the measures in force were justified on the grounds mentioned above, it would have allowed the monitoring as only in this case reasonable expectations of privacy could not be founded. But the reasoning used by the US Court falls completely out of line with the jurisprudence of the ECHR. As analysed at the relevant part of the book, the US Court ruled that there were no reasonable expectations of privacy because every user should be aware of the fact that any telephone company possesses the technological means necessary to record the relevant information. Thus, awareness of the risk is equivalent to the introduction of limitations on the expectations of privacy. In contrast to that, the ECHR would have demanded the application of the specific derogations included in legislation in order to legitimise the limitations imposed on privacy. In the case in question it is highly unlikely that the ECHR would have produced the same ruling as its US counterpart. The same goes for *United States v*

Miller where the US court as stated above, explained that there were no expectations of privacy in transactional bank records because the individual in question voluntarily conveyed this pieces of information to the bank and should have been aware of the ability of the latter to make use of it. Again the rationale behind the ruling is sharply opposed to the reasoning usually used by the ECHR on the relevant doctrine. The ECHR would not have produced the same ruling and definitely not on the same grounds since it consistently refused to use awareness of risks or technological opportunities as a legitimate ground for privacy abuse. Similarly, in *United States v Simons* the US Court as analysed above ruled that employees do not have a reasonable expectation of privacy related to their on line activities at work because they ought to know that there is the possibility to be monitored by their employer. In the European context the ruling would have been wholly different. In accordance with a very recent case (*Copland v the United Kingdom (2007)*), the ECHR provided us with a different ruling. In *Copland,* the ECHR accepted on the contrary that telephone calls from business premises are *prima facie* covered by the notions of "private life" and "correspondence" for the purposes of Article 8 § 1 of the Convention. The ECHR insisted that it follows logically that e-mails sent from work should be similarly protected under Article 8, as should information derived from the monitoring of personal internet usage. The applicant in the present case had been given no warning that her calls would be liable to monitoring, therefore she had a reasonable expectation as to the privacy of calls made from her work telephone. The same expectation should apply in relation to the applicant's e-mail and internet usage. The Court recalls that the use of information relating to the date and length of telephone conversations and in particular the numbers dialled can give rise to an issue under Article 8 as such information constitutes an "integral element of the communications made by telephone. *The mere fact that these data may have been legitimately obtained by the employer, in the form of telephone bills, is no bar to finding an interference with rights guaranteed under Article 8.* Accordingly, the Court considers that the collection and storage of personal information relating to the applicant's telephone, as well as to her e-mail and internet usage, without her knowledge, amounted to an interference with her right to respect for her private life and correspondence within the meaning of Article 8. This ruling does not allow any doubt that the aforementioned US case (United States v Simons) would have been judged on a wholly different basis if brought in the European judicial context. The relevant comparative analysis illuminates and underlines the great differences in the perception and enforcement of privacy at the two sides of the Atlantic.

As Jeffrey Rosen observes "the expectation driven conception of privacy is vulnerable as people's subjective expectations of privacy tend to reflect the amount of privacy they subjectively experience; and as advances in the technology of monitoring and searching have made ever more intrusive surveillance possible, expectations of privacy have naturally diminished, with a corresponding reduction in constitutional protection"[1085]. "At this point, the balance of rights is so heavily tilted in favour of collectors, that it is probably unreasonable to expect that our personal information will not be abused"[1086]. Thus, if web sites record all data of the citizens then the latter will have no expectation of privacy. If the employers monitor the traffic data and the phone calls of all employees and that is presumed to be an acceptable workplace method, then there is no expectation of privacy. And according to US case law, if there is no expectation of privacy that can be reasonably accepted, then there is nothing to be protected, there is no scope of protection in the first place. The effect of such a policy would be fatal for personal liberties and societal needs, because if it was universally accepted that activities are being monitored then people would avoid expressing themselves freely, but would prefer to conform to the "acceptable" social norms to allay the chances of being in the centre of criticism or just being different. This policy, according to my opinion leads to exactly the same abuse that is supposedly at the heart of the US legal system: the abuse of the freedom of expression. In all its aspects, both as the inability to express a personal opinion, which can be seen as controversial and the natural human capacity to be original, as conformity to a uniform commonly accepted standard would be the means desired to escape being distinguished from the rest. This would have obvious effects also on the other characteristic of the US society, which is its pluralistic and diverse nature. Diversity cannot be achieved when individuals confuse the lines between private and public life and therefore, align their activities with the societal expectations of their public role. Their originality will have to be sacrificed on the way. Thus the stance adopted by the US courts is not only inefficient but also threatening to both freedom of expression and the right of privacy.

[1085] Spencer B. Shaun, supra note 1073, page 860.

9. Proposals

It is a central position in this book that regulation at central level is necessary in order to deal with the growing threats to privacy. The development of technology has rendered imperative a re-evaluation of the current legislative framework. The experience from the US has vividly proven that self regulation can by no means protect the citizens from abusive privacy practices. The social value of privacy as one of the essential fundamental rights has been underlined and extensively presented throughout this book. On the other hand nobody can dispute the social value vested in the development of technology and the positive repercussions that the latter can have on our lives. However, it is highly important that the modern democratic state will create all the safeguards to assure that developments in technology or the economy will not be at the expense of rights fundamental for individuals irrespective of whether they are acting in their capacity as citizens or consumers. This is a principle deeply embedded in European culture, which based on Greco-Roman traditions, the Magna Carta and the French Revolution has been centred on the respect of human rights. Europe after the second World War has managed to shape the delicate balance between economic development on the one hand and the respect of human rights on the other with great success. Similar dilemmas had been put to European citizens, legislators and leaders in the past as well, but the pursuance of further economic development with the simultaneous adherence to Europe's humanistic traditions seemed to be always the choice. It is strongly believed that this delicate balance need not be upset in the case of privacy either. Apart from the legislators and civil society the cooperation of scientists is absolutely necessary in order to find adequate solutions and produce the regulations which would be technologically up to date enough to deal with the new landscape. It is imperative that the solutions to be found will not compromise in any way the nature of the right to privacy as a fundamental human right, a status recognised by all basic treaties and constitutional texts adopted at European level during the last thirty years.

In the pursuance of designing the right policies to deal with this issue it is a central position of this book that the concept of "consent" should assume a core

---

[1086] Bergelson Vera, supra note 943, page 416.

position in the whole debate. Since, the aspect of privacy that is more heavily affected by the emergence of internet as a widespread commercial tool is the protection of personal data collected on line, the control of such data by the subject who provides them is imperative. The concept of control is highly significant since the debate is centred on the collection and unlimited dissemination of personal data. The sense of controlling what is collected about us, knowing the exact destination of our data and the rationale behind its processing stands as the basic premise on which an effective data protection legislation is built upon. The EU Directive encompasses all these principles but they should be further consolidated and placed at the very heart of the continent's data protection regime.

A policy of data protection centred on consent can shift the control over personal data from business to consumers. The latter will be able to exercise control over their personal data. Consumers will therefore, acquire better bargaining power and be able to urge businesses to take into account their privacy concerns. If data protection means the exercise of control over personal data then consent is the concept which can realise it. And the of consent can be found to entail lack of control over our personal data. Therefore, when it comes to the protection of data while making use of the commercial opportunities of internet on commercial web sites this can provide a satisfactory answer to the data protection issues which have been raised. However, as it is noted there is a drawback inherent in an approach centred on consent. "It seems plausible to argue that one can consent to give up one's privacy"[1087]. If one decides to divulge personal data even of sensitive nature on line it is true that there is nothing and no one able to prevent him from doing this. This is partly due to the lack of any formal definition of privacy which a variety of individuals can claim to perceive as encompassing divergent areas of activities based on different personal experiences and cultural perceptions. This argument goes back to the debate on whether privacy is a human right or just a property right. The European legal order correctly assumed the position that privacy deserves the status of a human right, which means a right inalienable, which can be neither sold nor renounced nor can one be deprived of it. The legislative responses to privacy should consequently take this form. Preventing businesses from making enquiries about sensitive personal data unless it is necessary

---

[1087] Lisa M. Austin, Is Consent the Foundation of Fair Information Practices? Canada's Experience under PIPEDA, 56 University of Toronto Law Journal, 2006, page 188.

due to the nature of the transaction in question (pharmaceutical industry) and when they do to strictly regulate the processing of such data, their future use, the reasons for their collection, the right of access to check the validity of the collected data and the forms of bringing challenges for compliance with the standards set. All of these issues should be brought to the attention of the consumer from the very initial stage as a subject of the agreement to which the consumer has to grant his consent. They should be drafted in a standard form approved by the relevant authorities so that the average consumer would deal with a familiarly set agreement whose terms he can comprehend so as to consciously grant his consent. The independent Data Protection Authorities in cooperation with the industry should draft such agreements as currently they are too lengthy and hugely complicated literally forcing the consumers to quickly bypass it by consenting to a list of obligations they didn't have the time and the skill to read. This agreement stating the data collected, the purpose of collection, future use and the rights of the consumers in case of abuse should be short and clearly written. It is important to have a standard form as the consumer will be able to get very familiar with this particular form and be able to comprehend its full content each time he makes an on line purchase. This practice will enhance consumer confidence and boost the potentials of internet.

It has to be noted, however, that a central point of this strategy lies in consumer education. It is absolutely necessary that consumers realise what exactly is at stake. Consumer awareness therefore, stands at the core of this strategy. It is a central position of this book that privacy awareness especially in the framework of the new digital era is urgently needed and should form a policy priority if any change is seriously intended. This campaign can be orchestrated by the relevant data protection authorities, consumer organisation and of course the state itself. If privacy is a fundamental human right, citizens must be fully aware of its content, the related threats and the consequences of abuse. In schools throughout the continent the younger Europeans learn the significance of certain human rights most of them common throughout European countries and they are very familiar with their significance from a very early stage of their social integration. Privacy and its current threats should be included in this list for Europeans to be aware of the risks they are taking in case of an abuse. The consequences of privacy abuses were thoroughly explained in other parts of the book, however it can be noted here that increased surveillance and the analysis of our data can lead to lack of control over our personal life, lack of the ability to freely develop our personality, loss of dignity from the dissemination of embarrassing personal data, a tendency not to be creative or controversial so as not to distinguish ourselves from the rest and attract attention and further scrutiny, thus at the very end lack of our freedom of expression since we will know that someone is watching so our views will have to be mitigated or even silenced. In simple words citizens should know that privacy albeit difficult to define is not a vague notion but a concrete right of ours of high social value which in case of abuse can seriously impair our freedom.

It should be pointed out that the provision of personal data on line is not a "one off" as the real danger lays with the aggregation of data, data mining and data matching which can lead to the creation of personal profiles to be used for commercial objectives as well as for criminal justice in a way which as explained before is neither scientific nor accurate. The impact of such practices is evident in several aspects of every day activity from the refusal of a visa because one fits the profile of a criminal personality and the refusal of insurance due to the analysis of previous collected data to the rejection of credit as according to the matching of data one does not appear credit worthy. Not to mention the more criminal use of this data for instance in cases of blackmail. Data collected about a person when he was young related to his personal life or political and other choices back then can be dug up and used later when for example he becomes wealthy or wants to become a politician etc. The citizens should know that the aggregation of data in massive databases takes place gradually and its effect is cumulative. Therefore, citizens from an early stage should be made fully aware of the content of the right to privacy, the new dangers and their rights. Those should be included in concrete legislation and include rights of access and redress in case of abuse. Privacy in general is a vague concept so it tends to lose when placed in the balance with other rights such as the right of expression or even security, which are more concrete in nature and with which the citizens due to their education and social upbringing are more familiar with. Thus, it is imperative that privacy will become a more consolidated right in the European legal order with a concrete content. Only in this way will Europeans be in a position to evaluate it on the right basis and act or demand form the state action accordingly to protect it. Consent can therefore be the tool to engage the citizens in this process. Consent should be explicitly granted for the primary use stated in the agreement and not for any secondary use for which the consumer has not granted his consent. In addition to that the sites should be urged to enquire only about the data which are necessary for the transaction and not for sensitive data. The latter should not be given unless, there is special need included in law.

A position taken by this book is to further extend the power of the already founded independent data protection authorities. The latter were founded by the European directive and their existence has enhanced the protection of data and privacy but not to the full extent of their potential capacity. They should be more active and assertive in their related fields. They should be well funded both by the state and by private individuals with interest in the area. The employment of both lawyers and social scientists and IP programmists is *sine qua non* for the success of their initiatives and proposals. They must be competent to scrutinise the privacy aspects of public and private projects, monitor the relevant activities of both the private and the public sector and seek judicial redress in case of abuse. The Data Protection authorities should be fully involved in awareness efforts and along with other consumer organisations should inform and assist citizens in asserting their rights of control, access and redress.

In conjunction with consumer organisations the Data Protection authorities have a very important role to play. They can contribute to link consumer preferences with data protection and privacy. The market responds to demands when they appear and seem attractive in market terms. If consumers learn to ask for privacy guarantees business will have to provide them if it is to stay competitive. Therefore, privacy can be linked with competitiveness. Usually, adhering to enhanced data protection standards is found to be a feature highly impairing competitiveness as it requires higher costs to comply with the process set by the directive. If however, privacy ranks at the top position of the consumer preferences and criteria list then the companies which do not reply to this demand will lose their competitive edge. This will serve as a strong stimulus for businesses to adhere to higher fundamental rights standards on market terms. In order to further serve this goal the data protection authorities can compile a list with companies which respect the privacy requirements as set by the relevant legislation and one black list of companies which process data irrespective of the requirements of law. Even if there are no fines attached to that, giving publicity to these lists will enlighten consumers about the companies which tend to comply with the law and create enormous pressure on those which do not to adapt their practices if they do not wish to be found in the market's margins. A proposal which would serve both as a reassurance towards the consumers and a competitive benefit for business is to allow the certification of sites in accordance with their adherence to data protection principles. In this way, commercial sites will be encouraged to align their practices with the demand of data protection law in order to receive the certification and be included in the list of companies which would attract consumers' loyalty and trust. This is not an ethical requirement, since loyalty and trust are components of consumer confidence. And where there is confidence there is choice. If consumers are urged to switch to privacy friendly companies then the latter will enjoy a competitive advantage. This does not need to happen independent of the commercial world but it would be even more effective if it could be a common initiative of for example the data protection authorities and the chambers of commerce. If privacy is seen as a competitive advantage it can attract the interest of commercial fora and become the subject of a common initiative. A useful pattern in this case is the newly emerged Company Social Responsibility initiatives. After public outcry about the practices of several companies which accumulated wealth while showing disregard for the environment, human rights or social obligations, many companies have incorporated this doctrine to deal with the pressure. They integrated social concerns into their list of priorities and ran pilot programmes funding environmental projects, even local schools or hospitals to meet their so called social obligations and return some of the value of their profits to the public in its wider sense. Some argued that this is a marketing exercise but even so, it was a result of public pressure and it has led to many companies funding social projects which would otherwise have been abandoned. It has also proved to be a competitive advantage for the companies concerned and they tend to occupy a prominent position in the respective commercial websites. Privacy can become a part of similar patterns, which will emphasise the function of companies on the basis of respect of basic rights, while enabling consumers to make the right choices. This can lead to the consolidation of a culture of privacy which will cover all aspects of corporate structure with emphasis on the data protection policies. Business should designate a person clearly responsible for the processing of data, the data controller, and make him publicly accountable for the enterprise's compliance with data protection standards. This will play a determining role in upgrading privacy to a criterion for consumer preference and will place the debate not only on a human rights basis but also viewed from an angle deeply related to a competitive edge and positions in the market.

Transnational cooperation on the issue would hugely help in shaping the right solutions to the problem but as illuminated by this book wide divergences in approach, different cultural values and diverse historical experiences render a common international policy on privacy if not impossible at least very difficult. The European Directive has been hugely influential at this point as with its extraterritorial effect it forced many other jurisdictions on the planet to adopt standards similar to European standards of data protection. In this sense it led to enhanced rules in several other countries, set the issue at the global agenda and rendered it a criterion for commercial relations. This Directive has been of profound practical and symbolic importance for data protection. However, it is difficult to see a common international stance on the issue.

As noted before since the nature of the new challenges to privacy is mainly technological, the need to incorporate technological solutions in the proposals is compelling. Technology and its evolution are not only the sources from which challenges to privacy originate, but also the scientific basis on which several proposals aiming at tackling the problem could be founded. One of the most prominent in the scientific world of such solutions could be cryptography. Cryptography is "the branch of mathematics concerned with establishing ways to encode information so that the encoded information has no meaning to anyone other than those in possession of the correct algorithm for transposing the information". Similarly encryption is "the process using cryptographic algorithms of converting information into a string of symbols that has no meaning or value to any person other than the one for whose use it is intended, who will be able to decrypt it"[1088]. Cryptography is considered effective because by using this method the content of the data can be obscured so radically so as to become unreadable and therefore decrypted only in case someone obtains access to the key. The latter is a secret code known only to the person aimed at decrypting the data. With the use of such technology data is known only to the people who have access to the key. Only they can become aware of the content of the data in a readable form. The rest will only access a set of intelligible symbols of no particular use and importance. Thus, encryption prevents an unauthorised interceptor from obtaining any access to the data. Due to its impact in enabling the security of transferred information, encryption

---

[1088] Definitions found in Perri 6, The Future of Privacy, Volume 1, Private Life and Public Policy, Demos, London, 1998, pages 333 and 334.

systems are used in sensitive industries and sectors of the economy such as banking and telecommunications. Recently, the relevant technology has been introduced to e-government projects ensuring the privacy of citizens' data in the framework of their dealings with the local municipal or governmental authorities. An even more advanced method of cryptography is the so called public key cryptography. "In a public key system data can be encrypted with one key which is kept private and secure by the sender (the private key) and divulged to no one, but can also be decrypted with the use of a second key which is available to the sender (the public key) but from which the private key cannot be deciphered. Clearly, if the private key is acquired the system's integrity is lost but as long as the public key is held only by individuals trusted by the sender, public key cryptography systems can provide a greater measure of security than traditional ones"[1089]. Encryption is absolutely vital for electronic commerce as well as it guarantees the security of transactions especially in relation to data such as the credit card numbers which the consumers tend to divulge while conducting their on line purchases. Therefore, encryption appears as one of the few ways of protecting the privacy of communications on internet. Of course there are always risks flowing from for example hackers who are usually focused on finding the codes of the key to crack the system and decrypt the information but cryptography can offer more guarantees than anything else available right now.

Because of the effectiveness of cryptography there were several worries over its use by criminal groups in order to obscure their on line communications. Therefore, the use of cryptography was held to be a threat to national security and to the efforts of the law enforcement agencies to develop their activities unimpeded from such obstacles. Thus, initially there was a lack of political will to allow such technologies to assume widespread use. However, those efforts were much resisted from the IT and internet industry and now the relevant technologies are in use by significant industries as mentioned above. It is imperative that any restrictions on the use of such programmes are lifted so as to promote their implementation by industry. The rationale behind this belief is not just the protection of personal data which can reach more safely the intended destination without any unauthorised interception but also the profound contribution which such systems will have to the consolidation of a climate of security of on line transactions fostering consumer confidence. It is imperative that funding

---

[1089] The same at page 116.

should be poured in such projects so as to ensure their evolution especially in the light of counter research on methods to break such codes and obtain access to encrypted material. The implementation of rules on internet cannot have as its central parameter that the latter is unfortunately used as a means of communication of criminals or terrorists as well. All efforts should be centred on the simple fact that the internet is the on line environment that hundreds of millions of people can access to conduct commercial transactions or communicate with other individuals. Initiatives analysed above such as the limited and strictly regulated retention of traffic data is believed by some governments to be in a position to assist them in their efforts to detect signs of criminal activity on line. Therefore, extending privacy insecurities to all aspects of internet would be futile and seriously harmful to its commercial potential.

In this framework the role of the so called Trusted Third Parties (TTP) is useful. These are private agencies which can assume a multiplicity of duties related to data protection and security of transactions. If the TTP are to contribute to the protection of data their functions and duties must be strictly regulated by law so as to be aware of their exact nature, the extent of their competence and the safeguards they provide. Proposals by computer scientists have included duties such as "certifying identity" in the sense of confirming that a certain consumer using a particular algorithm is the person he claims to be, "holding private keys"[1090] as a way of shaping a balance between the need for incorporating cryptography in data protection strategies on one hand and ensuring the law enforcement agencies on the other that when they have a warrant or a judicial authorisation they could obtain access to the identity and content of communications of certain individuals who are investigated for criminal activities. Therefore, widespread surveillance and monitoring of internet transactions could be avoided. These activities can take place in close cooperation with the independent data protection authorities and with the judicial authorities. After those proposals were put on the table by computer scientists it is the duty of the legislature to make sure that the function of such bodies can be vested with the necessary guarantees to successfully fulfil its objectives. To this end it is imperative for citizens to know that personal information could be retrieved from such agencies only in the cases, provided by law only with the demonstration of a warrant and only for the people involved in the activities investigated. The law should also clarify that the basic data protection

---

[1090] Page 119.

principles will apply to those bodies as well and that liability will occur in case of a breach. These agencies should be certified by the relevant authorities after recognition of their compliance with the requirements set by law.

Another solution recently found by the IT industry to deal with the privacy and security problems are the so called "on line wallets". They entail the creation of a database to which the consumers voluntarily provide their personal data such as name, address and credit card numbers. In exchange for that they acquire a number which is used as a personal code. The consumer will make all his purchases with this number and instead of providing his personal details to a variety of on line retailers the latter will turn to the "on line wallet" to receive its payment. Two prominent ones are Google's Checkout and eBay' Pay Pal. If one of its subscribers wants to purchase a book from Amazon she will order the book but Checkout will pay on her behalf charging her account in it. Therefore, the only body aware of her on line transactions, credit card details or even e-mail will be Google Checkout or Pay Pal. The latter assure the consumers that they can "shop safe in the knowledge that their financial information won't be shared with sellers or merchants"[1091]. This scheme is quite similar to the purchase and use in on line transaction of pre paid cards in the pattern of mobile telephony. The consumers can pay with their anonymous pre paid card without charging their credit card and without revealing their identity and habits. The "on line wallet" projects are a very good idea especially if they are accompanied by the same legal guarantees as the ones described above. The companies operating such schemes should receive the necessary legal safeguards that they should not convey the information they hold unless all legislative requirements are met. The latter should refer again to the existence of the warrant to take the information and data of people legally under investigation. These schemes could also receive the certification of the data protection authorities therefore enhancing their structure as trustworthy entities which handle the consumers' data in full compliance with law and the data protection principles. Companies which register to accept such methods of payment should be included in the lists of companies of the data protection authorities which openly

---

[1091] See Pay Pal's site at: https://www.paypal.com/uk/cgi-bin/webscr?cmd=xpt/cps/general/PayPalShoppers-outside A unique benefit of paying with PayPal is that merchants receive payments without ever seeing your financial details. When you choose to pay with PayPal, you are choosing one of the safest ways to pay online. Not only do we take measures to protect your financial information, we also offer extensive protection against unauthorised payments sent from

endorse privacy friendly policies. They could enjoy other privileges as well. Google for example offers companies which adhere to its scheme cheaper advertising on its websites and services. The consumers will know that the advertisements found on Google will mostly be from companies which are bound by the privacy friendly schemes. Exceptions to the rule related to national or public security and other legitimate premises should be provided for by law. These projects can serve as an important stimulus to e-commerce as they function as guarantees of privacy and security. The latter should not be underestimated as the fear of on line fraud is significantly lessened by the intervention of another significant entity paying on behalf of the consumer for his transaction. These entities can also guarantee transparency since the consumers are very well aware with whom they will have to deal in case of a breach. They will not have to pursue the liability of an obscure commercial entity somewhere in the world but with an agency with which they signed a contract with certain rights and obligations which was certified by the relevant authority. Therefore, the challenging issue of on line liability can be resolved. The development of such schemes with the necessary legislative regulation and safeguards could be proven as effective tools to deal with the privacy threats imposed by internet.

---

your account. See: https://www.paypal.com/uk/cgi-bin/webscr?cmd=xpt/general/Privacy-outside July 27th 2006.

10. Conclusion

The new reality created by the advent of internet as a means of conducting trade has created new legal challenges. In the light of technological evolution the issue of data protection assumes a central position in the debate over the proper solution to the recently emerged problem. It is not the first time that technology challenges the efficiency of the current legal framework but the extent of the threat to privacy and personal liberties renders a new approach imperative. The EU has moved towards policy choices which seem compatible with its legal and political traditions although the latest proposal on data retention as analysed above can be viewed as a deviation from the latter. It was extensively explained in the book that the EU assumed the conscious decision to include the right to privacy as one of the fundamental rights granted to its citizens. The book offered an analysis of the historical, cultural, legal and political developments in the two principal continental legal orders in order to shed light on the actual evolution of privacy from a value enjoyed by French aristocracy in the 19th century to a right currently recognised as fundamental at pan-European level. Privacy and the protection of personal data passed from the philosophical essays of Kant to assume a central position at the very core of the German constitutional and legal order. The historical events and conditions prevailing in Europe at the time of the Second World War painfully proved the importance of fully respecting human dignity as the core principle of democracy. The Europeans in the post war European Union placed certain rights at the core of their legal order in response to among others the experiences of that period. Therefore, the right to privacy and the protection of personal data found their prominent place within the European legal order in this context and in close relation to human dignity. The EU therefore, assumed the decision to respond to the technological challenges to privacy with a legislative framework which guarantees growth and development and simultaneously safeguards the rights of the European citizens. The landmark directive 95/46 on the protection of personal data which was thoroughly analysed before provided the general framework within which electronic commerce will evolve in the European context; in full respect of Europe's basic data protection principles. The Directive promoted a set of principles in accordance to which personal data can be lawfully processed. Therefore, the Directive and in effect the EU legal system placed a greater emphasis on the procedure. The processing of data can take place if the specific requirements of the EU law are specifically complied with. As an additional safeguard, sensitive personal data receive an additional layer of protection due to their character and nature which could entail a greater degree of risk in case of abuse. The EU has avoided as explained in the relevant part the theoretical complexities of the German legal order over several "personality circles" and in contrast to that chose to place the focus on the actual processing of data. However, it added further requirements and conditions to be met for the specifically defined sensitive data to be processed. Thus, the EU managed to maximise protection and to guarantee the existence of a system realistic enough to survive the challenges of the new era while avoiding unnecessary theoretical and legalistic complexities which would have created a great degree of legal uncertainty and therefore render the whole system unenforceable.

Due to the nature of the challenge and the global character of internet, the ideal solution would require close cooperation between the world's most significant trading partners the EU and the US and a set of proposals which would combine legal with technological responses. It is unfortunate that the US approach does not facilitate at all a common approach on the relevant issue. For historical and cultural reasons thoroughly presented in the relevant parts of the book, the US legal priorities present certain differences in comparison with the respective European one. The US legal order places the freedom of expression in the framework of a laissez faire society at the top of its principles' list. Liberty to express oneself or act as one wishes especially against the state occupies the top position in the priority agenda of the US legal order; it holds the place that human dignity enjoys in the European legal order. Therefore, the Americans have a wholly different approach as they fail to understand why they are called to regulate internet in the first place and limit the freedom of US citizens to act and express themselves freely. However, the rulings of the US Constitutional Court which were analysed at the respective part of the book proved that this legislative and judicial stance has resulted not only in the elimination of privacy in the US context but also in the serious undermining of the most important principle in the US constitutional order; the freedom of expression. According to the rulings of the Court, the US citizens are not justified in expecting to withhold their privacy in their employment premises, in relation to the phone numbers they dialled, while conducting their on line activities, when sending an e-mail and more frightening even at their own domicile when they cannot have reasonable expectations to maintain it. The construction of "reasonable expectations" of privacy has been used by the Court to limit the protection to a miniscule range of activities. The relevant concept has been intentionally shaped on a subjective basis so as to exclude protection from all areas of personal activities when one can expect that there is the ability of monitoring. By acknowledging ability of monitoring, the US citizen is unwillingly stripped of his expectations of privacy which cease to be treated as "reasonable" by the US judiciary. Therefore, in effect in the US the internet as a whole now can be deemed to fall out of the scope of any judicial protection of privacy as everyone is aware of the potential technological ability to have one's on line activities monitored. Thus, nobody can found "reasonable" expectations to keep his on line privacy. It is important to note the difference between the US Constitutional Court and the ECHR on the concept of "reasonable expectations" of privacy which provides an insight on the wholly different legal culture underlining the function of the two top Courts. As explained before, the ECHR has ruled that there is no reasonable expectation of privacy when a public authority interferes with one's privacy in compliance with the cumulative requirements of preventing crime, ensuring public safety, in the interests of national security and in accordance with law. Therefore, certain specific requirements have to be met so as to justify a privacy abuse in the European legal order, while the subjective perception of privacy limits is enough to condemn it in the US context. Interestingly enough, in its effort to exclude privacy from constitutional protection, the Court gradually resorted in the actual infringement of the literal content of the Fourth Amendment of Constitution which does protect privacy in one's house. In addition to that, the Court managed to fully undermine the right of expression as well since, individuals to tend to censor themselves and shift their opinions and behavioural patterns if aware that they are monitored or under scrutiny. Finally, this stance has an adverse effect even on the potential further growth in on line trade as this level of transparency and data gathering is a discouraging factor for many individuals to consume on line. The European approach has emphatically been a more appropriate response to the digital challenges to privacy as it laid on the premise of ensuring the fundamental rights of the European citizens. Europe chose to reconcile the demands of the new era with its humanistic traditions and rich legal culture which is based on the guarantee of freedom and democracy. It refused to accept that consolidating a data protection regime will prove irreconcilable with on line growth; and it was right to do so.

The evolution of technology and the significance of personal data in the framework of a knowledge based economy do not predetermine as futile any effort to deal with the problem. On the contrary as noted above, despite the evident cultural differences and historical experiences which render transnational cooperation more complex than initially perceived, consumer awareness in conjunction with the adequate legislative arrangements and technological responses can provide us with the necessary framework to protect privacy, combat insecurity and promote confidence in a means of trade which is now considered as transparent as never before. Europe for its part should restate its faith in its legal tradition and invent solutions which would be in compliance both with its humanistic traditions and with its legitimate aim of promoting on line growth. It has proved in the past capable of combining the respect of human rights with extensive growth and development. It is certain that it will manage to shape the right balance in the future as well provided of course that it possesses the necessary political will to do so. Data protection and the battle over privacy will dominate headlines and attract further attention if internet is to be left unregulated with the image and the reputation of a fully transparent instrument where nothing can be kept private. If this is the case its obvious potential will be further impaired and its reputation as a reliable means of trade will be seriously undermined. If there is a lack of confidence, there is a lack of will to use the full capacity of the net. However, the whole issue should be viewed in its full dimensions. It does not only concern a means of conducting trade but also the nature and the exact character of the society we choose to live in. Will it be a society which respects human rights and democratic values and is based on providing its citizens the scope to exercise their freedom of choice or will it be a society which will monitor all activities making Orwell's nightmare into a reality we will all have to live with? The answer to this question lies in the choices our societies have to make.

Bibliography

Articles

• A DeMarco David, Understanding Consumer Information Privacy in the Realm

of Internet Commerce: Personhood and Pragmatism, Pop Tarts and Six Packs,

84 Texas Law Review, 2006

• A Geist Michael, Doris Estelle Long, Leslie Ann Reis, David E Sorkin and

Fred Von Lohmann Copyright and Privacy: Collision or coexistence?

Conference Brochure: Copyright & Privacy, Through the Technology Lens, 4

The John Marshall Law School Review of Intellectual Property Law, 2005

• A. Levasseur Alain, Civil Law, Procedure and Private International Law: The

Boundaries of Property Rights: La Notion de Biens, 54 The American Journal

of Comparative Law, 2006

• A. Nova Todd , The Future Face of the Worldwide Data Privacy Push as a

factor affecting Wisconsin Businesses dealing with Consumer Data, 22

Wisconsin International Law Journal, 2004

• Abu Bakar Munir, Siti Hajar Mohd Yasin, Retention of Communications

Data: A Bumpy Road Ahead, 22 The John Marshall Journal of Computer &

Information Law 731, 2004

1

- Ah-Wong Jacqueline, Gandhi Puja, Patel Heena, Targett David, Shah Urvi, Tran ToDenh, E-Commerce Progress: inhibitors and the short term future, European Business Journal, 2001.

- Alboukrek Karen, Adapting to a New World of E-Commerce: The Need for Uniform Consumer Protection in the International Electronic Marketplace, 35 George Washington International Law Review, 2003

- Amelung Ulrich Tilman, Damage Awards for Infringement of Privacy, The German Approach, 14 Tulane European and Civil Law forum, 1999

- Arnulf S. Gubitz, The US Aviation and Transportation Security Act of 2001 in Conflict with the EU Data Protection Laws: How much Access to Airline Passenger Data does the United States need to combat Terrorism?, 39 New England Law Review 431, 2005

- Asfaw Tesfaye, Karunanayake Kanishka, Mehta Manish, Parnaik Amol, Shah Aarti, Targett David, Imperial College Management School, London, E-Commerce progress: International Comparisons, European Business Journal, 2001.

- Asim Z. Haque, Mathie H. Le, 2004 Privacy Year in Review Annual Update: International: Privacy Year in Review: Canada's PIPEDA and Japan's Personal Information Protection Act, 1 Journal of Law and Policy for the Information Society, 2005

- Austin Lisa M., Is Consent the Foundation of Fair Information Practices? Canada's Experience under PIPEDA, 56 University of Toronto Law Journal, 2006

- Azmi Madieha Ida, E-Commerce and Privacy Issues: An analysis of the Personal Data Protection Bill, 8(8), Computer and Telecommunications Law Review, 2002, 206-212.

- Baker R Wallace, deFontbressin Patrick, The French Refere Procedure and Conflicts of Human Rights, 25 Syracuse Journal of International Law and Commerce, Spring 1998

- Bale B. Robert, Informed Lending Decision v Privacy Interests in Great Britain: Technology Over the Edge of Infringement," 10 Transnational Lawyer 77, 1997.

- Banisar David, Davies Simon from Privacy International, Global Trends In Privacy Protection: An International Survey of Privacy, Data Protection, and Surveillance Laws and Developments, 18 The John Marshall Law School, The John Marshall Journal of Computer and Information Law

- Barcelo Rosa, Seeking Suitable Options for importing Data from the European Union, 36 The International Lawyer, Number 3, 2002.

- Barrington Moore in Daniel J. Solove, A Taxonomy of Privacy, 154 University of Pennsylvania Law Review, 2006

- Basho Kalinda, The Licensing of Our Personal Information: Is it a Solution to Internet Privacy?, 88 California Law Review, 2000

- Baumer L. David, Brande Earp Julia, Evers S. Pamela, Tit for Tat in Cyberspace: Consumer and Website Responses to Anarchy in the Market for Personal Information, 4 North Carolina Journal of Law & Technology 217, 2003

- Bejot Michel, European Treatment of Internet Privacy issues, Journal of Internet Law. At: http://www.gcwf.com/articles/journal/jil_jan01_1.html accessed on 5/02/2002.

- Bejot Michel, European Treatment of Internet Privacy Issues, Journal of Internet Law, GrayCary, available at: www.gcwf.com/articles/journal/jil_jan01_1.html , accessed on 5/02/2002.

- Bergelson Vera, It's Personal But is it Mine? Towards Property Rights in Personal Information, 37 University of California Davis Law Review, 2003

- Bergkamp Lucas, EU Data Protection Policy, The Privacy Fallacy: Adverse Effects of Europe's Data Protection Policy in an Information driven Economy, Computer Law and Security Report, Volume 18, number 1, 2002

- Bert Jaap Koops and Ronald Leenes, "Code" and the Slow Erosion of Privacy, 12 Michigan Telecommunications and Technology Law Review 115, 2005

- Bierlein Matthew and Gregory Smith, 2004 Privacy Year in Review Annual Update: Internet: Growing Problems with Spyware and Phishing, Judicial and Legislative Developments in Internet Governance and the Impacts on Privacy, 1 Journal of Law and Policy for the Information Society, 2005

- Bignami Francesca, Transgovernmental Networks v Democracy: The Case of the European Information Privacy Network, 26 Michigan Journal of International Law 807, 2005.

- Blanke M. Jordan, Safe Harbour and the European Union's Directive on Data Protection, 11 Albany Law Journal of Science and Technology, 2000.

- Bloustein J. Edward, Privacy is dear at any price: A Response to professor Posner's economic theory, Georgia Law Review, 12, 1978

4

- Bohlmal Erick, Privacy in the age of information, Journal of Information, Law and Technology, 2002, accessible at http://elj.warwick.ac.uk/jilt/02-2/bohlman.html

- Bourgoignie Thierry, European Community consumer law and policy: from Rome to Amsterdam, Consumer Law Journal, Andover, Sweet & Maxwell, 1998.

- Breslin John, Privacy – The Civil Liberties Issue, 14 Dickinson Journal of international Law, 1996

- Brown Russel, Privacy Law: Article: Rethinking Privacy: Exclusivity, Private Relation and Tort Law, 43 Alberta Law Review, 2006

- Brownsword Roger, Howells Geraint, Consumer Protection on the Internet: The impact of the information society on law, Institute for Commercial Law Studies, University of Sheffield, available at http://jsis.artsci.washington.edu/programs/europe/Netconference/HowellsPaper.htm Accessed on 5/02/2002.

- Butler Des, A Tort of Invasion of Privacy in Australia?, 2 Melbourne University Law Review, 339, 2005

- Bygrave Lee, Automated Profiling, Minding the Machine: Article 15 of the EC Data Protection directive and Automated Profiling, 17 Computer Law and Security Report, 2001

- Bygrave Lee, European Data Protection, Determining Applicable Law Pursuant to European Data Protection Legislation, Computer Law and security report, 2000

- C. McWilliams Martin , Applicants laid Bare: The Privacy Economics of University Application Files, 34 Hofstra Law Review, 2005

- Cardonsky B Lauren, Towards a Meaningful Right to Privacy in the United Kingdom, 20 Boston University International Law Journal 393, 2002.

- Carlin M Fiona, The Data Protection Directive: The Introduction of Common Privacy Standards, European Law Review, 21 (1), Sweet & Maxwell, 1996.

- Caruso Denise, Exploiting and Protecting Personal Information, The New York Times, March 1st 1999

- Castor A. David, Treading Water in the Data Privacy Age: An Analysis of Safe Harbour's first year, 12 Indiana International and Comparative Law Review 265, 2002.

- Catanzariti Therese, Swimmers, surfers, and Sue Smith, Personality Rights in Australia, Entertainment Law Review, 13 (7), 2002

- Catinat Michel, The National Information Infrastructure Initiative in the United States – Policy or Non Policy? Part 1, Computer and Telecommunications Law Review, 1998, 4 (3)

- Caulfield Timothy and Nola M. Ries, Consent, Privacy and Confidentiality in Longitudinal, Population Health Research: The Canadian Legal Context, 12 Health Law Journal, 2004

- Chissick Michael, Data Protection in the E-Commerce Era, Computer and Telecommunications Law Review, 5 (4), 1999.

- Chissick Michael, Data Protection in the Electronic Commerce Era, Computer and Telecommunications Law Review, Sweet & Maxwell, London, 1999

- Clausing Jeri, IBM takes stand for Consumer Privacy on the Web, April 1st 1999, The New York Times.

- Clear Marie, Falling Into the Gap: The European Union's Data Protection Act and Its Impact on US Law and Commerce, 18 John Marshall Journal of Computer and Information Law, 2000

- Coad Jonathan, Privacy – Article 8. Who needs it?, Entertainment Law Review, 2001,12 (8), 226-233

- Cole Richard, Authentic Democracy: Endowing Citizens with a Human Rig in their Genetic Information, 33 Hofstra Law Review, 2005

- Craig D.R. John, Invasion of Privacy and Charter Values: The Common Law Tort Awakens, 42 McGill Law Journal, 1997

- Craig John DR, Nolte Nico, Privacy and Free Speech in Germany and Canada: Lessons for an English Privacy Tort, 2 European Human Rights Law Review, 1998, Sweet & Maxwell

- Crisci L Camrin, All the World is not a Stage: Finding a Right to Privacy in existing and proposed Legislation, 6 NYU Journal of Legislation and Public Policy, 2003

- Crump Catherine, Data Retention: Privacy, anonymity and Accountability On – Line, 56 Stanford Law review, 2003

- Crutchfield Barbara George, Lynch Patricia, Marsnik F. Susan, US Multinational Employers: Navigating through the Safe Harbour Principles to comply with the EU Directive, The American business Law Association, 38 American Business Law Journal, 2001.

- D. Blackman Joshua, A Proposal for Federal Legislation Protecting Informational Privacy across the Private Sector, Santa Clara Computer and High Technology Law Journal 431, 1993

- D. Warren Samuel & Louis D. Brandeis, The right to Privacy, 4 Harvard Law Review 193, in 1890.

- D. Warren Samuel and Louis D. Brandeis, The Right to Privacy, Harvard Law Review, 4, 1890

- Da Jerker B. Svantesson, Geo Location Technologies and other Means of Placing Borders on the borderless Internet, 23 John Marshall Journal of Computer & Information Law, 2004

- Daemen Thomas, Book Review: The United States of Europe: The New Superpower and the End of American Supremacy by T.R Reid, 11 Columbia Journal of European Law 717, 2005

- Davidson J. Stephen, Andresen A. Katheryn, UCITA and other US Laws in an International EU Perspective, GrayCary, Journal of Internet Law, 2000, available at www.gcwf.com/articles/journal/jil_july00_1.html , accessed on 5/02/2002.

- De Bottini Renaud Par, La Directive "Commerce Electronique du 8 Juin 2000, La Revue du Marche Commun et de l'Union Europeenne, 2001, Paris

- De Burca Grainne, The Constitutional Challenge of New Governance in the European Union, European Law Review, 2003, 28 (6), 814

- de Cock Buning Madeleine, Marc de Vries, Ewoud Hondius, Corien Prins, Consumer@ Protection.EU. An analysis of European Consumer Legislation in the Information Society, Journal of Consumer Policy 24, Kluwer Academic Publishers, 2001.

- deBeer Jeremy, Employee Privacy: The Need for Comprehensive Protection, 66 Saskatchewan Law Review, 2003

8

- Debusserea Frederic, The EU E-Privacy Directive: A Monstrous Attempt to starve the Cookie Monster?, International Journal of Law and Information Technology, March 2005.13 (70).

- DiLascio Tracey, How safe is the Safe Harbour? US and EU Data Privacy Law and the Enforcement of the FTC's Safe Harbour Programme, 22 Boston University International Law Journal, 2004

- Dmytrenko Olena, Ali Nardali, .NET Passport under the Scrutiny of US and EU Privacy Law: Implications for the Future of Online Authentication, 1 The Ohio State University, Journal of Law and Policy for the Information Society, 2005

- Dmytrenko Olena, Cara D. Cutler, Does Ukraine need a Comprehensive Statute to "control" private data controllers?, 5 Washington University Global Studies Law Review, 2006

- Douglas Scott Sionaidh, The Charter of Fundamental rights as a Constitutional Document, European Human Rights Law Review, 2004, 1, 37-50

- Drews Ludwig Hans, Data Privacy Protection in German, The Effects of the German Federal Protection Act from the perspective of Siemens AG, updated special reprint, February 2003. Available at Siemens intranet at: http://dsb.siemens.de/dspages/InfoSchulung.htm

- Du Pont George F., The Criminalisation of True Anonymity in Cyberspace, 7 Michigan Telecommunications Technology Review 191, 2001

- Dupre Catherine, The Protection of Private Life Against Freedom of Expression in French Law, European Human Rights Law Review, 6, 2000

- Durie Robyn, An Overview of the Data Protection Act 1998, Computer and Telecommunications Law Review, 2000, 6 (4), 88-93

- E. Frazier Leah, Extraterritorial Enforcement of PIPEDA: A multi-tiered Analysis, 36 George Washington, International Law Review, 2004

- Eberle J Edward, Human Dignity, Privacy and Personality in German and American Constitutional Law, Utah Law Review 963, 1997

- Edwards Lilian, Consumer Privacy, On line Business and the Internet: Looking for Privacy in all he Wrong Places, International Journal of Law and IT, September 2003.11 (226).

- Elbert Lin, Prioritising Privacy: A Consitutional Response to Internet, 17 Berkeley Technology Law Journal, Summer 2002.

- Emerson Thomas I., The Riht of Privacy and the Freedom of the Press, Harvard Civil Rights, Civil Liberties Law Review, 14, 1979

- Endeshaw Assafa, Consumer Protection in Cyberspace: Back to Caveat Emptor?, Consumer Law Journal, Andover, Sweet & Maxwell, Volume 7, Number 1.

- Epstein Richard A., A Taste for Privacy? Evolution and the Emergence of a Naturalistic Ethic, The Journal of Legal Studies, 9, 1980

- Euobserver article, Helena Spongenberg, US Could Access EU Data Retention Information, 12 May 2006

- Evans D. Mark, Protection of Data on the Internet, Intellectual Property Quarterly, 2002.

- Ewing Mike, The Perfect Storm: The Safe Harbour and the Directive on Data Protection, 24 Houston Journal of International Law, 2002

- Finkin W. Matthew, Employee Privacy, American Values and the Law, 72 Chicago Kent Law Review, 1996.

- Finkin W. Matthew, Information Technology and Workers' Privacy: A Comparative Study: Part IV: The Comparative Historical and Philosophical Context: Menschenbild: The Conception of the employee as a person in Western Law, 23 Comparative Labour Law & Policy Journal, 2002

- Fitzgerald L. Peter, Hidden Dangers in the E-Commerce Data Mine: Governmental Customer and Trading Partner Screening Requirements, The International Lawyer, Spring 2001, Volume 35, No1, American Bar Association, Chicago, Illinois.

- Fried Charles, Privacy, The Yale Law Journal, 77, 1968

- Fried Frank Harris Shriver & Jacobson, Data Protection v Privacy: United States and EU come to Terms on a Safe Harbour, Cyberspace Lawyer, May 2000, Volume 5, number 3.

- Friedemann Caitlin, Legislative Development: Council Decision Regarding Agreement Between the European Community and he United States on the Use of Passenger Name Record Data, 1 Columbia Journal of European Law 207, 2004 – 2005.

- Fromholz M. Julia, Foreign Law: a) Data Privacy: The European Union Data Privacy Directive, 15 Berkeley Technology Law journal, 2000.

- Froomkin Michael A, Symposium: Cyberspace and Privacy: A New Legal Paradigm? The Death of Privacy?, 52 Stanford Law Review, May 2000

- Gallagher David F., Amazon Tries to Ease Privacy Worries, August 30th 1999, The New York Times.

- Gavison Ruth, Privacy and the Limits of Law, The Yale Law Journal, 89, 1980

- Gerety Tom, Redefining Privacy, Harvard Civil Rights, Civil Liberties Law Review, 12, 1977

- Gigante Alexander, Ice Patch on the Information superhighway: Foreign Liability for Domestically Created Content, 14 Cardozo Arts & Entertainment Law Journal, 1996

- Gladstone Julia, The impact of e-commerce on the laws of nations. The US privacy balance and the European Privacy Directive: Reflections on the United States privacy policy, Willamette Journal of International Law and dispute Resolution, Volume 7, 2000

- Glancy Dorothy, Symposium on Internet Privacy, At the Intersection of Visible and Invisible, 16 Santa Clara Computer and High Technology Law Journal, May 2000.

- Glover Rodney, Worlton Amy, Rein Wiley, United States: Trans-National Employers must harmonise conflicting Privacy Rules, World Data Protection Report, November 2002, Volume 2, number 11.

- Gomez Velez Natalie, Internet Access to Court Records, Balancing Public Access and Privacy, 51 Loyola Law Review, 2005

- Gross Emanuel, The Struggle of a Democracy against Terrorism, Protection of Human Rights: The Right to Privacy versus the National Interest – The Proper Balance, 37 Cornell International Law Journal, 2004

- Gross Hyman, The Concept of Privacy, New York University Law Review, 42, 1967

- Guirguis Max, Electronic Visual Surveillance and the Reasonable Expectation of Privacy, Journal of Technology, Law and Policy, Vol 9, December 2004

- H. Tomas Gomez Arostegui, Defining Private Life under the European Convention on Human Rights by referring to Reasonable Expectations, 35 California Western International Journal Law, 2005

- Harris R. Peter, International Developments, European Directive, Implementation Issues with Application of directive 95/46EC to Third Countries, 33 World Data Protection Report, May 2002

- Haubold Jens, Kaufman Winn Jane, Electronic Promises: Contract Law Reform and E-Commerce in a Comparative Perspective, European Law Review, 2002, 27 (5)

- Hauch M Jeanne, Protecting Private Facts in France: the Warren & Brandeis Tort is Alive and Well and Flourishing in Paris, 68 Tulane Law Review 1219, 1994.

- Hetcher A Steven, The Emergence of Website Privacy Norms, 7 Michigan Telecommunications Technology Law Review, 2001

- Hetcher Steven, Changing the Social Meaning of Privacy in Cyberspace, Harvard Journal of Law and Technology, Harvard Law School, Vol 15, number 1, 2001.

- Heydrich W. Michael, A brave new world: Complying with the European Union Directive on personal privacy through the power of contract, 25 Brooklyn Journal of International Law, 1999

- Hildner Laura, Defusing the Threat of RFID: Protecting Consumer Privacy through Technology Specific Legislation at the State Level, 41 Harvard Civil Rights – Civil Liberties Law Review, 2006

- Hirshleifer Jack, Privacy: Its Origin, Function, and Future, The Journal of Legal Studies, 9, 1980

- Howells Geraint, United Kingdom's Consumer Policy White Paper- A step in the right direction? , Consumer Law Journal, Volume 8, Number 2, Andover, Sweet & Maxwell.

- Howells Geraint, Wilhelmsson Thomas, EC Consumer Law: Has it come of Age?, 28 European Law Review, 2003, 370

- Hull John, Privacy as an Aspect of Public Law: Reflections on R v Broadcasting Complaints, Entertainment Law Review, Sweet & Maxwell, London, 1995

- Iglezakis Ioannis, Consumers' Access to Justice in the European Union, Revue Hellenique De Droit International, L'Institut Hellenique de Droit International et Etranger, Sakkoulas Editions, Thessaloniki, 2000.

- J King Nancy, Sukanya Pillay, Gail A Lasprogata, Regulation of Electronic Employee Monitoring: Identifying Fundamental Principles of Employee Privacy through a Comparative Study of Data Privacy Legislation in the European Union, United States, Canada, 2004 Stanford Technology Law Review 4

- J King Nancy, Sukanya Pillay, Gail A Lasprogata, Workplace Privacy and Discrimination Issues related to Genetic Data: A Comparative Law Study of the European Union and the United States, 43 American Business Law Journal, 2006

- J Sylvester Douglas, Sharon Lohr, Counting on Confidentiality: Legal and Statistical Approaches to Federal Privacy Law after the USA Privacy Act, 2005 Wisconsin Law Review

- J. Cockfield Athur, The State of Privacy Laws and Privacy Encroaching Technologies after September 11th: A Two Year Report Card on the Canadian

Government, 1 University of Ottawa Law & Technology Journal 325, 2003 / 2004.

- J. Garcia Flora, Bodil Lindqvist: A Swedish Churchgoer's Violation of the European Union's Data Protection Directive should be a Warning to US Legislators, 15 Fordham Intellectual Property, Media & Entertainment Law Journal, 2005

- J. Steinbock Daniel, Data Matching, Data Mining and Due Process, 40 Georgia Law Review, 2005

- J. Sylvester Douglas and Sharon Lohr, The Security of Our Secrets: A History of Privacy and Confidentiality in Law and Statistical Practice, 83 Denver University Law Review, 2005

- J. V. McHale, Regulating Genetic Databases: Some Legal and Ethical Issues, Medical Law Review 2004.12 (70).

- Jabbour Vivianne, Rowe Heather, The Proposed Data Protection Directive and the Data Protection Act 1984, Computer and Telecommunications Law Review, 1 (2), 1995, 38-46

- Jay Hoofnagle Chris, Big Brother's Little Helpers: How ChoicePoint and other Commercial Data Brokers collect and package your Data for Law Enforcement, 29 North Carolina Journal of International Law & Commercial Regulation 595, 2004.

- Justin Kent Holcombe, Solutions for Regulating Offshore Outsourcing in the Service Sector: Using the Law, Market, International Mechanisms, and Collective Organisations as Building Blocks, 7 Univesity of Pennsylvania Journal of Labour and Employment Law, 2005

- K. Baker Roger, Offshore IT Outsourcing and the 8th Data Protection Principle with reference to Financial Services, International Journal of Law and Information Technology, 2006

- K.A. Taipale, Data Mining and Domestic Security: Connecting the Dots to Make Sense of Data, 5 Columbia Science and Technology Law Review 2, 2004

- K. Katyal Sonia, Privacy v Piracy, 9 International Journal of Communications Law and Policy 7, 2004/2005

- Kallel Sami, Arbitrage et Commerce Electronique, Revue de droit des affaires internationales, number 1, 2001.

- Kalven Harry Jr, Privacy in tort Law: Were Warren and Brandeis Wrong?, Law and Contemporary Problems, 31, 1966

- Kambas J William, A Safety Net in the E-Marketplace: The Safe Harbour Principles offer comprehensive Privacy Protection without stopping Data Flow, 9 ILSA Journal of International and Comparative Law, 2002

- Kang Jerry & Benedikt Buchner, Privacy in Atlantis, 18 Harvard Journal of Law and Technology, 2004

- Kang Jerry, Information Privacy in Cyberspace Transactions, 50 Stanford Law Review 1212, 1998.

- Kao C. Audiey, Linden Ozanne Erica, Direct to Consumer advertising and the Internet: Informational Privacy, Product Liability and Organisational Responsibility, Saint Louis University Law Journal, Volume 46, Number 1, 2002

- Karas Stan, Enhancing the Privacy Discourse: Consumer Information Gathering as Surveillance, Journal of Technology Law & Policy, 2002, Volume 7, Issue 1

- Kariyawasam Rohan, Internet Interconnection: Where are we going?, Computer and Telecommunications Law Review, 2000, Sweet & Maxwell limited and Contributors.

- Kaufman Winn Jane, Haubold Jens, Electronic Promises: contract law reform and electronic commerce in comparative perspective, 27 European Law Review, August 2002, Sweet & Maxwell, London

- Kennedy Gwen, Thumbs Up for Biometric Authentication, 8 Computer Law Review & Technology Journal, 2004

- Kenny Mel, Globalisation, Interlegality and Europeanised Contract Law, 21 Penn State International Law Review, 2003, 569

- Kesan P Jay, Cyber Working or Cyber Shirking?: A First Principles Examination of Electronic Privacy in the Workplace, 54 Florida Law Review

- Kotzker Jason, The Great Cookie Carer: Internet Privacy and Target Marketing At Home and Abroad, 15 Saint Thomas Law Review, 2003

- Koussoulis Stelios, Regulating Electronic Commerce, Revue Hellenique de Droit International, L'Institut Hellenique De Droit International et Etranger, Thessaloniki, Greece, 2002

- Kramer Chuang Lynn, Private Eyes are Watching You: Consumer On-line Privacy Protection – Lessons from Home and Abroad, 37 Texas International Law Journal, 2002

- Krotosnynski J Ronald, Autonomy, Community and Traditions of Liberty: The Contrast of British and American Privacy Law, Duke Law Journal, 1990.

- Kuner Christopher, Beyond Safe Harbour: European Data Protection Law and electronic Commerce, The International Lawyer, American Bar Association, Chicago, Illinois, Volume 35, number 1, 2001.

- L. Rustad Michael & Thomas H. Koenig, Harmonising Cybertort Law for Europe and America, 5 Journal of High Technology Law, 2005

- L. Rustad Michael, Sandra R. Paulsson, Monitoring Employee E-mail and Internet Usage: Avoiding the Omniscient Electronic Sweatshop: Insights from Europe, 7 University of Pennsylvania Journal of Labour and Employment Law, 2005

- L. Weaver Russell, Andrew T. Keynon, David F. Partlett, Clive P. Walker, Defamation Law and Fee Speech: Reynolds v Times Newspapers and the English Media, 37 Vanderbilt Journal of Transnational Law 1255, 2004

- L. Woodard Rebecca, Is Your Medical Information Safe? A Comparison of Comprehensive and Sectoral Privacy and Security Laws, 15 Indiana International & Comparative Law Review 147, 2004

- L'Hoest Raphael, The European Dimension of the digital Economy, Intereconomics, January/February 2001.

- Labman Shauna, Genetic Prophecies: The Future of the Canadian Workplace, 30 Manitoba Law Journal 227, 2004.

- Leenheer Zimmerman Diane, Is there a Right to have Something to say? One View of the Public Domain, 73 Fordham aw Review, 2004

- Legorburu Bruce, Doing Business between the EU and New Zealand: What do you have to do to protect Personal Information these days, Computer and Telecommunications Law Review, 2000, Sweet & Maxwell

18

- Linda S. Spedding, An Overview on Outsourcing, Advising Business: Law & Practice, 2005

- Lindsay David, An Exploration of the Conceptual Basis of Privacy and the Implications for the Future of Australian Privacy Law, 29 Melbourne University Law Review 131, 2005

- Lipton Jacqueline, Protecting Valuable Commercial Information in the Digital age: Law, Policy and Practice, 6.1 J.Tech.L & Pol'Y2, 2000

- Litan Robert, Cate H. Fred, Constitutional Issues in Information Privacy, 9 Michigan Telecommunication Technology Law Review, 2002

- Long J. William, Quek Pang Marc, Personal Data Privacy Protection in an age of globalisation: the US-EU Safe Harbour Compromise, Journal of European Public Policy, June 2002, Taylor & Francis Ltd.

- Loon Wee, Emergence of a Right to Privacy from within the Law of confidence?, 18(5) European Intellectual Property Rights Review, 1996

- Lorber Steven, Data Protection and Subject Access Requests, Industrial Law Journal 2004.33 (179).

- Lord Gordon Slynn, The Development of Human Rights in the United Kingdom, 28 Fordham International Law Journal 477, 2005

- Loring B. Tracie, An Analysis of the Informational Privacy Protection Afforded by the European Union and the United States, University of Texas at Austin School of Law Publications, 37 Texas International Law Journal, Spring 2002

- M Blanke Jordan, Robust Notice and Informed Consent: The Keys to Successful Spyware Legislation, 7 Columbia Science and Technology Law Review 2, 2006

- M. Richards Neil, Reconciling Data Privacy and the First Amendment, 52 UCLA Law Review, 2005

- M. Ries Nola, Privacy Law: Patient Privacy in a Wired ad Wireless World: Approaches to Consent in the Context of Electronic Health Records, 43 Alberta Law Review, 2006

- M. Young Jason, Surfing while muslim: Privacy, Freedom of Expression & the Unintended Consequences of Cybercrime Legislation: A Critical Analysis of the Council of Europe Convention on Cyber Crime & the Canadian Lawful Access Proposal, 9 International Journal of Communications Law and Policy 9, 2004/2005

- MacDonnell John, Exporting Trust: Does E-Commerce Need a Canadian Privacy Seal of Approval?, 39 The Alberta Law Review 346, 2001

- Mackenzie P. Andrew, Privacy – A new Right in UK Law, 12 Scots Law Times, 2002, 98-101.

- Maier Lothar, Institutional Consumer Representation in the European Community, Journal of Consumer Policy 16, Kluwer Academic Publishers, 1993.

- Mailland Julien, Freedom of Speech, the Internet, and the Costs of Control: The French Example, 33 New York University Journal of International Law and Politics, 2001

- Marta Pardo Leal, La directiva 2000/31 CE sobre el comercio electronico: su aplicacion en el ambito del Mercado Interior, Gaceta Juridica de la Union Europea y de la Competencia, 2000.

- Martin Craig, Mailing Lists, Mailboxes, and the Invasion of Privacy: Finding A Contractual Solution to a transnational Problem, 35 Houston Law Review, Fall 1998

- Mayer-Schoenberger Viktor, 1 West Virginia Journal of Law and Technology 1.1,1997. At: http://www.wvu.edu/%7Ewvjolt/Arch/Mayer/Mayer.htm, accessed on 22/06/2003.

- Mc Closkey H.J., The Political Ideal of Privacy, Philosophical Quarterly, 21, 1971

- McBride Jeremy, Disclosure of Crime Prevention Data: Specific European and International Standards, European Law Review, 2001, Sweet & Maxwell

- McClurg J. Andrew, A Thousand Words are worth a Picture: A Privacy Tort Response to consumer Data Profiling, 98 Northwestern University Law Review, 2003

- McColgan Aileen, The EU Charter of Fundamental Rights, European Human Rights Law Review, 1, 2004

- McDonald Barbara, International and Comparative Perspectives on Defamation, Free Speech, an Privacy: Privacy, Princesses and Paparazzi, 50 New York Law School Law Review 205, 2005 / 2006

- Micklitz W. Hans, Weatherill Stephen, Consumer Policy in the European Community: Before and After Maastricht, Journal of Consumer Policy 16, Kluwer Academic Publishers, 1993.

- Moakes Jonathan, Data Protection in Europe – Part 1, Journal of International Banking Law, 1986, 1(2), 77

- Mohd. Salman Waris, Indian law-a semblance of data privacy, Privacy and Data Protection, 2005

- Monahan Amy, Deconstructing Information Walls: The Impact of the European Data Directive on US Businesses, 29 Law and Policy in International business, 1998

- Morton Jeremy, Data Protection and Privacy, European Intellectual Property Review, 18 (10), 1996, Sweet & Maxwell, 558-561

- Moshell Ryan, And then there was one: the Outlook for a self-regulatory US amidst a Global Trend toward Comprehensive Data Protection, 37 Texas Technology Law Review, 2005

- Mullen Kenneth, UK Developments: Data Protection and on line Privacy, Cyberspace Lawyer, Volume 6, Number 7, 1998.

- Murphy T Caitlin, International Law and the Internet: An Ill Suited Match Case Note on UEJF & LICRA v Yahoo Inc, 25 Hastings International and Comparative Law Review, 2002, 405.

- Murray J Patrick, The Adequacy standard under Directive 95/46: Does US Data Protection meet this Standard?, 21 Fordham International Law journal, 1998

- Myers M Jennifer, Creating Data Protection Legislation in the US: An Examination of the Current Legislation in the EU, Spain, and the United States, 29 Case Western Reserve Journal of International Law, 1997

- Nevenko Misita, Reconstructing the Consumer Committee: Glossae marginalis, Consumer Law Journal, Volume 8, Number 1, Andover, Sweet & Maxwell, 2000.

- Nonnie L Shivers, Firing "Immoral" Public Employees: If Article 8 of the European Convention on Human Rights Protects Employee Privacy Rights, then why can't we?, 21 Arizona Journal of International and Comparative Law, 2004

- P. Nehf James, Incomparability and the Passive Virtues of ad hoc Privacy Policy, 76 University of Colorado Law Review, 2005

- P. Nehf James, Shopping for Privacy on Line: Consumer Decision Making Strategies ad the Emerging Market for Information Privacy, 2005 University of Illinois Journal of Law, Technology and Policy

- Parent W. A., A New Definition of Privacy for the Law, Law and Philosophy, 2, 1983

- Pearson E. Hilary, E-Commerce Legislation: Recent European Community Developments, Journal of Internet Law, accessed on 5/2/2002 at www.gcwf.com/articles/journal/jil_aug00_1.html

- Peers Steve, The European Parliament and Data Retention: Chronicle of a "sell out" foretold?, Statewatch Analysis, accessed at: http://www.statewatch.org/news/2005/dec/sp_dataret_dec05.pdf on July 15th 2006.

- Posner A. Richard, The Right of Privacy, Georgia Law Review, 12, 1978

- Post Robert, The Social Foundations of Privacy: Community and self in the common Law tort, California Law Review, 77, 1989

- Ramberg Hultmark Christina, The E-Commerce Directive and formation of a contract in a comparative perspective, 2001, 26 European Law Review, Sweet & Maxwell

- Rebeiro Michael, A Glancing Blow to Computer Privacy, Computer and Telecommunications Law Review, 2(3), 1996, 122-124

- Rees Christopher, Brimsted Kate, The twelve stages of data protection, IT Law Today, December 2002

- Rehm Gebhard, 32 University of West Los Angeles Law Review, 2001

- Reich Norbert, Consumer Law and E-Commerce- Initiatives and Problems in Recent EU and German Legislation, ERA- Forum- 2-2001.

- Reidenberg R. Joel, E-Commerce and Privacy Institute for Intellectual Property & Information Law Symposium: E-Commerce and Trans Atlantic Privacy, Houston Law Review, 2001.

- Reidenberg R. Joel, E-Commerce and Trans-Atlantic Privacy, 38 Houston Law Review, Fall 2001.

- Reidenberg R. Joel, Restoring Americans' Privacy in Electronic Commerce, 14 Berkeley Technology Law Journal, 1999.

- Reynolds B. John, European Data Privacy Regulation and its Impact on American Business, Washington Legal Foundation, Contemporary Legal Notes Series, Number 35, September 2000, www.wlf.org

- Ribstein E. Larry, Kobayashi H. Bruce, State Regulation of Electronic Commerce, 51 Emory Law Journal 1, 2002

- Ritter B Jeffrey, Hayes S Benjamin, Judy L Henry, Emerging Trends in International Privacy Law, 15 Emory International Law Review, 2001

- Robin Olivier Sophie, Immigration Law and Human Rights: Legal Line Drawing Post September 11: Symposium Article: Citizens and non Citizens in Europe: European Union Measures against Terrorism after September 11, 25 Boston College Third World Law Journal, 2005

24

- Roch P Michael, Filling the void of Data Protection in the US: Following the European Example, 12 Santa Clara Computer & High Technology Law Journal

- Rojas Hugo, La, Culture and Society: Lancrit Theory and Transdisciplinary Approaches: Law, Land and Labour: Constructions of Property and Status in Local and Global Contexts: Labour Law and Genetic Discrimination on Chile, 16 Florida Journal of International Law, 2004

- Rotenberg Marc, Agre E. Philip, Technology and Privacy: the new Landscape, 11 Harvard Journal of Law & Technology 871, 1998.

- Rotenberg Marc, Fair Information Practices, Stanford Technology Law Review 1, 2001

- Rowland Diane, Data Retention and the War against Terrorism – A Considered and Proportionate Response? 2004 (3) The Journal of Information, Law and Technology (JILT)

- Rowland Diane, Griping, Bitching and Speaking your Mind: Defamation and Free Expression on the Internet, 110 Penn State Law Review, 2006

- Rubenfeld Jed, The Right of Privacy, Harvard Law Review, 102, 1989

- Ruttley Philip, E.C. Competition Law in Cyberspace: An Overview of Recent Developments, [1998] ECLR 4, Sweet &Maxwell, 1998.

- Sadiq Reza, Privacy and the Criminal Arrestee or Suspect: In Search of a Right, in Need of a Rule, 64 Maryland Law Review 755, 2005.

- Saltzman Ilana, Cassidy Joanna, The Data Protection Directive: How is UK Data Protection Law Affected, International Company and Commercial Law Review, 1996, 7(3), 110-114

- Satish M. Kini and James T. Shreve, Notice Requirements: Common Themes and Differences in the Regulatory and Legislative Responses to Data Security Breaches, 10 North Carolina Banking institute 87, 2006

- Scherer Joachim, European Telecommunications Law: The Framework of the Treaty (of Rome), European Law, Review, Sweet & Maxwell, 1987, 12 (5), 354

- Scherzer H. Dov, EU Regulation of Processing of Personal Data by wholly non Europe based websites, European Intellectual Property Law Review, 2003, Sweet & Maxwell.

- Schiller C. Julia, Information Privacy v The Commercial speech Doctrine: Can the Gramm Leach Bliley Act Provide Adequate Privacy Protection?, 11 CommLaw Conspectus, 2003

- Schriver R. Robert, You cheated, you lied: The Safe Harbour Agreement and its Enforcement by the Federal Trade Commission, 70 Fordham Law Review, 2002.

- Shaffer Gregory, Globalisation and Social Protection: The Impact of EU and International Rules in the Ratcheting Up of US Privacy Standards, 25 The Yale Journal of International Law, 2000.

- Shubhankar Dam, Remedying a Technological Challenge: Individual Privacy and Market Efficiency; Issues and Perspectives on the Law relating to Data Protection, 15 Albany Law Journal of Science & Technology, 2005.

- Sideek Mohamed, Consumer Protection in the EC Financial Market, Consumer Law Journal, Volume 8, Number 3-4, Andover, Sweet & Maxwell, 2000.

- Siebecker R. Michael, Cookies and The Common Law: Are Internet Advertisers Trespassing on our Computers?, 76 Southern California Law Review, 2003

- Singh Rabinder, Strachan James, The Right To Privacy in English Law, 2 European Human Rights Law Review, 2002, 129

- Skok Gavin, Establishing a Legitimate Expectation of Privacy in Clickstream Data, 6 Michigan Telecommunication Technology Law Review 61, 2000

- Slobogin Christopher, The Search and Seizure of Computers and Electronic Evidence: Transaction Surveillance by the Government, 75 Mississippi Law Journal 139, 2005.

- Smith Seagrumn, Microsoft and the European Union Face Off over Internet Privacy Concerns, Duke Law and Technology Review, August 2002.

- Smitherman W Charles, The New Transatlantic Marketplace: A Contemporary Analysis of the US – EU Trade Relations and Possibilities for the Future, 12 Minnesota Journal of Global Trade, 2003, 251.

- Sookman B. Barry, E-commerce, Internet and the Law – A Survey of the Legal Issues in Canada, Computer and Telecommunications Law Review, 1999, 5(3)

- Sookman Barry, Legal Framework for E-Commerce Transactions, Computer and Telecommunications Law Review, 7 (4), 2001

- Sovern Jeff, Protecting Privacy with Deceptive Trade Practices Legislation, 69 Fordham Law Review, 2001

- Spencer B. Shaun, Reasonable Expectations and the Erosion of Privacy, 39 San Diego Law Review, 2002

- Steele K. Betty, Privacy, Confidentiality and Consumer Protection on the Internet, accessed at www.tntech.edu/www/acad/mayberry/2000N-BettySteele.htm , accessed on 11/02/2002

- Stiles Allison, Everyone's a Critic: Defamation and Anonymity on the Internet, 2002 Duke Law & Technology Review

- Stokes Simon, Data Protection, European Intellectual Property Review, Sweet & Maxwell, 1995, 17 (7)

- Stuyck Jules, European Consumer Law after the Treaty of Amsterdam: Consumer policy in or beyond the internal market? , Common Market Law Review 37, Kluwer Law International, 2000.

- Swire P Peter, Litan Robert, None of Your Business: World Data Flows, electronic Commerce, and the European Privacy Directive, 12 Harvard Journal of Law and Technology, 1999

- Szafran Emmanuel, Overstraeten Van Tanguy, Data Protection and Privacy on the Internet: Technical Considerations and European Legal Framework, Computer and Telecommunications Law Review, 2001, Sweet & Maxwell.

- T Thai Joseph, The Jurisprudence of Justice Stevens: Panel I: Criminal Justice: Is Data Mining ever a search under Justice Steven's Fourth Amendment?, 74 Fordham Law Review, 2006

- T. McKay Alexandra , The Private Sector Amendment to Australia's Privacy Act: A First Step on the Road to Privacy, 14 Pacific Rim Law & Policy Journal, 2005

- Tal Z. Zarsky, Institute for Information Law and Policy Symposium State of Play: II. Article: Information Privacy in Virtual Worlds: Identifying Unique

Concerns Beyond the Online and Offline Worlds, 49 New York Law School Law Review 231, 2004 / 2005.

- Tal Z. Zarsky, Thinking Outside the Box: Considering Transparency, Anonymity, and Pseudonymity as Overall Solutions to the Problems of Information Privacy in the Internet Society, 58 University of Miami Law Review 991, 2004

- Tal Z. Zrsky, Desperately Seeking Solutions: Using Implementation Based Solutions for the Troubles of Information Privacy in the Age of Data Mining and the Internet Society, 56 Maine Law Review, 2004

- Tanus Daniel Gustavo, Alguien te esta mirando, Information Technology, Mind Opener SA, Edicion Number 50, Noviembre 2000, Buenos Aires, p144. Also available at www.protecciondedatos.com.ar/doc6.htm. Accessed on July 1st 2003.

- Targett David, B2B or not B2B? Scenarios for the future of e-commerce, European Business journal, 2001, volume 13, number 1.

- Taylor Nick, Policing, Privacy and Proportionality, European Human Rights Law Review, 2003, 86-100.

- Tedeschi Bob, Net Companies Look Offline for Consumer Data, July 21st 1999, The New York Times

- Teh Jeanette, Privacy Wars in Cyberspace: An examination of the Legal and business tensions in information privacy, Yale Journal of Law & Technology, 2001/2002.

- The Economist, "E-business or out of business", June 30th-July 6th 2001.

- The Economist, Spyware, A Hidden Menace, June 5th 2004

- The writer is not mentioned in the article. However, the article can be found in Consumer Law Journal, Consumer Policy Action Plan 1999-2001, Volume 7, Number 1, Andover, Sweet & Maxwell, 2000.

- Thomas Kyle Sammin, Any Port in a Storm: The Safe Harbour, the Gramm Leah Bliley Act and the Problem of Privacy in Financial Services 36 George Washington International Law Review, 2005

- Thomson Jarvis Judith, The Right to Privacy, Philosophy and Public Affairs, 4, 1975

- Thwaite J Gregory, Brehm Wolfgang, German Privacy and Defamation Law: The Right to Publish in the shadow of the Right to Human Dignity, 16 (8) European Intellectual Property Law Review, 1994

- Torfs Rik, On the Permissible Scope of Legal Limitations on the Freedom of Religion or Belief in: Belgium, 19 Emory International Law Review 2005

- Ulrich Christian, Consumer Protection in Electronic Commerce Transactions in Germany and in the United States, Part II, GrayCary, Journal of Internet Law, 2000, available at www.gcwf.com/articles/journal/jil_dec00_1.html , accessed on 5/02/2002

- Vallelersundi Ana Palacio, Le commerce electronique, le juge, le consommateur, l'entreprise et le Marche Interieur: nouvelle equation pour le droit communautaire, Revue du droit de l'Union Europeenne, Number 1, 2001, p19.

- Vilasau Monica, The Right to Privacy and to Personal Data Protection in Spanish Legislation, Computer and Telecommunications Law Review, Sweet & Maxwell, 2003, 9 (7), 196.

- Vitale Angela, The EU Privacy directive and the Resulting Safe Harbour: The Negative Effects on US Legislation concerning Privacy on the Internet, 35 Vanderbilt Journal of Transnational Law, 2002

- Volokh Eugene, Symposium: Cyberspace and Privacy: A new legal paradigm? Freedom of Speech and Information Privacy: the Troubling Implications of a Right to stop People from speaking about you, 52 Stanford Law Review, 2000

- W Downing Richard, Shoring Up the Weakest Link: What Lawmakers around the World need to Consider in developing comprehensive laws to combat cybercrime, 43 Columbia Journal of Transnational Law, 2005.

- Wacks Reymond, The Poverty of Privacy, The Law Quarterly Review, 96, 1980

- Wagner DeCew Judith, The Scope of Privacy in Law and Ethics, Law and Philosophy, 5, 1986

- Walden Ian, Regulating Electronic Commerce: Europe in the Global Economy, European Law Review, Sweet & Maxwell, 2001

- Warner Jeremy, The Right to Oblivion: Data Retention from Canada to Europe on three Backward Steps, 2 University of Ottawa Law & Technology Journal, 2005

- Warner Richard, Surveillance and the Self: Privacy, Identity and Technology, 54 DePaul Law Review, 2005

- Warren Adam, Sources of Literature on Data Protection and Human Rights, 2001 (2) The Journal of Information, Law and Technology. Available at http://elj.warwick.ac.uk/jilt/01-2/warren.html

- Webb Philippa, A Comparative Analysis of Data Protection Laws in Germany and Australia, (2) Journal of Information, Law and Technology, 15 December 2003, (JILT).

- Weiss Charles, The Coming Technology of Knowledge Discovery: A Final Blow to Privacy Protection?, 2004 University of Illinois Journal of Law, Technology & Policy 253, 2004

- White Antony, Data Protection and the Media, European Human Rights Law Review, 2003, 25-36.

- Whitman Q James, The Two Western Cultures of Privacy, Dignity versus Liberty, 113 Yale Law Journal, April 2004

- Winer M. Jonathan, Regulating the Free Flow of Information: A Privacy Czar as the Ultimate Big Brother, 19 John Marshall Journal of Computer and Information Law, 2000.

- Wuermeling U. Ulrich, Harmonisation of European Union Privacy Law, 14 John Marshall Journal of Computer & Information Law, Spring 1996

- X Dempsey James & Lara M. Flint, The Future of Internet Surveillance Law: A Symposium to discuss Interne Surveillance, Privacy & the USA Patriot Act: Surveillance, Records & Computers: commercial Data and National Security, 72 The George Washington Law Review, 2004

- Yohei Suda, Monitoring E-mail of Employees in the Private Sector: A Comparison between Western Europe and the United States, 4 Washington University Global Studies Law Review, 2005

- Zimmerman L. Diane, Requiem for a Heavyweight: A Farewell to Warren and Brandeis Privacy Tort, Cornell Law Review, 68, 1983

Books

- Amitai Etzioni, The Limits of Privacy, Basic Books, USA, 1999

- Asch David, Wolfe Brian, New Economy – New Competition, The Rise of the Consumer?, Palgrave, New York, 2001.

- Bainbridge David, Computer Law, Fourth Edition, Longman, London, 2000

- Bainbridge David, EC Data Protection Directive, Butterworths, London, 1996

- Bainbridge David, Introduction to Computer Law, Fifth Edition, Pearson Longman, London, 2004

- Barrington Moore JR, Privacy, Studies in Social and Cultural History, M.E. Sharp Inc, New York, 1984

- Bennett Colin J. and Charles D. Raab, The Governance of Privacy, Policy Instruments in Global Perspective, Ashgate, 2003

- Bennett Colin J. and Rebecca Grant, Visions of Privacy, Policy Choices for the Digital Age, University of Toronto Press, Toronto, 1999

- Boling Patricia, Privacy and the Politics of Intimate Life, Cornell University Press, Ithaca and London, 1996

- Bygrave Lee A , The Place Of Privacy In Data Protection Law, University of NSW Law Journal, [2001] UNSWLJ 6

- C. Nicoll, J.E.J Prins, M.J.M. van Dallen, Digital anonymity and the Law, Tensions and Dimenions, T.M.C. Asser Press, The Hague, 2003

- Campbell Dennis, Fisher Joy, Data Transmission and Privacy, Martinus Nijhoff Publishers, London, 1994

- Chissick Michael, Kelman Alistair, Electronic Commerce, Law and Practise, Third Edition, Sweet and Maxwell, London, 2002.

- Clayton Richard, Hugh Tomlinson, Privacy and Freedom of Expression, Oxford University Press, 2001

- Colvin Madeleine, Developing Key Privacy Rights, Hart Publishing, Oxford and Portland, 2002

- Conor Foley, Liberating Cyberspace, Civil Liberties, Human Rights and the Internet, edited by Liberty, Pluto Press, London, 1999

- Douglas Thomas and Brian D. Loader, Cybercrime, Law Enforcement, security and surveillance in the information age, Routledge, London and New York, 2000

- Ernst Morris L. & Alan U. Schwartz, Privacy: The Right to be Let Alone, Milestones of Law Series, The MacMillan Company, New York, London, 1962

- Fairfield Paul, Public/Private, Rowman & Littlefield Publishers Inc, New York, 2005

- Gregor Mary, Groundwork of the Metaphysics of Morals, Cambridge University Press, New York, 1998

- Hadley Steve, The Law of Electronic Commerce and the Internet in the UK and Ireland, Cavendish Publishing Limited, London, 2006

- Hendrickx Frank, Employment Privacy Law in the European Union: Surveillance and Monitoring, Intersentia, Antwerpen , Oxford , New York, 2002

- Henry Michael, International Privacy, Publicity & Personality Laws, Butterworths, 2001

- Hick Steven, Edward F. Halpin, Eric Hoskins, Human rights and the Internet, Macmillan Press Ltd, London, 2000

- Howells Geraint, Wilhelmsson Thomas, EC Consumer Law, Ashgate, Dartmouth, Sydney, Singapore, 1997.

- Iglezakis Ioannis, The Protection of Personal Data on the Internet, National and EU Law Regulations, Commercial Law Review, Sakkoulas Publications, Thessaloniki, 2002, Greece

- J. Roland Pennock and John W. Chapman, Privacy, NOMOS XIII Yearbook of the American Society for Political and Legal Philosophy, Atherton Press, New York, 1971

- Jay Rosemary, Hamilton Angus, Data Protection, Law and Practice, Sweet & Maxwell, London, 2003

- Kendall Vivienne, EC Consumer Law, Wiley Chancery, London, New York, 1994.

- Klang Mathias and Andrew Murray, Human Rights in the Digital Age, Glasshouse Press, London, 2005

- Kuner Christopher, European Data Privacy Law and Online Business, Oxford University Press, Oxford, 2003

- Lace Susanne, The Glass Consumer, Life in a Surveillance Society, National Consumer Council, The Policy Press, University of Bristol, 2005

- Lloyd Ian, Legal Aspects of the Information Society, Butterworths, London, 2000

- Lloyd J. Ian, Electronic Commerce and the Law, Hume Papers on Public Policy: Volume 7, No.4, Edinburgh University Press, 2000.

- Long Edward V., The Intruders, The Invasion of Privacy by Government and Industry, Frederick A. Praeger, New York, Washington, London, 1967

- Lyon David & Eli Zureik, Surveillance, computers and Privacy, University of Minnesota Press, Minneapolis/London, 1996

- Lyon David, Surveillance Society, Monitoring Everyday Life, Open University Press, Buckingham, 2001

- Nagel Thomas, Concealment and Exposure, And Other Essays, Oxford University Press, Oxford, 2002

- Oughton David, Lowry John, Consumer Law, Second Edition, Blackstone Press Limited, London, 2000.

- Peers Steve , Angela Ward, The European Union Charter of Fundamental Rights, Hart Publishing, Oxford and Portland Oregon, 2004

- Perri 6, Briscoe Ivan, On the Cards, Privacy, Identity and trust in the age of smart technologies, Demos, London, 1996

- Perri 6, The future of Privacy Volume 1: Private Life and Public Policy, Demos, London, 1998

- Reed Chris , John Angel , Computer Law, Fifth Edition, Oxford University Press, 2003

- Reed Christopher, Internet Law: Text and Materials, Butterworths, London, Edinburgh, Dublin, 2000.

- Reich Norbert, Woodroffe Geoffrey, European Consumer Policy after Maastricht, Kluwer Academic Publishers, London, 1994.

- Renée Marlin Bennett , Knowledge Power, Intellectual Property, Information and Privacy, Lynne Rienner Pblishers, Boulder London, 2004

- Rosemary Jay, Hamilton Angus, Data Protection, Law and Practise, Sweet and Maxwell, London, 1999.

- Rössler Beate, Privacies, Philosophical Evaluations, Stanford University Press, California, 2004

- Rowland Diane, Elizabeth Macdonald, Information Technology Law, Cavendish Publishing Limited, London, 2005

- Rowland Diane, Macdonald Elizabeth, Information Technology Law Second Edition, Cavendish Publishing Limited, London, 2000

- Shapico Eric, All is not fair in the Privacy Trade: The Safe Harbour Agreement and the World Trade Organisation, 71 Fordham Law Review, 2003

- Singleton Susan, Data Protection, the New Law, Jordan's, 1998

- Singleton Susan, Data Protection, Tolley, London, 2001.

- Sjaak Nouwt, Berend R. de Vries, Roel Loermans, Reasonable Expectations of Privacy, Eleven Country Reports on Camera Surveillance and Workplace Privacy, T.M.C Asser Press, The Hague, 2005

- Smith J H Graham, Internet Law and Regulation, Third Edition, Sweet and Maxwell, London, 2002.

- Stanley Benn, Privacy, Freedom and Respect for Persons, Nomos, XIII, 1971

- Tridimas Takis and Paolisa Nebbia, European Union Law for the Twenty-First Century, Rethinking the New Legal Order, Volume 2, Internal Market and Free movement Community Policies, Hart Publishing, Oxford and Portland Oregon, 2004

- Tridimas Takis and Beatson Jack, New Directions in European Public Law, Hart Publishing, Oxford, 1998.

- Tridimas Takis, The General Principles of EU Law, Second Edition, Oxford University Press, 2006

- Weinstein Michael, The Uses of Privacy in the Good Life, Nomos, XIII, 1971

- Weinstein W.L., The Private and the Free: A Conceptual Inquiry, Nomos, XIII, 1971

- Weintaub Jeff, Krishan Kumar, Public and Private in Thought and Practice, Perspectives on a Grand Dichotomy, The University of Chicago Press, Chicago & London, 1997

- Westin Alan F. , Privacy and Freedom, Atheneum, New York, 1967

- Westin Alan, Privacy and Freedom, Bodley Head, London, 1970

- Young John B., Privacy, John Wiley & Sons, New York, 1978

Reports

- Article 29 Data Protection Working Party, Privacy on the Internet, An Integrated EU Approach to On-line Data Protection, 21st November 2000, WP37, see: http://europa.eu.int/comm/internal_market/privacy/docs/wpdocs/2000/wp37en.pdf accessed on August 10th.

- 2002 Regular Report of the DG Enlargement of the European Commission on the progress made by candidate countries on the issue of consumer protection. Available at:
  http://www.europa.eu.int/comm/enlargement/negotiations/chapters/chap23/index.htm

- A Study on practical consumer experiences with electronic commerce, Consumers International with the financial support of the DG Health and Consumer Protection of the European Commission,
  http://europa.eu.int/comm/dgs/health_consumer/library/surveys/sur12_en.html, accessed on 23/01/2002.

- Article 29 Data Protection Working Party, Opinion 4/2000 on the level of protection provided by the "Safe Harbour Principles", adopted on May 16th 2000, CA07/434/00/EN, available at

http://europa.eu.int/comm/internal_market/privacy/docs/wpdocs/2000/wp32en
.pdf

- Article 29 Data Protection Working Party, Working document on determining the International Application of EU Data Protection Law to Personal Data Processing on the Internet by non-EU based websites, Adopted on May 30th 2002, 5035/01/EN/Final, WP56, European Commission, Internal Market DG, Brussels.

- Baker & McKenzie, Doing E-Commerce in Europe, A Report, 2001.

- Commission of the European Communities, Green Paper on European Union Consumer Protection, Brussels, 2.10.2001, COM (2001) 531 final

- Commission Staff Working Paper on the application of Commission Decision 529/2000/EC of July 26th 2000 on the Safe Harbour Privacy Principles and related Frequently Asked Questions issued by the US Department of Commerce, Brussels 13.02.2002, SEC (2002) 196. See Decision 529/2000/EC at:

  http://europa.eu.int/smartapi/cgi/sga_doc?smartapi!celexapi!prod!CELEXnum
  doc&lg=en&numdoc=32000D0520&model=guichett

- Committee of consumer protection final report, Board of Trade, Committee of Consumer Protection, Sessional Papers, 1961-62, Cmnd 1781, accessed on 22/6/2003 at http://www.bopcris.ac.uk/bop1955/ref477.html .

- COMMON POSITION (EC) No 51/98 adopted by the Council on 24 September 1998 with a view to adopting European Parliament and Council Directive 98/ /EC, on certain aspects of the sale of consumer goods and associated guarantees
  Official Journal C 333, 30/10/1998 p. 0046, available at

http://europa.eu.int/smartapi/cgi/sga_doc?smartapi!celexapi!prod!CELEXnum
doc&lg=EN&numdoc=51998AG1030(04)&model=guichett

- Communication from the Commission to the Council and the European
  Parliament: An Internal Market Strategy for Services: COM (2000) 888

- Communication from the Commission to the Council, the European
  Parliament, the Economic and Social committee and the Committee of the
  regions, Implications of the Information Society on EU policies: Preparing the
  next steps, COM (96) 395final, July 24th 1996.

- Council Resolution of 19 January 1999 on the consumer dimension of the
  information society, OJ C 023, 28/1/99, p1-3, available also at:
  http://europa.eu.int/eur-lex/en/lif/dat/1999/en_399Y0128_01.html

- Data Privacy and the challenge to business, An e-briefing from the Economist
  Intelligence Unit, Written in Co-operation with Baker & Makenzie, October
  2001.

- Drews Ludwig Hans, Data Privacy Protection in German, The Effects of the
  German Federal Protection Act from the perspective of Siemens AG, updated
  special reprint, February 2003, page2. Available at Siemens intranet at:
  http://dsb.siemens.de/dspages/InfoSchulung.htm

- Electronic Privacy Information Centre, Privacy & Human rights, An
  International Survey of Privacy Laws and Developments in association with
  Privacy International, Washington and London, 2003

- Electronic Privacy Information Centre, Report on the use of Cookies, available
  at: http://www.epic.org/privacy/internet/cookies/

- Electronic Privacy Information Centre, Surfer Beware III: Privacy Policies without Privacy Protection, 2000, available at www.epic.org/reports/surfer-beware3.html

- European Commission, Directorate General, Internal Market and Financial Services, 1998, Handbook on cost effective compliance with Directive 95/46/EC.

- European Consumer Law Group, Consumer Transactions on the Internet, ECLG/194/2000, Brussels, 2000.

- European Data Protection Supervisor, Public Access to Documents and Data Protection, Background Paper Series, July 2005, No 1: http://www.edps.eu.int/publications/policy_papers/Public_access_data_protect ion_EN.pdf accessed on July 10th 2006

- European Parliament Resolution on "A European Initiative on Electronic Commerce", COM97 (157).

- FTAA Joint Government- Private Sector Committee of Experts on Electronic Commerce, Issue Briefing Notice by the Chair, Consumer Protection Issues in Electronic Commerce, accessed on 22/3/2002 at www.ftaa-alca.org/SPCOMM/derdoc/eci27e.doc .

- Global Information Infrastructure Commission, Consumer Protection in Electronic Commerce, An overview of Current Initiatives, August 1999, available at www.giic.org/focus/ecommerce/ , accessed on 24/06/2003.

- http://ec.europa.eu/justice_home/fsj/privacy/thridcountries/adequacy-faq_en.htm#1   and http://europa.eu/rapid/pressReleasesAction.do?reference=IP/02/46&format=H

TML&aged=1&language=EN&guiLanguage=en Report on EU-Australia Data
Transfer

http://www.coe.int/T/E/Legal_affairs/Legal_co-
operation/Data_protection/Documents/International_legal_instruments/Amendem
ents%20to%20the%20Convention%20108.asp#TopOfPage

- http://www.privacyinternational.org/survey/phr2003/countries/japan.htm
  Survey of Japan

- In 1999 the Committee of Ministers of the Council of Europe issued a
  recommendation (No R (99) 5) concerning the protection of privacy on the
  internet. See: http://www.coe.fr/cm/ta/rec/1999/99r5.htm#02 . The
  recommendation offered non-binding guidelines on the protection of
  individuals with regard to the processing of their personal data on internet.

- In 2001 the COE proceeded to amend the Convention in order to allow to
  European Communities to accede. See:

- Korff Douwe, EC Study on Implementation of Data Protection Directive,
  Comparative Summary of National Laws, Cambridge, September 2002.

- Korff Douwe, Study on the protection of the rights and interests of legal
  persons with regard to the processing of personal data relating to such persons,
  page   17,   see:
  http://europa.eu.int/comm/internal_market/privacy/docs/studies/legal_en.pdf ,
  accessed on August 10, 2004.

- Michael James, Privacy and Human Rights, An International and
  Comparative Study, with special reference to developments in Information
  Technology, Unesco Publishing, Dartmouth, Paris, France, 1994

- OECD, Electronic Commerce: Opportunities and Challenges for Government, Paris, 1997

- Press Release 2709th Council Meeting, Justice and Home Affairs, Brussels 21 February 2006. See: http://ue.eu.int/uedocs/cmsUpload/88467_06EN.pdf July 24th 2006. See also the Press Releae of September 21st 2005 at: http://europa.eu.int/rapid/pressReleasesAction.do?reference=MEMO/05/328& format=HTML&aged=1&language=EN&guiLanguage=en July 24th 2006

- Principles of Consumer Protection for electronic commerce, A Canadian Framework, Working Group on electronic Commerce and Consumers, Industry Canada, accessed on 22/2/2002, at http://strategis.ic.gc.ca/SSG/ca01185e.html

- Privacy On-Line: A Report to the Congress, Federal Trade Commission, 1998, available at http://www.ftc.gov/reports/privacy3/toc.htm

- Recommendation (73)22 of the Committee of Ministers. COE

- Recommendation (74)29 of the Committee of Ministers. COE

- Report of the US General Accounting Office on the use of data mining at: http://www.gao.gov/new.items/d04548.pdf

- Resolution of the European Parliament on the application of the principle of subsidiarity to environment and consumer protection policy, Official Journal C042, 15/02/1993 p. 0040, Available also at http://europa.eu.int/servlet/portail/RenderServlet?search=RefPub&lg=en&nb_ docs=25&domain=&in_force=NO&year=1993&month=&day=&coll=JO&nu _jo=42&page=40

- Speech by David Byrne, European Commissioner for Health and Consumer Protection, The e-confidence barrier – New regulatory models - Conference on

the e-Economy in Europe – European Parliament, Brussels, 2 March 2001, available   at
http://www.europa.eu.int/comm/dgs/health_consumer/library/speeches/speech
86_en.html

- Speech by David Byrne, European Commissioner for Health and Consumer
  Protection
  "Cyberspace and Consumer Confidence", Annual Conference of the Kangaroo
  Group of MEP's, 19 September 2000, available at
  http://www.europa.eu.int/comm/dgs/health_consumer/library/speeches/speech
  55_en.html

- Study produced by PriceWaterhouseCoopers for Health & consumer
  Protection DG.   A summary can be accessed at
  http://europa.eu.int/comm/dgs/health_consumer/library/surveys/sur20_en.html

- Tenth Annual Report of the Data Protection Registrar, 1994, London, HMSO.

- The European Commission, DG Internal Market, Existing case law on
  compliance with data protection laws and principles in the Member States of
  the European Union, Korff Douwe, Annex to the Annual Report 1998, of the
  Working Party established by article 29 of the Directive 95/46EC,
  Luxembourg.

- The European Commission, DG Internal Market, Fifth Annual Report on the
  Situation regarding the Protection of Individuals with regard to the Processing
  of Personal Data and Privacy in the European Union and in third Countries,
  Covering the year 2000, Part II, Adopted on March 6th 2002, Luxembourg.

- The European Commission, Directorate General Internal Market, Application
  of a Methodology designed to Access the Adequacy of the Level of Protection

of Individuals with regard to Processing Personal Data: Test of the Method on Several Categories of Transfer, Final Report, September 1998, Luxembourg.

- The European Commission, Directorate General Internal Market, IDA Projects: A Guide to Data Protection Compliance, Final Report, 1998, Annex to the annual Report of Article 29 Working Party,

- The European Commission, Directorate General Internal Market, Reidenberg R. Joel, Schwartz M. Paul, On-line Services and data protection and privacy, Volume II, Luxembourg, 1998.

- The European Commission, Final Report by Douwe Korff (contractor), The feasibility of a seamless system of data protection rules for the European Union, Directorate General XV, Internal Market and Financial Services, 1998, Luxembourg.

- The European Commission, On-line services and data protection and the protection of privacy, Volume I, Annex to the Annual Report 1998 (XV D/504/98) of the Working Party established by Article 29 of directive 95/46/EC, Directorate General Internal Market and Financial Services, 1999, p49.

- The European Commission, The Amsterdam Treaty, A comprehensive Guide, Luxembourg, Office for Official Publications of the European Communities, 1999.

- White Paper on Growth, Competitiveness and Employment, The challenges and ways forward into the 21st Century, COM (93) 700 final, Brussels December 5th 1993, see:

http://www.gencat.es/csi/pdf/eng/soc_info/basic/WP_growth.pdf

- Working Party Opinion 3/2001 on the level of protection of the Australian Privacy Amendment (Private Sector) Act 2000:

  http://ec.europa.eu/justice_home/fsj/privacy/docs/wpdocs/2001/wp40en.pdf

Sites

- http://www.cnil.fr/traces/traces.htm CNIL comments on line privacy issues
- 1968 Brussels Convention on jurisdiction and the enforcement of judgments in civil and commercial matters, Official Journal C027, 26/01/98, p1-27. Article 13. Also available at

  http://europa.eu.int/smartapi/cgi/sga_doc?smartapi!celexapi!prod!CELEXnum doc&lg=EN&numdoc=41998A0126&model=guichett .

- 98/257/EC: Commission Recommendation of 30 March 1998 on the principles applicable to the bodies responsible for out-of-court settlement of consumer disputes (Text with EEA relevance)

  Official Journal L 115, 17/04/1998 P. 0031 – 0034, available at

  http://europa.eu.int/smartapi/cgi/sga_doc?smartapi!celexapi!prod!CELEXnum doc&lg=EN&numdoc=31998H0257&model=guichett

  Accessed on 21/02/2002

- Article 100 of the Treaty of Rome at

  http://europa.eu.int/abc/obj/treaties/en/entr6d05.htm#Article_100

- Article 13 of 88/592 EEC, Convention on Jurisdiction and the enforcement of judgments in civil and commercial matters, Lugano September 16th 1988, Official Journal L319, 25/11/1988, p 9-33. It can also be accessed at

  http://europa.eu.int/smartapi/cgi/sga_doc?smartapi!celexapi!prod!CELEXnum doc&lg=EN&numdoc=41988A0592&model=guichett .

- Article 29 Data Protection Working Party, Opinion 2/2002 on the use of unique identifiers in telecommunication terminal equipments: the example of IPV6, 30 May 2002, WP 58, see at:

  http://europa.eu.int/comm/internal_market/privacy/docs/wpdocs/2002/wp58_en.pdf accessed on August 10th

- Article 2 (4) of the Package Travel Directive, Council Directive 90/314/EEC of 13 June 1990 on package travel, package holidays and package tours, Official Journal L 158, 23/06/1990 P. 0059 – 0064, also available at

  http://europa.eu.int/smartapi/cgi/sga_doc?smartapi!celexapi!prod!CELEXnumdoc&lg=EN&numdoc=31990L0314&model=guichett

- Article 8 of the European Convention for the protection of Human Rights and Fundamental Freedoms www.europa.eu.int/eur-lex/en/treaties/dat/C_2002325EN.000501.html

  at: http://conventions.coe.int/Treaty/EN/Treaties/Html/108.htm

- Cable Communications Policy Act

  http://www.buskegroup.com/Conducting_a_Community_Needs_Assessment.pdf

- Case GB Inno BM v Confederation du commerce luxembourgeois., Reference for a preliminary

  ruling: Cour de cassation - Grand-Duchy de Luxembourg. Case C-362/88. European Court reports 1990 Page I-00667. See Grounds of the judgment number 18. Also available at

  http://europa.eu.int/smartapi/cgi/sga_doc?smartapi!celexapi!prod!CELEXnumdoc&lg=EN&numdoc=61988J0362&model=guichett#MO

- Children's Online Privacy Protection Act

  http://www.ftc.gov/bcp/conline/pubs/buspubs/coppa.htm

- Comcast Angers Privacy Groups But For What?, February 13th 2002, available

  at: http://www.internetnews.com/bus-news/article.php/974451

  accessed on   5/7/2003.

- Commission Decision 2000/518/EC of 26.7.2000, O. J. L 215/1 of 25.8.2000,

  also available at:

  http://europa.eu.int/smartapi/cgi/sga_doc?smartapi!celexapi!prod!CELEXnum

  doc&lg=en&numdoc=32000D0518&model=guichett

- Commission Decision 2000/519/EC of 26.7.2000, O.J. L 215/4 of 25.8.2000,

  available at:

  http://europa.eu.int/smartapi/cgi/sga_doc?smartapi!celexapi!prod!CELEXnum

  doc&lg=en&numdoc=32000D0519&model=guichett

- Commission Decision 2002/2/EC of 20.12.2001 on the adequate protection of

  personal data provided by the Canadian Personal Information Protection and

  Electronic Documents Act, O.J. L 2/13 of 4.1.2002, also available at:

  http://europa.eu.int/smartapi/cgi/sga_doc?smartapi!celexapi!prod!CELEXnum

  doc&lg=en&numdoc=32002D0002&model=guichett

- Commission Decision C (2003) 1731 of 30 June 2003, available at:

  http://europa.eu.int/comm/internal_market/privacy/docs/adequacy/decision-

  c2003-1731/decision-argentine_en.pdf

- Confidential Information Protection and Statistical Efficiency Act (CISPEA)

  www.eia.doe.gov/oss/CIPSEA.pdf

- Council Directive 85/577/EEC of 20 December 1985 to protect the consumer

  in respect of contracts negotiated away from business premises, Official

Journal L 372, 31/12/1985 P. 0031 – 0033, also available at

http://europa.eu.int/smartapi/cgi/sga_doc?smartapi!celexapi!prod!CELEXnum
doc&lg=EN&numdoc=31985L0577&model=guichett

- Council Directive 92/59/EEC of 29 June 1992 on general product safety
  Official Journal L 228, 11/08/1992 P. 0024 – 0032, available at
  http://europa.eu.int/smartapi/cgi/sga_doc?smartapi!celexapi!prod!CELEXnum
  doc&lg=EN&numdoc=31992L0059&model=guichett

- Council Directive 93/13/EEC of 5 April 1993 on unfair terms in consumer
  contracts, Official Journal L 095, 21/04/1993 P. 0029 – 0034, available also at
  http://europa.eu.int/smartapi/cgi/sga_doc?smartapi!celexapi!prod!CELEXnum
  doc&lg=EN&numdoc=31993L0013&model=guichett .

- *Council of Europe*, Convention for the Protection of Individuals with regard to
  Automatic Processing of Personal Data
  http://conventions.coe.int/Treaty/en/Treaties/Html/108.htm

- Council Regulation (EC) No 44/2001 of 22 December 2000 on jurisdiction
  and the recognition and enforcement of judgments in civil and commercial
  matters, Official Journal L 012, 16/01/2001 P. 0001 – 0023. Article 15.
  Available also at
  http://europa.eu.int/smartapi/cgi/sga_doc?smartapi!celexapi!prod!CELEXnum
  doc&lg=EN&numdoc=32001R0044&model=guichett

- D. Ian Hopper, Associated Press writer, Microsoft tracks habits of users,
  available at http://www.s-t.com/daily/02-02/02-24-02/c03bu090.htm

- Data protection: Commission takes five Member States to court, available at:
  http://europa.eu.int/rapid/start/cgi/guesten.ksh?p_action.gettxt=gt&doc=IP/00/
  10|0|AGED&lg=EN&display= accessed on 16/8/2003.

- Declan McCullagh, You? A Terrorist? Yes!
  http://www.wired.com/news/politics/0,1283,19218-
  2,00.html?tw=wn_story_page_next1

- Directive 1999/44/EC of the European Parliament and of the Council of 25
  May 1999 on certain aspects of the sale of consumer goods and associated
  guarantees. Official Journal L 171, 07/07/1999 P. 0012 – 0016. Available also
  at
  http://europa.eu.int/smartapi/cgi/sga_doc?smartapi!celexapi!prod!CELEXnum
  doc&lg=EN&numdoc=31999L0044&model=guichett

- Directive 2000/31/EC of the European Parliament and the Council of 8 June
  2000 on certain legal aspects of information society services, in particular
  electronic commerce, in the internal market, available at
  http://europa.eu.int/smartapi/cgi/sga_doc?smartapi!celexapi!prod!CELEXnum
  doc&lg=EN&numdoc=32000L0031&model=guichett

- Directive 2002/58 of the EP and of the Council of 12 July 2002 concerning the
  processing of personal data and the protection of privacy in the electronic
  communications sector, OJ L201, 31/07/2002, p37-47, available at
  http://europa.eu.int/smartapi/cgi/sga_doc?smartapi!celexapi!prod!CELEXnum
  doc&lg=EN&numdoc=32002L0058&model=guichett

- Directive 2006/24/EC
  http://www.ispai.ie/DR%20as%20published%20OJ%2013-04-06.pdf

- Directive 95/46EC of the European Parliament and of the Council of 24
  October 1995 on the protection of individuals with regard to the processing of
  personal data and on the free movement of such data, OJ 281, 23/11/1995,
  p31-50, available at

http://europa.eu.int/smartapi/cgi/sga_doc?smartapi!celexapi!prod!CELEXnum
doc&lg=EN&numdoc=31995L0046&model=guichett

- Directive 97/7/EC of the European Parliament and of the Council of 20 May
  1997 on the protection of consumers in respect of distance contracts, Official
  Journal L 144, 04/06/1997 P. 0019 – 0027, available at
  http://europa.eu.int/smartapi/cgi/sga_doc?smartapi!celexapi!prod!CELEXnum
  doc&lg=EN&numdoc=31997L0007&model=guichett

- Directive 98/27/EC of the European Parliament and of the Council of 19 May
  1998 on injunctions for the protection of consumers' interests
  Official Journal L 166, 11/06/1998 P. 0051 – 0055, available at
  http://europa.eu.int/smartapi/cgi/sga_doc?smartapi!celexapi!prod!CELEXnum
  doc&lg=EN&numdoc=31998L0027&model=guichett

- Directive 98/43/EC of the European Parliament and of the Council of 6 July
  1998 on the approximation of the laws, regulations and administrative
  provisions of the Member States relating to the advertising and sponsorship of
  tobacco products
  Official Journal L 213, 30/07/1998 P. 0009 – 0012, available at
  http://europa.eu.int/smartapi/cgi/sga_doc?smartapi!celexapi!prod!CELEXnum
  doc&lg=EN&numdoc=31998L0043&model=guichett

- Directive 98/6/EC of the European Parliament and of the Council of 16
  February 1998 on consumer protection in the indication of the prices of
  products offered to consumers
  Official Journal L 080, 18/03/1998 P. 0027 – 0031, available at
  http://europa.eu.int/smartapi/cgi/sga_doc?smartapi!celexapi!prod!CELEXnum
  doc&lg=EN&numdoc=31998L0006&model=guichett

- DoubleClick site at
  http://www.doubleclick.com/us/product/database/default.asp?asp_object_1=&
  accessed on August 1st 2003

- EC Convention on the Law applicable to contractual obligations, Rome 1980,
  available at

- Electronic Privacy Information Centre: www.epic.org

- Financial Services Modernisation Act
  http://www.ftc.gov/privacy/glbact/index.html

- French Constitution of September 3rd 1791, at: http://www.premier-
  ministre.gouv.fr/fr/p.cfm?ref=15008

- Frequently Asked Questions on the Commission's adequacy finding on the
  Canadian Personal Information Protection and Electronic Documents Act
  (March 2002), available at:
  http://europa.eu.int/comm/internal_market/privacy/adequacy/adequacy-
  faq_en.htm

- Guidelines for Consumer Protection in the Context of Electronic Commerce.
  See: http://www1.oecd.org/publications/e-book/9300023E.PDF

- Hellenic Constitution, article 9A,
  http://confinder.richmond.edu/greek_2001.html

- http://ec.europa.eu/justice_home/fsj/privacy/docs/wpdocs/2004/wp87_en.pdf
  Working Party Opinion on Transfer of Data Decision between the EU and the
  US

- http://europa.eu.int/abc/obj/treaties/en/entr6d05.htm#Article_85 Art 85 Treaty
  of Rome.

- http://europa.eu.int/comm/internal_market/privacy/law/implementation_en.htm#germany

- http://europa.eu.int/comm/internal_market/privacy/modelcontracts_en.htm Contractual Clauses

- http://europa.eu.int/comm/internal_market/privacy/studies/legal_en.htm accessed on August 10th 2004. Internal Market

- http://europa.eu.int/eur-lex/en/treaties/dat/amsterdam.html. Also available at Official Journal C 340 of 10 November 1997. The Treaty of Amsterdam.

- http://europa.eu.int/rapid/pressReleasesAction.do?reference=MEMO/01/228&format=HTML&aged=1&language=EN&guiLanguage=en the same

- http://www.bfd.bund.de/information/bdsg_eng.pdf German Federal data protection act in 2001

- http://www.bfd.bund.de/information/bdsg_eng.pdf German Federal Data Protection Act

- http://www.cnil.fr/traces/traces.htm CNIL Privacy Test

- http://www.dpa.gr/legal_eng.htm Hellenic Data Protection Law

- http://www.europa.eu.int/comm/consumers/overview/index_en.htm , Overview of Consumer Policy as expressed by the relevant DG Consumer Protection. It constitutes the official position adopted by the Commission.

- http://www.europa.eu.int/eur-lex/en/archive/2003/c_16920030718en.html The Constitutional Treaty

- http://www.europa.eu.int/eur-lex/pri/en/oj/dat/2001/l_181/l_18120010704en00190031.pdf , Commission Decision 2001/497/EC of 15 June 2001 under the Directive 95/46/EC - O.J. L 181/19 of 4.7.2001

- http://www.europemedia.net/shownews.asp?ArticleID=16526 accessed on 23/7/2003. Internet figures.

- http://www.europemedia.net/shownews.asp?ArticleID=4374 accessed on 23/7/2003. European internet penetration figures.

- http://www.hmso.gov.uk/acts/acts1998/19980029.htm   UK passed in 1998 a new Data Protection Act.

- http://www.hmso.gov.uk/acts/acts1998/19980029.htm UK Data Protection Act

- http://www.ita.doc.gov/td/ecom/Principles1199.htm Safe Harbour principles http://www.jus.uio.no/lm/ec.applicable.law.contracts.1980/doc.html#1

- http://www.law.cornell.edu/constitution/constitution.billofrights.html#amendmentvi The First Amendment

- http://www.law.cornell.edu/constitution/constitution.billofrights.html#amendmentvi The Fourth Amendment

- http://www.nua.ie/surveys/analysis/weekly_editorial/archives/issue1no197.html accessed on 22/7/2003. On line figures.

- http://www.polk.com/products/polkone.asp (examples of methods of the collection of data)

- https://www.paypal.com/uk/cgi-bin/webscr?cmd=xpt/cps/general/PayPalShoppers-outside Paypal site

- Le Senat, La Protection des Donnees Personnelles, Les Principaux Textes, Allemagne, accessed at: www.senat.fr/lc/lc62/lc621.html on 30/06/2003.

- Le Senat, La Protection des Donnees Personnelles, Note de Synthese, accessed at: www.senat.fr/lc/lc62/lc620.html , accessed on 30/6/2003.

- Misleading Advertising Directive, Directive 97/55/EC of European Parliament and of the Council of 6 October 1997 amending Directive 84/450/EEC concerning misleading advertising so as to include comparative advertising, Official Journal L 290 , 23/10/1997 P. 0018 – 0023, available also at http://europa.eu.int/smartapi/cgi/sga_doc?smartapi!celexapi!prod!CELEXnum doc&lg=EN&numdoc=31997L0055&model=guichett .

- OECD Guidelines on privacy and data protection http://www.oecd.org/document/18/0,2340,en_2649_34255_1815186_1_1_1_1 ,00.html

- Opinion 2/2001 of the Art. 29 Data Protection Working Party, available at: http://europa.eu.int/comm/internal_market/privacy/docs/wpdocs/2001/wp39en .pdf

- Opinion 4/2002 of the Art. 29 Working Party, available at: http://europa.eu.int/comm/internal_market/privacy/docs/wpdocs/2002/wp63_e n.pdf

- Opinion 5/99 of the Art. 29 Data Protection Working Party, available at: http://europa.eu.int/comm/internal_market/privacy/docs/wpdocs/1999/wp22en .pdf

- Opinion 6/99 of the Art. 29 Data Protection Working Party, available at: http://europa.eu.int/comm/internal_market/privacy/docs/wpdocs/1999/wp24en .pdf

- Orwell George, 1984, published in 1949. Available on line at http://www.online-literature.com/orwell/1984/ , accessed on August 1st 2003.

- Preamble of the founding Treaty of Rome, 1957, accessed at: http://europa.eu.int/abc/obj/treaties/en/entr6a.htm#11

- President Clinton's position on e-commerce at http://www.pbs.org/newshour/cyberspace/

- Press Release IP/03/81 of the Commission of the March 11th 2002. Accessed on July 23rd 2003 at http://www.europa.eu.int/rapid/start/cgi/guesten.ksh?p_action.gettxt=gt&doc= IP/02/381|0|RAPID&lg=EN&display= on "Most consumers not yet confident enough to shop cross border".

- See all the text of the draft Constitution at: http://european-convention.eu.int/docs/Treaty/cv00850.en03.pdf

- See article 12 at: http://www.un.org/Overview/rights.html of the Universal Declaration of Human Rights.

- See article 17 of the International Covenant on Civil and Political Rights of December 16th 1966 at: http://domino.un.org/unispal.nsf/0/dda106bf303c3cee85256368005960a0?OpenDocument

- See article 18 of the Single European Act that supplements article 100a to the EEC Treaty. Available in pdf form at: http://www.eurotreaties.com/singleuropeanact.pdf

- See article 8 of ECHR at: http://www.echr.coe.int/Convention/webConvenENG.pdf

- See http://europa.eu.int/abc/obj/treaties/en/entr6d05.htm#Article_86 Art 86 Treaty of Rome

- See the announcement of the Centre of Democracy and Technology at http://www.cdt.org/action/doubleclick.shtml on the double click issue.

- See the chronological progress of the adoption of the implementing legislation at the site of CNIL: http://www.cnil.fr/frame.htm?http://www.cnil.fr/textes/directiv.htm

- See the Double click statement at

  http://www.cdt.org/privacy/000302doubleclick.shtml

- See the Guidelines for the Regulation of Computerised Personal Data Files issued at the UN level on December 14th 1999 at

  http://www.unhchr.ch/html/menu3/b/71.htm .

- See the guidelines on "the protection of privacy and transborder flows of personal data" on September 23rd 1980on line at:

  http://www1.oecd.org/publications/e-book/9302011E.PDF

- See the High Commissioner's for Human Rights statement at:

  http://www.unhchr.ch/tbs/doc.nsf/(symbol)/CCPR+General+comment+16.En? OpenDocument

- See the OECD Guidelines also at:

  http://europa.eu.int/comm/internal_market/privacy/instruments/ocdeguideline_ en.htm

- See the Press Release at:

  http://europa.eu.int/rapid/pressReleasesAction.do?reference=IP/05/1167&for mat=HTML&aged=0&language=EN&guiLanguage=en on data retention.

- See the site of the company at:

  http://www.acxiom.com/default.aspx?ID=2548&Country_Code=USA&Top_ Mind=T

- See Treaty of Amsterdam: Questions and answers. Available at:

  http://europa.eu.int/abc/obj/amst/en/qa.htm#7

- See: http://europa.eu.int/abc/obj/treaties/en/entr6d02.htm#Article_39 Title II of the Treaty of Rome dedicated to agriculture in article 39 (1) (e).

59

- Special message to the Congress on protecting the consumer interest, March 15 1962, President Kennedy, accessed on 25/6/2003 at http://www.presidency.ucsb.edu/site/docs/pppus.php?admin=035&year=1962&id=93 .

- Statewatch: www.statewatch.org

- The Centre of Democracy and Technology at http://www.cdt.org/action/doubleclick.shtml

- The Centre of Democracy and Technology: www.cdt.org

- The Constitutional Treaty, Part II, Artilce II-8. See http://europa.eu.int/eur-lex/pri/en/oj/dat/2003/c_169/c_16920030718en00010105.pdf

- the Council of Europe adopted the Convention for the Protection of Individuals with regard to Automatic Processing of Personal Data

- The Double Click Privacy statement at http://www.doubleclick.com/us/corporate/privacy/privacy/default.asp?asp_object_1=&

- The European Commission, DG Internal Market, Commission decisions on the adequacy of the protection of personal data in third countries, available at: http://europa.eu.int/comm/internal_market/privacy/adequacy_en.htm

- The European Commission, DG Internal Market, Status of implementation of Directive 95/46 on the Protection of Individuals with regard to the Processing of Personal Data, available at: http://europa.eu.int/comm/internal_market/privacy/law/implementation_en.htm

- The legislative act in question can be accessed at: http://www.cnil.fr/textes/docs/CNIL-Loi78-17_modSenat1-VI.pdf

- The TEU at http://europa.eu.int/en/record/mt/title2.html

- The USA Patriot Act 2001 at:

  http://www.epic.org/privacy/terrorism/hr3162.html

- Title III of the Treaty of Rome. Available At

  http://europa.eu.int/abc/obj/treaties/en/entr6d03.htm#112

- Video Privacy Protection Act

  http://www4.law.cornell.edu/uscode/html/uscode18/usc_sec_18_00002710----000-.html

- Working Paper "A Framework for Global Electronic Commerce" at

  http://www.technology.gov/digeconomy/framewrk.htm#5.%20PRIVACY

CASE LIST

ECJ

- *Bodil Lindqvist* Case C-101/01 See:http://curia.europa.eu/jurisp/cgi-bin/gettext.pl?lang=en&num=79968893C19010101&doc=T&ouvert=T&seance=AR RET&where=() July 16th 2006. Judgment of 06/11/2003, Lindqvist (Rec.2003,p.I-12971)

- C-106/89 *Marleasing SA v La Commercial Internacionale de Alimentacion* [1990] ECR I-4135 [1992] 1 CMLR 305.

- Case 42/74, *Van Duyn v Home Office*, [1974] ECR 1337

- *Case GB Inno BM v Confederation du commerce luxembourgeois*, Reference for a preliminary ruling: Cour de cassation - Grand-Duchy de Luxembourg. Case C-362/88. European Court reports 1990 Page I-00667. See Grounds of the judgment number 18. Also available at

  http://europa.eu.int/smartapi/cgi/sga_doc?smartapi!celexapi!prod!CELEXnumdoc&lg =EN&numdoc=61988J0362&model=guichett#MO

- Cases C-6 & 9/90 *Francovich & Bunifaci v Italy* [1991] ECR I-5357, [1993]2 CMLR66

- *Criminal Proceedings against Patrice Di Pinto*, Reference for a preliminary ruling from the Cour d'Appel de Paris, Case C-361/89, [1991] ECR I-1189.

- *Rechnungshof* (C-465/00) http://www.curia.europa.eu/jurisp/cgi-bin/gettext.pl?lang=en&num=79969479C19000465&doc=T&ouvert=T&seance=ARRET&where

- The transfer of the passenger personal data to the United States Bureau of Customs and Border Protection decision: http://curia.europa.eu/jurisp/cgi-bin/form.pl?lang=EN&Submit=rechercher&numaff=C-317/04 Joined Cases C-317/04 and C-318/04 July 16th 2006

European Court of Human Rights

- *Halford v UK*
http://cmiskp.echr.coe.int/tkp197/view.asp?item=1&portal=hbkm&action=html&highlight=Halford%20%7C%20v%20%7C%20UK&sessionid=7791922&skin=hudoc-en
- *Lüdi v Switzerland*
http://cmiskp.echr.coe.int/tkp197/view.asp?item=1&portal=hbkm&action=html&highlight=L%FCdi%20%7C%20v%20%7C%20Switzerland&sessionid=7791885&skin=hudoc-en
- *Niemietz v Germany*, ECHR, December 16th 1992. See the judgement at:
http://cmiskp.echr.coe.int/tkp197/view.asp?item=1&portal=hbkm&action=html&highlight=Niemietz&sessionid=7862396&skin=hudoc-en

- *P.G & J.H v UK*

http://cmiskp.echr.coe.int/tkp197/view.asp?item=1&portal=hbkm&action=html&high light=P.G.%20%7C%20v%20%7C%20UK&sessionid=7791960&skin=hudoc-en
- *Peck v UK*

http://cmiskp.echr.coe.int/tkp197/view.asp?item=2&portal=hbkm&action=html&high light=Peck%20%7C%20v%20%7C%20UK&sessionid=7792003&skin=hudoc-en
- *von Hannover v Germany*

http://cmiskp.echr.coe.int/tkp197/view.asp?item=3&portal=hbkm&action=html&high light=Hannover%20%7C%20v%20%7C%20Germany&sessionid=7792003&skin=hu doc-en
- *Z v Finland* (1997) 25 EHRR 371

USA

- *Griswold v Connecticut 381 US 479 (1965).*

- *James Woolsey v Owen B. Judd (1855)*

- *Katz v United States 389 US 347 (1967)*

- *Kyllo v United States 533 US 27, 2001*

- *McIntyre v Ohio Elections Commission 514 US 334, (1995)*

- *O'Connor v Ortega 480 US 709, 1987*

- *Pollard v Photographic Co (1888)*

- *R v Dyment, [1988] 2SCR 417*

- *Reno v ACLU 521 US 844 (1997).*

- *Smith v Maryland 442 US 735 (1979)*

- *Talley v California 362 US 60, (1960)*

- *United States v Charbonneau, 979 F.Supp. 1177, (1997)*

- *United States v Dionisio 410 US 1 (1973)*

- *United States v Miller 425 US 435 (1976)*

- *United States v Simons United States v Simons, 206 F.3d 392, 2000*

- *Whalen v Roe 429 U.S. 589 (1977)*

France

- *Décision 94-352* du Conseil Constitutionnel du 18 Janvier 1995

- *Rachel.* Tribunal du Premiere Instance de la Seine, 1858, June 16th, DP III 62

- *Dumas.* Appeals Court, Paris, May 25th 1867

Germany

- *Census Case, 65 BVerfGE 1, 64, 1983.*

- *Cf Bundesgerichtshof Betriebs Berater 1990*

- *Elfes, 6 BVerGE 32, 1957*

- *Lebach 35 BVerfGE 202, 1973.*

- *Mephisto 30 BVerfGE 30, 173, 1971*

- *Mikrozensus, BVerGE 27,1.*

• *Tagebuch, BVerfGE 80, 367, 1989*

UK

• *Coco v AN Clark, [1969] RPC 41*

• *Douglas v Hello Ltd, 2 WLR, 2001, 992*

• *Hellewell v Chief Constable of Derbyshire [1995] 1 WLR 804*

• *Kaye v Robertson [1991] FSR 62*

• *Malone v Metropolitan Police Commissioner[1979] Ch 344, 372*

• *Morris v Beardmore [1980] 2 All ER 753*

• *R v Brown [1996] 1 All ER 545*

• *R v Department of Health, ex parte Source Informatics Ltd [2001] QB 424.*
• *Re X (1974), [1975] 1 All ER 697 (CA) at 704*

•*[1990] 1 A.C. 109 (H.L.) A.G. v Guardian Newspapers Ltd (No2).*

Wissenschaftlicher Buchverlag bietet

kostenfreie

Publikation

von

wissenschaftlichen Arbeiten

Diplomarbeiten, Magisterarbeiten, Master und Bachelor Theses
sowie Dissertationen, Habilitationen und wissenschaftliche Monographien

Sie verfügen über eine wissenschaftliche Abschlußarbeit zu aktuellen oder zeitlosen
Fragestellungen, die hohen inhaltlichen und formalen Ansprüchen genügt,
und haben **Interesse an einer honorarvergüteten Publikation**?

Dann senden Sie bitte erste Informationen über Ihre Arbeit per Email
an info@vdm-verlag.de. Unser Außenlektorat meldet sich umgehend bei Ihnen.

VDM Verlag Dr. Müller Aktiengesellschaft & Co. KG
Dudweiler Landstraße 125a
D - 66123 Saarbrücken

www.vdm-verlag.de

www.ingramcontent.com/pod-product-compliance
Lightning Source LLC
LaVergne TN
LVHW022301060326

832902LV00020B/3208